Swedenborg's Principles of Usefulness

Swedenborg Studies No. 23

Swedenborg's Principles of Usefulness

Social Reform Thought
from the Enlightenment
to American Pragmatism

By John S. Haller, Jr.

Foreword by James F. Lawrence

**SWEDENBORG
FOUNDATION**
West Chester, Pennsylvania

Library of Congress Cataloging-in-Publication Data
Names: Haller, John S., Jr., 1940- author.
Title: Swedenborg's principles of usefulness : social reform thought from the enlightenment to American pragmatism / John S. Haller, Jr., ; foreword by James F. Lawrence.
Description: West Chester, Pennsylvania : Swedenborg Foundation, 2020. | Series: Swedenborg studies ; No. 23 | Includes bibliographical references and index. | Summary: "Swedenborg's Principles of Usefulness presents a possibly unsuspected historical undercurrent that further evidences Emanuel Swedenborg's pervasive influence on a whole host of historical figures-from poets and artists to philosophers and statesmen-whose contributions to the evolution of self and society have resonated throughout time and into the present. Besides having an impact on individual thinkers, Swedenborg's ideas worked their way into the various social reform traditions that vitalized the American landscape during the nineteenth and early-twentieth centuries. His concept of usefulness, best demonstrated in the competing worldviews of the nation's liberal and conservative traditions, involved a commitment made by Swedenborgians, New Church members, and others to energize the nation and its people by envisaging the possibility of a much-desired Universal Human"-- Provided by publisher.
Identifiers: LCCN 2020005825 | ISBN 9780877853565 (hardcover) | ISBN 9780877857105 (ebook)
Subjects: LCSH: Swedenborg, Emanuel, 1688-1772. | Utilitarianism. | Pragmatism.
Classification: LCC B4468.S84 H355 2020 | DDC 289/.4092--dc23
LC record available at https://lccn.loc.gov/2020005825

Edited by John Connolly
Design and typesetting by Karen Connor

The scripture quotations contained herein are from the New Revised Standard Version Bible, copyright © 1989 by the Division of Christian Education of the National Council of the Churches of Christ in the USA, and are used by permission. All rights reserved.

Printed in the United States of America

Swedenborg Foundation
320 North Church Street
West Chester, PA 19380
www.swedenborg.com

The essence of uses is the public good.

(Swedenborg, *Apocalypse Explained* §1226:7)

Contents

Foreword

John Haller persuasively demonstrates how Swedenborg's concept of usefulness played a profound yet previously undetected behind-the-scenes role in shaping American social reform movements and the philosophical tradition of American pragmatism. First, usefulness provided critical perspectives for Ralph Waldo Emerson, William James, and Charles Sanders Peirce, the most important early architects of this distinctive American contribution to world philosophy, and second, it contributed in surprising ways to numerous evolving arenas of social reform in the widening wake of this "can-do" school of thought. Haller illuminates how Swedenborgian aspects of pragmatism have manifested themselves up through the first quarter of the twentieth century in American philosophical thought, social reform movements, economic theories, and the fields of psychology and spirituality.

As a distinguished historian of ideas in nineteenth- and twentieth-century American studies, Haller has an impressive publication record of discovering and interpreting Swedenborg's complex reception in the United States during that period. His adept study contributes toward shaping what has become a revolutionary project in understanding Swedenborg's reach, a project that has continued to grow in scholarship over the past three decades, as studies of his influence have become a veritable cottage industry. *Swedenborg's Principles of Usefulness: Social Reform Thought from the Enlightenment to American Pragmatism* might be one of the most, if not *the* most, important studies yet offered, as it insightfully frames a complex web of conversations and grounded movements that have been enlivened by the principles expressed through Swedenborg's concept of usefulness.

Recognized as one of the most beloved aspects of his spiritual philosophy, the concept of usefulness is as profound an idea as it is rare a topical term in the history of Christian thought. Carrying a large cargo in Swedenborgian thought, usefulness performs an integral role in divine functioning on the one hand, and it serves as a primary method and practice for personal spiritual development on the other. As a scientist turned theologian, Swedenborg worked in ways that were not common in the history of Christian theology. Because of his long first career in natural philosophy, which we would today refer to as theoretical and applied natural science, Swedenborg abides in a minor category of religious thinkers who also made historically significant contributions to the scientific community; and since he made notable advances in both fields, he can arguably be identified as foremost in that category.

Swedenborg demonstrated his earliest prowess in mechanical engineering, which lends itself to understanding how to build a machine to actually work and perform a use, or something that is good and needed. His subsequent accomplishments in mathematics, astrophysics, metallurgy, and cognitive and neurological anatomy, along with his ongoing slew of inventions, continued to establish that Swedenborg instinctively focused on "how things work." Marveling in delight over concrete results when things actually work, he not only became a believer in the value of use as a guiding principle, but also became fulfilled emotionally and spiritually by the goodness he experienced as a result. Swedenborg is distinctive in that he sought a metaphysics for theology: he wanted a cosmos that works as functionally as would any mechanical science, his earliest love. The empirical results demonstrated through a thing's usefulness played a striking role of necessity for Swedenborg's theological universe: the only reason why anything exists is that it provides a use; in other words, usefulness is intrinsic to purpose, which itself is the force for being.

So when turning to theology and an overarching philosophy of the divine life well past the midpoint of his own, Swedenbor carried through with his focus on how to make love and wisdom practically effective for people both individually and as a society. Usefulness became the measuring instrument that completed his trinity of heart, head, and hands, but he expressed this in his own attuned way of how success looks and feels. Following Swedenborg's lead, the philosophy of American pragmatism essentially operates under the perception that *when something actually works,* one recognizes that a love for good has propelled it and that there is truth surely in it.

We can imagine three arenas of discourse central to a study of Swedenborg's concept of usefulness: how it functions within the Swedenborgian tradition, how it manifests in the larger context of historical Christian theology, and how it plays on the vast canvas of a broader cultural reception. Haller tackles the third discourse in a manner hitherto never attempted—or even comprehended—either inside or outside Swedenborgianism.

As for the first arena, it is quite fascinating to see the gradual growth of usefulness inside the Swedenborgian tradition. Though Swedenborg had begun preparing a separate volume in 1761 focused primarily on usefulness, he stopped work on it and instead incorporated a fulsome discussion of the subject in *Divine Love and Wisdom* (1763). Despite the fact that he discusses usefulness in more than a hundred passages throughout his writings, Swedenborg did not feature such terms as *uses* or *usefulness* in the book titles, chapter titles, or section headings of any of his published works. In fact, the first few subsequent generations did not seize upon usefulness, at least in print, with any particular emphasis. Other Swedenborgian concepts, such as the reality of the spiritual world, the inner sense of scripture, and the Second Coming having already occurred, were far more dramatic in the immediate religious social situation in which the earliest Swedenborgians found themselves. The Swedenborgian tradition, therefore, started a little slowly in recognizing the profundity of Swedenborg's discussion of usefulness.

In the longest-running early Swedenborgian journal, *The Intellectual Repository,* a few articles shaped the initial conversation on usefulness near the end of the eighteenth century, emphasizing the concept's philosophical and metaphysical foundations. This pattern of there being a modest quantity of published discourse on

Swedenborgian usefulness continued into the nineteenth century, even though it is now clear that its oral usage began to rise significantly in sermons and in the spiritual life of the church. There would later appear two books on the subject: B. F. Barrett's *Ends and Uses* (1887) and John Bigelow's *The Useful Life: A Crown to the Simple Life* (1905).

In the latter quarter of the twentieth century, though, the doctrine of usefulness spiked to the forefront of spirituality discourse among Swedenborgians. A 1981 article turned pamphlet (*Uses: A Way of Personal and Spiritual Growth*) by the American psychologist Wilson Van Dusen struck a chord and rapidly progressed into a runaway favorite among the Swedenborgian branches. Implementing usefulness as a spiritual growth method is now at the forefront of Swedenborgian practices, and the overall concept of usefulness competes with that of correspondences as the most beloved of Swedenborgian ideas.

As for the second arena, it is quite provocative and even perplexing that *usefulness* does not appear as important terminology among any prominent theological writings in Christian history. Whether considering the categories of common topics, the schema of fields, or the "systematics" of any particular major theologian from late antiquity to the present (from Origen to Wolfhart Pannenberg), you won't find the doctrine of usefulness explicitly framed except in Swedenborg. Even zeroing in on the subfield of practical theology—the skill-building and performance disciplines in theology that include preaching, teaching, worship, pastoral care, social outreach, ethical living, and spiritual practices—which one might identify with various particular *uses* of Christian theology in practice, the vocabulary of usefulness is absent and the philosophy of usefulness as a "way" is missing.

Finally, as for the third arena, up until *Swedenborg's Principles of Usefulness,* the larger philosophical and cultural engagement with Swedenborg's concept of usefulness was likewise mute. This welcome volume, however, explores some undiscovered country and reports Haller's findings. For both Swedenborgian and American studies alike, this book tells stories and builds perspectives that will prove without a doubt to be very *useful.*

Dr. James F. Lawrence, Dean of the
Center for Swedenborgian Studies, Piedmont, CA

Acknowledgments

Those to whom I am indebted include Julie McDaniel and the staff in the Swedenborg Memorial Library at Urbana University in Ohio; the Morris Library at Southern Illinois University Carbondale; the Flora Lamson Hewlett Library at the Graduate Theological Union in Berkeley, California; the Harvard Library; Stanford Libraries; the University of Michigan Library; the New York Public Library; the HathiTrust Digital Library; Google Books; and JSTOR. Equally important is the Swedenborg Foundation, who I want to thank for encouraging my research over the years. In particular, I extend my heartfelt gratitude to Jim Lawrence, Dean of the Center for Swedenborgian Studies at the Graduate Theological Union, for providing the book's foreword, and to the anonymous reviewers for their comments, suggestions, and careful reading of the manuscript in its various iterations. Along with my appreciation of their help, my thanks go to the generous advice and expert counsel from Editor John Connolly and Executive Director Morgan Beard, who helped measurably with the final product. Lastly, I thank my wife Robin, who not only provided the index but also offered encouragement and criticism along the way. Any errors of fact or interpretation that remain are mine alone, and for them I take full responsibility.

Introduction

For many today, the significance of Emanuel Swedenborg (1688–
1772)—the eighteenth-century Swedish scientist, mystic, and noble-
man—remains a puzzle. How is it, they ask, that his writings and
doctrines have had such an influence in Europe, America, and even
Asia over the course of the nineteenth and twentieth centuries and
into today? How did this prodigy become associated with such a wide
variety of belief systems—from philosophical (transcendentalism,
idealism, and pragmatism) and social reform (Owenism, Fourierism,
single tax, social gospel, socialism, nationalism, and progressivism)
to religious (Spiritualism, Zen Buddhism, mysticism, New Thought,
Theosophy, and the New Church) and therapeutical (homeopathy,
eclecticism, osteopathy, and New Age)? Why did his inspiring and
penetrating thoughts offer meaning, purpose, and authority to so
many people? How did his unimpassioned writings spur reform that
threatened to overthrow the reigning systems of theology and ecclesiasticism? And why did this unpretentious and devout man resonate
among so many Christians, unburdening them of ancient rituals and
dogmas dealing with God's tri-personality, the vicarious atonement,
bodily resurrection, salvation by faith alone, and biblical literalism?

Swedenborg began his study of the human being by way of anatomy, his preferred point of entry into the workings of the soul. In his
study of the human organism, he accumulated evidence on the functions of the organs and the relation of their fluids to the whole body.
A scientific prodigy, he incorporated ideas of Euclid, Copernicus,
Vesalius, Galen, and Boerhaave into his life's work. A discoverer and

inventor, he helped formulate the elements of crystallography and differential and integral calculus; and he experimented in the fields of astronomy, cosmogony, geology, metallurgy, anatomy, physiology, chemistry, mathematics, and mechanics. He mastered several languages; and he served as a poet, metaphysician, financier, member of the Swedish Parliament, and man of letters. Swedenborg's early contributions included the publication of the scientific periodical *Daedalus Hyperboreus* (1716–18); various mechanical and mathematical discoveries, including the invention of the air-tight stove; revisions to the currency, decimal system, balance of trade, and liquor laws; innovative ideas on the manufacture and assaying of iron, steel, copper, and brass; a nebular hypothesis for the formation of the planets and the sun; and the idea that the motion of the brain was synchronous with respiration.

The scion of two distinguished families—his mother's in mining and his father's in Pietism—Swedenborg lived a life indelibly marked by a spiritual crisis that he experienced in 1745. Convinced that the event had changed his life, he left his colleagues in the Cartesian world of materially enlightened science and technology for a spiritual world of visionary insight that turned the cold orthodoxy of his Lutheran countrymen into a religion of love and good works. Joining the great tradition of Western and Eastern mystics, he claimed to have communicated with the world of spirits, offering revelatory soundings on scripture. Out of these ecstasies emerged his doctrines of forms, series, degrees, influx, correspondences, and usefulness. These concepts that he lived and breathed connected his thoughts to daily endeavors, made clear the distinction between the literal and universal senses of things, and revealed the significance of divine influx. As a self-proclaimed servant of the Lord, he turned his attention to scripture and the dry catechism of the Church, infusing both with ethical and moral wisdom, correcting popular errors, and rearranging the universe according to God's ruling loves.[1]

As a result of his mystical experiences, Swedenborg wrote three volumes of visionary interpretations of scripture that he chose not to publish, and these were followed by eighteen volumes of theology, scripture interpretation, and spiritual experiences that he did publish. Viewing himself as a vessel through which God's teachings could be spread, he dedicated his life to addressing the inner meaning of scripture, which, for most Protestants, was the only authentic medium of communication between God and humanity—the form God took to reconcile life's contradictions. Knowing that the strict literalness of the Bible was a veil concealing important internal meanings, Swedenborg wrote a corpus of works that presented a picture of cosmic unfoldment according to an ascending ladder of degrees, series, and potentialities that are tethered to the providential action of divine influx. In *Secrets of Heaven* (1749–56), *Heaven and Hell* (1758), *Divine Love and Wisdom* (1763), *Divine Providence* (1764), *Apocalypse Revealed* (1766), and *True Christianity* (1771), Swedenborg redefined Christianity, addressing such ideas as justification by faith alone, which he rejected; the doctrine of the Trinity, which remained a gray area for traditional Christians; the meaning of creation; and the type of life that followed physical death. By the end of his life's work, he claimed to have discovered the relationship between the soul and body and, in accordance with the concept of degrees, between the soul and God.

Swedenborg's writings were noted for both their dullness and depth of insight. Many readers, in fact, found his work to be unreadable, if not unfathomable. Still, he astonished admirers—then and now—with solutions to many of Christianity's most puzzling questions, including those related to the nature of free will, the humanity of Christ, and the identification of God with humanity. Unitarian preacher Octavius Brooks Frothingham (1822–95) suggested that Swedenborg "transcended his limitations and opened an original path for thought." His "brilliant flashes of insight" and the "astonishing penetration of single utterances" gave him passage "beyond the limitations of time and place."[2]

With ideas that were quite unorthodox, if not verging on heretical, Swedenborg proposed a conception of heaven as the Universal Human, something unlike anything found beyond a few Christian mystics, such as Gregory of Nyssa and Meister Eckhart. His questions and responses forced proponents and detractors alike to reimagine the meaning of religion, belief, salvation, creation, evil, consciousness, freedom, and even God. His thoughts penetrated to the very roots of Christianity and to the mystery of the divine economy, namely, God's actions to bring about the world's salvation and redemption. His success in providing a more integrated understanding came without the accoutrements of formal institutions or, for that matter, organized forms of ritual and belief. Church membership was not a prerequisite to understanding the intricacies of his doctrines. This explains how and why so many different political, religious, and intellectual leaders saw few restraints in applying his beliefs to their particular endeavors. In time, Swedenborg's doctrines of forms, series, degrees, influx, correspondences, and usefulness; his visions of divine love and wisdom; and his depictions of heaven and hell appealed to Christians across Europe and America—particularly to those whose faith trembled as a result of their growing disbelief in the harshness of the Christian God.

Swedenborg's **doctrine of correspondences,** which describes the relationship between things in the natural and spiritual worlds, offers the key to understanding the Word, as it provides a cause-and-effect relationship between those worlds. Everything in the natural world "corresponds" to its counterpart in the spiritual world from which it springs as the effect of a cause. Despite the seeming infinity of beings in nature, each species originates from a spiritual cause and is subordinate to the Creator's purpose in the formation of a heaven: "Since there is nothing created that lacks [a purpose, a means, and a result], it follows that the universe and everything in it has been created by the Lord by means of the sun where the purpose of everything resides."[3]

The **doctrine of forms** explains the principles by which nature ascends from the mineral kingdom to the human species, with all forms deriving their perfection from the "form of forms," a paean to Plato's theory of Ideas, which describes a transcendent or archetypal property or quality that is separate from the object itself.

According to the **doctrine of series,** all substances are organized alongside those similar to themselves in their properties. This, in turn, leads to the **doctrine of degrees,** where substances ascend, each in its series, from least to greatest. Overall, each series forms an impassable boundary or barrier; no substance can leap from one series to another. By degrees, nature ascends and descends in one continuous distinct and discrete form or substance.

According to the **doctrine of influx,** the energy that makes the connection between the natural and spiritual worlds is divine influx, which accounts for the presence of God in everything. Creation is the process by which finite things form from things that are infinite and are then sustained by influx from the Creator. The natural and spiritual worlds are not identical in substance; neither is nature identical with humanity. Each product of creation receives and manifests its purpose from the Creator. God creates all things from himself but is also perfectly distinct from his creation. That said, God is not nature; nor is nature God. All things are both finite and distinct from God, though they are derived from him. In God, human beings live under the law of influx. But humanity is neither divine nor destined to somehow merge into the oversoul of God.[4] Thus, when speaking of these different doctrines, Swedenborg notes how all things are connected, operating by the sustaining power of their Creator in a relationship of cause and effect: "People who propose a creation of the universe and everything in it with no constant intermediate steps from what is first cannot help but formulate theories that are fragmentary and disconnected from actual causes."[5]

The **doctrine of usefulness,** arguably the most philosophical and practical of Swedenborg's many contributions, holds that all being is created "from use, in use, and for use."[6] The whole of creation fulfills a heavenly purpose at the same time that it serves the material world. From the lowest inanimate forms of being to the highest and most complex living organism—what Western thinkers from the Neo-Platonists to the philosophers of the seventeenth and eighteenth centuries identified as the "Great Chain of Being," or *scala naturae*—all of creation exists not just for its own sake but for purposes of the whole. All existence, both living and nonliving, has its place in the chain, and each link performs its appointed duty, which, as a consequence, sustains the whole.[7] Like the Enlightenment's

Great Chain of Being, Swedenborg's concept of creation consists of distinct planes of activity that developed progressively. In the realm of human beings, the regions of the mind are divided into degrees called natural, spiritual, and heavenly, with each individual's final destiny being dependent upon the mind's development, namely, its degrees of love, wisdom, and use. Since every effect represents the particular nature of an individual's usefulness, by following the chain or sequence of effects, one can track the degree to which a particular individual is drawn to or from divine love.[8]

Beginning with the first act of creation, God intended the universe to become his "theater of useful functions," and it is in its application that each individual forms the breadth and depth of his or her spiritual sight or influx. "All useful functions from beginnings to limits and from limits to beginnings have a relationship and a responsiveness to everything in humans, so that we are a kind of image of the universe and conversely the universe, from a functional point of view, is in our image."[9] All things in the physical and spiritual universe are conjoined to assist the natural mind in seeking its heavenly end. At the heart of the doctrine of usefulness is the mind's ability to identify a connection between objects in the natural world and their transcendent archetypes, revealing a use on the natural plane that provides the means for attaining its spiritual end. The soul, having love as its object, pursues usefulness through the body that, in turn, fuels the direction the individual takes to or from divine love. Useful activities pass into forms that shape the soul to the body, shape the effects produced by the individual on the natural world, and, in turn, shape the particular province in the heavens that best reflects the fullness of an individual's affections. While the causes of all things are in the spiritual world, the effects are in the natural world. For humankind, there is an added difference between those whose greatest love is goodness and those whose greatest love is to work toward selfish ends. In both, what the doer perceives as useful translates into either good or harmful works: If an individual's highest priority is to do good, then he or she will choose to help others in order to make him or herself useful. On the other hand, if an individual is focused on their own personal gain, then the outcome of their works is likely to be harmful to others. Both choices are free choices of the will.[10]

So what does it mean to be useful? According to Swedenborg, it is "simply to do work benefiting one's neighbor, one's native land, the church, and the Lord's kingdom."[11] The defining nature of life is in the performance of useful actions, whether done for selfish interests or for the benefit of others, the latter of which he regards as a way of worshiping God.[12] Useful actions are not of equal value.[13] Swedenborg identifies three forms of useful action: those sustaining the body, those perfecting the rational mind, and those receiving the spiritual from the Lord. All of these useful actions are proper to humanity's rationality and freedom, and any one of them could be acted out for good or evil purposes. Whether carried out for selfish love or for unselfish love, they constitute a general order or sequence that defines the person's ascent to or descent from the Lord. The individual puts to use, together with the will, that which he or she deems to have the higher ends—whether for material purposes, for the benefit of others, or for spiritual purposes.[14] "We all possess [rationality and freedom] from creation and therefore from birth—they are given us by the Lord."[15]

"Serving the Lord," says Swedenborg, "means performing useful deeds because true worship consists in acting usefully and therefore in exercising neighborly love." This does not imply praying or listening to sermons; instead, it refers to the discharge of those responsibilities that are integral to everyday duties, regardless of any particular station in life. Usefulness is the mode that, performed in total sincerity, an individual acts out in his or her choices, each according to that particular end perceived as good. Thus, each individual becomes a reflection of his or her choices. "Good spirits [are] forms embodying a good ambition," while "evil spirits [are] forms embodying an evil ambition." In choosing their ways of being useful, individuals act on their loves, creating the sphere or persona that flows from them. Each person is who he or she is according to the ways in which they can be useful. The end (i.e., for the sake of which one acts) ultimately becomes that which one loves above all else.[16]

In the Lord's view the whole human race is as one [person]. . . . It is not the [people] themselves that are thus seen together, but the uses with them. They that are good uses, that is, that perform uses from the Lord, when viewed together, are seen as a [person] perfect in form and beautiful. . . . But they that perform uses, not for the sake of uses, but for the sake of themselves alone, or the world alone, likewise appear before the Lord as one [person], but as an imperfect and deformed [one].[17]

The same reasoning applies to charity, or loving one's neighbor and selflessly doing good things for others, which, like love, exists in use. To the extent that individuals express their love for the Lord, they do so in useful actions that are performed out of charity toward their neighbors. By contrast, actions taken for one's own good are not done out of love for the Lord and so are not performed out of true charity but are derived from evil. Only those who perform charitable acts naturally and spiritually out of love for the Lord, with their neighbor as the object of this love, can conjoin with the Lord. If charity is not expressed in unselfish acts of love, then it is of little purpose.[18] Love serves as the basis of Swedenborg's view of charity. Like will and action, charity and works are distinct from one another. Charity belongs to the inner self, while good deeds are the product of the outer self. Only when good deeds are spontaneous and derived from charity, and not concealing an intention or purpose that is self-centered, does the individual become a temple of God. The whole being of the individual, evident in works that represent love's affections, forms the composite of a person's inner nature.[19]

The religious philosophy of Swedenborg is all-inclusive, binding the Creator to the origin of all things (animate and inanimate), revealing an external universe of creation, and sustaining it along with an internal universe of mind and spirit. In Swedenborg's worldview, all things proceed from love and wisdom, where heaven consists of human society perfectly organized as the Universal Human who reflects the image and likeness of the Divine-Human One, and where the fully elucidated principles on which the world rests are based on the doctrines of degrees, influx, and correspondences. With the universe created by divine love and wisdom and with a cosmic orderliness implying both a purpose and an end, Swedenborg conceptualizes humanity not as something that will eventually be absorbed into the Infinite but as something serving a heavenly use in the Universal Human. Like all created beings, human beings exist not for themselves alone but for purposes of the whole. Each person is directed by a ruling love, which, in turn, forms a place in heaven or hell. Love is the end, wisdom is the cause, and usefulness is the effect.[20]

Overall, Swedenborg's doctrines portended a new approach to Christianity: the sacraments are signs; religion is not senseless formality; true religion consists in love of God and charity to humankind; heaven is the Universal Human; scripture is deceptive in appearance only, not in reality; Satan has no being or existence; and no individual is predestined to hell. Absent from the equation were original sin and personal atonement, which were replaced by Old Testament primitivism, with its view of sin as a collective rather than personal failing.[21] Being a Christian no longer meant living with dogma and ritual; instead, it meant a combination of performing services in the forms of good works and having a renewed spirituality. Unlike those Protestant churches that continued to teach the culpability of the individual before God, social reformers before and after the Civil War, including the social gospelers and progressive reformers, were urging a collective sense of guilt, with redemption through practical activities such as revising penal codes, treating better the poor and insane, paying attention to the needs of the Native American and African American, making improvements in the educational system, attacking political corruption, and making democracy less of an illusion.

Those Americans who found comfort in Swedenborg's writings and revelatory visions included the New England Transcendentalist Ralph Waldo Emerson; biblical scholar George Bush; jurist Theophilus Parsons; poets John Greenleaf Whittier and Philip Freneau; publishers Francis Bailey and William Cooper Howells; theologian and philosopher Henry James, Sr.; lawyer and statesman John Bigelow; author and literary critic William Dean Howells; and New Thought authors Warren Felt Evans and Timothy Shay Arthur. Besides his impact on individual authors, philosophers, and statesmen, Swedenborg influenced the Harmonist ideas of George Rapp, the utopian socialist project of Robert Owen in Indiana, and the Fourierist initiatives of William Henry Channing and Albert Brisbane. From Edward Bellamy's nationalism and Henry George's single-tax theory to the social gospel and the emergence of the philosophy of pragmatism, a surprising kinship existed between Swedenborg's writings and those persons searching for answers to underscore the purposes of the will as played out in the natural world. Equally important is that all sought meaning through a common genotype, namely, the practical and functional consequences of one's actions.[22]

Swedenborg's doctrine of usefulness has long been embedded in American thought and culture, best understood in the competing worldviews of the nation's liberal and conservative traditions. This included, respectively, the Jeffersonians—who advocated for an agrarian society, with its core values founded on the will of "plain folk," limited government, and a strict interpretation of the Constitution—and the Hamiltonians—whose ideals formed around the British model of strong government, banking, industrialization, and expansionism. During the nation's growth, as evidenced by the raw statistics on immigration, urbanization, railroad expansion, steel production, episodes of boom and bust, and an ever-emerging middle class, these two competing philosophies often changed sides in their efforts to reconcile ends and means. To the extent that this changing of sides took place, spiritual currents and intellectual sparks resulted in a procession of ideas and dreams that crossed political and class boundaries in the nation's experiment with democracy. With sources deep in the American and European experience, America's reformers set out to address the nation's problems with both moral and social engineering that was Jeffersonian in rhetoric but oftentimes Hamiltonian in outcome.[23] Ultimately, the nation's reformers learned by trial and error that achieving their objectives required a centralized power that was enlightened by concepts of Christian social democracy. For those Swedenborgians and New Church members who acted out their faith within these two political traditions, the doctrine of usefulness involved a commitment to energize the nation and its people by envisaging the possibility of a much-desired Universal Human.

Chapter 1 ("Love's Affections") explains how the first half of the nineteenth century could be recognized as, according to Emerson, the age of Swedenborg: a pre-Darwinian world whose philosophy was constant, whose truths were intuitive, and whose morals were absolute. From there, it recounts the extent to which that age's representative spokespersons were able to connect the ideal with the real, bridging the divide between their contemplative worldview and the world of change and contingency. Yet, despite the emphasis on spirit over matter and an attention to a higher reality, the age remained fixated on a subtle but real discrepancy between the nation's democratic faith and its acquiescence on matters of race and ethnicity.

Chapter 2 ("Incantatory Delusions") traces the efforts of communitarians as they set out to transform into brick and mortar the perfectionist beliefs of Emanuel Swedenborg, Robert Owen, and Charles Fourier. Brook Farm, arguably the most famous of the communities, began as a society formed in 1841 by a group of Transcendentalists before converting to Fourierism in 1843 and Swedenborgianism in 1844. A study of contrasts, its combination of Emerson's individualism, Fourier's faith in communal perfection, and Swedenborg's doctrine of usefulness represented an effort to connect subjective with objective, contemplation with action, and innermost with outermost.

Chapter 3 ("In Search of a Vision") analyzes the nation's soul-searching as it transitioned from a Jeffersonian-centered democracy built around Lockean principles and Emerson's self-reliant individual to a Darwinian worldview whose individuals had little or no control over the biological and socioeconomic forces controlling their destiny. Working at the edges of an evolutionary and highly deterministic philosophy, the nation's writers and artists sought in different ways to leave behind the romantic generalities of their youth for an unmediated view of reality. Early concepts of social evolution clashed with the detritus of industrial capitalism, turning the once-optimistic view of American exceptionalism into an existential questioning of the nation's core values. The central appeal of the representative writings of Edward Bellamy and William Dean Howells remained their ethicality, as they were always concerned with the morality and fairness of what happens to individual character. Nevertheless, they viewed their fellow human beings as living and working in an environment that often prevented them from being good even though they desired in their heart to be so. Here was located the nexus of the challenge to the New Church. Was it possible to carry Swedenborg's undiluted belief in the Universal Human into the second half of the century, or must the New Church seek some alternate way to accommodate the new worldview? How much, if any, would Swedenborgianism need to change to remain relevant?

Chapter 4 ("Single Tax") recounts the displacement of the nation's agricultural democracy by a plutocracy of special interests whose control of the land caused irreparable damage to the body politic. As seen through the eyes of Henry George and his disciples, the solution lay in the imposition of a single tax on the unearned increment to the value of land. Neither socialist nor utopian in intent, the single tax represented a heavy dose of Christian virtue mixed with Jeffersonian democracy, and it quickly became a cause célèbre among many in the New Church, as they sought ways to transform the tawdry materialism of the age into a more rational and kindlier society based on the doctrine of usefulness.

Chapter 5 ("Social Gospel") explains how American Protestantism, whose elements of repentance, salvation, and sanctification were premised on a highly individualistic relationship between a person and his or her God, fell short of the needs stemming from unfettered capitalism. Rather than extolling the personal relationship between

God and humanity, the social gospelers sought a collective sense of responsibility by motivating individuals toward the salvation of a society based on the principles of brotherhood and love of one's neighbor. Without breaking into naïve optimism, they projected a vision of the future built on a combination of Christian hope, applied Christianity, evolutionary science, and a politically engaged clergy. For Swedenborgians, the social gospel movement represented a crisis not of ends but of means, challenging whether issues involving the referendum, the Australian ballot, strikes, labor unions, arbitration, and political activism should take front and center for their Church and its members.

Chapter 6 ("Loose Ends") identifies a list of unresolved issues that overshadowed the ability of the Swedenborgians to unify in the late nineteenth century. Included among them were questions regarding the proper sphere of women, the nature of true charity, the unanticipated consequences of political activism, the consequences of race and ethnicity, and the higher criticism. Each of these issues resulted in recriminations between and among Swedenborgians and the leadership of the Church.

Chapter 7 ("Pragmatism") explains the connection between Swedenborg's doctrine of usefulness and the action philosophy of pragmatism, two belief systems focused on how we think and how we act. Together, they forced the abandonment of age-old beliefs and practices, replacing them with a philosophy that defined truth not as something fixed once and for all time but as a set of actionable beliefs that worked to the best possible purposes. "The ultimate test for us of what a truth means," wrote William James, "is indeed the conduct it dictates or inspires."[24] Pragmatism fit the criterion of usefulness, with its emphasis on self-reliance, individualism, insight, instinct, intuition, optimism, and practice. The idea became true in the process of making it true. This was not anything transcendental but was instead the realization that thought is instrumental or, using the language of Swedenborg, a form of good. By taking experience as it comes and resisting the temptation to intellectualize it, the world becomes a place of unlimited opportunities for making connections, distinctions, and decisions; even more, the world becomes radically pluralistic, bereft of all its idealistic monism. Like Swedenborgianism, pragmatism deprecated rigid determinism, distrusted dogma and abstraction, replaced Cartesian dualism with the indivisibility of experience, and saw no meaning or value to an idea without factoring in its use. Value comes in the doing, where ends and means combine in the immediacy of the moment.

Chapter 8 ("Pastoral Clinical Movement") recounts one of the more durable outcomes of the social gospel movement, which involved the fusion of German-based psychoanalytic experimentation with Swedenborgian idealism and a Phineas Quimby-inspired theory of mental healing. Together, they produced a nondogmatic and nondenominational form of psychotherapy that made its way into professional as well as laitized efforts to use the power of thinking to improve health and well-being.

Conclusion ("American Spirit") seeks to capture in summary form the facts that neither did Swedenborgianism represent any conventional house of Christian theology nor did those in the New Church allow themselves to be shallow followers of their own ecclesiastical leaders. Faith consciousness, conditioned by a mixture of American and British philosophical thinking, encouraged Swedenborgians to dispense with conventional solutions to life's challenges. Having lived through the central issues of the day and awakened by the nation's shortcomings, they worked with progressive thinkers—both churched and unchurched—to reinvigorate the founding principles of government.

Those who read Swedenborg's revelatory writings believed that they had discovered in them the hermeneutical meanings behind the stories, symbols, and representations in scripture, in the spiritual fullness of the natural world, and in the deeper meanings hidden but still discernible in the structure of the human body. Each material thing had a functional value as well as a deeper spiritual meaning, the latter of which rose to the level of awareness through correspondences and usefulness. This combination stoked the efforts of those who sought to reconcile religion and politics with concepts of reason and nature. There was a dimension to Swedenborg's beliefs that suggested a political element operating on the fringes of his mystical thinking. His doctrine of correspondences, linking the material and spiritual worlds, suggested a conduit for ideas that became a portent for both spiritual and political regeneration—all resulting in the Universal Human.[25]

Swedenborg's Principles of Usefulness

Swedenborg Studies No. 23

1 Love's Affections

Love and wisdom are nothing but abstract notions to think about, notions that pause in the mind for a little while and then vanish like a breeze. The two come together in service, though, and in service become virtually one entity, something we can call real. Love cannot rest until it does something. Love is the essential active element of life. Wisdom cannot emerge and last either, except when it is doing something out of and together with love. "Doing something" is service; so we define service as doing something good out of love by means of wisdom. The service is that "something good" itself.

(Swedenborg, *Marriage Love* §183:3)

In the period of social ferment between 1820 and 1860, the age of Jacksonian democracy was best symbolized by an ethic of individual responsibility, faith in the nation's exceptionalism, obsessive interest in reform, the proliferation of voluntary associations, and an optimism that was truly American, with its vision of a glorious future. In all subjects of discourse, including especially humanity's capacity for moral improvement, advocates brought forth both religious and secular ideas that gave free rein to the imagination and, in particular, to the desire to distinguish humankind's uniqueness from its generality. The age was filled with mesmerists, vegetarians, electrobiologists, clairvoyants, and phrenologists—all of whom saw no barrier between the mind and the solutions to age-old mysteries such as death and immortality. As waves of reform swept over the young republic in the 1840s, men and women like Charles A. Dana, Louisa

May Alcott, Lydia Maria Child, Julia Ward Howe, Bronson Alcott, Theodore Parker, and James Freeman Clarke made frequent references to Swedenborg in their lectures, books, and personal correspondence. His name and doctrines became common currency among the leading minds of the day, whose articles in *The Christian Examiner, The American Quarterly Review, The New England Magazine,* and *The Massachusetts Quarterly Review* gave proof to the breadth of Swedenborg's influence.

"This age is Swedenborg's,"[1] said Ralph Waldo Emerson about the first half of the nineteenth century, noting the influence of the mystic's gentle and optimistic theology, which are characteristics that resonated with antebellum society. Harvard literary critic Francis Otto Matthiessen reaffirmed Emerson's description, explaining it as an alignment of Swedenborg's mysticism with the period's embrace of idealism. Swedenborg's doctrines of correspondences and usefulness counteracted the materialism of the age by enchanting generations with the prospect of divine influx; influencing the visionary and ecstatic writings of its Transcendentalist poets and authors; explaining away the occasional eruptions of eccentricity that followed in the wake of the Fox sisters' Spiritualist rappings; and encouraging the sublimation of selfhood for the more encompassing Universal Human.[2]

Swedenborgianism

The movement that would become known as Swedenborgianism originated in England, which is where Swedenborg's works were first published by an admiring group of followers. Initially, the term referred to a core of mystically inclined believers who found comfort in Swedenborg's spiritual view of the world. Scattered across Protestant denominations, their intent was to inculcate a practical morality built on free will, piety, spiritual regeneration, and a much-simplified set of religious principles that were augmented by Swedenborg's revelatory visions. Over time, the London-based Swedenborgians formed themselves into a denomination called the Church of the New Jerusalem (the "New Church"), which attracted small numbers of believers in England, France, Germany, Sweden, and the United States.[3]

The New Church held to the belief that at the close of the third century, there had been a marked decline in the Apostolic Church's spiritual power, with much of its message having been forgotten. Though the Post-Nicene Church exercised enormous political influence, it, too, continued to lose spiritual power, especially that of the redemptive spirit that characterized the early Church. Once "Romanized," the rituals of Catholicism replaced the spiritual life of the early Church. With this change, "sacramentarianism," or "salvation by magic," became the new apostolic message. The Protestant Reformation succeeded in restoring some of the fundamental teachings, but it introduced a new doctrine, "salvation by faith alone," which Swedenborgians considered to be a "retrograde movement." The erroneous teachings of both the Roman and Reformed Churches brought forth the divine judgment, with the New Church "instituted by a new revelation to do a work without which salvation would be impossible."[4]

Long before 1769, the year marking Swedenborg's return to his homeland to answer to the charge of heresy made by prelates of the Lutheran state church against "those leading men who [were] reported as favoring [his] principles," rumors abounded suggesting Swedenborg's participation in conspiratorial activities among Europe's intellectual dilettantes. As early as 1706, there were allegations that he had joined the ranks of Freemasonry, making numerous visits to its lodges across Europe, and claims that he had even been arrested in Paris in 1737. In 1799, Abbé Barruel singled out the Swedenborgian Masons, accusing them of involvement in questionable activities bent on overthrowing the established churches and governments. In defense of Swedenborg, Rudolph L. Tafel, in his *Documents Concerning the Life and Character of Emanuel Swedenborg* (1877), dismissed the claims as fraudulent. Robert Hindmarsh drew similar conclusions in *Rise and Progress of the New Jerusalem Church in England, America, and Other Parts* (1861). More recently, however, Marsha Keith Schuchard accused Swedenborg of working on behalf of the Swedish government and using secret Masonic networks to relay intelligence. She perceptively pointed out the close relationship between Swedenborg and his brother-in-law Eric Benzelius, who had served as both a father figure and tutor in Swedenborg's youth. It was

Benzelius, she noted, who worked on cabalistic interpretations of the New Testament and the Rosicrucian ideals of science and religion. For these reasons, Schuchard and Barruel viewed Swedenborg and those of the New Church as catalysts for change.[5]

While these views are indicative of differences of opinion regarding Swedenborg's personal involvement in reform activities, there seems to be little evidence that he openly endorsed revolution, much less civil disobedience. However, he did share with many his fear of absolutism.[6] Nevertheless, a compelling case can be made that Swedenborg's ideas influenced Freemasonry, members of which dabbled in occultism, alchemy, cabalism, mesmerism, and spiritism. Freemasons found in his revelatory writings a much-welcomed defense of their activities.[7] Those who had long been associated with the occult considered his writings to be the fulfillment of enduring convictions concerning spiritual enlightenment and prophecy. Freemasonry openly endorsed Swedenborg's writings—especially his central idea of correspondences, which linked the material and spiritual worlds.[8]

Given the tradition of prophecy and millenarianism that jostled amid the rational, classical, and liberal components of the Enlightenment, it was not surprising that mystically inclined artists, poets, novelists, and publishers supported a lively subculture whose beliefs in social and moral improvement crossed geographical, secular, and religious boundaries. Swedenborg's writings influenced first chaplain to the Continental Congress Rev. Jacob Duché, Swedenborgian preacher Ralph Mather, novelist and playwright Honoré de Balzac, and dramatist August Strindberg, notable figures whose efforts and works contributed to the emotional and spiritual dimension of the late eighteenth and early nineteenth centuries.[9]

Swedenborgianism became a repository for the period's collective expressions of the soul and the interrelation of human beings in society. It touted an exalted idea of dignity, a growing impatience with outdated rules, and a distinct deference to the power of collective attainment. Those influenced by his writings carried away from them an artist's interpretation of their inner meaning, which more often than not exalted imagination over reason, assigned the primacy of spirit over matter, encouraged self-sufficiency and a far-sighted sense of mission, and possessed a willingness to challenge the old order. Though it can be argued that Swedenborg was not disposed to performing heroic actions, those who studied his works perceived a sense of direction, persuasion, and perseverance that often provoked their making unpopular but necessary decisions.

William Blake

In the arts and literature, this reform dimension was nowhere more evident than it was in the polemical and apocalyptic works of William Blake (1757–1827). Along with Blake's claim to the gift of "vision," which he asserted gave him access to Socrates and Christ, his mytho-visionary writings (especially his poetry) were provoked by not only the French Revolution itself, which he cheered, but also by the indeterminacy of its meaning. John Gould Fletcher described Blake as having "no God except the God comprehensible to man, the divine spirit of humanity incarnated historically in Jesus, and capable of reincarnation in Everyman."[10] His prophetic books and poetry became encoded attacks on conventional morality, targeting love and marriage in particular, as well as on nature in general. He challenged historical prophecies with his own brand of visionary and irrational enthusiasms that were infused with extremist rhetoric, contradictions, intertextual conflict, and larger-than-life characters with otherworldly prophecy. At the heart of his writings was his fundamental disagreement with the nature of revolution and his obsession with the chief conservative voice of the time, Edmund Burke, whose *Reflections on the Revolution in France* (1790) eroded much of England's sympathy for the overthrow of the *ancien régime* and its decadent ways. Burke's rhetoric transformed the French Revolution not only into a volcanic force of destruction, social instability, and class struggle but also into a war on ideas. The Revolution became a subversive force seeking to undermine Europe's intellectual and political foundations.[11]

Blake acquired an education and competence in several languages, placing him among an elite group of intellectuals. A lover of verse, his compositions were varied and spontaneous, demonstrating a clear predilection for a mystical habit of thought, a consummate mastery of language and its meanings, and a genuine delight in lyrical imagination. His *Marriage of Heaven and Hell* (1790), a skillful reinterpretation of biblical episodes, replaced reasoning and ecclesiastical authority with intuition. Similarly, his *The French Revolution* (1791), which embodied a "visionary" interpretation of the events that took place in Paris and Versailles in 1789, reflected his utter disdain for authority, whether taking the form of Louis XVI or clericalism. These works, along with *A Song of Liberty* (1792), *America a Prophecy* (1793), and *The Book of Urizen* (1794), made it clear that he was on the side of unrestricted freedom and license.[12]

A radical in both politics and religion, Blake viewed Swedenborg's revelatory interpretations as cause for replacing the corrupted beliefs of the existing churches in Christianity. The illumination that drew him to Swedenborg's mysticism also promoted a sense of empowerment to remove the ecclesiastical detritus that was clinging to Christianity. Blake's writings reflected the ideological biases of a circle of authors and artists who not only welcomed the French Revolution but also looked toward the general reconstitution of social systems. Individuals such as writer and advocate of women's rights Mary Wollstonecraft, who was a reader of Swedenborg; dissenting theologian and natural philosopher Joseph Priestley; Scottish political writer Thomas Christie; and political theorist and revolutionary Thomas Paine lent themselves to the welter of thought reflective of the Enlightenment's skeptical regard for all things orthodox and traditional. The distinctions between politics, religion, and more personal matters fell before their harsh rationalism.[13] Anxious as they were to test ideas of spiritual regeneration and millennial awakening, their visions of a reborn society made their debut among groups in Germany, England, France, and the United States. As explained in Robert Rix's *William Blake and the Cultures of Radical Christianity,* "The politicization of Swedenborgian doctrines penetrated the [New] Church to its very core.... There was a widespread tendency among Swedenborgians to turn their prophet's teaching into a social gospel that fitted a radical and anticlerical outlook of the late eighteenth century."[14]

The Peculiar Institution

From ancient Egypt, Babylon, and Assyria, to classical Greece and Rome, and on to medieval Europe, India, China, and the New World, societies and their governments almost universally permitted or acquiesced in the practice of slavery. Not until the Scientific Revolution of the sixteenth and seventeenth centuries, and the subsequent struggles to reformulate science, philosophy, society, and politics, did the authoritative norms of Western tradition, superstition, and prejudice face harsh questioning. Still, in the Enlightenment's classification of the natural world, including humankind's place in the hierarchical Great Chain of Being, each species and its attendant varieties held an assigned position and status. Exemplary of this type of thinking was the Scottish historian and empirical philosopher David Hume (1711–76) who, in his essay "Of National Characters," wrote:

> I am apt to suspect the negroes, and in general all the other species of men (for there are four or five different kinds) to be naturally inferior to the whites. There never was a civiliz'd nation of any other complexion than white, nor even any individual eminent either in action or speculation. No ingenious manufactures amongst them, no arts, no sciences. On the other hand, the most rude and barbarous of the whites, such as the ancient *Germans*, the present *Tartars*, have still something eminent about them, in their valour, form of government, or some other particular. Such a uniform and constant difference could not happen, in so many countries and ages, if nature had not made an original distinction betwixt these breeds of men. Not to mention our colonies, there are *Negro* slaves dispersed all over *Europe*, of which none ever discover'd any symptoms of ingenuity; tho' low people, without education, will start up amongst us, and distinguish themselves in every profession. In *Jamaica*, indeed they talk of one negro, as a man of parts and learning; but 'tis likely he is admir'd for very slender accomplishments, like a parrot, who speaks a few words plainly.[15]

By the second half of the eighteenth century, a period in Western Europe more self-directed in thought and action than in previous ages, there emerged an awakening to the unfulfilled aspects of human existence. In Britain, France, and their colonies in North America, a growing number of critics weighed slavery's perceived economic benefits against the fact that it was a social evil to which humankind had for too long been blind. What for centuries had been rationalized as a natural aspect of Western culture now faced a more personalized judgment. The belief in natural rights, and the idea that history progressed in a linear direction rather than simply repeating itself, challenged the peculiar institution, but not to the degree that it threatened the Europeans' view of themselves. Despite the competing hereditarian and environmental notions of species origination and differentiation, both theories ascribed to a hierarchical view of the races, with the European, or Caucasian, stationed at the very top.

The earliest antislavery activity came not from science or organized religion but from individuals—both religious and secular—seeking a truer purpose for creation. Secularists such as Rousseau, Montesquieu, Voltaire, and Locke were not above calling out the institution of slavery as a despotic practice, while, on the religious side, particularly among evangelicals, opposition to the slave trade was becoming understood as a reflection of the changing nature of sin. Societies such as the Quakers followed the lead of these individuals, questioning the morality of slavery in spite of what most felt to be the "natural order" of the races. Still, if it were not for the blatant examples of slavery's brutal realities, the abolitionist movement would most likely not have succeeded so quickly and effectively.

As many great thinkers of the time were formulating arguments in support of antislavery, it is useful to explore Swedenborg's writings to learn just how much he inspired opposition to this ghastly enterprise. For him, the work of creation was not the result of blind forces acting without direction; nor was it the result of an arbitrary order. There was a connection of all things by intermediates and an order in which the world had been created. All of creation (mineral, vegetable, and animal) had a role, with each part conjoined to the whole for a purpose and an end subsumed in love, wisdom, and use from the Lord.[16] In accord with the Enlightenment's Great Chain of Being, each species existed according to its kind and was distinguished from every other species.[17]

Because each species was viewed as having a fixed place in the Great Chain, it followed that the races, or varieties within the species, held their place as well. Swedenborg did not comment on the idea of a hierarchical order of races, except to infuse into the discussion a description of each race's inner nature, which in the case of Africans included their gentler and more spiritual aspects. A contemporary of Rousseau, Swedenborg adhered to the Enlightenment's concept of primitivism, or the natural superiority of primitive peoples, which explained his admiration of the African race and of its ability to experience more immediate perceptions of truth and perform acts of unselfish cooperation. He noted that Africans were "more receptive than others in this earth" because they "willingly receive, from the angels, the doctrine concerning the Lord." More than any other people, they had "implanted in themselves that the Lord must appear altogether as a man, and that it can by no means happen otherwise. They are in the capacity of receiving not only the truths of faith, but especially its goods. They are of the celestial genius." Swedenborg also stated that while the Church was "perishing in Europe," it had the potential of being "renewed in Africa."[18] For this reason, he opposed missionary efforts, believing them to be harmful to the truths that Africans intuitively received from divine influx. Swedenborg's identification with primitivism reflected the general tenor of the Swedish government's humanitarian approach to slavery and the slave trade. His views inspired many supporters who, together with Quakers and other "inner light" groups, energized the antislavery movement in both Europe and America.[19]

Swedenborg also commented on the different characteristics he observed among the heavenly angels (former humans from the natural world), discovering differences and likenesses in their garments that he attributed to individual as well as to broader racial/ethnic temperaments. Those groups that he chose to comment on were the Dutch, British, Germans, Roman Catholics, Muslims, Africans, and Jews. Each group displayed garments with a certain color, texture, and design and demonstrated an attentiveness to certain "loves," whether they be of a worldly or spiritual nature. The Africans' peculiarities, which came partly from climate and partly from heredity, gave them an "inner rationality" that enabled them to understand religion more than did most other groups. That is to say, the Africans' "love" sought no other end than to unite themselves with God.[20] Unlike Europeans who thought externally, receiving their truths in the form of memory, and who therefore lived their religion "for the sake of reputation, honors and opportunities for material gain, . . . the African people are more capable of enlightenment than all other peoples on this earth, because they are of such a character as to think interiorly and thus to accept truths and acknowledge them."[21]

In the 1788 edition of Swedenborg's *A Treatise Concerning the Last Judgment, and the Destruction of Babylon,* the translator took note of the changes that had taken place in the minds of men. With the accomplishment of the Last Judgment in the spiritual world, which according to Swedenborg occurred in 1757, the hold of the "Shackles of Church Power" had become diminished and a greater freedom of thought had spread to all parts of Europe, resulting in "a more enlarged Spirit of universal Toleration" than ever before. Along with this enlarged spirit had come a "national benevolent Desire of emancipating from Slavery those wretched Victims to Avarice, the African Negroes."[22]

The Swedenborgian Carl Bernhard Wadström (1746–99) became a central figure in the abolitionist movement. Sent in 1787 by the Swedish King Gustaf III with authorization to establish a West African colony, he chose instead to relocate to England, where he worked with British abolitionists Thomas Clarkson, Granville Sharp, and William Wilberforce to expose the brutality of the slave trade. The very next year, he joined the New Jerusalem Church in Great Eastcheap, where he and other members proposed a set of rules for a colony in Sierra Leone that would be administered according to Swedenborg's beliefs concerning the African race.[23] His work entitled *An Essay on Colonization, Particularly Applied to the Western Coast of Africa, with Some Free Thoughts on Cultivation and Commerce*

(1794–95) not only exposed slavery's dark side but argued that persistence in its cruelties reduced the potential benefits that could emerge from a more humanitarian form of colonization. Wadström's most long-lasting contribution to the antislavery movement has been his engraving of a cross-section rendition of a typical slave ship. Republished time and again, this image visualized for readers the utter inhumanity of the slave trade.[24]

American members of the New Church did not initiate the antislavery movement and were generally late to the antislavery position, compared to the majority of other denominations, but a number of antislavery voices were those of committed Swedenborgians such as George Bush, Richard DeCharms, Robert Carter, and William Cooper Howells. The sectarian element contained few antislavery or even social reform voices, due to a widespread perspective in the churches that society was not going to be reformed until there was a theological revolution. This position held church-based Swedenborgians mostly on the sidelines of both the antislavery and temperance movements. As a result of Swedenborg's *Marriage Love* (1768), which built a metaphysical basis for segmenting roles in culture around gender, Swedenborgians were also late on feminism and suffrage. Yet George Bush, in particular, proved to be a powerful force in pressing forward with antislavery work within the Swedenborgian theological framework, and he inveighed against the idea that social reform could only occur through theological revolution. In a much earlier phase in the American republic, Swedenborg's writings seemed to have inspired Thomas Fairfax and Col. Robert Carter of Virginia to emancipate their own slaves.[25]

In matters of Christian philosophy and doctrine, including the principles of universal love and charity, the New Church stood on the liberal side of most issues. These principles proved elusive, however, with regard to social and political matters external to the Church since, temperamentally, its associations, unions, and conventions preferred to distance themselves from the day-to-day affairs of state. The early New Church considered its main duty to be teaching doctrine, so when questions of political, social, and moral life were raised, "the

New Church felt that she must not so much as touch upon them with a single outspoken word, for she regarded them as entirely beyond her sphere and province." As a consequence, when the nation became torn over the evils of slavery, New Church pulpits were "almost as silent as the tomb."[26] Lydia Maria Child, who left the Boston Society of the New Jerusalem when its pastor would not perform a marriage ceremony unless both members of the couple were Swedenborgian, later reported to her abolitionist coworkers her frustrations with the New Church's silence and even declared that it amounted to being proslavery. Child became editor for *The National Anti-Slavery Standard.* The same applied to Richard DeCharms, the only Swedenborgian antislavery voice who worked primarily in congregational ministries. His abolitionist stance and gripping stories of slavery stood apart from those pastors who feared being drawn into sectional politics.[27]

During the dark years leading up to the Civil War, New Church magazine editors were conspicuously silent, as they were reluctant to voice any position that might upset a particular region. "By entering the field of social and political reform," explained the editor of *The New Jerusalem Messenger* in 1855, "the Church would destroy its own influence and lose sight of its proper work."[28] Even the annual reports from Swedenborgian societies chose to ignore the conflict. And, when notice was made, the language was couched in carefully crafted words.

> The political troubles and excitement of civil war in which our country is now engaged, absorb the minds and demand the attention of the people to a degree that leaves but little room for any other subject, even though that be the church as a visible body among us. Still we believe the *spirit* of the church is really more active than ever before. The Lord is with the disciples. He is "asleep on the pillow" of the ship. When the disciples awake him, and cry, "Lord save, or we perish," He will arise and "rebuke the winds and the sea," saying, "Peace, be still;" and they will obey him.[29]

As late as 1865, the editors of *The New Jerusalem Magazine* remarked, "It is not for us, as members of the New Church, to say what shall be done [as] these things belong rather to the civil government to decide." Setting aside the abuses connected to slavery, the editors explained that human bondage was permissible according to divine order provided the bondage had no spiritual motivation and "all that was required of [those in bondage] was to regulate their outward actions by certain prescribed forms." This the editors rationalized by recognizing that "there must always have been those of superior wisdom . . . and there must also have been others of well-developed but humbler powers, who obeyed the direction of those wiser than themselves, and thus were assisted in applying their gifts to the welfare of the community in the most useful possible manner." [30]

Ralph Waldo Emerson's "Great Men"

In the rough and tumble days of early industrialism and the emerging issues that would eventually challenge the nature of the Union, Ralph Waldo Emerson (1803–82) brought to the discussion a contemplative and rarefied mind that resonated with people from all walks of life. Emerson's cornerstone beliefs in benevolence (with respect to God), immanence (with respect to Nature), and self-reliance (with respect to humanity) helped remove the absolute, the arbitrary, and the inscrutable elements of historical Puritanism, replacing them with an intelligent, relational principle, with a joining of God and the world. The term *benevolence* suggests that there is a "good" God who has made the earth his home. From this arises the optimism that humanity feels as it begins to have a sense of the Divine and, as a consequence, becomes conscious of a universal soul within each individual.

As literary critic Alfred Kazin noted, Emerson served as "the teacher of the nation," [31] as his essays and lectures made an indelible imprint at a time when questions of philosophy, theology, and society stood foremost in the minds of his fellow Americans. From his Phi Beta Kappa address, "The American Scholar," to "Man the Reformer," this much-loved poet/philosopher demonstrated a gift for imparting values to a generation struggling to find its moral compass as it worked through the meanings and consequences of Jacksonian democracy. An honest thinker molded by nearly two centuries of Puritan dissent and offset with the virtues of individualism and self-reliance, he offered a treasury of insight into the workings of American politics and culture. From the pulpit to the dais and printed page, he radiated the spirit of an invigorated new American. For Emerson, life's journey had brought humanity to a divide in the road, forcing it to choose between reason and intuition, evidence and speculation, the literal and the figurative, the homily and the creed, the metaphysical and the pietistic, and the old theology and something entirely new but as yet unformulated.

Few writers affected educated men and women as much as did Emerson. An exponent of the nation's democratic ideals, he drew wisdom from the world's best-known philosophers while also showing antipathy to church-door warrants announcing humankind's depravity or reprobation. The son of a Unitarian clergyman, he could easily have joined with his father's spiritual ancestors to reinforce the world of his inheritance. Instead, he challenged conventional truths, advocating for a broader view of life and duty; inspired a culture of creative democracy; and retained a filial duty to both his Creator and to the brotherhood of humankind. With essays the caliber of "Nature" (1836), "Self-Reliance" (1841), "The Over-Soul" (1841), "Manners" (1844), and "Experience" (1844), the last of which is considered his most important essay and text for protopragmatism, Emerson demonstrated his ability to sit pensively while sketching the mood of the nation. Building upon his gift for encapsulating insight, he started a cottage industry producing proverbs and aphorisms for useful living.[32]

Democracy was an essential component of Emerson's oracular philosophy. Beginning with the term "created equal" and ending with "consent of the governed," he imparted an intuitive respect for others that served as a focal point for his emphasis on individualism and self-reliance. He had a knack for supporting democratic dissidents, questioning the probity of elected officialdom, and idolizing an almost Nietzschean *ecce homo;* he was an unashamed moralist holding to his own set of inner laws. Unlike Thoreau, however, his individualism did not renounce societal obligations in favor of isolation. An introspective thinker, Emerson's judgments did not come easily, and his journals give ample evidence of a nursery where his ideas were first tended before the cuttings were shared.

In his theory of human greatness, Emerson included faith in the individual, distrust of the masses, the transcendence of conventional morality and ethics, and the exuding of optimism above all else. A partisan of the ideal, he drew his heroes from Swedenborg's *Divine Love and Wisdom* (1763), Sampson Reed's *Observations on the Growth of the Mind* (1826), Victor Cousin's *Introduction to the History of Philosophy* (1832), and Thomas Carlyle's *On Heroes, Hero-Worship and the Heroic in History* (1841). From these sources, he prepared six lectures that he presented to sympathetic audiences in both Boston and England. The first of these dealt with the tests of what Emerson termed "great men," while the subsequent lectures presented biographical accounts of Michael Angelo (Michelangelo), Martin Luther, Milton, George Fox, and Edmund Burke. Based on the ideas of these figures, he reasoned that true leadership came from either thinking great things or reproducing great things that had fallen off others' lips. These men whom he so greatly admired spoke beyond literal truths to spiritual truths worthy of distinction.[33]

Drawing from a large list of great individuals that he discussed over several years, Emerson chose to focus on Plato, Swedenborg, Montaigne, Shakespeare, Napoleon, and Goethe in his *Representative Men* (1850). The book's introductory chapter, "Uses of Great Men," could easily have been written by Swedenborg, as its title suggests. According to Emerson, the written record of humanity was infused with the names of those whose deeds became the dreams of youth and whose legends formed the beliefs of peoples and cultures. "I count him a great man who inhabits a higher sphere of thought, into which other men rise with labor and difficulty," he explained. "He has but to open his eyes to see things in a true light and in large relations, whilst they must make painful corrections and keep a vigilant eye on many sources of error. His service to us is of like sort." A person's greatness grew from within outward—a concept that loomed large in Swedenborg's *Divine Love and Wisdom*.[34]

According to Emerson, the world respected two types of usefulness from superior individuals. One was their giving of *things;* the second was their contribution of *ideas.* Central to both was a core set of ethics that moved from the soul outward. The genius of these representative men was in their ability to present their ideas in such a way that those ideas would be accepted as the new reality. True genius did not impoverish the soul; it liberated it, adding new senses, creating a new consciousness, and opening people's eyes to new advantages. What superior individuals of this kind knew and were able to communicate, they did for the sake of humankind. "These men correct the delirium of the animal spirits, make us considerate and engage us to new aims and powers." They were thus "a collyrium to clear our eyes from egotism and enable us to see other people and their works." A person with such abilities could change or enlarge the thoughts of many. In their presence, "all are wise, so rapid is the contagion." Genius kept society alive and moving forward by focusing its members on universal ideas rather than on the frenzied notions of the moment.[35]

Simply put, Emerson's portraits of "great men" demonstrated a remarkable consistency: all of them had turned their thought into action and their action into usefulness. The thought of each pulsed in sync with the heartbeat of a nation whose countrymen yearned for oneness, universality, and morality. Among the mass of humanity, these men emerged as leaders and molders of that mass, making life more intelligible for all its members. They not only made things present that were once absent, but they also put before humanity's eyes the very real possibility that all could understand and eventually say, "Now I see it." By following their intuition, Emerson's representative men spoke on behalf of a greater self—they were messengers for ideas that resonated with both the individual and with the soul of humanity, speaking to the few as well as to the many.[36] Depending on individual temperament, the sentiments of representative men took hold spontaneously, as if capturing the soul's deepest yearnings.[37]

To this end, Plato, the philosopher, offered his insightful allegory of the cave. While greatness might be relative to place and time, Emerson revealed in Plato's discourse the possibility for all individuals to act in such a manner that genius could sometimes replace pettiness and the monotony of life with an overpowering sense of reason, imagination, discovery, and beauty. Plato stood for the greatness of philosophy. The constellation of his ideas drew a litany of followers who transcended race, religion, and nation. Having absorbed the learning of his day, including that of his master, Socrates, Plato conceptualized an even larger synthesis that would be needed by later generations. "Great geniuses have the shortest biographies," noted Emerson. Plato was no exception. Still, if philosophy represented the account by which the mind explained the constitution of the world, his writings "preoccupied every school of learning, every lover of thought, every church, every poet—making it impossible to think, on certain levels, except through him." Viewing Plato from the point of conjecture, faith, understanding, and reason, Emerson taught the importance of beauty in all things; the need for wisdom as the soul's organ of sight; and the significance of virtue, which in and of itself could not be taught. His fame did not stand or fall on a syllogism but in both the power of his intellect, which saw that the order of nature was from the mind to the body, and the resolve of his moral conclusions—that it was "better to suffer injustice than to do it."[38]

Montaigne, the skeptic, represented the "cool head" who opposed exaggeration, wearied of dogmatizers, and shunned the extremes of philosophizing beyond one's depth. In explaining Montaigne's equanimous counsel, Emerson asked, "Why fancy that you have all the truth in your keeping? There is much to say on all sides." The proving ground of the skeptic was not one of unbelief but was a field imbued with a sense of probity—of questioning before judging. Keeping to the middle of the road, Montaigne's actions were guided more by example than by choice. Making his way by means of sober equilibrium, he sought out the checks and balances in nature as a weapon against "bigots and blockheads."[39]

Just as Montaigne tapped into the existing forces of nature, Shakespeare's genius was pushed forward by the ideas and necessities of contemporary society, through which he was able to find new angles of vision that were worthy of the most sublime contemplation. As Emerson put it, genius "consists in not being original at all; in being altogether receptive; in letting the world do all, and suffering the spirit of the hour to pass unobstructed through the mind." Shakespeare, the poet, became a scribe to the human race, expending his gifted powers in lyric poetry and dramatic theater to offer it glimpses of magic, perfidy, treason, and fortune. In his profound understanding of morals, manners, philosophy, taste, and the conduct of life, Shakespeare was a gentleman sage; "he converted the elements which waited on his command, into entertainments."[40]

Napoleon, the man of the world, was surely the most powerful of Emerson's representative men, if judged by his armies. "If any man is found to carry with him the power and affections of vast numbers, if Napoleon is France, if Napoleon is Europe, it is because the people whom he sways are little Napoleons." Napoleon reflected the virtues and vices of the middle class, whose tendency was to attain material success, even at the expense of the intellectual and spiritual forces of the age: "to be the rich man, is the end." As the "idol of common men," he demonstrated a thoroughly modern capacity to usurp the mind of the masses, transforming France into a behemoth of power while never losing his native sense and sympathy with things. Even though there was "this identity between Napoleon and the mass of the people, his real strength lay in their conviction that he was their representative in his genius and aims, not only when he courted, but when he controlled, and even when he decimated them by his conscriptions." Risking much and sparing little, he worked at the edges of possibility before bringing his followers to ruin.[41]

Goethe, the writer, represented that class of scholar whose power of expression was widely imitated but never equaled. What separated him from all others was his inward illumination, or interior truth, that opened every subject to scholarly scrutiny. As a philosopher, Goethe was able and happy to cope with an enormity of facts and sciences, and "by his own versatility to dispose of them with ease." Not only was he able to set his philosophy to poetry, but he showed himself to have an encyclopedic grasp of history, mythology, science, and literature. "He was the soul of his century," observed Emerson. "Amid littleness and detail, he detected the Genius of life."[42]

Emerson's formal introduction to Swedenborg came in 1826 from reading Sampson Reed's *Observations on the Growth of the Mind.* Before that, he made only a vague reference to Swedenborg in his journal dated December 10, 1824.[43] Later references, approximately sixty in number, came by way of Rev. Thomas Worcester, pastor of the

New Jerusalem Church of Boston; Nathaniel Hobart, author of *Life of Emanuel Swedenborg* (1831); and his friends Theophilus Parsons, James John Garth Wilkinson, and Thomas Carlyle. All of these references culminated in his lecture entitled "Swedenborg; or, the Mystic," which he gave before appreciative audiences in New England and Great Britain in 1847, before its inclusion in *Representative Men*. Emerson's choice of this "colossal soul" not only signaled the already broad influence of the man and his ideas, but it also gave credence to the validity of his doctrine of correspondences for understanding the fullness of the world. It spurred new editions and translations of Swedenborg's writings, the formation of reading circles dedicated to his work, renewed interest in the New Church, and proponents of his teachings to put them into practice.[44]

Swedenborg, the mystic, "who appeared to his contemporaries a visionary and elixir of moonbeams, no doubt led the most real life of any man then in the world." As Emerson explained, Swedenborg learned the sciences "to find images fit for the measure of his versatile and capacious brain" before venturing to "pass the bounds of space and time . . . into the dim spirit-realm." Swedenborg's observations and speculations anticipated later discoveries in astronomy, atomic theory, and physiology; but his proximity to so many other geniuses made it difficult for him to prove his own originality. Emerson considered Swedenborg understandable without instruction, but questioned whether he could be appreciated for long as his books had "no melody, no emotion, no humor, [and] no relief to the dead prosaic level." To be sure, he found in Swedenborg's "golden sayings" a "singular beauty [of] the ethical laws." Among those he admired most were "The perfection of man is the love of use" and "Man, in his perfect form, is heaven." Despite his admiration, Emerson thought Swedenborg's view of the world lacked spontaneity since there was no "individual in it." Instead, the universe was "a gigantic crystal, all whose atoms and laminæ lie in uninterrupted order and with unbroken unity, but cold and still."[45]

> The universe . . . suffers under a magnetic sleep, and only reflects the mind of the magnetizer. Every thought comes into each mind

by influence from a society of spirits that surround it, and into these from a higher society, and so on. ... His heavens and hells are dull; fault of want of individualism. ... Though the agency of "the Lord" is in every line referred to by name, it never becomes alive. There is no lustre in that eye which gazes from the centre and which should vivify the immense dependency of beings.[46]

Even though he placed Swedenborg among the world's greatest men, Emerson found him an irritant, one whose judgments were filled with caveats and an impossible theology. On balance, he saw him as a modern Jacob Behmen [Böhme] (1575–1624), albeit accusing him of believing in devils and other peculiarities, and suggesting that he ultimately failed to transcend these limitations.[47] According to Marguerite Beck Block, Emerson's difficulty was in figuring out "how logically to accept him as a philosopher and scientist, but reject him as the prophet of a new religion." Block suggests that by calling him a "mystic," Emerson chose a middle ground between having to accept that his visions were divinely inspired and insisting on his insanity.[48]

Not everyone in the New Church agreed with Emerson's characterization of Swedenborg. Rev. John Goddard of Newtonville, Massachusetts, for example, considered inappropriate the use of the term *mystic* to describe Swedenborg since, unlike the well-known mystics throughout history, he had never relinquished his own freedom and rationality, he remained always calm, and he never allowed illumination to substitute for his own will or reason. More to the point, Swedenborg "was not seeking to enjoy blessedness, but to find the truth, wherever it might lead." Genuine mystics left the earth behind and sought communion with the unseen. For Swedenborg, the scientific, philosophical, and religious elements of life were always present. The secret of his uniqueness, explained Goddard, was his "long and wonderful preparation in all the knowledge of this world before he became aware of his mission." Thus his revelatory wisdom remained connected with the natural world, as opposed to the genuine mystic who separated the inner from the outer. "Swedenborg's revelations of the inner world, both subjective and objective, furnish the spiritual intuitions of men with an earthly and rational basis, removing superstition, banishing mystery, and investing this world and its experiences with a meaning, an importance and a sacredness which they never had before."[49]

Unlike Thomas Carlyle's divinely gifted heroes who stood apart from the crowd (much like Dostoyevsky's heroes), Emerson's "great men" were geniuses whose sphere of thought inspired others to see in themselves their own liberating capabilities. Each of these six representative men opened the eyes of their generation to new possibilities. While they did not all persevere through time in equal measure, each was an exhibition of a new possibility that served well its time and place, creating a union of minds and influencing generations to come.

Henry James's Spiritual Socialism

Henry James, Sr., (1811–82) made it his life's work to bring about the spiritual liberation of others by explaining the problem of evil, the concept of free will, the nature of the state and society, and the promise of democracy. He also elaborated a Christian form of socialism founded on the doctrine of usefulness. Supported by a wealthy inheritance, James lived comfortably. Instead of entering the business world or frittering away his wealth in self-indulgence, he matriculated at Princeton Theological Seminary, only to later be repelled by doctrines (e.g., human depravity) he could no longer in good conscience accept. After visiting Great Britain in 1837, where he discovered the primitivism of theologian Robert Sandeman (1718–71), he returned to marry the sister of a seminary classmate. Residing first in New York City, and then in Massachusetts, James and his family divided their time between Cambridge and abroad. As best explained by biographer Frederic Harold Young, James spent his life "trying to tease out of his soul and brain a satisfying religious metaphysics of creation."[50]

In 1843, James experienced a profound religious epiphany, followed by a debilitating sense of exhaustion that an acquaintance friend diagnosed as *vastation,* which is a term employed by Swedenborg to explain the early stage of purification that accompanies religious illumination. Intrigued by both this term and its author, James read *Divine Love and Wisdom* and *Divine Providence* to see if he could learn the nature of his malaise. As explained by scholar Paul Croce, after turning to Swedenborg's writings, James's world became "a theater of symbols, with Swedenborg and those who followed his readings holding the hermeneutical key."[51]

From the 1840s onward, James produced a steady stream of theological and philosophical works that included *What Constitutes the State?* (1846); *Tracts for the New Times* (1847); *Moralism and Christianity* (1850); *Lectures and Miscellanies* (1852); *Love, Marriage, and Divorce* (1853); *The Church of Christ Not an Ecclesiasticism* (1854); *The Nature of Evil* (1855); *Christianity the Logic of Creation* (1857); *The Social Significance of Our Institutions* (1861); *Substance and Shadow* (1863); *The Secret of Swedenborg* (1869); and *Society the Redeemed Form of Man* (1879). These were followed by *The Literary Remains of the Late Henry James* (1885), a posthumous collection of unpublished writings edited by his son William.

James imbibed heavily in the intellectual currents of the day, including Calvinism, Unitarianism, Swedenborgianism, transcendentalism, Fourierism, and Christian socialism. In each, he was both an advocate and a critic, selecting only those ideas that matched his idiosyncratic view of the world. An intense thinker whose metaphysics was both Neo-Platonic and Gnostic, he was not at all averse to calling out the opinions of contemporaries, including his friend Emerson, when they deserved criticism. In search of a centerpiece for his religious and spiritual thinking, James found comfort in the customs and bold faith of Apostolic Christianity, which, unencumbered by the rituals of ecclesiasticism and its sacramental magic, offered a simple and immediate comprehension of faith. Against the backdrop of an age operating between the extremes of Calvinism, with its doctrines of salvation for the few and damnation for the many, and Emerson's self-reliance, James placed his faith in a spiritually democratic society that excluded no one from his vision of a "Divine-Natural-Humanity." This great spiritual verity symbolizes the majesty and mystery of life, incorporating the importance of the incarnation, the natural inheritance of every individual being capable of spiritual life, the infinitude of divine love, the prerogative of revelation to reveal the scope and substance of divine intent, and the promise of redemption.

Having immersed himself in the Swedenborgian world of spirituality, which he believed stood behind the purposes of divine creation and its connection to humanity, James rebelled against the Baconian world of facts, choosing revelation over the sensory world. Not all knowledge derived exclusively from observation, experience, or reasoning; while science yielded an appealing explanation to life's questions, it played second fiddle to revelation, as "science is the organ of the distinctively finite intellect, the intellect tethered to sense." Revelation disclosed the existence in humanity of a much higher moral purpose.[52] A logical and thoroughly objective response to those who claimed the priority of reason and science, revelation would always remain the highest source of truth.[53]

As a profoundly complex thinker, James stood in the tradition of Paul, Augustine, Pascal, Calvin, and Swedenborg. Making free use of his own experiences, he speculated that, unlike the rest of creation, each human being consisted of two forces: a material force that *finited* that being and a spiritual force that *infinited* it. Unique among creation, human beings had the power to separate from their animal appetites in order to become fitting tabernacles of God. It was this adjustment of the finite to the Infinite that constituted the secret of human history. Both worlds were embraced in human consciousness and connected by the doctrine of correspondences. Since human history involved revelation and realization that Jesus was the perfect union of God and humanity, it stood to reason that Jesus was the inmost and vital selfhood of every individual. As explained by J. A. Kellogg, "whatever life was in him [Jesus], actually is potentially in all men." Beginning first with the consciousness of selfhood distinct from God, humanity gradually attained the consciousness of selfhood *with* God. This truly divine element of regeneration, or growth from the natural to the spiritual life, was a privilege that no other of God's creatures possessed.[54]

Hostility toward human pride dominated much of James's work. Society's failure to acknowledge the equality of humankind in the eyes of God led him on a journey to reassert the importance of Christ's redemptive work and the necessity of reconnecting humankind with

God. His was a religion of community and one that sought to remove the physical and intellectual barriers separating human beings from the divine life. Looking outside the chaos of institutions, James promoted the fusion of denominations and sects into a grand Christian fellowship whose members chose not to glorify themselves at the expense of others but instead to create a spiritual entity that annihilated selfhood.[55] Here was not merely the transcendence of the conscious individual self but the development of a shared consciousness—a redeemed human community that was spiritually connected to each other and to God.

A thorough believer in Protestantism's victory over ecclesiasticism, including the hierarchically structured and visible church, James turned his efforts toward the realization of the Divine-Natural-Humanity. This explains his "Letter to a Swedenborgian" in *Tracts for the New Times* (1847) and his criticism of the Swedenborgians in his *The Church of Christ Not an Ecclesiasticism* (1854).[56] "The history of the church," he insisted, "is the history of human corruption; and the only emphatic testimony it bears is to the slender reliance which is to be placed upon the most devout pretensions."[57] James denied the ability of any institution to sanctify a human being. Similarly, he denied the ability of government to do anything more than promote those freedoms already divinely present in a human being. "The real divinity of the nation, its vital imperishable holiness, resides not in any dead parchment, but only in the righteous unselfish lives of those who see in any constitution but the luminous letter of their inward spiritual faith ... and rally around it ... with the joyous unshrinking devotion not of slaves but of men."[58]

In a series of lectures delivered in New York City in 1850–51, James celebrated democracy as marking the end of humankind's puberty, as it transformed institutions into vehicles intended for the welfare of the people rather than for the "yoke of kings and nobles." While still imperfect, democracy affirmed the sovereignty of the people, granted that they took precedence over institutions, and heralded the promise of a "universal human heart." No longer did government's fiduciary obligation result in purely political ends; it now had a moral and social purpose whose benefits came from the increase of "just, amicable, and humane relations" among its members. Democracy looked toward a time in the not-too-distant future "when all coercion and restraint shall be disused in the conduct of human affairs." The purpose of democratic government was "to proclaim the unity of man." Eventually, all other functions would harmonize with this objective.[59]

The genius of democracy was that it asserted the people's exclusive right to govern themselves. This did not mean a portion of the people, or even a numerical majority, but the *whole* people. James anticipated moral rather than political benefits from democracy, namely, the crafting of relations between members of society to prepare the way for the reign of infinite love. Democracy portended a time when, in the conduct of human affairs, "man will *freely* do unto others as he would have others . . . do unto him." Its function was to create the conditions for the perfect society. This was requisite "to inaugurate the divine life on earth," with the presence of God in every soul and so expressing humanity's inward spirit.[60] Democracy was a metaphysical concept embodying the ideal of the Divine-Natural-Humanity, a redeemed society more concerned with what its members did than with what they believed.

Democratic society implied a quality of unity in which each member was equal to every other member and every person had the aptitude for some divine end through love. Here was the Universal Human whose fellowship, from the least to the greatest, revealed the presence of God in all. The human race, not the individual, was the natural end of history in which all creatures were bound together as one. This occurred when people found their ruling loves authenticated not by attention to themselves but in the social sentiment of the whole. Society was the instrument through which individuals were able to unite their inward and outward life. It enabled them to resist the domination of the outward, or sensible, sphere as the sole agent for gratifying their wants. It also aided them in overcoming poverty, acquiring property and other natural wants, rising above brutality, and pursuing the refinement of art.[61] Embodied in democratic society were the dual ideas of Protestantism and constitutional liberty, the former "denying the Church as an absolute Divine substance" and the latter "denying the State as an absolute Divine form." Though Americans had inherited these ideas from Europe, the difference was that *"we begin where they leave off.* Like all heirs, we enter upon a full fruition of the estate which it cost them their best blood to found and mature."[62]

Property, an artifact of society, represented "the perfect sovereignty which man is destined to exercise over nature" and the means by which individuals came to understand their spiritual being. Thus, to the extent that individuals subdued the earth, they acquired self-consciousness and self-knowledge. However, their sovereignty over nature could never be realized except through the fellowship of humanity. Property was not an end but a means for humanity to find its inner spiritual attributes. No property was sacred in itself; it was representatively sacred only when used for purposes of benevolence.[63]

With property as an expression of human society's sovereignty over the natural world, it became the function of society and of the moral law to protect the right of private property so that humanity could fulfill its God-given talents. Still, property was only symbolic of human sovereignty, as it was not the defining characteristic of humanity. Being a transient good in and of itself, property was a shadow of a higher good. In a true society of fellowship, there would be no such thing as exclusive privilege or unequal property. A true society "would guarantee to [everyone], for the whole term of [their] natural life, food, clothing, shelter, and the opportunities of an education adapted to [their] tastes; leaving all the *distinction* [they] might achieve to [themselves], to [their] own genius freely influencing the homage of [their fellow citizens]." By removing the incitements that came with exclusivity and inequality, property became not the "scum and froth of society attaching to [the] extremes [of both] rich and poor alike" but a servant to the interests of the Universal Human. This became the basis of James's justification for the doctrine of usefulness and the source for what would later become the rationale for Henry George's single-tax theory, Edward Bellamy's nationalism, and the social gospelers' Christian socialism.[64]

Although James disdained the Calvinist tenet of original sin, he discovered in Jonathan Edwards's *A Treatise Concerning Religious Affections* (1746) and *The Nature of True Virtue* (1765) the idea of disinterested benevolence, which he adopted to buttress his spiritualized form of socialism. The commingling of Edwardian and Swedenborgian concepts seemed, at first, counterintuitive, yet James's visionary theology indicated a more positive relationship with them than it did with the models of social organization drawn from Thomas Malthus, Herbert Spencer, or Karl Marx. Disinterested benevolence, or love of being, proved much more relevant to James's vision of the world. It was this emphasis on benevolence without the prospect of an angry and unforgiving God that allowed him to turn Calvinism on its head, socializing the doctrine of election so as to focus on collective, not individualized, salvation. Here, at last, was a philosophy that merged creation with a spiritualized form of socialism. Christian socialism represented the redeemed form of humanity.[65] It was the preferred remedy for civilization's problems, offering to "lift man out of [his] harassing bondage." It enabled humanity to fulfill the Christian hope of perfection by revealing a perfect harmony between itself and God. Socialism, as James explained, "lifts us out of these frivolous and pottering responsibilities we are under to man, and leaves us under responsibility to God alone, or our inmost life."[66] In Swedenborg's loving God and Edwards's disinterested love of being, James found justification for his socialist philosophy and for his stand against what he considered to be the counterfeit philosophy of self-righteousness and the prescriptive moralism of the churches. James's Christian socialism was the embodiment of the Divine-Natural-Humanity, which replaced the randomness of a chaotic universe with a spiritual creation bent on redeeming humanity from its selfishness and moving toward selfless love.[67]

James's preference for the triadic phrase "Divine-Natural-Humanity" represented what biographer Frederic Young called a philosophy of "theo-pragmatism" and "theo-utilitarianism" because it stressed the natural world as the realm of use for the power and purpose of divine spirit. In other words, it was the *natural* aspect of the Divine-Natural-Humanity that drew James's undivided attention. It was central to God's incarnation (i.e., his coming into human nature) and humanity's redemption (i.e., its ascent to become divine humanity).[68] "Nature is properly nothing more than the robe or garment of spirit," observed James. "It is only the tabernacle or house of spirit, only the subservient instrument or means by which spirit subsists and becomes conscious. Every thing in nature . . . embodies an internal use or capacity of operation, which constitutes its peculiar spirit." In this manner, nature had a very concrete relationship to humanity, furnishing the operational theater for its creative spirit.[69]

From 1845 to 1882, James made continual reference to Swedenborg's *True Christian Religion* (*True Christianity*), which became a model for the terminology, principles, and concepts in his own writings. The philosophical concepts that James expounded began and ended with the Divine-Natural-Humanity, the absolute divinity of Christ, and the contemplation of the divine essence as understood through creation, redemption, and regeneration. While he would be identified as a genuine Swedenborgian theologian, James was not a spokesperson for American Swedenborgianism. Above all else, he was an independent thinker, utilizing Swedenborg's ideas in a very idiosyncratic manner. One of the most searching intellects of the nineteenth century, James utilized his faith in human nature and his belief in democracy to formulate a concept of Christian socialism intended to realize the Universal Human. Secure in his faith in individual liberty, he advocated for bringing peace, freedom, and unity through a collective democracy in which all were members of a moralized Christian community. His vision of humanity had the grandeur of an imposing piece of architecture stretching far into the night sky. While James's philosophical and religious thought remained largely unappreciated during his lifetime, he successfully constructed an intensely spiritual philosophy that profoundly impacted his sons William and Henry, who, in turn, made significant and generous contributions to American thought and culture.

James became the unofficial spokesperson for those Swedenborgians who, like himself, chose to remain outside the ecclesiastical

Church. For them, he presented Swedenborgianism in all its relevancy and beauty. Not only did he penetrate into the deeper undercurrents of Swedenborg's writings, but he used them in an unapologetic manner to broaden the concept of democracy, transforming love of neighbor into a visionary world of the Universal Human through Christian socialism. Even with a spirituality that was cosmic in scope, he focused on its practical consequences in everyday life. Overcoming the negative sense of self, or *proprium,* by demonstrating an outpouring of love, a continuity between human reason and reason in nature, and the importance of community, he left a legacy for future generations of reformers. His approach to change was gradualistic, with a vision of redemption that favored the universal over the particular, the general over the personal. Henry James, Sr., certainly deserves a more prominent place than he has received in the history of American social thought.

William Blake's mytho-visionary attacks on conventional morality and his larger-than-life disagreement with Edmund Burke spilled over into causes for replacing corrupted Christianity with Swedenborg's dissenting theology. Like others among the Enlightenment's skeptics, when it came to traditional politics and religion, the Swedenborgians were part of a cultural radicalism that a few of its members used as a way of challenging slavery and the slave trade. Waiting, however, on a theological revolution that would precede such social reform, most Swedenborgians held back, allowing others to take the lead. Still, in matters of Christian philosophy and doctrine, they retained their eagerness for change.

Whether referring to Ralph Waldo Emerson or Henry James, Sr., the doctrine of usefulness was integral to each of their respective worldviews. Emerson explained usefulness in his descriptions of *"representative men." His views, which were influenced by Hellenism, French naturalism, English pantheism, New England Unitarianism, and German idealism, stood in stark contrast to the materialism of the age. In its stead, he insisted on the liberation of conscious-ness and the power of thought and inspiration. James also worked in favor of the ideal, with his study of the state and society, his fas-cination with Fourierism, and his endorsement of a democratically based Christian socialism that utilized a combination of Edwards's disinterested benevolence and Swedenborg's assent to the Divine-Natural-Humanity through the principles of love, wisdom, and use. James's writings represented a frank expression of individual taste and temperament, a militant conscience, and an idealistic metaphysics intended to awaken a nobler faith in human destiny. Much of Henry James's attention to virtue would later emerge in the radical empiri-cism, pragmatism, and pluralism of his son William James, whose highly personal dimension of cognitive reality projected a vision of human society that drew from his father's "redeemed form of man."

2 Incantatory Delusions

All natural existence may be classified into forms of use; all spiritual existence into forms of power. . . . But in thus classifying all natural existence into forms of use, and all spiritual existence into forms of power, we must not forget to observe that the use promoted by the one class is never absolutely but only relatively good, nor the power exerted by the other class absolutely but only relatively benignant. That is to say, it is good and benignant not in itself, but in opposition to something else. Thus every natural form is a form of use, but some of these uses are relatively to others good, and some evil.

(Henry James, Sr., *Substance and Shadow*, 1863)

America once lived with dreams of utopia—not only a radical concept considered feasible but a valid option within the national imagination. Perfectionist aspirations—from secular utopian schemes to visions of Christian eschatology—were once a vibrant part of the nation's heritage, offering a fundamental challenge to existing institutions, not to mention to the prevailing beliefs regarding property, polity, marriage, and family life. Opportunistic about what could be achieved historically, utopians offered the biblical kingdom of God as something immanent and within reach. Often overlooked or misunderstood is the fact that the writings of Swedenborg, along with the efforts of many in the New Church, played a significant role in the history of the nation's perfectionist and millenarian aspirations. Adrift in a world of spiritual planes, armed with exalted ideas of human dignity, and marked by a preference for ecstatic intuition and introspection, millenarians set out to construct a world that complemented the Universal Human. Blurring the difference between the actual and the possible in their willingness to reconcile dichotomies, they assayed their circumstances and moved quickly to prepare themselves and their brethren for a celebration of their chiliastic enthusiasms.

Nineteenth-century communitarians abandoned the static presuppositions underlying history and instead looked toward a perfectionism that, though by no means fully defined, assumed a better tomorrow, except when retarded by human folly. Drawing upon rational, empirical, eschatological, and liberal ideas emerging from the Enlightenment, they contributed to the building of Owenite and Fourierist communities—earthly paradises drawn in part from visions of Swedenborg's Universal Human and from the idealistic philosophies of the French Encyclopedists. Numerous communitarian societies took root among small patches of believers whose social experiments ranged from moderate to adventuresome and sometimes to extreme. In carrying out the spiritual regeneration of the world, one society at a time, they sought a sense of peaceful harmony in their individual and collective lives, the acceptance of what they believed to be the rightful use of property, and a self-imposed isolation from worldly affairs.[1]

Communitarianism

The tectonic changes resulting from the impact of the French Revolution and from the beginnings of a proletariat class of wage-earners dependent on the fortunes of industrialization produced a generation of reformers intent on constructing a more humanized society. Leaving scientists to the work of understanding the natural world, reformers busied themselves with psychology, logic, sociology, ethics, and politics to determine if it was possible to construct new and better models of human organization. Supported by many different tributaries of thought, including those proposed by Rousseau's *Emile, or On Education* and *The Social Contract,* Welsh social reformer Robert Owen (1771–1858) and French social theorist Charles Fourier (1772–1837) gave the term *society* a whole new meaning in both theory and practice. Their extraordinary appeal resulted from the fact that hopes ran high that the old order was changing, that aristocracy was disintegrating, and that human destiny was about to turn a corner. Though different in their approaches, Owen and Fourier promised a fairer equalization of property that would provide context for a more purified morality. Essentially, they offered a socialized expression of romantic idealism.

Using terms of universal application, their model societies centered around eleven communities connected to Owen and more than forty established by the disciples of Fourier. From New Harmony, Hopedale, and Northampton to Brook Farm, Fruitlands, and the North American Phalanx at Red Bank, New Jersey, self-contained communities sought to harness individual and collective perfectibility without disrupting the body politic. With the exception of three or four communities that lasted upward of twelve years, and Oneida which lasted thirty-three, most ended within anywhere from two years to months of their creation. Few of these communities had leaders of recognized authority, and most of them offered realities that stood in sharp contrast to their aspirations. Nonetheless, both leaders and followers believed they could build societies that were universally adaptable.[2]

Most of the experiments that marked the first half of the nineteenth century strove to reconcile individualism with some form of communal cooperation. For example, Owen and Fourier constructed their respective visions of society by substituting family dwellings for "unitary dwellings." Their communal edifices, though based on competing principles of capitalism and communism, tended toward a certain sameness in their day-to-day activities. John Humphrey Noyes, the author of *History of American Socialisms* (1870) and founder of the Oneida community, blamed their lack of success on spiritual *afflatus*, a term he used to describe the preponderance of selfishness that stemmed from the absence of any form of religious or structural "glue" to hold members' devotion to the cause.[3] Others attributed their lack of sustainability to a loss of faith in the democratic process; their lack of flexibility in learning from mistakes; the unintended consequences of buying too much land and assuming too much debt;

romantic insensibilities; and the practical everyday economic factors that contributed to the instability of community life. Despite these impediments, their visions seemed very much in tune with the needs of the day, focusing on religious freedom, social equality, and the integrity of a community structure.[4]

Fourier's *Theorie des Quatre Mouvements* (1808) and Owen's *A New View of Society* (1813) offered the first broadly shared and popularized secular plans for societal reorganization. That said, the word *socialism* did not exist in either man's lexicon. In its place, Fourier offered the term *harmonie* as the newest and highest stage of social organization, while Owen referred to the "change from the individual to the social system; from single families with separate interests, to communities of many families with one interest."[5] In other words, there were no so-called socialists, only groups called Shakers, Rappites, Anabaptists, Owenites, and Harmonists, all of whom held the concept of a collective society. Even Fourier's disciple Albert Brisbane used the term *associationist*, or *phalanstérien*, to convey Fourier's communal intentions. Not until the 1830s did the term *socialiste*, or *socialist*, appear in England and the United States.[6]

Owenism

An indomitable reformer and environmental determinist, Owen put his ideas to practice in the Scottish village of New Lanark as early as 1800. Determined to do more, he looked westward to the United States, where he introduced his theory before audiences whose numbers included the president and president-elect, members of the Supreme Court, and members of both houses of Congress, inviting all to consider his thirty-thousand-acre experiment at New Harmony in Indiana, a community purchased from the Rappites.[7] Though Owen's hopes were dashed in a short span of time by hordes of freeloaders bent on exploiting his good will, belief in his vision continued through the efforts of his son Robert Dale Owen and fellow Scottish-born social reformer Frances Wright. Owen's eleven communities included Blue Spring, Forrestville, Macluria, and New Harmony (*Feiba Peven*) in Indiana; the Co-operative Society in Pennsylvania; Coxsackie, Franklin, and Haverstraw in New York; Kendal and

Yellow Springs in Ohio; and Nashoba in Tennessee. All were examples of industrial reconstruction without the social evils that grew out of unimproved government. By 1829, the movement had run its course and subsided. Nevertheless, Owen anticipated many of the features of modern socialism.[8]

One of Owen's disciples was Daniel Roe, minister of the New Church in Cincinnati, who replicated the New Harmony experiment when he and seventy-five church families purchased the village of Yellow Springs. Known for the medicinal qualities in their waters, the springs, located seventy miles north of Cincinnati, had become a health resort. They were also home to numerous mills powered by the Little Miami River. The most significant piece of the purchase was the acquisition of the town's hotel and rental cottages, which catered to clientele using the waters. Thus, the Owenites did not build a new community but, like New Harmony, acquired the town and its environs from Presbyterian and Quaker citizens who had already demonstrated their economic prowess.

The "Constitution of the Yellow Springs Community," which was signed January 9, 1826, put into practice a form of communism that quickly proved unsustainable. Within a matter of months, the stockholders acknowledged the community's failure to serve their individual and collective needs. Yellow Springs's problems, not unlike those of New Harmony, included the mismatch of classes, the avoidance of using common labor, and the inability to fulfill the land contract. Unselfish cooperation was fine in the abstract but difficult to practice.[9]

Fourierism

Born into a wealthy merchant's family in Besançon, France, Charles Fourier learned early in his life to dislike the world of business and what he perceived to be the deceptive manipulation of the free market for the sake of profit by bankers, manufacturers, and merchants. After losing his inheritance during the French Revolution's Reign of Terror, he turned his attention to preparing plans for a reorganization of society that would establish lasting peace in Europe. Surviving on a small legacy from his mother and occasional earnings that he made in the mercantile world, he managed to publish *The Theory of the Four Movements and of the General Destinies* (1808), followed by *Treatise on Domestic Agricultural Association* (1822), *The New Industrial World* (1829), and two volumes entitled *False Industry, and its Antidote Natural, Attractive Industry* (1835 and 1836). The first of these works contained the overall outline of his social system, while the subsequent works were largely elaborations on its particulars.

Fourier set his sights on building a uniform social structure similar to the harmony he found in the universe, likening his discovery of "social attractions" to Newton's law of gravitation. His plan involved the creation of self-contained communities, or phalanxes, populated with 1,500 to 1,800 individuals who, working as a social unit, fulfilled the free and peaceful exercise of their passions. The phalanx was not a communist organization but a joint stock company, with seven-eighths of the members being farmers and mechanics and the remainder consisting of capitalists, scientists, and artists. At the end of each year, the profits would be distributed: five-twelfths to labor, four-twelfths to capital, and three-twelfths to those with special skills or talents. Fourier intended his phalanxes to extend across the globe, eventually unifying humanity into a single brotherhood. Although he did not live to see the popularity of his theories, when he died in Paris in 1837, he was surrounded by disciples dedicated to spreading his ideas. Just Muiron, one of his earliest disciples, noticed distinct similarities between the phalanx and Swedenborg's Universal Human. These similarities would become important when Fourierism later transitioned into Spiritualism.[10]

Representative Fourierist communities included Alphadelphia and Washtenaw in Michigan; Brook Farm and Northampton in Massachusetts; Marlboro and Trumbull in Ohio; Integral and Sangamon in Illinois; Moorhouse Union and Sodus Bay in New York; Leraysville and Sylvania in Pennsylvania; Garden Grove in Iowa; Lagrange in Indiana; Raritan Bay Union in New Jersey; and Spring Farm in Wisconsin.[11] Though members of the New Church rarely rushed headlong into questionable ventures, the phalanxes at Jasper Colony in Iowa; the Hopedale community in Massachusetts; and the Leraysville, PA, and Canton, IL, communities contained considerable numbers of Swedenborgians among their members. New

Churchman Dr. Solyman Brown served as the general agent of the Leraysville Phalanx, an industrial association founded in 1844 by Dr. Lemuel C. Belding. Leraysville began with a stock subscription of nearly $50,000 and 1,500 acres of land secured for the society's use. With several farms joined together, and with most of the inhabitants having membership in the Church of the New Jerusalem, the intent of the phalanx was to construct a community whose faith in order, economy, and justice matched their Swedenborgian convictions. It lasted less than a year. The Canton Phalanx was founded in 1845 by John F. Randolph, the president of the Illinois Association of the New Church, who contributed his own property for the good of the project. It, too, lasted less than a year.[12]

Fourier was never personally involved with any of the American communities. In the United States, his most vocal spokesperson was Albert Brisbane (1809–90) of New York. Well-educated and well-traveled, Brisbane learned philosophy under Victor Cousin (1792–1867) in Paris and under Georg Wilhelm Friedrich Hegel (1770–1831) in Berlin. Keen on devising a system of social organization, he identified first with Henri de Saint Simon's (1760–1825) socialist ideas before turning to Fourier's *Treatise on Domestic Agricultural Association* for guidance. After spending two years studying with Fourier and his disciples in Paris, he returned to the United States, where he embarked on a campaign to spread the ideas of associationism. Following the publication of his *Social Destiny of Man* (1840), an exposition of the most basic elements of Fourier's system, Brisbane devoted his energies to styling the movement to the needs of American society. At the time, there were many well-publicized debates over the strengths and purposes of associationism, so many so that it became a household word among educated circles along the East Coast and into the Midwest.

While Fourier's social design called for a phalanstery consisting of at least 1,500 individuals, none of the communities ever came close to realizing this size. Nor, for that matter, did any of them practice the full extent of his theories. Instead, his American followers adopted Brisbane's attenuated version; and the various communities were bound together by the National Convention of Associationists, who were headed up by George Ripley, Horace Greeley, Brisbane, Parke Godwin, and Charles A. Dana. The convention, in turn, formed a National Confederation of Associations, with *The Phalanx* as its official magazine.[13]

With religious sensibilities that were intense and symbolic, associationists saw Fourier as a new Christ image, a heroic figure in the drama of sin and redemption. His birthday developed into a socialist Christmas that utilized a pattern of religious symbolism to color his life and teachings. George Ripley's lecture titled "Fourier, the Second Coming of Christ!" harmonized the earth's inhabitants with their destined salvation in the providence of God. And by the time associationism had expended its energies, its leaders had managed to blend Christian rituals into their socialist communities. Their artifacts included a communal meeting house (Church of Humanity); candles and trays of fruit and bread (communion); public confession; a leader's pledge of loyalty (ordination); wall images and busts of Fourier (iconography); toasts (consecrations and communion); and socialist characterizations of earth (revelation).[14] The associationists expected society to repent its "social" sins as a way to arrive at godly living. In other words, they stressed a dual approach to unityism, or universal love—one that included recognition of personal wrongdoing and a commitment to much-needed social reorganization. This blend of Christianity and socialism gave the phalanx a distinctive look that resembled Auguste Comte's "Religion of Humanity."[15]

Brook Farm

The period from the 1830s to the 1850s in New England has sometimes been dismissed as an episodic and unnatural exhibition of effete intellectuals dallying in social, religious, and political voyeurism. Focused on what they perceived to be the shortcomings of their fellow citizens and of the nation at large, they initiated quests of a patronizing and quixotic nature that did little to turn heads from the business of making money. Their world was centered in Boston, the undisputed "intellectual hub" of the young republic, whose pulpits and publishing houses presented a national agenda that proved as intoxicating as it was self-congratulatory. Such self-appointed guardians as Ralph Waldo Emerson, Theodore Parker, William Ellery Channing, and Margaret Fuller were among those Transcendentalists who set out to redirect society away from its materialistic pursuits.

Like their European counterparts—best exemplified in Thomas Carlyle, John Ruskin, and Samuel Taylor Coleridge—New England's intellectuals railed against what they saw to be not only the material but also the philosophical detritus of the Industrial Revolution. They were repelled by the bourgeois society of Lockean liberalism, the utilitarianism of Jeremy Bentham, and the extreme rationality and empiricism of Auguste Comte's positivism. Instead, they drew upon a combination of neo-Platonism, German idealism, and Eastern mysticism, preoccupying themselves with the uniqueness of individual potential and the importance of spirit over matter. Having a need to break from tradition and custom, they experimented with myriad forms of self-expression as they confronted their demons in their inward search for truth. Restless in their search for meaning and order, these men and women reached out to all who would listen.

Transcendentalism attracted all types of reformers—from anarchists and abolitionists, to Unitarians, communists, and Swedenborgians. This movement came at a time when Henry James, Sr.'s, views on labor, government, women's rights, love, marriage, and crime were being delivered as heady medicine to the body politic. These were also the years in which thrived such movements as phrenology, Grahamism, mesmerism, homeopathy, and Spiritualism.

Viewing the American landscape from his privileged position among New England's Brahmin hierarchy, Emerson concluded that "the Church, or religious party, is falling from the Church nominal, and is appearing in temperance and non-resistance societies; in movements of abolitionists and of socialists … and … of seekers, of all the soul of the soldiery of dissent." As did the majority of sympathizers, he found the solution to society's ills a matter of removing the artificial impediments to humankind's quest for perfection. Perfectibility, a notion derived from religion, was based on the premise that each individual had the potential for unlimited improvement, provided that the impediments in society were removed to allow for unfettered progress.[16] In the new synthesis of romanticism, individualism, and liberalism, the safety of ready-made answers to questions of human development no longer seemed justified. The world was not understood as that which is, but as that which was possible. Political stability, social decorum, and economic success were in the eyes of the beholder who, in the case of the Transcendentalists, dreamed of more anarchic freedoms and elevated passions. "Our whole history," observed Emerson, "appears like a last effort of the Divine Providence in behalf of the human race."[17] Here was not the atheistic radicalism of Shelley or the melancholy of Keats. Emerson's words were a call to action to follow the God within, cease the thoughtless repetition of ancient creeds, and affirm the universal fellowship of humanity.

At the intersection of this synthesis of romanticism, individualism, and liberalism stood Brook Farm in West Roxbury, just outside of Boston, where liberal Christians undertook a joint stock communal experiment in agriculture and education. They believed that a society built around a combination of labor and intellectual pursuits would provide ample preparation for the kingdom of Christ. Brook Farm's constitution spoke of individuals coming together in a community of shared property to live a religious and moral life that would benefit from the "comfort of life, to the finest art" without the competitive "rules of trade." This implied living in "all the faculties of the soul" that the community valued—namely, education over labor, spiritual over bodily health, the value of reading over temporal distractions, and corporate responsibility over individual greed.[18]

The history of Brook Farm lies deeply embedded in the social, religious, and philosophical traditions of New England. In fact, without the contributing influence of Unitarianism and Congregationalism, it is hard to imagine its existence. Brook Farm was sired by Dr. William Ellery Channing, the nation's preeminent Unitarian theologian, who, in 1840, took counsel with George Ripley, Dr. John Collins Warren, Margaret Fuller, Orestes A. Brownson, and Frederic Henry Hedge, among others, to consider the wisdom of initiating the project.[19] That their collective efforts became identified as a "school" or "movement" proved more a reflection of the nation's narrow circle of intellectuals than it did any national consensus. According to Van Wyck Brooks in *America's Coming-of-Age* (1915), the Transcendentalists "were like high-minded weather-cocks on a windless day."[20]

The official name of the community was "The Brook Farm Institute for Agriculture and Education," and its articles of association included the following formulation of purpose:

> To more effectually promote the great purposes of human culture; to establish the external relations of life on a basis of wisdom and purity; to apply the principles of justice and love to our social organization in accordance with the laws of Divine Providence; *to substitute a system of brotherly cooperation for one of selfish competition* . . . to institute an attractive, efficient, and productive system of industry . . . and thus to impart a greater freedom, simplicity, truthfulness, refinement, and moral dignity to our mode of life.[21]

Made famous by the region's rich social, religious, and philosophical history, the two-hundred-acre community became a meeting place of the mind for its stockholding members, boarders, and visitors, each sojourner carrying a vision of society not yet realized but made into a real and joyous part of their conversations and sympathies. Like the Puritans of an earlier era, Brook Farmers felt as though they were participating in a community whose activities focused on realizing a time in the near future when the kingdom of God might arrive. However, with the roles of church and state remaining separate, and without claiming a particular denomination as the basis of their beliefs, they adhered to a very functional formulation of their civic duties, most of which centered around a more liberalized education for their thirty or more students. Grounded in the spiritualization of the individual whose politics and self-interest melded into a form of harmonized citizenry, they chose "to walk ever on the mountain tops of life."

Brook Farm was not much of a community. With its focus on education rather than on industry, there was little motive for its members to associate for any specific or ulterior purpose. According to member Charles Lane, Brook Farm was "merely an aggregation of persons, and lacks that oneness of spirit, which is probably needful to make it of deep and lasting value to mankind." Burdened with debt, its leaders knew only too well that their success depended upon a deeper involvement in and support from the very business world they endeavored to escape.[22]

Brook Farm's official organ, *The Dial,* was a modest quarterly magazine published from July 1840 to April 1844. Edited by Margaret Fuller for the first eight issues and by Emerson for the last eight, its four-year history deserves considerable recognition for what it brought before the public.[23] *The Dial*'s stable of authors contributed to the corpus of thought that took shape under the umbrella of transcendentalism, propagating their individual and collective views on the rights of labor, the corrupting influence of capitalism, the debasement of black people, and the offensive byproducts rising from materialism. *The Dial*'s more noted articles included George Ripley's review of Albert Brisbane's *Social Destiny of Man;* Emerson's "Man the Reformer," "Transcendentalism," "New Jerusalem Church," "Goethe and Swedenborg," and "Fourierism and the Socialists"; Elizabeth Peabody's "Fourierism"; and Charles Lane's "Fruitlands" and "Brook Farm." For the magazine's readership, reform had to be of deeper character than what had gone on before. In order to be justified, any improvements had to come with a certain degree of moral elevation.[24]

Fuller assumed her editorial tasks without any promise of remuneration, and as the work of editorship claimed more and more time, her health deteriorated, forcing *The Dial*'s brief suspension and her withdrawal from the position. Despite impediments, she did an admirable job marshalling authors and keeping tabs on meetings, subscribers, and correspondence. What began as a quasi-religious magazine that set out to explain "A Glimpse of Christ's Idea of Society"—an October 1841 article by Elizabeth Peabody—acquired an element of prophecy, as it equated the kingdom of heaven with Christ's idea of society. Thus, *The Dial* followed a very idiosyncratic social agenda—a blend of transcendentalism, Christian socialism, and "hard-scrabble Yankee ingenuity."[25]

When Emerson took over editorial duties for *The Dial* in 1842, the magazine quickly became an extension of his sympathies toward government, temperance, abolition, trade, and domestic life, making it an organ very much in line with the daily affairs of educated Americans.

For those who shared its pages, it became a must-read, even though its subscription list never exceeded more than three hundred people. To read about it today is to sense a gospel of freedom whose writers were at the heart of the nation's very soul. The truth, however, is otherwise. While prominent in the nation's intellectual history, *The Dial* preached to a narrow group of readers who were distant from the practical needs and aspirations of the common person.[26]

Long identified with liberal religion, individualism, democracy, and national identity, the Transcendentalists of Brook Farm made a larger-than-life imprint on American thought and culture. They were persons who, regardless of their relationship to the movement, stood as important thinkers and doers in their own right. This helps to explain why, after shedding their attachments to socialist experimentation, mesmerism, Spiritualism, innovative marriage, and Swedenborgianism, and even after renouncing the US Constitution, their reputations remained "protected."

Associationism

At the time of Brook Farm's formation in 1841, Ripley had reputedly been aware of Brisbane's *Social Destiny of Man* but was largely unimpressed with Fourier's theories. Once the Farm became a reality, though, Ripley took a more focused interest in these ideas. He was drawn by both Brisbane and Greeley, who at the time were the leading advocates of associationism, the term coined by Brisbane to describe the systematic set of economic, political, and social beliefs of Charles Fourier. By 1843, Ripley had joined the cause in advocating Fourierist social theory, urging that the Brook Farm community move in this direction for sustainability purposes. Greeley and Brisbane had connections with James John Garth Wilkinson in England, a translator of several Swedenborgian books, who served as the English correspondent to Greeley's *New York Tribune* and made frequent reference to the connection between Fourierism and Swedenborgianism.[27] The same was true of Emerson, who noted the "strange coincidences" between Swedenborg's writings and Fourier's theory.[28] Moreover, when William Ellery Channing's nephew, Rev. William Henry Channing, took up the torch of associationism in 1843, he demonstrated a lively curiosity as to how it might resonate with the Brook Farm experiment. Calling himself a Christian socialist, Rev. Channing was a frequent visitor to the North American Phalanx in New Jersey. He edited the magazines *The Present* (1843–44) and *The Spirit of the Age* (1849–50), both of which endorsed a religious union of associationists through the merger of Fourierism and Swedenborgianism.[29]

When Rev. Channing joined Ripley, Peabody, and the radical reformers gathering at Brook Farm, he gave full expression to his newfound beliefs.

> First, my fundamental conviction is that God, as the only self-existent and all perfect, is the source of all that is, and therefore of all goodness, wisdom, beauty, energy, and peace in human souls. . . . Second, . . . all events in the past, all influences which have been exerted, all causes which have coöperated to produce the present condition of the human race, have been from God, and have had his sanction, and are revelations of his will in proportion to their degree of importance. Third, it is a plain matter of fact that religion and morality are man's highest interest, and equally plain that the highest manifestation of these in ancient times was given through the Jewish nation in ever-increasing brightness, until the revelation through that people reached its perfect consummation in him who came, fulfilling their highest hope in the fullness of time.[30]

On December 26th and 27th in 1843, a convention of the Friends of Social Reform in New England met in Boston to take counsel on the cause of social reorganization and reform, to examine the truths of social science discovered by Fourier, and to consider the establishment of an association based on the broad goal of "attractive industry," which sought to remedy the drudgery of work. Organized by members of the Northampton, Hopedale, and Brook Farm communities, the delegates spent hours identifying similarities in the writings of Swedenborg and Fourier. Several Brook Farm delegates noted comparisons between Fourier's ideas and their own Transcendentalist community. Before long, the participants had no less a goal than building a living Universal Human that would consist of the working people of the country.

One of the principal challenges at the convention came from concerns that individuality might be lost in moving to associationism. In Rev. Channing's retort to this challenge, the answer seemed obliviously casuistic—namely, that individuality actually increased under associationism, as it opened its members to new interests, encouraging each of them to manifest his or her respective strengths. By bringing together the harmonies of each individual's natural passions, and securing the highest possible social good, the reverend intended their collective labors to result in the formation of the Universal Human, which would express the holiest and loftiest aims of humankind.[31]

Before the convention ended, its enthusiasts adopted several resolutions promoting efforts to create a spirit of Christian brotherhood, liberty, and peaceful reform. They also announced the law of love (i.e., usefulness) that stood behind their belief in associationism and the need to exercise the principles of freedom and human rights in the areas of abolitionism, pacifism, temperance, women's rights, banking, and tariffs.[32] By forming themselves into model societies, and showing the practical aspects of their principles, they thought it possible to realize these reforms without interference from the state. Guided by the law of love, they intended to test the influence of one intellect upon another and of one heart upon another, eventually reaching the larger circle of family and community.[33]

Over the winter of 1843–44, Brook Farm declared itself a Fourierist community and obtained incorporation status by act of the Massachusetts legislature. Its transition proved decidedly easy due to its existing administrative structure (Departments of General Direction, Agriculture, Education, and Finance) and leadership. With the change, the numbers of visitors and applications for membership increased, and the Farm experienced a robust two years focused on the construction of a unitary phalanx building representing their expanded purpose. For the first time in the history of associationism, its building design compared favorably to artists' renderings of what phalanxes might look like in years to come.

Brook Farm members rejoiced at their community's efforts to engage in "a practical manifestation of Association." Committed to the professed principles of Christian love and liberty, the phalanx demonstrated clear evidence of Fourier's doctrine of universal unity and of the practical arrangements derived from it. With property valued at $30,000, the community became the "poster child" for associationism across the Northeast and Midwest, but expansion into a "perfect phalanx" required even more capital.[34]

When Elizabeth Peabody reported in *The Dial* on the decision to align the Brook Farm community with the doctrines of associationism, she noted her surprise at the suddenness of the action. The community had begun as a reflection of the Unitarian and Transcendentalist frame of mind, but how was it that its founding principles had somehow transformed into Fourierism?

> The question is, whether the Phalanx acknowledges its own limitations of nature, in being an organization, or opens up any avenue into the source of life that shall keep it sweet, enabling it to assimilate to itself contrary elements, and consume its own waste; so that, Phoenix-like, it may renew itself forever in great and finer forms....
>
> The life of the world is now the Christian life. For eighteen centuries, Art, Literature, Philosophy, Poetry, have followed the fortunes of the Christian idea. Ancient history is the history of the apotheosis of Nature, or natural religion; modern history is the history of an Idea, or revealed religion. In vain will any thing try to be, which is not supported thereby. Fourier does homage to Christianity with many words. But this may be *cant*, though it thinks itself sincere. Besides, there are many things that go by the name of Christianity, that are not it.[35]

Peabody admitted that despite the suddenness of the change, most of her reservations had dissipated as a result of the explanations given by William Henry Channing and others. In general, the transition to associationism had proceeded on the assumption that "there is in the Divine Mind a certain social order, to which man is destined, and which is discoverable by man, according to his truth in thought to the two poles of Christian perfection, Love of God and Love of

Man." Over a period of forty years of diligent work, she explained, Fourier had discovered the divine order of things based on the law of attraction (i.e., correspondences) that aligned the universe of humankind with the universe of matter. "If Fourier had done nothing but suggest ... that the divine order of society was a possible discovery," she observed, "he would have done much." Now that Brook Farm had become a phalanx, she wished it godspeed and dubbed it worthy of its inheritance. But, she cautioned, if Fourierism stopped short of serving both the soul and the body, it might become a curse rather than a benefit to humankind.[36]

The year 1844 was ripe with anticipation as Brook Farm's phalanstery moved from theory to practice. *The Dial* ended publication and was replaced by *The Phalanx*, which assumed its subscription list and proceeded to explain Fourierism in much greater detail. Thus, while William Ellery Channing had fathered the original Brook Farm, his nephew, Rev. William Henry, served as the principal catalyst for converting the community into a phalanx of Fourierism. An enthusiastic Jeffersonian and a passionate reformer, William Henry had the reputation of lending his name to many different causes. "Our end is to do God's will, not our own; to obey the command of Providence, not to follow the leadings of human fancies," he explained to the Friends of Social Reform at Clinton Hall in New York. "We stand today, as we believe, amid the dawn of a new era of humanity, and as from a Pisgah look down upon a promised land." In the February issue of *The Phalanx*, its editors announced that the community had successfully blended the social and religious beliefs of Swedenborg into Fourier's departments of labor, agriculture, domestic industry, and the mechanical arts.[37]

Elsewhere, the nation's phalanxes formed into social units built on the combined teachings of Swedenborg and Fourier. Notwithstanding these newer communities, Brook Farm remained the centerpiece for the propagation of Fourierism, a turn of events that precipitated the transfer of leadership in the movement from New York to Boston. Until then, New York had claimed to be the seat of Fourierism, principally because it was home to the movement's executive committee. Now, under the leadership of William Henry Channing, operations moved to Boston, where *The Harbinger* replaced *The Phalanx* as the official magazine of the American Union of Associationists. *The Harbinger's* threefold motto was "Unity of man with man in true society/ Unity of man with God in true religion/Unity of man with nature in creative art and industry."[38] And as Rev. William Henry explained, the combination of Fourier and Swedenborg had opened "a whole new world of study, hope, and action . . . and revealed the means of living the law of love."[39]

With William Henry Channing's ascendancy as corresponding secretary of the American Union of Associationists, he quickly became a leading figure not just to Brook Farm but also to Fourierist associations across the country. In this leadership position, the so-called "Apostle of Fourierism" eclipsed the work of Brisbane, who returned to Europe. With Brisbane gone, William Henry Channing and Charles A. Dana toured through New England, Ohio, Pennsylvania, and New York, calling for action on behalf of promoting universal unity, forming societies, raising funds, and circulating the good news of *The Harbinger*.[40] During this time, many of the phalanxes, mindful of their intellectual heritage and of Swedenborg's feelings of primitivism and his hostility toward slavery, actively participated in the Underground Railroad.[41]

Second only to William Henry Channing and Albert Brisbane in their support of Fourierism was journalist Parke Godwin, whose *A Popular View of the Doctrines of Charles Fourier* (1844) drew further analogies between Fourierism and Swedenborgianism. In his chapter on "Universal Analogy," Godwin explained the remarkable similarity between the revelations of Swedenborg in the sphere of spiritual knowledge and Fourier's discoveries in the sphere of science. "These two great minds . . . were the instruments of Providence in bringing to light the mysteries of His Word and Works, as they are comprehended and followed, in the higher states of existence." Both men had been commissioned "to spy out the Promised Land of Peace and Blessedness." With Fourier's doctrine of universal analogy and Swedenborg's doctrine of correspondences, both had arrived at an understanding of the relationship between things material and things spiritual. As Godwin reasoned, that man was created in the image and likeness of

God to satisfy the love of God paralleled Swedenborg's explanation that man, "being the image and likeness of his Maker, must reflect all these properties of his Original." The Deity had not performed the work of creation as a random act or out of caprice, but formed everything after the pattern of the ineffable attributes stemming from divinity's infinite love and wisdom and recognizable in all objects of a material nature from the most inferior to the most complex.[42]

Addressing the complaint that Fourierism contained irreligious doctrines—namely, that persons should follow the dictates of their own conscience rather than established religious authority—Godwin responded that its principles were anchored in the "practical embodiment of religious truth and love." Associationism did not supplant religion but instead acted as its servant for the sake of the earth's redemption. "We look upon it as the mightiest auxiliary to Christianity that has ever been presented to men, because it is a direct outgrowth and manifestation of the Spirit of Christianity." Associationism conciliated all classes and parties on the basis of mutual interest and harmony, and it absolved no one from the obligations of morality. Fourierism represented a union of social and individual virtues that, in essence, was the objective of religion as well. His science offered a blueprint for the principle of unity and order that was essential to leading humanity from misery to happiness on earth. It was "a faithful Image, though perhaps but faint, of God himself."[43]

Along with Godwin, the English Fourierist Hugh Doherty, who was another frequent contributor to *The Phalanx* and *The Harbinger,* made efforts to explain the similarity between Fourier and Swedenborg.

> I am a believer in the truths of the New Church, and have read nearly all the writings of Swedenborg, and I have no hesitation in saying that without Fourier's explanation of the laws of order in Scriptural interpretation, I should probably have doubted the truth of Swedenborg's illumination from want of a ground to understand the nature of spiritual sight in contradistinction from natural sight; or if I had been able to conceive the opening of the spiritual sight, and credit Swedenborg's doctrines and affirmations,

I should probably have understood them only in the same degree, as most of the members of the New Church whom I have met in England, and that would seem to me, in my present state, a partial calamity of cecity. I say this in all humility and sincerity of conscience, with a view to future reference to Swedenborg himself in the spiritual world, and as a means of inducing the members of the New Church generally not to be content with a superficial or limited knowledge of their own doctrines.[44]

Swedenborgianism

The final phase of the Brook Farm Phalanx involved its formal adoption of Swedenborgianism. Since the community had its origins in Unitarianism and transcendentalism, Swedenborgianism carried much more appeal than did the scientific formulations of Fourier and Brisbane. Though Fourierist in theory, the Farm's taxonomy associated more closely with the passional vision of Swedenborg, whose spiritual tendencies were distant echoes of Christian millennialism. The scientific aspects of Fourierism had a certain charm, but the bold mysteries behind Swedenborg's intuition and the promise of heavenly planes inhabited by angels had even greater appeal. As a community whose centerpiece was the life of the mind, the Farm's members judged Fourierism too bold in its materialism. As noted earlier, the promotion of this more spiritual side of associationism came after Brisbane returned to Europe in the spring of 1844, leaving the movement in the hands of William Henry Channing, Godwin, and others who were more entrenched in Christian, albeit mystical, socialism.[45]

Comparisons between Fourier and Swedenborg were also made in William Henry Channing's *The Present* and William Cooper Howells's *The Retina* by New Church clergymen B. F. Barrett and Solyman Brown, as well as by Charles Julius Hempel and John Sullivan Dwight. As did others, they started with Fourier's doctrine of universal analogy and Swedenborg's doctrine of correspondences before coming to the none-too-subtle conclusion that Swedenborgianism was the spiritual version of associationism, drawing the material and spiritual worlds together in a system of practical "uses."[46] Admittedly, except for a sense of sublime optimism that wafted over the aspirations of the reformers, the issues of sin, self-love, and hell were unresolved. But even though Swedenborg interpreted the Second Coming as "[the Lord's] presence in everyone," there were sufficient numbers of utopian literalists whose vision of the afterlife corresponded easily with these earthly societies.[47]

With the Farm's transition to Swedenborgianism, George Ripley turned his energies outward, becoming a staunch missionary, traveling extensively, making speeches, attracting new members, raising money, organizing meetings, and writing articles. As editor and publisher of *The Harbinger,* he used its pages to summarize Fourier's life and writings, editing out those aspects of his theories that were embarrassingly silly or overly complicated. Well aware of the connection between Fourier and Swedenborg, Ripley reminded followers that Fourier had been born into the world "the same year in which it was left by another profound observer of the laws of Universal Harmony, the illustrious … Swedenborg." He went on to observe that Fourier's discovery of the "divine social code," which followed the same laws that governed the movements of the planets, had been "consecrated by the parting benediction of the sublime spirit [Swedenborg] whose earthly lie was irradiated with the glorious visions of celestial beatitude and harmony."[48]

It is more than a coincidence that interest in Swedenborg, including production of the newer English translations of his works, appeared during the rise of Fourierism. James John Garth Wilkinson not only translated several of Swedenborg's works, but he became a frequent contributor to both *The Phalanx* and *The Harbinger*—as did Augustus Clissold, then-president of the Swedenborg Association and a life member of the Swedenborg Society of London. In the writings of Dwight, Dana, Henry James, Sr., and Charles Julius Hempel, Fourier's doctrines of series, universal analogy, attractions, and destinies were compared to Swedenborg's doctrines of forms, orders, degrees, influx, and correspondences, giving character to the breadth of knowledge and the universality of themes in the works of these two men.[49]

Henry James, Sr., the most influential Swedenborgian among the proponents of Fourierism, drew on the law of correspondences in his claim that Fourier's blueprint for society provided a close approximation of Swedenborg's angelic planes; and he recognized the transformative work of divine influx in the exercise of human fellowship. James's outline confirmed that God's construct of human nature was broader than a world that began and ended with original sin and the foreordained disposition of the individual soul. He viewed Fourierism as an earthly representation of Swedenborg's revelatory vision of the divine order, with the latent divinity of humanity realized in its earthly communities.[50] This was not the world of Emerson's individual who sought self-culture, but instead was an association of like-minded individuals called into service on behalf of humanity. "The notion that humans possessed divine life jointly rather than individually," explained historian Carl J. Guarneri, "seemed to move the powerful self of Transcendentalism off center stage," underscoring the link between Swedenborg and a socialist definition of selfhood.[51] The redemption of the individual depended upon a social reorganization that did justice to the corporate whole. Fourier's phalanx was none other than the Swedenborgian idea of the Universal Human.[52] "Viewed from this perspective," wrote Guarneri, "Swedenborg emerged as a socialist prophet, and Fourier's phalanx became the true organization of the New Church."[53]

In *Moralism and Christianity* (1850), James included three lectures ("A Scientific Statement of the Christian Doctrine of the Lord, or Divine Man," "Socialism and Civilization in Relation to the Development of the Individual Life," and "Morality and the Perfect Life"), which, taken together, illustrated how individualism and spiritual socialism revealed the groundwork for his concept of the spiritual human being. This was not to be understood in the individual sense but instead as the divine human who offset self-love (i.e., *proprium*) with true charity and brotherly love. The goal of human freedom was a balance between Fourierist thought and the social implications of Swedenborg's union of love, wisdom, and usefulness. The striking resemblance between Swedenborgianism and Fourierism came with the associationists' emphasis on "action" and Swedenborg's emphasis on "effect" and "use."[54] Seen through the doctrine of correspondences, the doctrine of usefulness became not only deeper in its meaning but was also recognized as the true expression of divine intent in the natural world. When combined, the doctrines of correspondences and usefulness gave humanity a more integrated understanding of the natural world and its place in it.[55]

Initially hostile toward any form of official religious organization, Brook Farm's eventual conversion to Fourierism and then to Swedenborgianism changed its social dynamic. Though dogma did not surface, religious phraseology and emotional group activities took on devotional aspects that gave the phalanx a decidedly religious tone. Theodore Parker's sermons on social reform, William Henry Channing's lectures on socialism, John Sullivan Dwight's musical and theatrical events, and the semi-religious ceremonies suggestive of Christianized socialism gave the community a sense of providential mission and outlook. By 1844, the phalanx had become the springboard for humanity's spiritual and material salvation.[56]

In a lecture titled "New England Reformers" read at Amory Hall on March 3, 1844, Emerson took note of the new movements of abolitionism, mesmerism, homeopathy, and phrenology, as well as other "soldiery of dissent," that called into question established institutions and authorities. This spirit of protest, best expressed in impatience with societal conventions, had caused reformers to act like a "congress of kings, each of whom had a realm to rule, and a way of his own that made concert unprofitable." Despite the din of debate and "plentiful vaporing," Emerson saw a contest brewing between conventional institutions and dissenters who found the world too much governed for their "tender consciences." Rather than condemn this new spirit for its excesses, he chose to plumb its truths, discovering in the process that these efforts to reform society were wholly warranted. He seemed unperturbed by their attacks on convention and by the hypocrisy that sometimes accompanied it.[57]

Noting the impact of Fourier and Owen on communities that had formed in New England and elsewhere, Emerson questioned whether these societies, supposedly composed of individuals "of superior talents and sentiments," would continue to draw on people with the same energy or would instead "become an asylum to those who have tried and failed." While they were fine efforts of catholic purpose, he cautioned that "no society can ever be so large as one man." Essentially, he worried that their number, which seemed to double by the hour, placed too much hope in the *group* rather than in the *individual.* "There can be no concert in two, where there is no concert in one. When the individual is not *individual,* but is dual; when his thoughts look one way, and his actions another . . . what concert can be?" Until such experiments became "inward" and not just written covenants, he doubted they would succeed. "Society is a hospital of incurables," he noted. No amount of education, philosophy, or influence of genius will give "depth of insight to a superficial mind."[58]

Dénouement

Brook Farm remained an exception among the phalanxes in that its members expected its future would be sustained by wealthy patrons. When Brisbane left for Europe, that expectation went unfulfilled, leaving a series of broken promises that continued until the financial setback caused by the fire of March 3, 1846, which destroyed the Farm's communal building. Under construction since the summer of 1844, the three-story building included fourteen apartments, a kitchen and dining hall capable of seating four hundred persons, two public saloons, and a spacious lecture hall. The actual expenditures on the building at the time of the fire amounted to approximately $7,000, and as it was not yet in use, it carried no insurance.[59] "The destruction of our edifice makes no essential change in our pursuits," *The Harbinger* reassured the Farm's members. "It leaves no family destitute of a home; it disturbs no domestic arrangements; it puts us to no immediate inconvenience. . . . Our schools were attended as usual; our industry in full operation; and not a look or expression of despondency could have been perceived."[60]

While "nothing but the most inexorable necessity, will withdraw the congenial spirits that are gathered in social union here, from the work which has always called forth [our] most earnest devotedness and enthusiasm," wrote Ripley, "it is a total destruction of resources, on which we had confidently relied, and must inevitably derange our plans for the enlargement of the Association and the extension of our industry." The belief that had burned so brightly in their hearts—much like the Puritan forefathers who felt the eyes of the Christian world on their efforts—would end in ashes. Here had been their chance to illustrate associationism in the body politic. They, too, had an "errand" to fulfill and perhaps could make up for what the Puritans failed to achieve. "Upon the firm establishment of the Brook Farm Phalanx," corresponded a supporter, "depends in no small degree, the advance of our whole Cause."[61]

In the aftermath of the fire, the community seemed to be gasping for air, hoping against hope that the essential soul of the phalanx would prove more powerful than the charred evidence of their uninsured loss. Clearly, however, doubts about the phalanstery preceded the fire, because there is no way to explain the community's precipitous collapse. Within weeks, the association dismissed most of its residents, discontinued its ongoing activities, and questioned the future of their school. Lacking the presence of mind to accept the disaster and press on, the fire became an omen to individual joint stock owners, as they challenged the directors to either buy out their shares or sell the corporation.[62] In March 1847, unable to preserve the relationships that once sustained its members, Brook Farm was sold at auction to become an orphan asylum maintained by the Lutheran Church.[63] With its sale, the beacon of Christian socialist hope ended, and news of its demise precipitated the collapse of sister communities whose founders preferred closure to compromising on their blend of work and play, sharing profits equally, and experiencing the beauties of nature and a simpler life.[64]

Nine months after the fire at Brook Farm, the American Union of Associationists, with an estimated membership of seven hundred, called on all affiliated societies to uphold and diffuse the principles of associationism. In all, twenty-five affiliated societies were spread across Massachusetts; Vermont; Maine; Rhode Island; New York; Pennsylvania; Virginia; Ohio; Washington, DC; and Wisconsin.[65] Of all the member unions, Boston and New York had unquestionably been the most effective. Without their well-publicized events and activities, there would have been little for the American Union to herald. The Boston associationists, most of whom had affiliated with Brook Farm, supported a lecture series at the Masonic Temple on Tremont Street that included talks by Horace Greeley ("Tendencies of Modern Civilization"), Albert Brisbane ("The Practical Organization of Associationism"), Parke Godwin ("Charles Fourier"), William Henry Channing ("The Destiny of Man Upon the Earth"), and George Ripley ("The Ground of Association in the Spiritual Nature of Man").[66] The lectures were often printed in their entirety by newspapers sympathetic to associationism, especially Greeley's *New York Tribune,* reaching a broad array of readers living along the Eastern seaboard.[67]

With the fire putting an end to the dreams of Brook Farm, William Henry Channing went through an episode of soul-searching, wondering what it would take to "live united with fellow-seekers of a divine-humanity in societies of heartily cooperating men and women." Believing in the nearness of the kingdom of heaven, he continued to rally associationists in Europe and the United States to the symbol of "God-in-Man" and the spiritual world waiting to be realized.[68] On January 3, 1847, some forty stalwarts met at the Boston home of Mr. J. Fisher, where they joined in a Religious Union to devote their lives to establishing the kingdom of God on earth. After unanimously being elected as their minister and leader of the Union, Rev. William Henry Channing preached to a crowded assembly hall on the subject "The Kingdom of Heaven is at Hand."[69]

In October 1847, *The Harbinger* returned to New York under the editorship of Godwin, assisted by Ripley and Dana. As for the Fourier communities, only the North American Phalanx in New Jersey, the Trumbull Phalanx in Ohio, and the Wisconsin Phalanx remained. Within months, the Trumbull Phalanx disappeared; and the Wisconsin Phalanx ended a year later. Being near New York City, with Horace Greeley as vice president and stockholder, with numerous affiliated societies cooperating, and with property estimated at $80,000, the North American Phalanx had a better than even chance of succeeding. In truth, it was not at Brook Farm but at the North American Phalanx that Fourierism met with the most success. The phalanx lasted until 1854, when it, too, suffered loss by fire. There was little to recommend its continuance, as most of the capital was owned by nonresidents and the majority of community members were living from hand to mouth. With uninsured losses estimated at $20,000, the phalanx lingered for another year before dying. "As the generality of those on the ground gave no tangible indications of any particular interest in the movement, it is no matter of surprise that, notwithstanding the zeal of a few disinterested philanthropists engaged in it, the institution failed to meet the sanguine expectations of its projectors." With the extinction of the North American Phalanx, Fourierism ended.[70]

In his quieter moments, William Henry Channing wondered to a friend whether, in the impulses that prompted the movement, there had been "too much haste, too much spasm." Complaining that there was no prophet or king at its head, and too much "ambitiousness and jealousy" among individual members, he confessed that the movement had proved too "rash and risky," "ill contrived," and poorly executed. Not until "the whole nation was … awakened to a new comprehension of its mission [and] its essential principle" could associationism spread throughout the land and realize its promise.[71]

With the extinction of the last remaining phalanxes, a perceptible change took place in the tone and content of *The Harbinger.* The magazine continued to include references to Swedenborg, but with far less insistence on connecting his ideas with those of Fourier.[72] Articles reporting on the celebration in Boston of Fourier's birthday, for example, no longer included mention of Swedenborg.[73] Similarly, associationism made no reference to the establishment of the Swedenborg Association in London and its objective of publishing Swedenborg's scientific works.[74] In an article reviewing Wilkinson's translations of *The Animal Kingdom* (1843–44), *The Principia* (1845), *The Economy of the Animal Kingdom* (1845–46), and *Remarks on Swedenborg's Economy of the Animal Kingdom* (1846), the editor confessed of not being sufficiently competent enough to critique the writings. "Our acquaintance with them is not yet sufficiently intimate to authorize us to take such a position. At present we desire simply to advertise [to] our readers that such books can be had, and to commend them to their most serious attention." The editor was quick to admit, however, that with the exception of Fourier's publications, no others in recent years were as significant as those of Swedenborg, which were equally "invaluable, almost indispensable," to a wide variety of readers.[75]

In the May 1, 1847, issue of *The Harbinger*, there was a review of Wilkinson's translation of Swedenborg's *Outlines of a Philosophical Argument on the Infinite* (1847). What caught the eye of the reviewer were Wilkinson's "Introductory Remarks," which explained that the frequent references made by contemporaries to the similarity between Swedenborg and transcendentalism were wrong-headed. From the editors' point of view, transcendentalism "wanders in the vague, it hovers impracticable over the whole field of life, alighting nowhere, for the want of a science of correspondences, a doctrine of Universal Unity. It has dwelt so long upon the idea of the shaping mind, that it has come to regard the mind as all, its objects nothing."[76] In the same issue of *The Harbinger* was a review of *Tracts for the Times. No. I. Letter to a Swedenborgian*. In it, the reviewer warned against the proneness to "*Swedenborgianize*" associationism. "It is Fourierism … which alone does justice to the thought of Fourier."[77]

The 1840s marked the high tide of communitarianism, with its plans and projects exploring the possibilities of self-discovery, controlled experimentation, peaceful change, and the adaption of individual ethics and self-culture to groups and communities. Underlying these projects was Swedenborg's doctrine of usefulness, which directed the efforts of self-discovery and personal responsibility toward broader ethical and societal objectives.[78] Swedenborg's visions of heaven's spiritual partitions appealed to many would-be utopians who, disenchanted with the side-effects of industrial capitalism, read into his words the potential for ideal societies based on collective values and dedicated to the common good. Neither Owen nor Fourier was particularly religious, but their disciples saw value in Swedenborg's scheme for post-Judgment life on earth. As noted earlier, what Fourier called "universal analogy" appeared indistinguishable from Swedenborg's doctrine of correspondences and was an obvious lifeline between the natural and spiritual realm. Swedenborg's vision of a New Jerusalem, suggesting a renewed spiritual world following the Last Judgment, inspired liberal Christians to consider the possibilities of brave new worlds that would accommodate the arrival of Christ.[79]

While members of the nation's utopian communities were searching for both spiritual and religious solutions, it is difficult to say to what extent they exclusively pursued one or the other, as their inheritance of ideas was highly eclectic and their impact on the environment noticeably uneven. In both respects, though, they looked to the regeneration of heart and mind. Despite being incurable optimists with little concern for the past and whose passionate efforts often died stillborn, the perfectionists and their communities became both a cautionary tale and a vision of things yet to come. In the end, the communitarians did not measure up to the high standards they had set for themselves. Their promotion of justice, love, and freedom failed to match the ideals they preached and only occasionally practiced. Having dismissed the state as a vehicle for change, they saw their prize ideals burn brightly and then disappear. Their ambivalence with regard to the state left them advocating an unfulfilled virtue of self-reliance and making a succession of compromises that diluted their purposes. As critics of American society, they operated as a branch of the Romantic Movement, which later generations would dismiss with little more than a shrug. Nevertheless, the spiritual underpinning that marked their efforts, as explained by historian Carl J. Guarneri, represented "a striking anticipation of the theology of the Social Gospel and of late nineteenth-century Christian Socialism."[80] To the extent that religious thought and, in particular, the doctrine of usefulness played a role in millennialism, communitarianism, and in the later social gospel and progressive movements, it carried forward the liberal Protestant legacy of the New Church—a call to action, or as Emerson explained, paraphrasing Romans 8:28: "making all things work together for the good of those who love the Lord."[81]

3 In Search of a Vision

*The reformer is a poet, a creator. He sees visions and fills the
people with their beauty; and by the contagion of virtue his
creative impulse spreads among the mass, and it begins to climb
and build.*

(Henry Demarest Lloyd, *Man, the Social Creator*, 1906)

As the nation emerged from the Civil War with a half million dead
lingering in its collective memory, its once-bright path to righteousness and social justice took a decidedly different turn by embarking on
a journey of gilded excess. With the South's "forgotten man" standing
in feeble awareness of his region's collapsed economy and the obstacles impeding his future, the North and West acted out their tawdry
appetites spending and laying waste the nation's resources. Except in
the South, the rush of scientific and mechanical innovations changed
the pace of living, bringing new social realities into art, science, philosophy, religion, and literature.[1] In each of these areas, the intuitive
process, long regarded as the most satisfactory approach to truth, felt
the tremors of change resonating from the biological sciences.

In this new environment, Swedenborgians and New Church
members faced the difficult task of finding relevancy in a society that
Walt Whitman disturbingly viewed as having "hollowness at heart
[and] little or no soul."[2] The old harmony that had given the nation
cohesion and strength appeared to be gone. Now nature, which once
mirrored the thoughts of the soul, became a power with an obscure
will. On the threshold of a new era, there seemed to be no place for the
rustle of angels' wings or for an understanding that gave every material and living thing their fixed place in the world. While the theory

63

of evolution had won hearts and minds, the challenge of bringing the Universal Human into this new equation seemed difficult at best. For Swedenborgians, there were numerous questions that required answers: Would the New Church simply choose to parse its words rather than to take on the issues directly? Could the Swedenborgian criterion of usefulness meet the conditions of Spencer's "survival of the fittest"? Did Swedenborg's revelatory wisdom have a place in the material world of Darwin in which benign forces acted mechanically and without guidance?[3]

Changing Paradigm

Those Americans coming to maturity in the second half of the nineteenth century belonged to a generation who witnessed their world passing while another was rising to take its place, a new world in which the "divinities" of science and technology were reshaping patterns of life that had been patched together over centuries of furtive stitching. The age of great cities had arrived, stripping away autonomy and substituting it with factory life, faceless oligarchies, and countless millions tethered to machines. While a broad movement of thought passed through this period, it ended on a somber note that seemed to deny individual choice and freedom. This was in stark contrast to the preceding age in which, as Episcopal theologian Henry S. Nash explained, Christianity had made humanity at home in the universe by "bringing the heart of God" into their own hearts and by providing a faith that gave answers to life's enigmatic questions.[4]

When Darwin announced his theory in 1859 in his *On the Origin of Species*, the intellectual world was ready to welcome evolutionary thinking, with or without the mechanism of natural selection. It came at a time when people were looking for a new faith that would align with the emerging industrial world. Darwin introduced a purely naturalistic account of development, separating science from religion, and doing so not by attacking the latter but by ignoring its relevance. Concepts such as "geological change" and "species variation" turned away from arguments of harmonious and divinely ordained change for each species of plant and animal, instead dealing with theories of impermanence and chance variability, neither of which was tied to religion or the argument of design. Essentially, religion had become irrelevant to scientific assumptions and their implications.[5]

Evolution offered a new paradigm that applied not only to the biological sciences but also to the broader culture—from law and history to economics, sociology, philosophy, religion, and art. It created a climate of opinion that explained away the Creation story and what little remained of transcendentalism, while justifying unbridled competition, militarism, and imperialism. The newly acquired empirical methods challenged truths that were intuitively reached and held without proof, as well as laws that were deductively rather than inductively proven. A whole host of "self-evident" dogmas fell out of favor as a new generation of scientists and social scientists upended the foundations of their respective disciplines by projecting a universe that was ever-emergent, where philosophy was dynamic and not constant, and where fixed ideas were as out of place as was Emerson's self-reliant individual.[6]

Evolution precipitated a fearful toll on the century's assumptions, imposing a set of values that unsettled many with a sense of the universe's benign indifference to humanity's purpose, let alone its existence. Before the century ended, terms such as *determinism, chance, uncertainty, the unknown,* and *agnosticism* would become common currency among those sensitive souls troubled by the silence and presumed emptiness of the universe. The late Victorians, explained D. H. Meyer, "were perhaps the last generations among English-speaking intellectuals able to believe that man was capable of understanding his universe, just as they were the first generation collectively to suspect that he never would."[7]

From the safety of Down House in rural Kent, Darwin watched converts won and lost, alliances formed, and terms like *Darwinist, Darwinism,* and *Social Darwinism* packaged and politicized.[8] Despite living his professional life in relative seclusion, his thoughts and written words were continually examined and became topics of intense scrutiny. Darwin's work, though not itself a matter of metaphysics, opened minds to new and developing philosophical tendencies, making less plausible such natural theological claims as the argument from design and the uniqueness of humankind. Darwin "helped to extend scientific procedures into fields where they had seemed to be quite inapplicable and to bridge that gulf between man and animal which had once been assumed to be unbridgeable."[9]

Taking a backward glance into Darwin's life and times, one cannot help but see the enormous amount of rummaging performed by scholars who were looking for any signs of ambivalence, hesitation, or awkwardness in his writings that might suggest a chance feeling or belief. The fact remains that Darwin's legacy was weighted with religious implications and context due to his tendency to substitute words in each new edition, thus giving added nuance to this feeding frenzy. The evidence suggests a steady drift from youthful orthodoxy—much of it built upon William Paley's *Natural Theology*,[10] to the beginnings of doubt while at Cambridge,[11] to deism evidenced during his five-year voyage on the HMS Beagle, to agnosticism and possibly even atheism in his later years.[12] All claims to Darwin's ultimate position, however, remained tentative, since he refused to take any public stand other than his making a private confession to Asa Gray that he was "in an utterly hopeless muddle."[13] Darwin's lack of clarity opened the door for interpretation. Having rejected the traditional concept of a providential God and the argument from design, his reluctance to pronounce any final judgment led his acolytes to find positions somewhere between lukewarm theism and a reticent agnosticism.

With natural selection as the primary mechanism for evolution, the chance variations that determined survival or extinction were unconnected with the effort to survive. This was the very antithesis of natural theology's concept of purpose, or design, by a first cause. As a consequence, many of Darwin's supporters chose to soften the theory of natural selection by suggesting some form of directive agency. This explains why the true nature of Darwin's nondirectional theory differed dramatically from the ways in which the communities of scientists, theologians, and social scientists chose to interpret it. In fact, the concept of natural selection suffered heavily in the ensuing decades, as educated society sought a more purposeful role for the theory's functional power. Even among Darwin's strongest supporters there remained levels of interpretation. Alfred R. Wallace, the co-originator of the theory of natural selection, distinguished between humanity's physical and mental evolution; Benjamin Kidd and Arabella Buckley gave evolution a Spiritualist and non-Christian overtone; Henry Drummond, Asa Gray, and Lyman Abbott held that evolution stood for God's method in creation; George John Romanes transformed evolution into a "tenuous theism";[14] and St. George Jackson Mivart, a Transcendentalist Catholic Tory, maintained that "the prevalence of this theory [of evolution] need alarm no one, for it is, without any doubt, perfectly consistent with the strictest and most orthodox Christian theology."[15]

The fact that Darwin's *Origin* was embraced in both Christian and non-Christian teleologies should give pause to the depiction of evolutionary theory as symbolic of a tectonic separation of science and religion. To be sure, Darwin put traditional natural theology to the sword, but he opened nature to a "cosmological revolution" by individuals who transformed evolution into a combination of value, purpose, and novelty.[16] On balance, Darwin seemed more comfortable with those who gave evolution a cosmic or spiritual motif than he did with those avowed or militant atheists, such as Edward Aveling, Robert G. Ingersoll, Carl Vogt, and the monistic Prussian naturalist Ernst Haeckel, who approached the topic as radical freethinkers. Clearly, the relationship between the alleged godlessness of Darwin's theory of natural selection and those suggesting some form of directive agency has been overplayed by parties on both sides, but especially by those intent on blunting the growing acceptance of reductionist thinking as the rightful heir to the *a priori* claims of religion.[17]

Evolution and the New Church

Those New Church conservatives who were fixated on Swedenborg's infallibility found no conflict between *true* science and divine revelation. Like many of their contemporaries, they rejected the chance materialism implicit in natural selection and, instead, approached the natural world by relying on deductive methodologies best reflected in the German school of *Naturphilosophie,* or "nature philosophy"— most notably in the writings of Goethe and Lorenz Oken, both of whom built belief on the prospect of the immutability of species. Each species identified in Carolus Linnaeus's *Systema Naturae* (1735) was no artificial human endeavor but instead was a reflection of the distinct thoughts of the Creator. For this community of natural philosophers, science worked as an integral part of humanity's moral purposes to sustain conviction and so they were ready expositors of the harmony existing between science and religion. Even those who practiced their science separate from religion still understood that their reductionist methods worked under the same designing hand of the Creator. True science, even when left to its own devices and unguided by religious truths, was thought to find a path back to religion, the glory of creation, and the benevolence of the Creator.

Darwin avoided the "human" question until *The Descent of Man* (1871), in which he introduced the theory of probability and chance variation into how humans were cognitively organized, leaving little room for the prevailing moral schemes of the day, including those based on Swedenborg's revelatory interpretations. Darwin did not dispute the existence of a moral sense in humans, but he did dispute whether this sense was any different qualitatively from the natural instincts in animals. Moral systems were recognized as merely being the sum of innate instincts, a position that Darwin admittedly found unsatisfactory but that ultimately led him to take comfort in agnosticism.[18]

Among New Church conservatives, Darwin's theory unleashed a degree of moral anarchy that led to the acceptance of a form of social utilitarianism over a transcendent morality. As explained by Edmund Swift, Jr., in *Evolution and Natural Selection in the Light of the New Church*, "all things are created and continually controlled by the Love and Wisdom of God, according to a Divinely perfect plan and fixed laws, and for a Divine *end, this end being the creation of man, and the formation of the human race into an angelic heaven.*"[19] Insofar as one perceived humanity as the Universal Human, all of its members were conjoined in both the natural and spiritual worlds, defined by the like forms of their accumulated usefulness. As explained by Leonhard I. Tafel, "the doctrine of [usefulness] is the only 'evolutionary' factor the New Churchman allows, all organisms tending and striving to perform their highest use. . . . All other evolution is a *sine qua non* of New-Church faith."[20]

Even among liberals, there was a clash of opinions, with many performing ratiocinations that attempted to bridge Swedenborgian theology with both modern science and philosophy. Such efforts were made by the likes of John Worcester of the New England school of New Church theology; Carl Theophilus Odhner and Charles R. Pendleton of the Academy of the New Church in Bryn Athyn; Emanuel Goerwitz of the Swiss Church; H. Clinton Hay of the Boston Society; and John R. Swanton, one of the founding members of the Swedenborg Scientific Association.[21]

New Church members came to regard Swedenborg's scientific concepts as revolutionary for their time due to his willingness to use new knowledge to build upon, challenge, and revise existing assumptions. In other words, since science was always changing, each generation of scholars was required to illuminate the current knowledge with new information. It was Swedenborg's open mind that made the New Church a progressive body in the nineteenth century, and it was this open-mindedness that would remain a cornerstone of the New Church's future. Thus, without too much internal turmoil, Swedenborgians accommodated to the concept of evolution (albeit not to that of natural selection) in much the same manner as did the major denominations at the time. Arguably the best example of religion's relationship with science was in evidence at the World's Parliament of Religions in 1893, where speaker after speaker employed science and evolutionary theory to demonstrate Christianity's overpowering influence and destiny among the religions of the world.[22]

Arts and Letters

As political and economic power shifted irrevocably to the North and Midwest and class discontent showed its telltale signs, American culture began producing more critics than contented thinkers, more "politicians" than statespersons, and more disruptors than conservators of the past. Higher education still awaited a thorough house-cleaning by German-trained scholars, but increased material prosperity had generated a sophisticated class of readers who were eager to enjoy the fruits of the print industry. Cheaper newspapers and magazines captured more eclectic topics through greater specialization and departmentalization. Established monthlies like *The Atlantic, Harper's,* and *Scribner's* faced tough competitors in *The Century, Good Housekeeping, Munsey's, Cosmopolitan, Ladies' Home Journal, McClure's, Review of Reviews, Collier's, Everybody's,* and *Pearson's,* all of which were dedicated to exposure and opportunism, delighting in controversy, sensationalism, and muckraking. Those who had once been admirers of *The Dial* now subscribed to Benjamin O. Flower's *The Arena* and Paul Carus's *Open Court.*

As it did in the areas of philosophy, law, and science, evolutionary thinking took on multiple forms in American letters, beginning with a ferment of change among the century's last hold-outs of an earlier, simpler, and more sentimentalized literary world. This was the world of local colorists like Mary Hunter Austin (*The Land of Little Rain*) in the Far West; Booth Tarkington (*The Gentleman from Indiana*) in the Midwest; George Washington Cable (*Old Creole Days*), Charles Waddell Chesnutt (*The Conjure Woman*), and Mary Noailles Murfree (*The Story of Old Fort Loudon*) in the South; and Margaret Deland (*Old Chester Tales*) in the Northeast. Some of these writers chose to dwell on the order of things passing, seeking to return to places once haunted and the richness of lives once lived; others captured pictures of regional bravado marked by business and moneymaking. Artistically and philosophically, most seemed more at home with the past and its established values than they did with the disillusionment that came with the impact of naturalism and determinism. They did not repudiate the newness of the times so much as they desired to stand aloof from it—not out of arrogance but instead out of their concern for the preservation of tradition.

This sort of thinking was well-demonstrated by Sarah Orne Jewett (1849–1909), whose writings recorded the twilight years of America's cramped and ingrown provincialism, a time before a new school of writers would herald a protest against the misshapen souls left in the wake of modern society. Her arrestingly crafted stories of rural New England connected with the traditions of the Stoics and the

Shakers, with Thomas à Kempis's *The Imitation of Christ* (1418–27), and with Swedenborg's revelatory visions. From her meditative novels, *A Country Doctor* (1884) and *The Country of the Pointed Firs* (1896), to the correspondences between the worlds of matter and spirit that she documented in her letters to Harvard law professor and Swedenborgian Theophilus Parsons, Jewett's works are an apotheosis of the nineteenth century's female world of charity, solitude, friendship, love of neighbor, and usefulness.[23]

Brought up in a not-so-strict Congregationalist family, Jewett learned early in life that the harsh, scrappy Calvinism that lingered among New England's back regions was not to her taste. Its less-than-cheery approach made Swedenborg all the more appealing; instead of to the vindictive God of the Old Testament, she turned willingly to divine influx and the law of correspondences, bridging the divide between the material and spiritual worlds. Introduced to the writings of Swedenborg by way of Parsons's *The Infinite and the Finite* (1872) and *Outlines of the Religion and Philosophy of Swedenborg* (1876), she discovered a satisfying alternative to what had once been New England's prevailing beliefs.[24] Drawing on Parsons's advice, she employed her writing for a didactic moral purpose and, in the process, discovered Swedenborg's doctrine of usefulness, realizing that one's purpose on earth had less to do with matters of "cold selfishness" than it did with exerting a moral influence.[25] Accepting this approach in her life, Jewett made frequent reference to it in her writings and in her mentoring of younger writers.[26] When asked by a friend how much she had learned from Swedenborg's writings, she replied, "I keep a sense of it under everything else. How such a bit of foundation lifts up all one's other thoughts together, and makes us feel as if we really stood higher and could see more of the world."[27]

By contrast, poets Sidney Lanier (*Hymns of the Marshes*), Edwin Markham (*The Man with the Hoe*), and William Vaughn Moody (*The Masque of Judgment*), along with novelists Edward Watson Howe (*The Story of a Country Town*), Hamlin Garland (*Main-Travelled Roads*), Theodore Dreiser (*Sister Carrie*), Frank Norris (*The Octopus*), Robert Herrick (*The Memoirs of an American Citizen*), Willa Cather (*O Pioneers!*), and O. E. Rølvaag (*Giants in the Earth*), told in brutal detail the spiritual and material disintegration of lives once valued. Literary naturalism, sometimes identified as pessimistic determinism, depicted humankind swept along by forces that offered no purpose to individual human actions and no protection from the indifference of nature. As Frank Norris explained in *The Octopus,* "Nature was, then, a gigantic engine, a vast cyclopean power, huge, terrible, a leviathan with a heart of steel, knowing no compunction, no forgiveness, no tolerance; crushing out the human atom standing in its way, with nirvanic calm."[28]

From the moral confusion evident in the characters of Mark Twain to the determinism of Theodore Dreiser and the action stories of Frank Norris and Jack London, no single definition captured the full measure of this new genre of literature. Two individuals, however, seem to best represent the sympathies along with the challenges of the age and the promise of things to come: Edward Bellamy and William Dean Howells. As friends and fellow socialists, neither was shy in expressing his disdain for the world's economic ills; yet, neither was so dissatisfied with the American scene that he failed to see a silver lining. Both demonstrated the ability to capture with artistic accuracy the essence of middle-class Americans whose world of moral correctness stood aloof from the distasteful undercurrents depicted by literary realism. Both offered a kindlier picture of America, if only certain changes could be made. Finally, it can be said that both men were born in the age of Swedenborg, when the relationship between God and humanity came through nature and where, despite their acceptance of evolutionary theory and its application to economic and social issues, they refused to relinquish their faith in the purpose and dignity of the individual. Nurtured in the liberal Christianity of their childhood, Bellamy and Howells shared a sensitivity to social injustice, an optimism in the expectation of progress, and a trust in the natural evolution of a more cooperative state.[29]

Edward Bellamy

Son of a well-to-do Baptist minister and descended from a line of Calvinist-Baptist clergymen on both sides of his family, Edward Bellamy (1850–98) grew up in an age of religious controversy and unsettled national convictions. Matters of prayer, introspection, and individual responsibility dominated much of his youth. Having seen his home town of Chicopee Falls, Massachusetts struggle through industrialization and its accompanying cost of poverty, long working hours, strikes, stunted factory children, and lowered standards of living, Bellamy faced the prospect of having to balance his inherited faith with rising levels of doubt about his own future. His mother, who spoke obsessively on religious matters and on the need for him to experience conversion, triggered spiritual and psychological depression, including thoughts of suicide, during periods of his life. This may explain his search for some inner refuge against disenchantment with life, religion, and the outside world.[30]

A quiet romantic and moral idealist, Bellamy studied law and was admitted to the bar before deciding on a career in journalism. He joined the staff of the *New York Evening Post* in 1871, and a year later, he transferred to the *Springfield Union*. In 1874, at the age of only twenty-four, he wrote "The Religion of Solidarity," a fragmentary essay strongly flavored with Emerson; Henry James, Sr.; and the New Theology of Andover Theological Seminary in Massachusetts.[31] In it, he celebrated a love for the human race, the evolutionary potential of the spiritual man, a friendly universe, a God who was neither distant nor unknowable. Interpreting religion as the highest reach of both the individual and community, Bellamy placed supreme value on human potential. His was a world realizing its potential in an environment of progressive evolution.[32]

A seeker after faith due in part to his frail health, Bellamy imparted in his essay the germ of what would later become his philosophy of life. It also showed the influence Emerson held over his generation—the entire essay projected a preference for words, phrases, and imagery that reflected Emerson's style. This is not to demean the authenticity of Bellamy's statement, but instead to give an obligatory nod to the pervasiveness of Emerson's presence in late-nineteenth-century thought and culture. Like Emerson, Bellamy was riveted by the dual life of humanity—the individual and the universal—which is to say, the frailties of the individual who is driven by passions and appetites, the insufficiency of existence, the ideals of self-reliance and self-culture, and the dreams of immortality. Commenting on the human soul, he compared it to the Northern Lights that were born fresh each day, "ever rising and falling, wavering, undulating, ever glowing and fading, ebbing and flowing, as from some eternal reservoir." The essay combined Jonathan Edwards's love for Being in general with Emerson's "Over-soul," each disclosing a "citadel of being" that was "at once it and of it, itself, yet not all of it." It was the nature of the soul to be "one in you and in all things."[33]

A complicated young man whose ideas centered not on the individual but on the Infinite, Bellamy craved a friendly universe whose creatures enjoyed a common spiritual destiny. Too often, individuals lived out their lives as "cave dwellers" in some finite corner of the universe. Bellamy urged them to spread their wings, saying that "there are no barriers to the soul but such as sense-bound fancy imagines." In this respect, he took issue with Emerson's emphasis on the individual, which he concluded hindered the "universal fusion" of the soul with the universe. While he feared the loss of personal identity, considering it a "precarious possession, held by a thread," he nonetheless viewed the elements of the individual as "trifles, the rents of tinsel in the garment of a day." Urging individuals to hold their lives "loosely, and not with the convulsive grip of one who counts personal life his all," Bellamy looked longingly to every human united with "other lives and all life."

> In the religion of solidarity is found the only rational philosophy of the moral instincts. Unselfishness, self-sacrifice, is the essence of morality. On the theory of ultimate individualities, unselfishness is madness; but on the theory of the dual life, of which the life of solidarity is abiding and that of the individual transitory, unselfishness is but the sacrifice of the lesser self to the greater self, an eminently rational and philosophical proceeding *per se,* and entirely regardless of ulterior considerations.[34]

Recognizing that "the completest man lacks the completion of the rest of the universe," Bellamy sought solidarity with the universe—not as a logical abstraction but as a "felt and living fact." By this he meant that human beings were capable of living an immortal life if they chose to do so. A life of infinite range existed before humankind—not the mystical kingdom of the Christian heaven but the "infinite potentialities of their souls." His theory "was in no way inconsistent with belief in a personal God" since it "illustrates a possible mode of existence of . . . a Supreme Being . . . as distinctly personal as is man."[35]

Following a physical breakdown, Bellamy left journalism to try his hand at fiction, and for more than a decade he wrote imaginative stories and novels for *The Atlantic Monthly*, *Harper's*, and *Scribner's*. His first novel, *Six to One: A Nantucket Idyl* (1878), was followed by *The Duke of Stockbridge: A Romance of Shays' Rebellion* (1879), *Dr. Heidenhoff's Process* (1880), and *Miss Ludington's Sister* (1884). A novel serially published in the *Berkshire Courier*, *The Duke of Stockbridge* expressed his earliest concern with the widening gulf between the classes. A story of post-revolutionary armed uprisings between farmers and merchants in Massachusetts over growing indebtedness, high taxes, and an unresponsive government, it recounted a story of class guilt and class prejudice, a pressing issue until it was marginalized by a love affair between the leader of the rebels and the daughter of one of the village leaders.[36]

Bellamy's next book, *Looking Backward* (1888), though intended as a "mere literary fantasy" rather than as a critique of society, influenced more native-grown socialists than did any other piece of American literature.[37] Selling more than two hundred thousand copies within months of its publication, *Looking Backward* hypnotized the nation with its simplicity and power of persuasion. Bellamy's critique, though inoffensive in manner, brought readers face-to-face with the chaos produced by the competitive nature of society. It had a great impact on the political scene, challenging the complacency of those in the middle class who were reluctant to address the dogged issues of trusts, labor unrest, inflation, unemployment, and poverty. He saw clearly how the dominant social philosophers of the day—Herbert Spencer, John Tyndall, and Thomas Henry Huxley in England, as well as William Graham Sumner in the United States—had a direct impact on capitalism's failure to ensure social justice. These thinkers extolled the school of social Darwinism by explaining "struggle" as the sole means of improving the human species.

Herbert Spencer, in particular, exerted an inordinate influence over Anglo-American social thought. For Spencer, evolution meant the "integration of matter and concomitant dissipation of motion; during which the matter passes from an indefinite, incoherent homogeneity to a definite, coherent heterogeneity; and during which the retained motion undergoes a parallel transformation."[38] All living organisms, including human beings, partook in the struggle for existence through "survival of the fittest," and though the outcome saw many harsh fatalities, these did not affect the interests of humanity as a whole, which moved inexorably forward. Preaching the universal progression of all beings from simple to complex, Spencer demonstrated a level of authenticity equaled only by the familiar formulations of natural law. Respected more highly than was either Comte or Darwin, his evolutionism stood as a predictive model of the individual for whom there was never any real security, only an indifferent yet benign universe. Spencer's theory was so prestigious that academics who challenged his view of societal development put their own careers at risk.[39]

The year *Looking Backward* was published, sometimes known as "the year of ten thousand strikes," signaled a watershed moment in United States history, marking an increase in industrial expansion and, at the same time, the imminent closing of the western frontier. Huge corporate combinations had emerged, with the founding of the Southern Pacific, Santa Fe, and Northern Pacific railroads; the formation of Standard Oil, United States Steel, and International Harvester corporations; and the power and influence of trusts controlling several key industries. With these seismic changes came the Great Railroad Strike of 1877, the Leadville Coal Strike of 1880, the Great Southwest Strike of 1886, the Haymarket Riot of 1886, the Panic of 1893, and the Pullman Strike of 1894. Between 1881 and 1906, thirty-six thousand strikes and one thousand five hundred lockouts affected more than nine million workers. Out of this festering resentment between labor and capital were formed the National Labor Union (1866); the Order of the Knights of St. Crispin (1867); and the Knights of Labor (1869), which would go on to become the American Federation of Labor (1886). The rise of these unions would shatter middle-class complacency with evidence of the nation's extreme inequality and growing sense of discontent.[40]

Against this background of industrial strife, Bellamy offered the prospect of a peaceful solution to a society very much in doubt as to its future. *Looking Backward* begins with the novel's principal character, Julian West, a well-to-do Bostonian and troubled insomniac, going into a mesmeric sleep in a specially constructed underground sleeping room on a night in 1887. By peculiar happenstance, he awakens in the year 2000 into a world of harmonious social order. The troubling conflicts of his former society are gone, replaced by a world free from violent revolution, strikes, and class conflict. Here is middle-class optimism at its best, reflecting the time's confidence in the infinite possibilities of human development along with its reverence for a moral structure to the universe.

Essentially, Bellamy envisioned life as a choice between reality and possibility, between the anarchy of individualism and the concepts of right and justice, between progress and the breeding grounds of poverty and vice. Given these polarities, though, he proved to be neither radical nor pessimistic. All business, including the production and distribution of goods, was merged into one "Great Trust" that worked as the servant of humanity; and society was marked by universal education and industrial armies of altruistic men and women whose sense of value coalesced around accepting each other in human community.

The book's narrative consists primarily of conversations between West and a Dr. Leete, the man in whose backyard West emerges from his sleeping room. Leete recounts how the nation's resources were managed through long-range economic planning that estimated supply and demand and involved the employment of an industrial army whose laborers (each having a choice of occupation) worked until the age of forty-five. Behind this managed economy was a faceless bureaucracy that mediated the needs and choices of individuals and that managed foreign exchange, trade, immigration, and foreign policy. It was a state without prisons and with minimal judicial and legislative functions. Here, in a nutshell, was the moral divide between unselfishness and rational self-interest—a change guided by Christian moral values and Bellamy's faith in the essential nobility of humankind.

Bellamy was deeply religious. Though his newfound society did not lay out a specific church structure, it did include spiritual leadership. Sidestepping his Calvinist upbringing, he insisted that moral defects were similar to physical defects and therefore treatable with the right kind of therapy.[41] Much like Henry Drummond, whose *Natural Law in the Spiritual World* (1883) argued that evolution was not in conflict with spiritual beliefs, Bellamy embraced a community of brotherly love, the abolition of poverty, and a world blessed with justice. He described a society where private ownership and capitalism ceased to be a matter of right. In their place, everyone between the ages of twenty-one and forty-five served in a workforce without unions, strikes, or even elections, and whose government played no favorites. His ideals harkened back to the celebration of a preindustrial pastoral and upper-middle-class society that was class-bound and managed by antidemocratic authorities. Much less formative in his details than were the earlier French and English utopians, Bellamy centered on the idea of an industrial army and a nationalized economy to answer the material and spiritual needs of society.[42]

Within the span of a year, *Looking Backward* drew approval from a wide variety of proponents who applied its ideal of brotherly love through a constellation of clubs, societies, and political parties. Clubs were formed in Boston; Washington, DC; Hartford; Portsmouth; Chicago; and New York intent on spreading the idea of *nationalism*, which is the term Bellamy gave to the social system outlined in his utopia. While Bellamy's utopia was suffused with material accomplishments, its central appeal remained ethical. Society as it was structured and sustained at that time prevented its members from being good, even though they desired it in their hearts. In its fullness, nationalism offered a kingdom of fraternal equality as the alternative to the human cost of unregulated industrial progress.[43]

With financial support from Bellamy, the magazine *The Nationalist* (1889–91) began publication in Boston, carrying accounts of its participating organizations. Its supporters included Edward Everett Hale, Theosophist Helena Blavatsky, William Dean Howells, Julia

Ward Howe, Lucy Stone, and Frances E. Willard. The magazine also found an ally in Rev. William Dwight Porter Bliss, pastor of the Church of the Carpenter, which was a missionary outpost of the Episcopal Church in South Boston that advocated a Fabian form of socialism. In the Church's monthly publication, *The Dawn* (1889–96), Bliss, along with Rev. Francis Bellamy (Edward Bellamy's cousin), Hamlin Garland, and other sympathizers, advocated its plan for reconstruction through the Society of Christian Socialists. According to Richard T. Ely, author of *Social Aspects of Christianity* (1888), the future government required two things, religion and nationalism: "Put these together and we have religious nationalism." The tone and direction of the Church and of society were Christian rather than Marxian, interpreting the nation's needs in distinctly Christian terms.[44]

Within three years of the publication of *Looking Backward,* supporters in twenty-seven states had formed Bellamy clubs, with additional societies organized in Holland, Denmark, and Sweden. For them, *Looking Backward* was not a dream but was the future. *The Nationalist* and the weekly publication *The New Nation* (1891–94), also financed by Bellamy, supported the People's, or Populist, Party, which carried the states of Colorado, Kansas, Idaho, and Nevada in the presidential election of 1892. The party's platform called for public ownership of utilities, direct election of senators, a graduated income tax, and the nationalization of banking. With the slogan "Wealth belongs to him who creates it," the party collected more than a million votes for its presidential candidate, General James B. Weaver of Iowa.[45]

Bellamy's sequel *Equality* (1897), published the year before he died, follows the storyline of *Looking Backward* by offering an extended version of West and Leete's conversations, describing in sharper detail the replacement of currency, the purchasing of goods at public stores, and the end of private capitalism and wages. Bellamy includes forecasts on women's dress, youthful ideals, the aesthetics of equality, the relation of property to human dealings, and the role of religion minus its ecclesiastical pretensions. Neither of the two books displays the thoroughness or the distinctive features of Fourier's and Brisbane's. Instead, readers are left with a vague premise of social planning, perhaps the book's greatest weakness as well as its greatest strength. Bellamy offers a moderately progressive middle-class view of the future that was judged unrealistic by most socialists, who considered his solutions woefully immature given the complexity of the issues. Nonetheless, the books spurred the moral awakening of the middle class, including Swedenborgians, while rejecting more radical solutions to the problems at hand.[46]

Looking Backward served as catalyst to an entire genre of utopian literature that included Crawford S. Griffin's Nationalism (1889), Laurence Gronlund's Our Destiny: The Influence of Nationalism on Morals and Religion (1890), Robinson Crusoe's (pseud.) Looking Upwards: or, Nothing New (1890), Albert Chavannes's The Future Commonwealth (1892), Solomon Schindler's Young West (1894), and Harry W. Hillman's Looking Forward (1906). In all, nearly fifty novels imitating Bellamy's thematic structure were published between the years of 1889 and 1900. Most of these resolved class conflict by appealing for nonviolent change while reinforcing the genteel traditions of the middle class.[47]

One of Bellamy's admirers was the poet, performer, and author Vachel Lindsay (1879–1931) of Illinois who grew up in a family of devoutly strict Campbellites and attended Hiram College in Ohio, the Chicago Art Institute, and the New York School of Art before claiming visions of Old Testament prophets. His revelatory and millenarian visions appeared in many of his poems and collected works, which he sold as he tramped across the country. His poems were written to be read aloud, chanted, and in some cases danced. According to his friend Stephen Graham who sometimes accompanied him, "He did not starve when he used to tramp in America and recite to the farmers for a meal and a night's lodging." His spiritual message, which he expressed deeply in earnest, gained him great popularity.[48]

Lindsay's The Golden Book of Springfield (1920), a utopian and mystical story about his hometown of Springfield in the years 1918 and 2018, reads as a journal recounting the intense religious experiences of individuals belonging to "The Prognosticators' Club." His vision is that of a combined biblical, Swedenborgian, and Marxian society whose improvements in technology, education, and spirituality are seen through the eyes of a Campbellite minister, a black woman, a skeptic, and a Jewish boy. There is travel to the stars in visionary airships, war against Singapore, and the transformation of Springfield into a global village—a metaphor for an America of the future. One of the more compelling parts of the book concerns Johnny Appleseed (John Chapman), a dreamer and Swedenborgian mystic whose wanderings included the planting of magic apple tree seeds, the results of which bathed the landscape with their radiance as they grew toward the heavens. In the book, Chapman is looked upon as a mythic figure who, in his nation-building, carried Swedenborg's *Heaven and Hell* in his sack along with seeds that produced orchards laden with fruit, beneficent herbs, and acorn-forested palaces. More angel than man, he was an American saint—a blend of mysticism and yeoman mythology—whose seeds created the great Amaranth Apple Orchards in Springfield, contributing to the social fabric of the town. Lindsay described the Golden Rain-Tree brought from New Harmony in Indiana as a symbol of democracy: "It is said in Springfield, and taught with especial emphasis by the devotees of the Flower Religion," Lindsay wrote, "that he who enters under the shade of the Rain-Tree boughs and leaves and flowers, enters the gate of eternal democracy."[49]

Lindsay's combination of Swedenborg's heavenly planes, Henry George's single-tax theory, and Bellamy's *Looking Backward* resulted in the image of a community dedicated to the Universal Human. According to Lindsay, all three "seem to go together in the minds of many more Americans than our great universities realize.... Thousands of folks of our purest, most valuable, oldest stock, go to the Swedenborgian church on Sunday and work steadily and silently for the Single Tax all the week."[50] Clearly Swedenborgianism appealed to Lindsay, as he connected with the doctrine of usefulness and called for benefits to be accrued to the community as a whole. However, he was unable to give the Universal Human focus, as too many other concepts competed with it to give any assurance that a purpose and a means to attain it would be possible.

Another prominent Swedenborgian influenced by Bellamy's *Looking Backward* was Rev. Rudolph Leonhard Tafel (1831–93), former tutor at the New Church Theological School of London, who viewed the book as an illustration of "scientific socialism" in the tradition of the Fabian Society in England. While Bellamy's nationalism differed from his own idea of a New Church Commonwealth, Tafel much preferred it to those socialists elsewhere in Europe who intended to establish a social commonwealth through the nationalization of land and labor. Such efforts, he felt, went against the doctrines of the New Church, which saw humanity enjoying the goods of the world as part of its use of freedom and rationality. Tafel's idea of a New Church Commonwealth existed by virtue of inward (spiritual) rather than outward (natural) means, operating from the human conscience and therefore existing on a different level than did temporal societies. For if the New Church were to advocate a society based on outward means, it would have the effect of making the Church a state institution whose political panaceas were no different from the abortive systems of communism, nihilism, and anarchism.[51]

In his book *Socialism and Reform in the Light of the New Church: Lectures* (1891), Tafel remarked that over the past three or four centuries, enormous amounts of wealth and luxury had drifted into the hands of a few while leaving the great bulk of humankind in poverty. Between these two extremes lived "the middle class, who by dint of hard struggle are able, as a class, to preserve their position in the middle; and while some of them, in the end, manage to swell the number of the comparatively few wealthy ones, many, on the other hand, sink down to the level of the poverty-stricken, who drudge and live listlessly from one day to the other, not knowing, and often not caring what to-morrow will bring to them." Responding to this unsatisfactory state of affairs, economists and philanthropists had endeavored to place their economies on a more equitable basis through wholesale legislative measures concerning free trade and by various reforms involving education, child labor, working hours, and emigration. While these changes had improved the material position of some, a great many of those in the laboring classes were left behind. On the whole, governments were impotent with regard to abolishing the discrepancies between rich and poor. This situation lent itself to the working classes forming trade unions and cooperative societies, which belong to what has become known as Christian socialism, collectivism, and scientific socialism.[52]

True reform, by which the loves of self and of the world were conquered, came through the instrumentality of the Church focusing entirely on the inner self. For Tafel, the New Church Commonwealth began from within and extended outward, with the doctrine of usefulness as its goal. Uses are "higher if they are performed to the immortal souls of men, and lower if they are performed to their bodies." Everyone in the Commonwealth would be valued according to the use he or she performed, the use being "the neighbour, whom all serve." The highest intellects were thus employed for the uses of the Church and of the schools; for these uses had as their object the training of the minds of men for heaven. Eventually, the Commonwealth would include cooperative farms, manufactories, and stores that were mindful of the doctrine of usefulness. While it would not yet be a heaven on earth, its members would be striving to lead a heavenly life.[53]

The New Church, naturally, will not be limited to one nation; and hence there will not only be one, but many New Church Commonwealths; and the international relations between them will all be characterized by the same liberal, frank, and open spirit. Strangers on their arrival in a foreign country, will not be treated as strangers, but as friends. Wars then will have ceased; they will cease from the moment when the citizens of each Commonwealth look for their enemies not abroad, but in their own bosoms; for then by the individual reform in their own hearts, the feeling of charity will spread from one member of the State to another; until at last the nations in the world will be united into one grand fraternity of nations. All then will be one, because all will have and acknowledge one Father, even the Lord Jesus Christ in His glorified humanity. This brotherhood of nations seems now a vague, distant dream. Yet that dream will be realized, as soon as the true Law of Reform, according to which all true reform begins in the hearts of the individuals, will be recognized and practiced; and, indeed, as soon as the common enemies of humanity, namely, the loves of self and of the world, will be resisted first, and finally conquered by the individuals in a nation.[54]

The movement inspired by *Looking Backward* signified the depth of economic and social discontent prevalent during the 1870s and '80s, and it represented a message of social hope to troubled reformers seeking answers. The book did for futurist thinking what *Uncle Tom's Cabin* accomplished for the antislavery movement. In fact, *Looking Backward* was the third-largest bestseller at that time, behind *Uncle Tom's Cabin* and *Ben-Hur*. Decades later, the realization of Bellamy's many predictions spurred renewed interest from the likes of John Dewey, Ida Tarbell, and advocates of New Deal programs during the Great Depression. For them, *Looking Backward* was an act of pragmatism, an idea whose value would ultimately be judged by the results it produced. The creation of the Works Progress Administration and the Civilian Conservation Corps in the 1930s were clear reminders of Bellamy's industrial army and the need for national planning. The spirit of American liberalism that inspired so much of the New Deal; the economic philosophy of Thorstein Veblen; and reform groups such as Dr. Francis E. Townsend's Plan, Father Charles Coughlin's National Union for Social Justice, and Upton Sinclair's End Poverty in California were clear reflections of the hope inspired by Bellamy's books.[55]

William Dean Howells

William Cooper Howells (1807–94), the father of novelist William Dean Howells (1837–1920), once observed that the Methodist Church to which he belonged was continually "rent and distracted" by controversies between those who enjoyed the extortive style of preaching and those who preferred the decorum of more private forms of prayer. Disturbed by feuds that served only "to break the monotony of the country life," he turned to Swedenborgianism, became a minister and publisher of the New Church newspaper *The Retina,* and had his children re-baptized. Religion came easy to William Cooper, who his son described as living "in some sort a dream of love and good will, to conceive all tangible and visible creation as an adumbration of spiritual reality; to accept revelation as the mask of interior meanings; to regard the soul as its own keeper, and the sovereign chooser of heaven or hell, but always master of the greatest happiness possible to it." As William Dean noted in the introduction to his father's *Recollections,* "My father was always a very close and critical observer, both of nature and of human nature, and . . . equally a lover of both. . . . He was not a poet in the artistic sense, but he was a poet in his view of life, the universe, creation; and his dream of it included man, as well as the woods and fields and their citizenship."[56]

Believing that each of his children required a religion best adapted to their needs, William Cooper refrained from forcing his own comforting beliefs on them. Thus, while William Dean accepted his "inherited faith," he did so willingly and without any pressure to follow the same practices.[57] He enlivened the family's Sundays by welcoming visits from neighboring ministers and reading from Swedenborg's *Secrets of Heaven.*[58] When Rev. R. Heber Newton, Rector of All Souls' Church in New York, asked William Dean the source of his religious and economic beliefs, he replied that "in a loose and stumbling way I've thought about it, and from my early instruction in Swedenborgianism—I've had some doctrine concerning it."[59]

When his father took charge of the *Intelligencer,* a Whig newspaper in Hamilton, Ohio, William Dean worked for him as a typesetter and a printer's apprentice. "This was not altogether because he was needed there," William Dean opined, "but because it was part of his father's Swedenborgian philosophy that everyone should fulfill a use; I do not know that when the boy wanted to go swimming, or hunting, or skating, it consoled him much to reflect that the angels in the highest heaven delighted in uses; nevertheless it was good for him to be of use, though maybe not so much use."[60]

Largely self-taught, Howells wrote a campaign biography for Abraham Lincoln in 1860 and, a year later, was rewarded with an appointment as US Consul to Venice, Italy. On his return, he joined *The Atlantic Monthly,* where he became an assistant editor and then editor. Over time, he matured into a minor poet and judicious critic before mastering the novel and revealing a remarkably productive mind. As a literary critic and author of more than a hundred novels, poems, literary criticisms, plays, memoirs, and travel narratives,

Howells earned a reputation for fiction that exhibited a rare form of cultured realism, concealing itself beneath the intellectual and moral refinements of the age. Thus, while his novels were not primers gritty with the taste, smell, and look of later realists, they were truthful in their originality, in their commitment to observation for its own sake, and in their modest sympathy for the sufferings of the poor.[61] His more noted books included *The Undiscovered Country* (1880), *A Modern Instance* (1882), *The Rise of Silas Lapham* (1885), *Annie Kilburn* (1888), *An Imperative Duty* (1891), and *The Coast of Bohemia* (1893). A man of letters and a critic rather than a fighter, he joined in spirit with Ralph Waldo Emerson, James Russell Lowell, John Greenleaf Whittier, Henry James, Frank Norris, and Theodore Dreiser in forming an organic link between the past, present, and future. The moral and civic good that became so much of the inspiration behind his characters found close similarity to Swedenborg's own civic, moral, and spiritual good.[62]

Known as the "Dean of American Letters," Howells revealed in his novels the impact of the century's social, political, and economic forces upon the individual and community. As a socialist thinker in the Gilded Age, he found himself caught up in the Haymarket Trial, Henry George's single tax, the socialist writings of Karl Marx and Danish-American Laurence Gronlund, and Bellamy's nationalism. Each contributed to his understanding of the forces shaping the times.[63] Concerned with how these forces acted spiritually on his characters, he prepared the groundwork for a generation of younger writers, including ones from the New Church, who would expand on his portrait of American society.[64] Besides being the son of a Swedenborgian editor and printer, he belonged to the Church of the Carpenter in Boston, was a charter member of Bellamy's Nationalist Club in Boston, and was a long-time admirer of Christian socialism. These relationships formed the basis of his social and religious response to the industrial and business environment of his day.[65]

Though Howells placed a high value on realism, his morality spews forth from his fictionalized characters. A well-trained observer, he took care that "his slices of life were all . . . cut clear of imperfections." In choosing this route, he appealed to the highest motives, differentiating himself from those younger realists like Stephen Crane and Frank Norris who wanted to fully expose the reader to life's unpleasantries. Ever mindful of the safeguards against sensationalizing or pandering, Howells chose to live in a world of propriety, holding an idealized but selective view of morality that valued the more constructive side of life. In striking this balance, he made his writings appropriate for both sexes and for all ages. With all his desire to show life, he remained a very proper Victorian.[66]

In the decades following the Civil War, Howells joined with other writers who were struggling with matters of science and religion, with the implications of a naturalistic philosophy, and with the lingering romantic notions of humankind's ability to control its destiny. As his own confidence and faith diminished, he turned toward a democratic practice shorn of creeds, dogmas, and orthodoxies. But with his early training in Swedenborgianism predisposing him to the idea of a benevolent God, he remained optimistic even in his doubts. He was emotionally and intuitively yearning, hoping for immortality despite the evidence against it. His was a passive faith, skeptical and increasingly dismayed with the chaos and confusion of life.

Given his heterodox religious upbringing, which found him detached and on the fringes of the mainline denominations, Howells concluded early in his youth that the only thing that mattered was if he "did right from a love of doing right"—a concept straight out of his father's Swedenborgian belief system.[67] His was no easy path, and though he faced life with little hope that organized religion, spirituality, or the presumed historicity of the Bible carried any permanent meaning, he acknowledged a divine power outside the bigotry, parochialism, and dogmas of revealed religion.[68] Much of his anticlericalism stemmed from his view that organized religion had failed to live up to its own teachings.[69] He explained this in *Ragged Lady* (1899), when he described a certain religious character as having been "left over from a time when people didn't reason about their beliefs, but only argued."[70]

Gravitating toward a simple belief in the social responsibility of each individual to minister to humanity's welfare, Howells declared himself indifferent to whether this ministerial role had a spiritual or practical value just so long as society removed its self-contrived barriers to a better life. For too many, the churches had become inconsequential to society's needs, having dissipated their energies in pursuit of various political ambitions. Such was his verdict of the church during the Middle Ages.[71] Clearly, he felt that the Roman Catholic and Protestant churches were the least effective agencies in the correction of humanity's social evils, relying as they did on an impassioned belief in a "just" God whose punitive doctrines left the sick soul condemned and unforgiven. Calling attention to Richard T. Ely's *Social Aspects of Christianity* (1888) and Charles Dudley Warner's *A Little Journey in the World* (1889), he urged the churches to take up the cause of social gospelers by making better the conditions of the living.[72]

At a time when American taste in literature seemed unduly fixated on Sir Walter Scott, Charles Dickens, and William Thackeray, Howells championed the realistic literature of Russian novelist Leo Tolstoy in his numerous columns in *Harper's Monthly, The Forum, Cosmopolitan, Literature,* and *North American Review.* Despite criticism levelled at Tolstoy by Charles Eliot Norton and other respected writers and critics at that time, Howells found his *War and Peace* (1869) and *Anna Karenina* (1877), among other of his works, riveting in their realism.[73] They demonstrated a compassion for the lives of simple folk and working people, for their misery and suffering in a society motivated by materialism. Tolstoy had a facility for handling truth and morality, the cries of the soul, the simple practicality of village life, and the purpose of neighborly love. Over the years, Howells used Tolstoy's novels as the standard by which he evaluated his own and others' writings. Rejecting the romanticized and dishonest representations of life that had dominated literature for decades, his commitment to artistry implied a portrait of life that was simultaneously true, honest, and expressive of individual psychology.[74]

With Russia at the beginning of industrialization, Howells found Tolstoy's works refreshing in their prophecy and honest in their depiction of the parasitic and idle rich. The moral obligations of the artist/writer/reformer were for Tolstoy to portray life as it is, including the conditions of squalor and suffering. Through essays, books, poems, and literary criticism, Howells likewise took an honest look at the American economic landscape. Although he rejected Tolstoy's call for a return to primitivism, his increasingly progressive language conveyed a growing disappointment with the alarming disparities in the class structure and the irresponsible nature of the business-man. Devoted to a sympathetic presentation of middle-class life, he advocated a mild but sincere form of gradualism or Fabian socialism.

Howells wondered if Tolstoy had ever read Swedenborg, a speculation that derived from the Russian writer's thoughts on self-sacrifice, brotherhood, and the sanctity of work, which so resembled Swedenborg's doctrine of usefulness.

> Most things drop from the outer natural memory in the course of life, but there is an inner spiritual memory of all that the man did or said or thought. After the man's death, when the angels are sent to recall him to consciousness in the life eternal, they "explore" this receptacle for him, and make him know from its contents what he was and is. He is not so unhappy, though; he is not in the agony that Tolstoy felt himself in when exploring his memory; he goes freely and willingly away to the companionship of the good or the bad, which forms his heaven or hell. But as for the inner memory, absolutely nothing is lost upon it or from it. For that reason the whole of terrestrial literature exists in the spiritual world, and can be always read there from the memories of those who have read it here. . . . If remembering and suffering are one, as Tolstoy says, and if remembrance is a condition of individual existence here-after, as Swedenborg implies, one should look to every word as anxiously as to every act.[75]

With his renunciation of the egoistic impulse in *A Hazard of New Fortunes* (1889), *A Traveler from Altruria* (1894), and *Through the Eye of the Needle* (1907), Howells hoped to rid humankind of this diseased element of the self. Life in Altruria, his literary answer to Bellamy's *Looking Backward,* allowed for no ownership of property or labor. Such was his criticism of individual selfhood.[76] This was much like Henry James, Sr.'s, ideal of the regenerate society where each individual's accomplishments were subsumed into a much larger divine self.[77] The same was true of New Thought author Ralph Waldo Trine, whose Christian socialism downplayed the significance of the individual self for a more cooperative and sympathetic society—a more cosmic consciousness signifying unification of the individual with socialism.[78] Both James and Trine sought a metaphysic of tolerance and democracy banded together and working in harmony to create a cosmopolitan socialist future.[79]

In *Through the Eye of the Needle,* Howells tells the story of Aristides Homos, an emissary of the Altrurian Commonwealth who visited the United States in 1893 and whose letters to a friend in Altruria explained his impressions. The other half of the book tells the story of Aristides's American wife who returned with him to Altruria and espoused its principles to a friend in New York. Within this contextual and sociological basis, Howells identified the defects of American plutocracy. By contrast, Altruria was a place where work was obligatory to all except children and the infirm, and where religious services consecrated the day's work. It required only a small degree of familiarity with Swedenborg's writings to realize that Howells's account of Altrurian living reflected the orderly world of the Universal Human. In Altruria, all were prepared to work from the love of serving others and the love of being useful—a preparation of the heart and intellect that Swedenborg had clearly expressed in his *Heaven and Hell.*[80]

In Altruria, religion was separate from creed and dogma. Instead, it carried a social message to all who were saddened by the failures in economic, political, and social equality; by the narrowness that came with bigotry; and by the shortcomings of American democracy.

> In this, as in all other things, we believe ourselves the true followers of Christ, whose doctrine we seek to make our life, as He made it His. We have several forms of ritual, but no form of creed, and our religious differences may be said to be aesthetic and temperamental rather than theological and essential. We have no denominations, for we fear in this, as in other matters to give names to things lest we should cling to the names instead of the things. We love the realities, and for this reason we look at the life of a man rather than his profession for proof that he is a religious man.[81]

In Howells's novels, it is obvious that revealed religion and its teachings went unattended. Instead, he appealed first to the Enlightenment ideas of Paine and Jefferson before going on to seek a reconciliation of faith and science in John Fiske's *The Destiny of Man* (1884) and *The Idea of God* (1885), in the social aspects of religion propounded by William James, and in the writings of Tolstoy.[82] In fact, Howells's longtime friendship with philosopher and historian John Fiske helped him through some of his most obstinate problems concerning how to square these two fields. The manner in which Fiske's "Unknowable" worked through these challenges helped Howells and many Americans of the day who, starting with agnosticism, had moved from disbelief to hope, and eventually toward credence in an unknown but intuitively benevolent force. Among the many things that Howells learned from science, particularly the theory of evolution, was the painful realization of humanity's diminished place in the universe, a factor that firmly restricted humanity's potential to shape destiny.

Howells also turned to Alfred Russel Wallace, Darwin's counterpart in formulating a theory of evolution, who provided a modicum of hope for those who sought an alternative to the fragility of faith and the dysteleology, or purposelessness, implicit in natural selection. With guidance from Wallace's *Man's Place in the Universe* (1903), he took refuge in a more intuitive faith, turning away from despair, from the promises of Neo-Lamarckism, and from the impersonal and deterministic tendencies of natural selection.[83] As the child of a Swedenborgian, Howells fell back on this intuitionist approach when doubts arose. Swedenborgians demonstrated a generous tolerance, an indifference to ecclesiastical Christianity, and a focus on the teachings and practice of Jesus, all of which tended to check the meaner assets of orthodoxy and the harshness of "survival of the fittest."[84]

Nevertheless, Howells had his darker moments, an example of which is evident in his 1891 poem "What Shall It Profit?":

If I lay waste and wither up with doubt
The blessed fields of heaven where once my faith
Possessed itself serenely safe from death;

If I deny the things past finding out;
Or if I orphan my own soul of One
That seemed a Father, and make void the place
Within me where He dwelt in power and grace,
What do I gain, that am myself undone?[85]

Throughout the 1880s and '90s, Howells's novels tended to be overly economic and even socialistic in their critique of American society, drawing liberally from the works of Tolstoy, George, Bellamy, and Gronlund to make his point.[86] According to one observer, it was Gronlund's socialism and Norwegian Bjørnstjerne Bjørnson's pastoralism more so than any other form of social criticism that provided the formulation for Howells's social and economic philosophy. Both Gronlund and Bjørnson viewed the future as beginning with the nationalization of the larger corporate monopolies. Howells's association with *The Atlantic Monthly* and the social elites in the Northeast, however, repressed these more radical views and tendencies. As a consequence, the social weight of his economic novels remained concealed behind the genteel veneer of Boston's Back Bay society. Like most literature of this type, it had a Christian-social-democratic tone that was gradualist, idealistic, and content to resolve issues through the existing framework of government.[87]

Although Emerson did not care for fiction, the literary generation that followed in the wake of his oracular essays could think of little else. For them, the novel had become what D. H. Lawrence would later describe as "the book of life."[88] In fact, the novelist—in particular, the social novelist—became the portrait artist of the day, devoted to life that was real and true, capturing not only the life-affirming motivations of individuals but also the darker side of the human spirit. Here was middle-class American life, rural and small-town people, embittered agrarians, local peculiarities, regional speech, the lingering rhetoric of a once picturesque past, and the effects of environmental and hereditary forces on human character.

As hard times impacted traditional American optimism, much of the new literature was being written in the shadow of colossal changes to the working classes. The worldview that separated Theodore Parker's *A Sermon of the Dangerous Classes in Society* (1847) from Stephen Crane's *Maggie: A Girl of the Streets* (1893) was marked by the complexities of a new economic order and a growing dissent toward accepted standards. The distance between classes, the loneliness of lives, and the psychological crises embedded in ordinary experiences were conveyed with broad strokes. The best of these depictions—from writers like Jewett, Howells, Twain, Garland, Norris, Dreiser, and James—captured the marrow of human ambitions and delusions, the landscape of moral confusion, and the troubled sense of self-consciousness. Their social portraitures gave substance to the nation's immaturity, to the corruptibility of man, to the vulgarism of money, and to the burden of circumstance. Here, as nowhere else, the confusions and uncertainties of American life and culture were re-enacted from moment to moment, from book to book.

4 Single Tax

We plow new fields, we open new mines, we found new cities; we drive back the Indian and exterminate the buffalo; we girdle the land with iron roads and lace the air with telegraph wires; we add knowledge to knowledge, and utilize invention after invention; we build schools and endow colleges; yet it becomes no easier for the masses of our people to make a living. On the contrary, it becomes harder. The wealthy class is becoming more wealthy; but the poorer class is becoming more dependent. The gulf between the employed and the employer is growing wider; social contrasts are becoming sharper; as liveried carriages appear, so do barefooted children.

(Henry George, *Progress and Poverty*, 1879)

Between the Civil War and the Great Depression, a nation of farms was fast becoming a nation of cities. The United States underwent profound urbanization, with more than half the population making the shift. This was a stark contrast from 1870, when nearly 80 percent of the population was still rural. Added to this was the deluge of immigrants into urban areas, with the burden of adjustment falling on both new and old Americans, each of whom had to address their respective sense of identity. New ideas challenged established beliefs, as those advocating for reform identified themselves as "populists," "greenbackers," "Free Silverites," "single taxers," "free traders," and "progressives" while referring to their opponents as "trusts," "captains of industry," "robber barons," "lords of finance," "monopolies," "Wall Street," and "moneyed classes." Looking to protect the interests of the working class, reformers accused local, state, and federal governments

95

of acting as agents of special interests. Much less utopian than were the earlier romantic and evangelically motivated communitarians, and distancing themselves from Europe's ideologues, the reformers of the day focused on the immediate issues of working conditions, child labor, the granting of public lands to private companies, corporate monopolies and trusts, and women's rights.

During this same period, the nation underwent a painful realization that industrial democracy was far different from the agrarian democracy that ended at Appomattox in 1865. Economic leadership had been left in the hands of a class of plutocrats capable of buying and selling influence in ways that permanently affected the body politic and its moral leadership. The emergence of industrial society brought in its wake a new working class, along with disturbing changes to the landscape that questioned America's time-honored values. The economic individualism, political localism, and broad sectarian diversity that once marked the nation's democratic experiment weakened perceptibly, leaving large pockets of disenfranchised workers struggling in their impotence to understand both the nature of their plight and its solution. With his introduction of the single-tax theory, which proposed doing away with all government taxes but one that would be based on land, Henry George—who John Dewey described as "one of the world's great philosophers"—awakened society to the inequities that overshadowed the working classes.[1] Acknowledging the issues and loathing the injustices of his time, George and his proponents, including many members of the New Church, became trumpeters of reform, fighting for what they thought was common sense and common decency. Setting out to broaden democracy, they warned that without substantive reform, the nation might sink under the impact of its long-standing problems.

Henry George

As a reporter, amateur economist, and moralist, Henry George (1839–97) made his mark on the late nineteenth century by questioning assumptions that for too long had gone unchallenged. Born the second of ten children whose father was a clerk in the Custom House of

Philadelphia, he entered the workforce at fourteen as an errand boy before joining the English merchant service as a cabin clerk on a five-hundred-ton ship bound for Australia and Calcutta. After roughing it with his mates, he returned home none the worse for wear, finding a position as a printer's apprentice before working on a collier schooner operating between Philadelphia and Boston. Self-educated, he settled in California at age eighteen, where he took jobs on ships, prospected, wrote newsletters for the columns of the *Evening Journal* in San Francisco, and, when able, sent money home to his parents. Married at twenty-two, he faced poverty firsthand as he moved between jobs, scratching out a living doing occasional printing work and even peddling clothes-wringers to support his growing family. Eventually, he found work at the *San Francisco Times,* where he advanced from reporter to managing editor before moving to the *Herald.*[2]

In 1868, George visited New York, where he discovered grotesque inequality amid great and almost unimaginable wealth—a situation that struck him as horribly unfair. As he observed, "poverty is not merely deprivation; it means shame, degradation; the searing of the most sensitive parts of our moral and mental nature as with hot irons; the denial of the strongest impulses and the sweetest affections; the wrenching of the most vital nerves."[3] On returning to San Francisco, he became a self-possessed authority on political and economic issues, struck by the fact that in his native city—not unlike in New York, London, and all the great cities of the industrial world—wealth had fallen disproportionally into the hands of a few. Contrasting the lives of the princely rich with those of the teeming millions suffering from poverty, he perceived that, as populations grew, those who owned the land would hold it not for purposes of use but simply as a means to increase their wealth.[4]

In an article titled "What the Railroad Will Bring Us" (1868), which was followed by the pamphlet *Our Land and Land Policy, National and State* (1871), George delivered his earliest salvos against the monopolization of land. Observing firsthand the autocratic and ruthless power of the Central Pacific Railroad, which reduced its workers to helpless submission through its control of corrupt businessmen and politicians, he described the stark contrast between the railroad's aggrandizement and the nation's founding principles. In tightly reasoned arguments, he explained how the distribution of land ownership to the railroads through government financing and land grants had precipitated a systemic cycle of low wages and poverty. More than 16 percent of the entire land area of California had been granted to the railroads.[5] The fluid economics of the frontier that fostered egalitarian democracy had denigrated into an exploitive source of social injustice. In effect, the good intentions of the Homestead Act of 1862 had been reversed by huge grants to railroad promoters. This hardly squared with the long-held promotion of free and unlimited land opportunities. Instead, the government had differentiated the person who "counts his income by millions" from the laborer who worked for a bare living. To make matters worse, religion counseled humility and self-abasement, teaching that if laborers "patiently bear their lot here God will after death translate them to a heaven where there is no private property and no poverty." Rejecting such self-serving casuistry, George warned that no civilization, however promising, could endure such unwholesome disparities. A fool may declare that there was no God, but it was equally foolish to state that this was a world whose creatures, even in the most advanced of nations, should content themselves with perpetuating poverty.[6]

Watching the rise of "monstrous fortunes" among a few, George concluded that if the tyranny of misgovernment did not come to an end, the future of democracy would be irreparably imperiled. Far from enhancing economic growth, the spread of inequality had damaged the nation's potential. As a critic of this asymmetrical order, he claimed that unless the distribution of wealth was addressed, "the day may arrive when the 'Boss of America' will be to the modern world what Caesar was to the Roman world." The governing class's business of accumulating political and economic power could not continue without dire social consequences. This was especially troublesome since the American frontier was closing, leaving no outlet for "the restless, the dissatisfied, the oppressed, and the down-trodden." Land was still comparatively inexpensive, but the imminent passing of the frontier meant that it would not be long before the farthest corners of the nation would fall prey to the pressures of land speculation. It was with the absentee landlord that the teeming millions of immigrants would need to make terms.[7]

Widely distributed, George's *Our Land and Land Policy* became a political statement bearing regional and national significance. Finding himself at the center of public opinion, he joined with friends to start a new newspaper, the *San Francisco Evening Post*, using it as a sounding board for his thoughts on land policy. When the paper failed, he sought appointment as a state inspector of gas meters, during which time he continued to write, lecture, and participate in the work of the Land Reform League of California, which he founded in 1878.[8]

When George sent his manuscript *Progress and Poverty* to D. Appleton and Company in March of 1879, the publisher initially rejected the work, fearing it too revolutionary to generate sales. Only when he offered to provide the plates did Appleton agree to print the book. Four years and ten editions later, Appleton admitted that it had published the equivalent of Adam Smith's *The Wealth of Nations* (1776). Hailed at home and abroad, *Progress and Poverty* was translated into several languages and ran serially in newspapers. By 1924, more than five million copies had sold or been given away. The book was compared to such "stepping-stone" works as Marx's *Das Capital* (1867) and Pierre-Joseph Proudhon's *Solution du Problème Sociale* (1848), both of which provided all-encompassing explanations for the social and economic issues of the day. And like those, George's book stimulated many who made it their life's work to ensure social and economic justice.[9] It was his demand for the "rights" of the individual that drew to his cause people like playwright George Bernard Shaw; poet James Whitcomb Riley; reformer William Lloyd Garrison, Jr.; the young Frank Lloyd Wright; authors Hamlin Garland and William Dean Howells; and politician Tom L. Johnson.[10]

George's treatise began with the simple observation that his generation had witnessed an enormous increase in "wealth-producing power" due to the utilization of steam, electricity, time-saving machinery, and other inventions that improved labor's efficiency. Despite these innovations, chronic episodes of depression, involuntary idleness, wasted capital, and poverty persisted. An "immense wedge" separated the wealthy few from those crushed with debt and lacking the essentials of a healthy and productive life. This division became the "great enigma," the riddle that, if left unanswered, threatened to destroy Western civilization.[11]

In recounting the prevailing theories regarding labor, capital, land, rent, wages, and interest, George observed that they were not unlike the increasingly complex epicycles constructed by the Ptolemaic astronomers to explain why their theories didn't match visual observations. His job was to show these theories' inadequacy in accounting for the observable economic phenomena. Discounting the traditional antagonism between labor and capital, George set out to redefine the dynamics of material progress, beginning with the classic Malthusian theory regarding the relation between population and food supply. This deterministic theory, he insisted, was neither doctrine nor natural law; rather, it was an artifice designed to support the existing power structure. Worse still, it played into the hands of powerful interests by perpetuating the status quo for personal gain. As a Neo-Lamarckian, he had too much respect for individual ingenuity and inventiveness to accept Malthus's deterministic doctrine.[12] George was not alone in his criticism of the Manchester school of economics, as others like statistician F. B. von Hermann in Munich, economist William Thomas Thornton in Great Britain, and American economist Francis Amasa Walker were similarly opposed to the wage-fund and population theories that were held to be as sacrosanct as natural law.[13]

In studying the economic landscape of California, George discovered that systemic poverty had coincided with the building of the railroads. Holding the most valued land and refusing to sell it at a fair price, the railroads had robbed the common man of access to a commodity that was needed for the production of goods and services. Essentially, the railroads had negated Locke's doctrine of property along with the physiocratic concept of well-being—two key elements of Jeffersonian liberalism. Noting how the disparities in wealth affecting New York, London, and other European capitals were now manifesting themselves in San Francisco, he predicted that California would become a textbook example of how the allocation of land to the railroads had increased land values, speculation, and depression. What was happening there was occurring across the industrial world. "Everywhere that a railroad was built ... land was monopolized in anticipation, and the benefit of the improvement was discounted in increased land values." Sadly, worldwide depressions had followed similar land giveaways, which explained the unfortunate conjunction of poverty with wealth and low wages with high productivity. "To command the land which is necessary to labor, is to command all the fruits of labor save enough to enable labor to exist." In his mind, the ownership of land ultimately determined the social, political, and consequently the intellectual condition of a people.[14]

The only way to remedy the unequal distribution of wealth, George argued, was to make land common property. This did not, however, require appropriation or confiscation. "As every man has a right to the use and enjoyment of nature, the man who is using land must be permitted the exclusive right to its use in order that he may get the full benefit of his labor." In other words, all were equally entitled to *use* the land, a right proclaimed in the Declaration of Independence. Since land was a gift of the Creator and belonged to all humankind, it seemed axiomatic that "land rent," or its unearned increment, should belong to the community. This did not mean that there would be common ownership of land, its seizure by the state, or its nationalization, but it meant the use of land rent to support public services. "I do not propose either to purchase or to confiscate private property in land. The first would be unjust; the second, needless. Let the individuals who now hold it still retain, if they want to, possession of what they are pleased to call *their* land. Let them continue to call it *their* land. Let them buy and sell, and bequeath and devise it. We may safely leave them the shell, if we take the kernel. *It is not necessary to confiscate land; it is only necessary to confiscate rent.*" Stating that everything in nature had an intrinsic value and the capacity to satisfy some human need, George concluded that no object should become anyone's property until human labor chose to take and use it.[15]

A brilliant and passionate thinker who became a cult figure in his day, George understood clearly how economic forces, and in particular property rights, were in league against democratic ideals. Unless government could ensure the distribution of land at a fair price, poverty would remain a scourge. To correct this situation, he called for a tax upon the unearned increment to the value of land. In advocating this, he distinguished between "unearned" and "earned" income (i.e., between ownership of land and its use, respectively). Destroying the "land monopoly" by shifting the burden of taxation from labor and the products of labor to a single tax offered a quick and workable solution to poverty. George considered the approach not only ethical but also derivative of natural law in that it eliminated poverty in a fair and nonviolent manner.[16] Such a tax, he hypothesized, would raise wages and capital, increase employment, eliminate pauperism, abolish poverty, lessen crime, elevate morals, and improve government. With the confiscation of rent, not land, society would fulfill the ideal of Jeffersonian democracy by simplifying the legislative, judicial, and executive functions of government. Having fewer responsibilities, government could "become merely the agency by which the common property was administered for the common benefit."[17]

George enjoyed debunking long-held theories, including the idea that Old World monarchies had created the poverty of its downtrodden masses or that lack of personal industry, frugality, or intelligence was its cause. George likewise challenged the assertion that progress was the inescapable outcome of evolution, or, to use Spencer's more specific language, progress "from an indefinite, incoherent homogeneity to a definite, coherent heterogeneity." Such sweeping generalizations did not accord with the facts. Humanity's power of adaptation and invention was neither predetermined nor sure to happen, and too many civilizations had come and gone to justify a law of inevitable progress. True progress depended on there being a higher degree of social intelligence and a higher standard of social morality. It was society operating as a purposive organism that ensured advancement.[18] "Men tend to progress just as they come closer together," he observed, "and by cooperation with each other increase the mental power that may be devoted to improvement, but just as conflict is provoked, or association develops inequality of condition and power, this tendency to progression is lessened, checked, and finally reversed."[19]

George also did not agree that there were permanent differences separating the mental organization of civilized human beings from that of the savage. "The Hindoos and the Chinese were civilized when we were savages," he reminded readers. "They had great cities, highly organized and powerful governments, literatures, philosophies, polished manners, considerable division of labor . . . when our ancestors were wandering barbarians." Numerous civilizations had arisen and flourished only to go into arrest and stagnation. "The earth is the tomb of the dead empires, no less than of dead men." In truth, that which destroyed all previous civilizations had been "the conditions produced by the growth of civilization itself." As he believed in an underlying human nature, George deplored those who assumed that Western civilization had a tougher constitution than did the rest of human history. "We of modern civilization are raised far above those who have preceded us and those of the less advanced races who are our contemporaries. But it is because we stand on a pyramid, not that we are taller." Though he did not deny the influence of heredity and natural selection, it seemed likely that there was "a common standard and natural symmetry of mind, as there is of body, towards which all deviations tend to return." By this he meant that the differences between and among people were not inherent in the individual but in the society. "Each society, small or great, necessarily weaves for itself a web of knowledge, beliefs, customs, language, tastes, institutions, and laws."[20]

To the degree that people worked and cooperated together, progress occurred. But true civilization also came from a balanced distribution of wealth and power. Where this existed so, too, did democratic forms of government. In theory, Americans were "intense democrats," but in actuality, the foundations of their society had been sapped by the rapid aggrandizement of land. "That our civilization may possibly be tending to decline, seems like the wilderness of pessimism," George observed, but the signs had already appeared. Western civilization stood at the brink. "Either it must be a leap upward, which will open the way to advances yet undreamed of, or it must be a plunge downward, which will carry us back toward barbarism."[21]

George ended his book not in a cool dispassionate tone but in true social gospel style, calling on his fellow citizens not to degrade justice and the decrees of providence. "It is not the Almighty, but we who are responsible for the vice and misery that fester amid our civilization." In studying the great religions, the doctrines of the old philosophers, and the teachings of religious leaders, he sensed that even in the solar system where earth was but "an indistinguishable speck," eternal laws gave hope that what passed from sight did not disappear into oblivion.[22] His view of the future was not a secular one but was in the tradition of a preacher drawing on scripture to make his points, often referring to "the City of God on earth," "thou shalt not steal," "thy Kingdom come," and "the reign of the Prince of Peace." Deeply religious in a nonecclesiastical way, he expressed high regard for religious rhetoric and made frequent reference to Jesus and his disciples. In his speech titled "Moses," which he delivered on numerous occasions in the United States and abroad, he likened the perpetuity of land to the immorality of humankind.[23] A literalist, he interpreted Christian teachings in a manner similar to that of Russian novelist Tolstoy, whose goal was a "kingdom of God on earth." Father Edward McGlynn, a Catholic priest and strong advocate of the single tax, was a supporter of George and likened *Progress and Poverty* to "a poem; it is a prophecy; it is a prayer."[24]

Following the book's publication, George traveled to Manchester, Glasgow, and London, where he lectured on the long-simmering Irish land question, offering a much-welcomed solution with his theory on rent and land. In London, he sparred with Herbert Spencer and George Douglas Campbell, Duke of Argyll, a ferocious critic who called him "The Prophet of San Francisco," a term that became a sobriquet among his many admirers. Other mocking titles included "The New Mahdi," the "Second Messiah," and "George the Fifth."[25] Campbell depicted *Progress and Poverty* as a sober but overly pessimistic and poorly designed remedy for the ills of society. He accused

George of destroying institutional structures essential for the stability of society and substituting a communist-designed solution that stubbornly denied the validity of Malthusian theory and the laws of economics.[26] Pope Leo XIII added to the criticism by grouping him among the partisans of socialism and anarchism.[27]

Ironically, George argued that socialism carried four systemic faults: it lacked a scientific basis; it was antireligious and therefore destitute of any guiding principles; it failed to protect individual rights; and it demanded a type of social life that hindered the achievement of its objectives.[28] While "the ideal of socialism is grand and noble ... such a state of society cannot be manufactured—it must grow." This reasoning placed George among the American pragmatists rather than the nation's more dogmatic socialists. He did not propose, for instance, the public ownership of capital but instead insisted on free competition and individual enterprise.[29] His individualistic rhetoric, while predicated on a transcendent common good, remained consistent with the eighteenth-century Jeffersonian tradition, with William James's forward-looking conception of truth, and with John Dewey's "great community."[30]

In a subsequent book, *Social Problems* (1884), George reiterated his refusal to accept the comfortable theory that "it is in the nature of things that some should be poor and some should be rich, and that the gross and constantly increasing inequalities in the distribution of wealth" were expected outcomes of life. No such natural order existed; in fact, just the contrary was the case. The Carnegie, Vanderbilt, Fisk, Drew, Sage, and Gould fortunes, along with the Bessemer Steel Ring, the Whiskey Tax Ring, and the Lucifer Match Ring, were all artificial creations suppressing the working class. "I am not denouncing the rich, nor seeking ... to excite envy and hatred," he insisted, but "we must recognize the fact that it is to monopolies which we permit and create ... that some men are enabled to get so enormously rich while others remain so miserably poor." There were deep wrongs in the present structure of society that were not inherent in the constitution of humanity. They were wrongs resulting from bad adjustments and, more importantly, were within humanity's power to amend.

America's laborers could be more industrious and better citizens if given the opportunity to take their rightful earnings home to their families.[31]

George considered the phrase "The poor ye have always with you" to be a blasphemous denial of Christ's teachings. Similarly, he rejected any forced equalization in the distribution of wealth, as taking from those who have and giving it to those in need also created injustice and resulted in great harm to the people. Referring to the Declaration of Independence; the preamble to the Constitution; and the Declaration of the Rights of Man and of the Citizen, which was issued by the National Constituent Assembly of France in 1789, George insisted that these documents formed the only true basis for social organization. In fact, their tenets were antecedent to any laws devised by humankind. All true and just laws, whether societal or natural, must conform to the higher, moral law.[32] Not until such truths were valued and put to work could the correct economic, social, and political adjustments become a reality. "You will see," he promised, "that the true law of social life is the law of love, the law of liberty, the law of each for all and all for each."[33]

Many associated George's economics with so-called "Darwinism," but the expression was applicable only if understood as Neo-Lamarckism, since purposive evolutionism rather than natural selection dominated the social sciences in the United States. In company with Asa Gray, Alpheus Hyatt, Joseph LeConte, Edward Drinker Cope, and other American scientists and social scientists, George allowed individual intent to overshadow the randomness of natural selection.[34] It was this outer- and inner-directed evolutionism that formed the basis of his social evolutionary theory. Although there was no guarantee that any civilization would survive beyond a single cycle of growth, decline, and fall, he attributed failure to the wasted mental powers of a particular civilization in addressing its environment. His inquiry startled students of history and anthropology, as it argued that the differences found among civilizations, especially those that rose to great heights and then collapsed, were due to the degree of social inequality and not to any biological or mental differences. In any state of civilization, there existed the possibility of people work-ing collectively to provide a more equitable distribution of wealth.[35]

Though George's views were not as stark as those found in Jack London's *The People of the Abyss* (1903) or in his dystopian novel *The Iron Heel* (1907), both of which dictated the inexorable triumph of the strong, his depiction of advanced civilization cried out for an answer from social scientists. Using a combination of economic and moral theories, George challenged reformers to remove poverty forever. Analyzing society through the collection of statistics on crime, pros-titution, poverty, and destitution, he examined the waste of productive power that came with civilization. He also took account of the labor problems, economic dislocations, agrarian unrest, urbanization, and land monopolization that impeded progress by detracting from social justice, the rights of man, and Christian ethics. "I assert that the injus-tice of society, not the niggardliness of nature, is the cause of the want and misery which the current theory attributes to over-population."[36]

Observing that poverty and want were present in all advanced societies, George insisted they were needless conditions that govern-ments, if they so chose, could correct. Preaching through his books and from lecture halls, he demanded an end to the speculation of land and its resources, offering a reformulation of society using language native in context and profoundly religious in motive. Without cater-ing to the leveling demands of foreign ideologies, strikes, boycotts, or state appropriation of property, he offered with the stroke of the legis-lative pen to eliminate the nation's most systemic injustices.[37] Having mastered the teachings of the classical school of political economy, he became a social and economic ideologue whose influence extended beyond America to the United Kingdom, the Wilhelmine German Empire, the Hungarian Kingdom, and Denmark.[38]

The New Order

A significant number of George's followers were members of the New Church who identified his single-tax theory as representative of the very core of Swedenborg's doctrine of usefulness. In fact, as the single-tax movement moved into high gear in the 1890s, it was this realization more so than any other that caused Swedenborgians to join single-tax reform leagues in New York, New Jersey, Pennsylvania, Tennessee, Kansas, Louisiana, California, Maryland, and Texas.[39] Charles Hardon, an ordained minister and instructor at Urbana University in Ohio, and later president of the Pomona Single Tax League in California, kept up a steady stream of correspondence in *The New-Church Messenger,* as he hoped to spur discussion about the single tax among New Church associations.[40] *The New Christianity* (1888–98), which was published by the Swedenborg Publishing Association and edited by S. H. Spencer in Germantown, Philadelphia, not only advertised George's writings in each of its issues, but it also included a lengthy section providing questions and answers regarding the single-tax theory.[41]

John Filmer, founder of the New Churchman's Single Tax League (1889–1900) of Brooklyn, was a lifetime member of the Swedenborg Foundation. According to the League's bylaws, its aim was "to spread among receivers of the doctrines of the New Church a knowledge of the New Political Economy which advocates a single tax [and] to promote the study and practical application of the New Church and the New Economic System conjunctively." Its magazine, *The New Earth* (1889–1900), was dedicated to promoting the single tax, illustrating social problems on moral and religious grounds, and reporting on the progress made by the movement across the country as well as in England, Canada, British Columbia, New Zealand, and Australia.[42] Assisted by Alice Thacher, L. E. Wilmarth, and A. I. Auchterlonie, editor Filmer used the magazine to build a connection between the single-tax theory and Swedenborg's doctrine of usefulness.[43]

The first issue of *The New Earth* came out in November of 1889, and copies were sent to eleven thousand New Church members around the country. On average, each issue consisted of eight pages of articles on the relationship between the doctrines of the New Church and the single tax, as well as book reviews, poetry, and extracts from letters received by the New Churchman's Single Tax League. Most important, *The New Earth* contained articles comparing Edward Bellamy's nationalism with George's single tax, and it clarified the difference between the *right to own* and the *right to use.* Generally speaking, New Church members considered Bellamy's nationalist movement too utopian and much less defined in its particulars than was the single-tax movement.[44]

The painter Lemuel Everett Wilmarth, one of the founders of *The New Earth* magazine, explained how the doctrine of usefulness related to George's vision for the new political economy.[45] Drawing from Swedenborg's *Divine Love and Wisdom,* Wilmarth reasoned that the possession of land for use was the true order of things while the claim of private ownership of land was a perversion in that it obstructed and often destroyed that order. "While we do not propose to change the present laws which sanction private ownership in land, we advocate as an antidote to their direful results, the Single Tax on land values, firmly believing that if this system of collecting ground rent for the community were once carried into effect, it would become unprofitable for any man to hold land out of use."[46]

With the New Churchman's Single Tax League and similar organizations formed or supported by Swedenborgians, New Church members in Missouri, Massachusetts, and Kentucky were poised to take a significant role in the single-tax movement. *The Echo,* a short-lived Swedenborgian paper published by Rev. William Martin in Iowa, supported the single tax; socialism; the writings of Henry James, Sr.; and reading circles dedicated to the works of Swedenborg. Writing in 1909 in *The New-Church Messenger,* Rev. Junius B. Spiers of Richmond, Virginia, reported visiting the single-tax town of Fairhope, which was on the shores of Mobile Bay, Alabama, and subsequently requesting contributions from fellow members of the league to construct a chapel in the town. He earnestly believed that the doctrines of the New Church would appeal to the moral sense of the townspeople because the concept of usefulness supported their application of the single tax.[47]

A new genre of reform literature, much of which George radicalized with his single-tax theory, included *In His Steps* (1896) by Charles Sheldon, and *Jesus Christ and the Social Question* (1900), *Jesus Christ and the Christian Character* (1905), and *The Christian Life in the Modern World* (1914) by Francis Greenwood Peabody. Sheldon's agitation for social change began with the simple question "What would Jesus do?" Once asked, its answer took precedence over age-old debates on predestination, free will, and redemption. Almost all the well-meant efforts of these authors centered on labor, housing, public corruption, the distribution of wealth, the inadequacies of private philanthropy, and the repudiation of classical political economy that lay at the core of *laissez-faire* capitalist society.[48]

Swedenborgians discovered in the subtleties of George's arguments a powerful rebuttal to the inequities of the age. They found him to be a platonically incorruptible pragmatist whose will, ability, and vision offset the sense of helplessness and uncertainty that seemed to threaten the nation's future. Unafraid of the growing plutocracy that he saw undermining democracy, George had countered with a powerful alternative that captivated the imagination and invigorated those who had begun to doubt a future for themselves and their families. In George, they spied a Samson wrecking the temple of the plutocracy, not out of fury but in response to the workings of a society that was marvelously disciplined. Here was a clear-thinking individual whose passionate beliefs were poised to liberate a generation or more from their doubts.

Though strong pressure was brought by individual Swedenborgians to commit the New Church to the single-tax cause, the Church declined to formally join the reform movement. It had no objection to individuals putting their religion into practice as citizens by seeking this particular type of reform, but "when a church assumes the functions of the State and begins to endorse and advocate ... this or that political, or industrial, or social measure of reform," warned managing editor H. Clinton Hay of *The New-Church Review*, "it is time for every patriot to take alarm, and array himself against that particular form of Church organization as a menace to his civil liberty." Thus, those who did choose to advocate for the single-tax theory generally did so from outside the Church.[49]

George Inness

Known for his Hudson River school landscape paintings, George Inness (1825–94) participated in numerous reform movements over his lifetime, the most prominent of which was the single-tax movement.

Born of well-to-do parents, Inness was the fifth of thirteen children, all of whom built successful lives in the business world. As a dreamer and idealist from youth, he decided to be a painter at a time when "an artist was little short of a disgrace." An individual with deep spiritual needs, he learned of Swedenborg from William Page, a portrait-painter and one-time president of the National Academy of Design in New York, with whom he had become close friends. Immersing himself deeply in Swedenborg's writings, Inness became a quick learner.[50]

Biographers and historians have long made the connection between Inness and Swedenborg. Not only was the painter a member of both the Brooklyn Swedenborgian Church and the New Churchman's Single Tax League, but Swedenborg's ideas shone through Inness's personal writings, his own ideas on art, the symbolic elements in his depiction of humanity and nature, and the form and color in his paintings.[51] Former Harvard psychologist Eugene Taylor carried this interpretation even further by proposing that Inness used his art "as the primary vehicle for communicating what was spiritual to all who saw his paintings."

> That is, when we try to look at one of his landscapes from a Swedenborgian point of view, as Inness in all likelihood himself saw it when he looked at the canvas, the picture ceases to be for us the mere depiction of a scene in nature and becomes instead a representation of one of the artist's own interior states of consciousness. In each picture Inness said that he was attempting to communicate an emotion to his viewers, who in turn bring their own interior states of feeling to bear in their reactions to the picture. . . . Between these interior domains of the painter and the viewer, both Swedenborg and, I think, Inness have suggested that there can be a fusion in which the spiritual dimension of experience is revealed.[52]

"Art is the endeavor on the part of Mind (Mind being the creative factor) to express through the senses ideas of the great principles of unity," wrote Inness, for whom color became the means for expressing his spirituality.[53] Color was the way he connected to the metaphysical system of Swedenborg. His essay "Colors and Their Correspondences," which was published in *The New Jerusalem*

Messenger in 1867, became a clear testimony to the artist's feelings: "Having given the study of color great attention during the larger portion of my life, I have been frequently impressed with numerous beautiful correspondences of the same, while reading the Word and the writings of Swedenborg." Inness went on to explain that red corresponded to love; blue to faith; and yellow to what was natural and external: "In a work of art red in excess produces fineness, or what is artistically called hardness. Blue in excess produces coldness. Yellow in excess produces vulgarity, but the perfect combination of these three colors in their relative proportions produces harmony."[54]

The doctrine of correspondences lent a spiritual meaning to Inness's art, as it suggested that all reality emanated from the Divine. That which one sees in the natural world had more than just a symbolic relationship to the spiritual; it was ultimately derived from it.[55] By turning within and drawing upon the intuitive faculties, there was a greater likelihood of "seeing" the correspondence between the natural and the spiritual worlds. Once understood, the love and wisdom that underpinned this seeing was best expressed through usefulness. Buddhist Daisetz T. Suzuki and radical empiricist William James would later identify this understanding as the primacy of immediate experience in which the object intermingles with the perception, thus eliminating the space between subject and object. In such works as *The Valley of the Shadow of Death*, *The Vision of Faith*, and *The New Jerusalem*, for example, Inness shared with the viewer an inward spiritual journey to an awakened consciousness that was both solitary and reflective. In viewing these paintings, observers not only could intuit the artist's interior state of consciousness, but they could also map that interior state onto their own personal experience.

Inness's reading of *Progress and Poverty* served as a catalyst for his realism, which portrayed working class realities without the sentimentality of previous ages and acknowledged in the process the impoverished predicament of their conditions. His art focused on manual laborers, the harsh reality of tedious work, the lack of interpersonal communication, physical strain, the squalor of old age, and the concern for human dignity and spiritual welfare. As an energetic member of the New Churchman's Single Tax League of Brooklyn, he participated in the organization's activities, using his artistic abilities to inform colleagues of the issues, sometimes to the point of pros-elytization. One evening after dinner, recalled George Inness, Jr., his father cornered a Canadian gentleman "and for hours poured into him his theories of Swedenborg, Henry George, the single tax, and paint, pounding each word in with a jab of his forefinger, until the poor fel-low, in utter desperation, tore himself away and retired."[56]

Louis and Alice Post

Another activist working on behalf of George's single-tax theory was Louis F. Post (1849–1928), a native of New Jersey whose legal career brought him expertise in the area of copyrights. Attracted to the Irish land question, he identified the land-holding system as Ireland's systemic cause of poverty and the single tax as the key to its solu-tion. A writer, reformer, and self-styled atheist, he was nonetheless a staunch believer in Swedenborg's philosophy of life. Post worked as editor of *The Standard,* the *Cleveland Recorder,* and later, *The Public* in Chicago and the *National Single Taxer* in New York. He also served as assistant US attorney for the southern district of New York and as assistant United States secretary of labor in the Wilson administra-tion in 1913. A respected progressive and loyal supporter of the single tax, he advocated municipal ownership of utilities, educational reform, and anti-imperialism. Regularly contributing in *The New Earth* mag-azine, he advertised his services as a lecturer willing to travel to any part of the United States and Canada to speak on the single tax, the political economy, free trade, and protectionism.[57] As chairman of the American Tax Reform League, he brought together land, labor, free trade, and union advocates to form the New York United Labor Party; the Manhattan Single Tax Club, of which he served as presi-dent from 1889 to 1892; and the National Single Tax Conference that was held in New York in 1890.

Post set out to resolve society's ills by reiterating the Sweden-borgian doctrine of usefulness. This became the centerpiece of his book *Social Service* (1909), which he dedicated to his friend Tom

Johnson, "who also sat at the feet of Henry George and learned of him." With chapters on the use and abuse of money, frequent references to the single tax, and a comparison of Marxism with Bellamy's nationalism, he explained the fundamentals of social service and the differences between the socialization of "natural capital" and the individualization of "artificial capital."[58] What bothered Post most was the undisciplined use of the word *radical,* which critics had applied to proponents of the single tax. "I am one of those people who do not believe in allowing the devil to take over the good words," he insisted. "'Radical' is a good word. Radicalism is absolute justice; it is not the antithesis of conservatism.... It is the antithesis of superficialism."[59]

Post's wife, Alice Thacher (1853–1947), who came from an old Boston family of Swedenborgian preachers, was a social reformer in the progressive tradition, having joined the Anti-Imperialist League and the American Proportional Representation League.[60] She helped edit two Swedenborgian-based papers, *The New-Church Messenger* and *The New Earth,* the latter of which, as noted above, was supported by the New Churchman's Single Tax League of Brooklyn.[61] In addition to tracing the work of single-tax societies at the local and national levels, the magazine opposed the war in the Philippines and advanced the cause of socialism, altruism, women's rights, and land reform across Europe and the Far East. Supportive of Henry George, Henry James, Sr., and Swedenborg, *The New Earth* defined socialism as the altruism that Jesus taught: "Love thy neighbor as thyself." Until the state was called "I," humankind would continue to face the egoism lodged within its consciousness.[62]

Thomas Lewis Nugent

Thomas Lewis Nugent (1841–95) was another Swedenborgian who advocated for the single tax, viewing it as a visible representation of the doctrine of usefulness. Born in Opelousas, Louisiana, in 1841, his father was an immigrant from Queen's County, Ireland, and his mother was the daughter of the chief justice of the Mississippi Territory. He inherited from his parents a strong love of music, religion, practicality, and fixed principles. After graduating from Centenary

College in 1861, he settled in Texas and enlisted in the Confeder-
ate Army. Though belonging to a slaveholding family, he opposed
slavery's continued existence, arguing that it had been God's plan to
reach down and, through the Northern abolitionists, find the most
practical way to free the African from slavery. At the close of the war,
he taught school in Austin before joining the bar in 1870. In 1873, he
moved to Stephenville, where he served as a member of the Constitutional Convention, urging an end to the government's subsidy of
the railroads. Less than a decade later, he endorsed the efforts of the
Farmers' Alliance in advocating government ownership of railroads.[63]
Appointed judge in 1879, he presided over the 29th Judicial District and
was subsequently elected twice to the office before resigning in 1888
for health reasons. A year later, he left the Democratic Party because
he considered it an empty shell on account of its moneyed interests.
"I parted company with the Democratic party," he said, "because I
became dissatisfied with its inconsistency in principle, the corruption
of its national management and the continual surrender to the interests of Wall Street." In 1891, he moved to Fort Worth, where, in 1892
and 1894, he twice ran as the People's Party candidate for governor.[64]

Nugent admired Esoteric Christianity; Buddhism; the doctrines of Swedenborg; the single-tax theory of Henry George; the
utopian sentiments of Edward Bellamy; and the social morality of
Henry James, Sr.—the last of whom pursued what the Rev. E. Payson Walton, founder of the Ontological Society, described as a "lonely
but lofty pathway of theology and philosophy."[65] Much like James,
Nugent was independent in his beliefs, demonstrating little desire to
become a church-going Christian. Neither he nor his wife attended
church services, not because he considered religion unimportant but
because he admitted to receiving no particular good from it. "I have
done no church work for years," Nugent admitted to a New Church
minister, "believing that the ecclesiastical era is nearing its end and
that the coming church is to be a redeemed and glorified social state in
which the Lord will stand as the man of the people, the Divine chief
of the world's organized industries." Religion, for him, had outworn
its usefulness. On another occasion, he noted that "orthodoxy throws

a blight over the whole intellectual man, and precludes a normal, free evolution of the faculties."[66] Observing that he had "passed through this transition," he nonetheless admitted that others might require an "earthly priest."[67] Still, he insisted that all were saved, as God could never have created human beings to suffer eternal torture. "As long as there is, in all the universe, one single thing in pain or torture or sorrow," he wrote, "God himself feels that pain, and continues to be crucified as long as the wrong-doing and suffering of humanity endure.... Even the devils in Hell would be redeemed."[68]

A Swedenborgian in the Henry James, Sr., tradition, Nugent felt detached from creeds and practices, preferring quiet reading, contemplating the analogies between the natural and spiritual worlds, and supporting the fundamental rights to happiness and personhood.[69] Above all else, he came to understand "that no church was exclusively the key to Heaven, and that all must finally enter the Lord's kingdom who live in the love and practice of the truth." The purposes of Christianity and its churches had been subverted and so required a total house-cleaning before they could earn back the allegiance of the people. In effect, the ecclesiastical church had overstayed its purpose. The kingdom of God that the major denominations had placed in the distant future could and should be realized by the living.[70]

Like Henry James, Sr., Nugent did not regard the New Church as the only option, referring to it as "a small ecclesiasticism centered around a high system of spiritual philosophy, but possessing little of the genuine inspiration of an unselfish, vital religion."

> I am a Protestant of the most pronounced type, and believe most faithfully in the fundamental teachings of the Christian religion—particularly in the vital doctrine of Christ's divinity and that of the saving efficiency of the divine truth—divine truth applied to the life, that is, accepted, believed and obeyed. I am no enemy of church organizations, but believe that the concentration of all ecclesiastical power in the hands of any one religious body would result in the destruction of both political and religious freedom. I regard it as a singular manifestation of the divine good will that Protestantism has led to the development of so many forms of religious

belief and to the establishment of so many churches. Thus the tendency to extreme intolerance is counterbalanced, the humane sentiment liberated and set free and social evolution along the lines of a true fraternity made possible. Thus tyranny over thought is broken, or so far restrained that, from this on to the end, it must always be felt as a spent force. As you will see, so far from believing church organizations to be a "menace to free institutions," I regard them as singularly promotive of individual and social freedom, and of all institutions in which the spirit of freedom seeks to employ itself. But I believe that any effort to thrust religious controversies into the arena of party politics must be attended with evil consequences—especially evil to the cause of political and social reform.[71]

Nugent decried the concentration of wealth in the hands of the moneyed classes. In doing so, he turned to Swedenborg, with his emphasis on the improvability of humankind. Nugent believed in the presence of a divine quality in each individual and in humanity's capacity for goodness and perfectibility. Human beings were both natural and spiritual, a physical body wearing spiritual clothes and capable collectively of achieving godliness. Like Swedenborg, he denied the doctrine of the elect and of eternal damnation. The kingdom of God was realizable while on earth through the regeneration of individuals, awakening the working class to the promise of a better life and using popular sovereignty to cast off oppressive economic obstacles.[72]

Land being the basis of livelihood, Nugent called for an end to the land monopoly and the aggregations of wealth stolen from the laboring class. Believing that land was a basic human right, he insisted that "any tradition, custom or power that denies or prevents this right is morally wrong." Since the "people" rather than the individual created the unearned increment of land value, he intended the single tax to replace the confiscation of private property. It represented a fair and appropriate way to diffuse the blessings of the land and use the revenues raised to free labor from the burdens of other taxes. He saw himself not as a revolutionist but as an educator advocating on behalf of the Farmers' Alliance; the Knights of Labor; and Brotherhoods of

Railway-men, Printers, Mechanics, Brick-layers, and Stone-masons. Claiming that the land was the heritage of the people, he insisted that taxation upon the unearned increment would return to the people the benefits that accrued by its private ownership.[73]

Throughout his speeches, Nugent drew on the writings of Henry George to demonstrate his points—whether advocating free trade in place of protective tariffs, destroying monopolies, supporting a single tax, prohibiting money hoarding, affording relief to farmers and laborers, opposing the gold standard, or fixing railroad rates. At times in his speeches, he even read directly from *Progress and Poverty* to make his point. Always reminding his listeners of the world's "despairing multitudes" and of his boundless confidence in the human race, he pled the cause of Christ's mission to the landless. This was the nature of his Christian socialism—namely, the public's ownership and control of public utilities.[74]

Nugent's issues also included tariff reform, free trade, the public ownership of railroads, telephone lines and other public utilities, free coinage of silver at the ratio of sixteen to one, and postal savings banks. Often accused of being a communist, anarchist, and socialist—terms that were frequently used interchangeably—Nugent found such comments amusing, and rather than being alarmed or defensive, he accepted them proudly. He expressed a strong adherence to the life and writings of Jefferson and to the importance of agriculture, free government, and an independent yeomanry. Similarly, he lamented the increase in pauperism, penitentiaries, and juvenile reformatories. He also showed a profound respect for the African American and spoke openly against mob lynching.[75]

Equipped with arguments that abounded with statistics, Nugent took on his opponents with devastating effect. As a statesman, jurist, philosopher, and reformer, he spoke as a messenger of hope in an age of greed to those whose lives had been bypassed in the "survival of the fittest." As leader of the People's Party in his state, he kept the reform movement practical and unaffected by ill-timed tactics or goals too distant to realize. As a consequence, he opposed inserting religion into politics, as individuals should be left in "undisturbed freedom" to seek their own religious destiny. "The People's Party," he advised, "will have its hands full if it devotes itself with full and complete abandonment to its great mission, which contemplates nothing less than the elimination of monopoly, both in spirit and fact, from our entire industrial scheme."[76]

For Nugent, life rested in love, service, and usefulness. This was the outgrowth of divine humanity and a dictum that stood at the center of his worldview. "Christ worked for love; by love produced, enriched, uplifted, amplified gifts, and was prepared to save the race. He is our Truth; thus we would embody His truth. He is our way; thus we would follow Him in service." Accordingly, he spent his efforts awakening others to the benefits of labor guilds, alliances, and mutual cooperatives. He praised the Farmers' Alliance's "Declaration of Intentions," which called on its members to demand that farmers be educated in the science of economical government, in nonpartisanship, and in fraternity. "The Farmers' Alliance is of God," he once stated. "The Peoples' Party is of the Farmers' Alliance; therefore the People's Party is of God.... If God be for us, who can be against us?"[77]

Given Henry George's notoriety, it seems somewhat ironic that by the 1940s, he all but vanished from view, seldom referenced among liberal and progressive circles. As explained by George R. Geiger, philosopher and founding editor of *The Antioch Review*, it was almost as if the single tax had been a "utopian panacea" advocated by "vegetarians, theosophists, spiritualists, Esperantists [and] believers in chiropractic and anarchism." Once a pioneer in American political economy, he had been eclipsed by the economist and socialist Thorstein Veblen and removed from the universe of academic discourse. According to Geiger, the land that had once been the centerpiece of George's philosophy had now "become old-fashioned, something bucolic which may affect a few Southern novelists with wistful nostalgia" but that no longer justified comment.[78] Until then, the concept of land usage had made a formidable impact on the social gospel and progressive thinking, causing sweeping changes in the popular mind and yielding a variety of socially conscious and reform-oriented measures designed to address the injustices that came out of a polarization between wealth and poverty. Reformers saw in George's single tax a palliative that would assure the world that they had no intention of using force for change. With Christian rhetoric, the single taxers found a way to cast aside both social Darwinism and socialism for a program promising to build on the strengths of the nation's democratic traditions.

5 Social Gospel

*The essence of Swedenborg's Doctrine of Use is that a man real-
izes the central purpose of good human life by the faithful performance of the duties of his office, profession, calling, or occupation.
According to this doctrine every one ought to have some useful
employment, ought to do some kind of work which benefits the
community and which is his chosen way of doing good to others.*

(Chauncey Giles, *The New Jerusalem Magazine*, 1872)

As the effects of industrial and finance capitalism hardened into a
determinism that all but perverted the ideal of Emerson's self-reliant
individual, a new period of reform commenced that far outdistanced
the fractured efforts of the earlier communitarians. With less than
a percent of the population controlling half the nation's wealth, and
whole armies of workers made idle at any one time due to recession,
overproduction, or banking collapses, regions of the country were
routinely thrown into economic depression. Adding to the confusion, streams of immigrants continued to arrive—all hoping for a
new life. A source of cheap labor, they became easy prey for employers
and were subject to the animosity of American-born workers. With
the near end of the frontier functioning as a "safety-valve" to class
conflict, cities became glutted with unskilled labor and the accompanying tenement housing and atmosphere of vice. Throughout the
Northeast and Midwest, strikes led to militias who were ordered to
combat workers with force. With the specter of anarchism looming
and with a sense of despair rising among discouraged workers, the
stage was set for class warfare.

With slums, strikes, and recurrent depression challenging the nation's sense of exceptionalism, a cadre of urban Protestant ministers, including many from the New Church, launched efforts to realize God's work in the world. Seeking to avoid the threat of violence that comes with class conflict, they were urged to take ameliorative steps toward endorsing cooperation between capital and labor, supporting arbitration to deal with strikes and lockouts, and advocating for the protection of women and children. They sought to replace the nation's overindulgence in individualism with an alternate vision that took its cue from Swedenborg's spiritual person, or inner self, and one's capacity for implementing the doctrine of usefulness. Denying any attempt to restore some idyllic past, they emphasized the creation of a moral community—a just society realized without force of arms and whose members were connected to each other and to God. The leading representatives of the social gospel movement turned away from dogma and creed to a more centrist form of theology that accepted the findings of science without surrendering religious ideals to the dysteleology of natural selection. Neo-Lamarckian in their view of progressive change, these pastoral leaders sought a middle ground between class-driven self-interest and God's willful purposes. They viewed democracy as more social than it was political or economic, affirming their faith in the idea of equality without challenging the status quo, and they were bent on improving the general conditions rather than giving in to the selfish consideration of a few to the detriment of society.

Early Warnings

As the upwardly mobile middle class bore witness to the transformation taking place in urban America, many of its members did so with a sense of God-given entitlement and respectability. Applying ratiocinations that looked outward rather than inward, they projected an aura of self-importance that held individuals morally accountable for their condition. From their pulpits, the clergy—society's moral compass—reflected this thinking by teaching that wealth was a reflection of hard work, divine justice, and personal piety. This explains why respect for the rich and the prevailing economic doctrines continued unshaken within those Protestant circles whose churches took comfort in the adage, "The poor we have with us always; and this is not the greatest of our hardships, but the choicest of our blessings." The middle class judged with a sense of righteous condescension those who failed to rise to their own standards and expectations. For all intents and purposes, the values of classical economics and a belief in the natural depravity of the "vicious poor" held equal standing with theology. Such was the nature of the moral truths preached in the churches and taught in the schools. Sadly, this resulted in a harshness of social conscience that caused many mainline denominations to lose the laboring classes from their pews, leaving ministers with the dubious luxury of speaking to a homogeneous group of believers. Accused of being mercenaries for capitalism and willing participants in the social crisis, the clergy were perceived as having little in common with the plight of the laborer and even less with that of the poor.[1]

As corruption engulfed the highest levels of government and business, even the least prudent clerics found it difficult to defend unregulated capitalism. Simply put, inequality had become too obvious and too harmful to be ignored. While the work of the nation was being done by many, the rewards accrued to the few. Society, always thought to be fluid, seemed in the process of disintegration, causing religious reformers to sympathize with the helplessness of individual workers and to distrust the unhealthy collusion between politicians and businessmen. The doctrines of the classical wage-fund theory and *laissez-faire* economics drew righteous criticism as a few stalwart critics came forward to challenge their application and universality. Sincere but misguided efforts to speak to and on behalf of the working classes—efforts that at various times excluded farmers, African Americans, and immigrants—often led to greater harm. Nevertheless, increasing numbers of liberal and evangelical Christians, particularly those living in urban communities, found the issues of capital and labor festering at the center of the nation's malaise. Essential to their thinking was the emphasis on Jesus's teachings and his ethical character, on the kingdom of God emerging *within* history, and on a collective rather than an individual view of sin.[2]

Those religious reformers who spoke from the pulpits and from the editorial offices of their magazines and newspapers advocated for a social gospel that led away from an otherworldly heaven, emphasizing rather a kingdom of God on earth.[3] This predominantly Protestant movement sought to retain as much of the older evangelicalism as possible while calling for a new religion designed to address the sociopolitical and economic forces of the day. This collective awakening of society's conscience took the form of a generation of reformers engaged in efforts to find common ground amid the turmoil of change. Their solution was a "theology of experience," where intuition replaced dogma.[4]

As a largely urban middle-class initiative, the social gospel movement included several highly renowned church figures keen on constructing a new social order based on the teachings of Jesus. The movement's religious approach was not necessarily theological, since there was little in its agenda that required justification by eliciting inherited dogmas. Rather, the doctrine of usefulness once again made itself evident, in that good works were the order of the day. The social gospel literature spoke of the need for charity and public morals, urging that corporations be more responsive to the will of the people. Sensitive to the mood of the nation, the social gospelers grasped the disillusionment, false idealism, and hypocrisy that lay behind the churches' past expressions of professed empathy.[5]

Rather than become entangled in metaphysical matters and awkward theological roadblocks with regard to sin, the social gospelers treated it as an "atavism," a reversion to humanity's primitive origins and an obvious deviation from any postmillennial society imbued with the immanence of the Divine. Moral evil was temporal, a condition that society could eliminate by means of useful practices (e.g., a single tax, initiative and referendum, an Australian ballot, an eight-hour work day, municipal socialism, nationalization, and other providential changes that would advance the kingdom of God).[6] It was a challenge that social gospelers expected to win, provided society recognized and addressed its collective sins; but they struggled to balance their liberal optimism, including their confusion concerning the relationship between evolution and human freedom, with an evangelical sense of those sins.[7]

Three individuals who best represent the breadth and depth of the social gospel were Washington Gladden, Lyman Abbott, and Walter Rauschenbusch. As social gospelers, their writings had an almost ecumenical acceptance across urban American Protestantism, including the New Church. Each of them proposed a form of Christian socialism, with its goal of brotherhood (i.e., from the love of God to the love of neighbor) as the solvent of the nation's social problems. The term "Christian socialism"—a catch-all phrase whose sources included English precedents in French utopianism, the gradualist theories of the Fabians, German socialism, Tolstoy, and Henry James, Sr.—referred to a movement that stood in opposition to unregulated capitalism and made efforts to arrive at a common understanding of its more glaring failures. From time to time, it meant cooperation for the common good, democratic practices, unselfishness, and social justice. Surprisingly, it remained silent on the free market and the private ownership of property, provided that the economic sphere was democratically managed. In effect, the nature of Christian socialism changed over time and seldom were its aspects defined in public discourse. A better term may have been "social Christianity," since Christian socialism did not really imply true socialism. Marxism stood largely outside its framework of optimism, meliorism, religious evangelism, and pragmatic impatience. From the Owenite community at New Harmony to the Fourierist association at Brook Farm to Bellamy's brand of nationalism, the types of socialism that Americans either attempted to practice or discussed in theory were those that Marxists detested. As Americans tended to dislike abstruse theories and philosophies, their politics, like their religion, leaned toward the practical.[8]

Washington Gladden

An authentic American who urged the application of Jesus's teachings to contemporary social problems, Washington Gladden (1836–1918) grew up in humble circumstances, carrying vivid memories of boisterous Methodist camp revivals, his work as a printer's apprentice, Bible study, abolitionist agitation, and the Civil War. Born into a nation of only twenty-five states, he lived to see the first telegram, the first ocean cable laid across the Atlantic, the wireless telephone, and the Roentgen ray. A man of great influence, he knew personally nearly all the notable political, religious, and financial minds of his generation.

After graduating from Williams College in 1859, Gladden prepared for the ministry, formulating his beliefs after a deep spiritual experience that he described as "being a Christian." Distressed by the divisiveness within Protestantism over the issues of predestination, baptism, temperance, and other matters, he delivered a series of lectures that were later combined into a book titled *Working People and Their Employers* (1876); and this became the basis of his lifelong search for the application of Christian law to industrial society. "Nothing was more needed," he insisted, "than the enforcement upon the consciences of men of the truth that the Christian law covers every relation of life, and the distinct and thoroughgoing application of that law to the common affairs of men." In Gladden's mind, "young ministers should understand how men ought to live together [rather] than ... be familiar with the Gnostic philosophy of the second century, or the Supralapsarian theories." This meant sympathizing with unions, supporting a living wage, and knowing how to be a Christian in the modern world. "Thou shalt love thy neighbor as thyself," he repeated over and over in his sermons and writings. This was the Christian law that both labor and capital needed to incorporate into the world of the employer and employee. Troubled by the widening breach between the classes, by misplaced paternalism, and by the prevailing social philosophy of *laissez-faire*, he urged the cooperation of capital and labor as essential to the future peace and welfare of the nation.

> The present state of the industrial world is a state of war. And if war is the word, then the efficient combination and organization must not all be on the side of capital. While the conflict is in progress, labor has the same right that capital has to prosecute the warfare in the most effective way. If war is the order of the day, we

must grant to labor belligerent rights. The sooner this fact is recognized, the better for all concerned. The refusal to admit it has made the conflict, thus far, much more fierce and sanguinary than it would otherwise have been.[9]

During his tenure as pastor of the First Congregational Church in Columbus, Ohio, Gladden grew increasingly impatient with capitalism and with those religious beliefs that reinforced the inequalities that it created. He postulated that ritualism, dogmatism, and sentimentalism had taken ownership of Christianity, causing its motives to be unsound and misdirected. By teaching the consequences of original sin and ignoring the social laws of Jesus, ministers had lost the message handed down through the gospel. Indeed, the true gospel commanded love of one's neighbor, an obligation largely forgotten in contemporary culture. Having focused on individual sin and repentance, Christianity had become indifferent to the broader social issues.[10]

Contributors to Gladden's beliefs included the president of Williams College Mark Hopkins; English theologian Frederick Robertson; and Horace Bushnell, whose *God in Christ* (1849) deepened the young minister's thinking. Admitting he had no intention of writing like a "theological troglodyte," a term Gladden applied to colleagues whose metaphysical ruminations dominated their conversations, he transformed Christianity into a religion of the present. His *Applied Christianity* (1886), *Burning Questions* (1890), *How Much Is Left of the Old Doctrines?* (1899), *Christianity and Socialism* (1905), and *Present-Day Theology* (1913) were all intended for the average individual, not for scholarly theologians equivocating over doctrinal deadwood. The pragmatic intent in his writings outshone any theological purpose.[11]

Gladden objected to any economic theory that regarded labor as a commodity arising out of a relationship with the employer. The assumption that labor was regulated solely by supply and demand was a pernicious and self-defeating notion that augmented human degradation and suffering. The welfare of any nation required a high degree of good health and the independence of its citizens. The laboring class was society's lifeblood, not to be bought at the cheapest price. Rejecting scientific socialism, with its doctrines of economic determinism and class conflict, Gladden called for labor's right to organize, for government reform, for improved race and industrial relations, and for a new approach to poverty. Socialism, he explained, was the "reaction of a scourged and outraged humanity against the greed and rapacity of the individualistic régime." If forced to decide between *laissez-faire* capitalism and socialism, he willingly chose the latter, admitting that he was "nearer to Karl Marx and the Socialists than to Herbert Spencer and the Anarchists." But genuine socialism was of the heart and spirit, not in the letter. Socialism's single most important commandment, "Thou shalt love thy neighbor as thyself," trumped all. Everything else was ancillary.[12]

In his *Applied Christianity*, Gladden noted that as the world grew richer, millions were left in poverty. Attempting to reconcile the scriptural connection between prosperity and righteousness, and the long-held belief that wealth was indicative of God's favor, he concluded that wealth was not itself an evil; in fact, it came as a blessing to humankind. The problem lay in its inequitable distribution. Referring frequently to Henry George, Henry James, Sr., and Edward Bellamy, Gladden advocated for a social contract between the churches and the communities they served. The social service aspect of Christianity became both a motive force and an ideal. As someone schooled in the Puritan tradition, he reached out for an ethical and practical interpretation of the Christian experience—one that was free of doubts and misunderstandings. "It was not an individualistic pietism that appealed to me; it was a religion that laid hold upon life with both hands, and proposed, first and foremost, to realize the Kingdom of God in this world." Noting the changes that had taken place over the course of his lifetime, from politics and science to the higher criticism, one particular phenomenon caught his attention—namely, that "Religion is nothing but Friendship; friendship with God and with men."[13]

Not unlike other social reformers in his day, Gladden protested private ownership of the railroads, telegraph, oil, gas, water, and other service commodities. These "outrageous monopolies" demanded public justice. He likewise took exception to the stock exchange, a venture that routinely gambled on "the life-blood of our commerce." Although he admitted that no solution could remove *all* inequities, he insisted that humankind find fairer ways to share in the advantages of civilized society. He supported the redistribution of wealth through taxation while leaving untouched the laws of trade. He opposed private charity because it left able-bodied working people carelessly dependent. At the same time, though, he felt that much could be done to support the physical and moral welfare of the poorer classes. This included making available free public libraries and good schools; giving labor the right to organize; bringing capitalists and laborers together in associations; and, most importantly, recognizing that economic laws, like moral laws, could never be fulfilled without love.[14]

Gladden applauded the Knights of Labor and similar organizations that supported the laboring class; he likewise encouraged the efforts of wage laborers to introduce cooperative industries, referring to the need for a well-regulated phalanstery, a concept borrowed from Fourierism.[15] Gladden referred to the United States as a plutocracy in the making since political power resided in a Congress paid to carry out the wishes of the moneyed class. Only Christian socialism could end this threat peaceably. This did not, however, imply a centralized bureaucracy, widespread government ownership, or limits to individual freedom. Private property and private enterprise could remain if they were infused with "a larger measure of good-will." Only when Christian law applied to the relationship between worker and employer would the twin elements of selfless love and benevolence— ideas derived from Henry James, Sr., and Jonathan Edwards—bring progress and happiness to humankind, secure individual and social welfare, eliminate the evils of intemperance, and remove the antisocial forces assailing the family.[16]

Treating the social sciences as support mechanisms for achieving his goal, Gladden relied on them to predict with greater probability the nature and circumstances of the path being taken by humankind. "I do not think I am claiming too much when I say that Sociology, the Science of Human Welfare, is at once the most comprehensive and the noblest of the sciences." It provided the tools and methodology to understand and direct Christian care and philanthropic sentiment toward the poor, offered practical ways to address social issues such as intemperance, and rendered a clearer elucidation of Christianity's theological truths. In effect, the social gospelers combined religion and sociology to nourish and support the demand for reforms, supplying ideas that would eventually be realized in the later progressive movement.[17]

Gladden avoided comparing the social gospel with European-style socialism, fearing that it would lead to economic and political inertia. He did not doubt that true socialism would eventually succeed in some distant future, but few people were of sufficient intelligence and educational background to make it work during his time. Up to that point, no state or population had attained the standard required for its success. "With the vast illiterate and unassimilated elements of our national life, with so many millions who are separated from the commonwealth and from one another by the barriers of race and language, it would be, indeed, a mock Socialism which we should succeed, at this juncture, in setting up." Until the realization of true socialism, the ingrained tendency of human nature would continue to direct "every man for himself." Thus, Gladden encouraged industry to establish departments dedicated to public service and the principle of good will, a clear reflection of Swedenborg's doctrine of usefulness.[18]

In his *Christianity and Socialism,* Gladden treated the Sermon on the Mount as the cornerstone for societal reconstruction. As it represented the core of Jesus's teachings, it should be looked upon as the obligation of every political democracy. Unfortunately, under the economic system at that time, labor had become a commodity "bought in the cheapest market and sold in the dearest," causing personal relations to fall into the hands of blind fate. Instead of wars between nations, there were class wars within each nation's borders. Worse still, the churches upon which the working classes depended for support were "mostly on the employer's side in this warfare." With industrial conflict raging and with power concentrated in the hands of a few, the laborer was helpless in bargaining for his needs, forcing a condition that Gladden identified as "practical vassalage."[19]

Along with other social gospelers, Gladden shared a great fondness for Theodore Roosevelt, whom he identified as having a vision for the nation and the wisdom needed to harness its vast combinations of capital. Roosevelt alone had the energy and the capacity to address the many injustices that were carried out under the flag of *laissez-faire*. Gladden also admired the work of New York City mayor Seth Low; the municipal experiments that were taking place in Galveston, Texas and Des Moines, Iowa; and the numerous town and city governments in Great Britain whose boards, councils, and commissions governed in place of single individuals. These distributive forms of authority enabled municipal ownership of public service industries— such as light, gas, trolley, and water—that rightfully belonged to the people. "No such control as this over the public welfare," he insisted, "can rationally be delegated by the people to any private agency." Sounding remarkably similar to Henry George, Gladden reminded his readers that private ownership of the public service industries had corrupted government. "If in any city there are ten or twenty or two hundred millions of dollars invested by private persons or corporations in public-service industries, these millions, as human nature goes, are directly interested in having bad government in that city."[20]

Gladden's work in the Congregational Church led to his appointment to the American Christian Commission, an organization that initially provided medical supplies and religious literature to Union troops in the Civil War but that later became a vehicle for broad ethical and altruistic programs across different sectors of society. Observing that "nothing walks with aimless feet," he stood at the forefront of the social gospel movement, warning that if corrections were not made to the outstanding injustices of the day, including the so-called "Negro Problem," the nation's fragile democracy might devolve into antisocial impulses, antipathies, and resentments of calamitous proportions. These concerns emerged out of what he called the "foolishness" and outright "vindictiveness" of Reconstruction politics, the unprincipled and "despotic brigandage" of the Tweed Ring and the Crédit Mobilier, and the rapacious power of corporations "wielding and controlling immense aggregations of money" to advance their own selfish purposes.[21]

The building blocks for Gladden's pragmatic theology stressed "God working in us," Christ as "the ideal man," the Church as "the central organ of the social organism," the Bible as inspired but not infallible, and belief in love. These became the shibboleths that he applied to the individual and to society.[22] That Christianity could save society was best explained in his *Tools and the Man* (1893) and *Ruling Ideas of the Present Age* (1895), the latter of which grew out of lectures delivered at Yale, Oxford, and Dartmouth. With unsparing precision, he attacked the economic principles of Adam Smith, David Ricardo, and Thomas Malthus, pointing out the fact that pursuing one's own welfare was consistent with both good economics and good Christianity. Adopting Orestes A. Brownson's definition that "property is communion with God through the material world," he proclaimed his support for a Christian form of socialism as the preferred path to the future.[23] Gladden repeatedly looked for answers in some form of Christian socialism, noting that "in many of their ideas and methods, Socialists and Christians are in closest sympathy."[24] Though plainly influenced by European socialism, Gladden's program of reconstruction remained more faithful to American middle-class values than to any desire to equalize property or opportunity.

Despite his clear advocacy of social reform, Gladden shared a blind spot with many other white Americans of the post-Reconstruction era. Specifically, he sought an accommodation with the South by agreeing that emancipation had thrown tremendous burdens on its white citizens, in much the same way that immigration from Southern and Eastern Europe (particularly of Catholics) threatened to undermine democratic institutions in the North. Gladden's views were not unlike those of the Immigration Restriction League—formed in 1894 by New Englanders Prescott F. Hall, Robert DeCourcy Ward, Charles Warren, and John Fiske—which represented a partnership between Northern legislators fearful of the consequences of accepting immigrants from nondemocratic countries and Southerners seeking sympathetic ears for their post-Reconstruction race issues. Working together, they produced the most restrictive immigration law in the nation's history, including differential immigration quotas that gave preference to those from Western Europe. As a condition for Southern votes, Northern legislators acquiesced to the South's legislative efforts at disenfranchisement and segregation. Having accepted the implications of social Darwinism, both sections of the country found it reasonable to argue that black people, along with the "lesser races" from Southern and Eastern Europe, were incapable of progressing at the same pace as were whites from Western Europe. Science became an "objective" tool for justifying immigration restriction and segregation. As there was no science or social science whose data dismissed the significance of racial differences, common opinion held that it was a grave mistake for civilized societies to ignore or otherwise minimize what physical and cultural evolution had "proven." Society first had to be made safe before it could be made democratic.[25]

Gladden nonetheless considered it the duty of the Northern states to assist their Southern brethren in providing elementary education for the vast numbers of illiterate black people. Choosing not to challenge the Southern insistence that the races be kept socially separate, he countered by arguing that the nine or more million black people were justified in having their own teachers and leaders who must be well-trained and competent. "If all social contact between the races is to be prevented, then it will not be seemly for a white physician to practice medicine in a black man's home, nor for a white lawyer to do business for a black client; the race must have its own doctors and lawyers, and they must be men of skill and learning." Accordingly, he supported the work being done for the benefit of black people by the American Missionary Association at many colleges and universities in the South.[26]

Lyman Abbott

A native of Roxbury, Massachusetts, whose lineage extended back to the Puritans, Lyman Abbott (1835–1922) graduated from New York University in 1853 and joined the bar in 1856 before abandoning it for the ministry in 1860. Following successful pastorates at the Congregational Church in Terre Haute, Indiana (1860–65), and the New England Church in New York City (1865–69), he was associate editor for *Harper's Magazine;* was editor of the *Illustrated Christian Weekly;* and held joint editorship with Henry Ward Beecher of *The Christian Union,* where he eventually became editor-in-chief. In 1888, he succeeded Beecher as pastor of the prestigious Plymouth Avenue

Congregationalist Church in Brooklyn, earning himself a reputation as one of the nation's premier preachers. An advocate of social reform, the single tax, and progressive evolutionism, Abbott taught that humankind was approaching the perfection of Jesus. As a leader among the pro-Darwin forces in the Congregational Church, he considered science and faith compatible in that evolution conformed to Christian thinking—the immanent God working toward universal harmony. In effect, evolution certified a universe governed by law and offering an idea of human destiny more dazzling than that which any of the early perfectionists could have imagined. Evolution made the problem of evil little more than a maladjustment in nature, destined to disappear in time. It forced the abandonment of age-old beliefs and practices, replacing them with a philosophy that defined truth not as something fixed once and for all time but as a set of beliefs that worked toward the best possible purposes.[27]

Abbott's writings included *Christianity and Social Problems* (1896), *The Theology of an Evolutionist* (1897), *The Rights of Man* (1901), *The Personality of God* (1905), *Christ's Secret of Happiness* (1907), and *The Spirit of Democracy* (1910). His *Christianity and Social Problems*, consisting of lectures delivered at the Meadville Theological School in Pennsylvania and articles contributed to *The Forum, North American Review, Century Magazine, Cosmopolitan,* and *Outlook,* announced that the kingdom of God would be at hand following a spiritual revolution in which each individual became servant to the many. Treating sin as a disease that evoked compassion, and religious rituals as an empty "sackcloth and ashes," Abbott called for charity toward all, an end to autocratic governance, and the transition to more democratic organizations, like the YMCA and Salvation Army, dedicated to teaching and service.[28]

Abbott enjoyed the admiration of those in the New Church who found common cause in his beliefs. Several Swedenborgian periodicals, including *The New Christianity,* tracked his reform efforts and reported on his speeches and sermons.[29] In one of many letters published in *Outlook,* Abbott attributed his beliefs to the writings of Swedenborg, noting that, "My friends say that I am a good deal of a Swedenborgian."[30] Accordingly, he criticized the country's unabashed individualism, which he said ignored the social obligations that came with humanity's stewardship of earth. Christianity was a social religion that relied on the principles and precepts of Jesus to address the contemporary scene. Socialism and Christianity agreed in the need for a reorganization of society to "give a greater diffusion of virtue, intelligence, and power." This was not an imperative drawn from the environment but an understanding that growth began with the individual and worked outward to the social regeneration of the whole society.[31]

Abbott urged the adoption of the referendum and the direct election of senators; remonstrated against the concentration of wealth and the perils of corruption; endorsed both the progressive income tax and the inheritance tax; advocated for the single tax; and argued against communism. Humanity's rightful use of property was an essential test of its judgment before God. Each person who owned property was a trustee, not to acquire special privilege or exclusive possession, but to work for the good of humanity. Only the use of one's abilities and capacities on behalf of the larger community justified the acquisition of wealth. "Christianity agrees with Socialism in recognizing the mutual dependence of men, and classes of men, on each other . . . ; but it differs from Socialism in putting first, both as an end in itself and as a means to social reconstruction, the reconstruction of the individual."[32]

Abbott aligned Christian socialism with democracy, protecting legitimate property rights, advocating for the pursuit of happiness, endorsing the sanctity of the family, and relegating all aspects of life to the teachings of Jesus. He believed that Jesus's teachings abolished class distinctions between capitalist and laborer by directing both to the law of *service*. "Labor is honorable, service is honorable; to live without labor, without serving, is dishonorable." As the son of a carpenter, Jesus had shown the importance of honest labor and the imperative of making the world a better place. His standard for success did not include the accumulation of material things but instead involved the achievement of an ethical state for which individual character was the true test. "The condemnation of an evil use is not the same as the condemnation of all use; and the mere fact that it is always the abuse, not the use, of property which is condemned, implies that there is a use which is commendable." Christian socialism placed no prohibition on industry or acquisitiveness, provided that it furthered love and service.[33]

As explained by Abbott, industrial capitalism had failed to provide employment to all who wanted work and had failed to provide a living wage for those who did. Even worse, it allowed the employer to hire labor in the cheapest market, a condition that placed workers in a perpetual conflict with the capitalist system. With labor defined as a commodity, there could be no "common enterprise" between capital and labor. Not until the precepts of Jesus coincided with the principles of sound political economy would the welfare of the laborer and the prosperity of the capitalist both be assured. Accordingly, he urged government to act as peacemaker and impartial tribunal to reconcile the differences between capital and labor, support the principle of nonresistance, and substitute reason in place of force in determining matters of social justice.[34]

Just as aggregations of capital existed to further management's interests, so too, labor was entitled to form associations to protect its interests. Abbott endorsed the Railway Union, the Brotherhood of Carpenters and Joiners, the Iron Molders' Union, the International Typographical Union, the Knights of Labor, and similar organizations to counter the power of the corporation and trust. Drawing from Daniel J. Ryan's *Arbitration between Capital and Labor* (1885) and Richard T. Ely's *Labor Movement in America* (1886), he recommended boards of arbitration and conciliation as substitutes for the strike. "Christ's first principle for the settlement of controversies is conciliation; his second, arbitration; the third is law." In this manner, labor and capital could cooperate in a common enterprise, adjusting their self-interest with love and brotherhood. A champion of a modified capitalism, Abbott aimed to rescue the nation's middle class from classical economics by replacing the prevailing wage-labor theory with a more compassionate worldview postulated on the progressive evolution of humankind and society.[35]

Walter Rauschenbusch

Considered the most articulate of the social gospelers and the leading theologian of their movement, Walter Rauschenbusch (1861–1918) urged Christians to carry Christ's communal message to the world. Alongside such reformers as Richard Ely, Jane Addams, and Theodore Roosevelt, Rauschenbusch offered a spiritual and evangelical message emphasizing collective repentance and a rebirth of society. In many ways, he represented the collaboration of the liberal and evangelical traditions within Protestantism. The liberal tradition brought to his social gospel optimism, a denial of sin's permanence, an acceptance of the higher criticism, and the benefits of science and evolutionary theory. The evangelical tradition emphasized a hunger for the kingdom of God, a fervor for an urgent end to injustice and inhumanity, and a belief in the immediacy of God's hand in the tasks ahead. By bringing these two together, Rauschenbusch's social gospel valued action over belief, and modest goals over idealistic crusades, in an agenda that treated secular and religious solutions with equal enthusiasm.

Born into a German immigrant family that had turned from Lutheran to Baptist, Rauschenbusch experienced conversion at age seventeen; studied economics and theology at the University of Berlin; became an admirer of Fabian socialism; and began his ministry in 1886 as pastor of the Second German Baptist Church, which stood on the edge of New York City's Hell's Kitchen. With his inaugural sermon based on Jesus's words, "Thy Kingdom Come," he explained that the spread of Christianity worldwide signaled that the kingdom was close at hand. An admirer of Henry George, Tolstoy, Jacob Riis, and Italian liberal Giuseppe Mazzini, he envisioned the church as a force to end poverty, disease, and lawlessness. A passionate advocate for social change, and optimistic about what could be achieved, he deliberately avoided what he saw to be the unnecessary distraction of abstract religious theories. Instead, he committed his energies to a reconstruction of society—a kingdom of God marked by democratic changes to the economy—leaving others to spend their time addressing the tortured theology of sin and redemption. The hope for the future of humanity lay under the pall of such social sins as war, militarism, religious bigotry, the combination of graft and political power, and class contempt more so than it suffered by the sins of individuals. This difference lay at the heart of the social gospel and in particular of Rauschenbusch's distinctive blend of social justice and spiritual regeneration.

Rauschenbusch witnessed poverty firsthand among struggling families on Manhattan's West Side. Thus, when the Society of Christian Socialists formed in 1889, he quickly associated himself with its reformist agenda. In 1892, he, along with Nathaniel Schmidt and Leighton Williams, founded the Brotherhood of the Kingdom, a nondenominational society of social gospelers whose members endorsed the spirit of brotherhood intended by Jesus. Its publications included numerous influential works, the most important being Rauschenbusch's *Christianity and the Social Crisis* (1907), which became a bestseller among pastors and seminarians. Not unlike the Society of Jesus in Roman Catholicism, the Brotherhood set forth as its goal the realization of the ethical principles of Jesus and the social justice aspects of Christianity. With issues that included the single tax, direct legislation, and municipal governance, the Brotherhood affirmed the goals of Christian socialism while standing apart from Marxism and from any formal party structure. They were faithful to a more practical form of socialism that focused on inheritance taxes, unions, and selective areas of public ownership.[36] "We are concerned with principles, not with methods," Rauschenbusch insisted. "We are evolutionists, not revolutionists. . . . In this sense we are Socialist . . . in the spirit rather than the letter."[37]

After eleven years as pastor, Rauschenbusch returned to his former Rochester Theological Seminary, where he taught that mainline Protestantism had lost its moral compass by allying almost wholly with the nation's economic and political establishment. Calling on the churches to address the lives destroyed by unregulated capitalism, he made one of the more powerful statements in the literature of prophetic Christianity by indicting religion's ceremonialism and priestly hierarchy for its neglect of the common man. Believing that Jesus's authentic teachings corrected this complacency, he called for the displacement of the status quo.[38] His indictment of industrial society was trenchant, particularly his reference to the supremacy of corporate property rights over the lives and welfare of the people. "The most fundamental evils in past history and present conditions were due to converting stewardship into ownership." He thus implied that Jesus had revolutionary aims that were social in nature. When Jesus spoke of the kingdom of God, Rauschenbusch reasoned, he did not intend a heavenly future, but one attainable *in* history, toward which all must work. "Theology must become christocentric; political economy must become anthropocentric. Man is Christianized when he puts God before self; political economy will be Christianized when it puts man before wealth. Socialistic political economy does that." Intending to make Christianity a vital force in the conflict between rich and poor, between ceremony and morality, he called for a return to Jesus's writings. "Jesus was not a mere social reformer. . . . He has been called the first socialist."[39]

In his *Christianizing the Social Order* (1912), a reworking of lectures delivered at Pacific Theological Seminary and Ohio Wesleyan University, Rauschenbusch suggested a Fabian form of socialism in which quality of life was guided by the ethical teachings of Jesus. His contrast between Christianity and capitalism remained sharp. "Christianity teaches the unity and solidarity of men; capitalism reduces that teaching to a harmless expression of sentiment by splitting society into two antagonistic sections, unlike in their work, their income, their pleasures, and their point of view." This contrast appeared on almost every page. Similarly, he cautioned against placing too much faith in personal salvation or in human perfectibility since evil existed in every social organization; evil was not a defect that would disappear over time. While sympathetic to the goals of modern or scientific socialism, he felt true reform had to be spiritual above all else, with good works resulting from the experience of God's grace. Otherwise, reform resembled the furtive efforts of good works that were tainted by personal impulses, none of which reflected spiritual renewal.[40]

In his *A Theology for the Social Gospel* (1917), a classic expression of theological liberalism, Rauschenbusch expressed a moral passion for the welfare of humankind that exceeded his belief in individual salvation. Dedicated to Augustus Hopkins Strong, former teacher and president of the seminary at Rochester, Rauschenbusch's book treated the social gospel as a permanent addition to Christian religion. In partnership with the social and psychological sciences, the social gospel sought to restore the democratic teachings of Jesus to the institutions of the Church. Rather than according with the order of traditional thinking that held the individual's relationship to God to be the dynamic by which one was judged, Rauschenbusch claimed that moral and social relationships counted more. Sin was social, not individual; it existed beyond any interior sense of one's own personal transgressions, afflicting the greater human sphere (e.g., disease, wars that created public debt, and churches that introduced "unbelievable creeds"). This social conception of sin became Rauschenbusch's most valuable contribution to the social gospel.[41]

In no small measure, Rauschenbusch's emphasis on service and sacrifice recast Christian spiritual life by projecting it onto a larger stage—a composite humanity searching for the kingdom of God. In this expanded context of power and aggrandizement, militarism, and corporate greed, individual culpability diminished and sin jumped to the societal level. "If unearned gain is the chief corrupter of professions, institutions, and combinations of men," he wrote, paraphrasing Henry George, "these super-personal beings will be put on the road to salvation when their graft is in some way cut off and they are compelled to subsist on the reward of honest service."[42] Without disregarding critical elements of doctrinal theology, he introduced an enlarged vision that involved whole communities in a renewal of spiritual life, projecting a kingdom on earth that matched the vision of Swedenborg's redeemed society of the Universal Human.

A popularizer more than an original thinker, Rauschenbusch set out to convince middle-class America of the dangers caused by the distorted and unequal distribution of wealth and power. The essential radicalism of his thought lay in his solidarity with the oppressed and his view of government as a source of security in an increasingly insecure world. Still, the social gospel movement remained predominantly religious, with cautious recognition of the limitations of legislation. In its clearest form, it redeemed the historical life of humanity from the social wrongs that impeded redemption. Salvation required the individual to turn from self to God and humanity. "The saint of the future will need not only a theocentric mysticism which enables him to realize God, but an anthropocentric mysticism which enables him to realize his fellow-men in God. The more we approach pure Christianity, the more will the Christian signify a man who loves mankind with a religious passion and excludes none."[43]

The First World War, the Great War, discouraged Rauschenbusch, who saw its moral complexity threatening much of what he believed in. As Europe's Christian nations became consumed in the conflict, it pained him to see that Americans had taken sides with the Allies. Believing that Germany was not as villainous as it was portrayed in the press, he wrote "Be Fair to Germany," an article whose publication caused a backlash and called his patriotism into question. Abandoned by friends, including fellow Baptists, he watched from the sidelines as the United States declared war in April of 1917. He died on July 25, 1918, four months before the Armistice.[44]

New Church Dissonance

The specter of strikes, lockouts, depressions, boycotts, and violence that had influenced the labors of Gladden, Abbott, and Rauschenbusch drew an inordinate number of Swedenborgians to question the New Church's perceived aloofness to worldly events. In the opinion of the Church's center-left elements, the history of civilization had been the story of humanity's slow but steady progress, accompanied by the rise of democracy and the expansion of individual freedoms. Governments that had shown the most advancement were those whose citizens were public-spirited and unselfish toward each other. Notwithstanding these milestones, chronic poverty continued to fester in pockets of society, forcing the creation of a labor movement that aimed for a standard of living to which the working classes felt entitled by virtue of their hard work. Labor's objectives were not so much ideological pursuits as they were demands for improvements to existing conditions—shorter working hours, better pay, and improved sanitary surroundings. These demands were not based on greed but instead on an honest belief that laborers were society's real producers, entitled to the benefits of their contributions. The New Church's advocacy of the sphere of usefulness meant tracing all things to their respective causes, including discerning the role of a person's will and understanding, the progressive degrees of love or charity present, and the states of potential regeneration. A new era had arrived (1880–1920), one in which—the New Church had concluded—a period of constructive change was at hand.[45]

Individual Swedenborgians and New Church members—albeit without official church support—became active participants in and promoters of the social gospel movement. Exemplary of this was Rev. Lewis Pyle Mercer, president of the Chicago Society, who delivered a sermon titled "Christianity and Society" before a meeting of the Christian Socialists in 1891. This was followed by Rev. Chauncey Giles of Philadelphia, who initiated a series of talks on "The Application of Christian Principles to the Administration of Public Affairs."[46] Others, like the Swedenborgian artist and philosopher Thomas Mower Martin, noted that the New Church had found the body politic "adrift without competent leaders [and] prey to trusts, combines, and corporations who sap the very foundations of the laws of justice and equity by bribing the law-makers and altering the laws for their own aggrandizement." Society had fallen into a "state of turmoil and unrest, no longer satisfied with the old order or the old leaders and teachers, and yet not knowing where to look for better ones, and very much in need of guidance on the natural and spiritual-natural planes of its life." In response to this extremity, Martin urged the New Church to broaden its field of social activity, saying that it must awaken to "the fact that the era of destructive criticism is passing and that of constructiveness beginning." This did not require that every minister become a social reformer, but only that they repeat the principles set forth in Swedenborg's writings. "As it is only in the New Church that knowledge of such civil and moral laws as correspond to spiritual laws can be acquired," he continued, "it follows that to teach concerning them is the plain duty of that Church."[47]

Despite Martin's encouragement, the Church declined such advice. As one of its members remarked, there was "too much surrendering of pulpit conscientiousness to the worldly wishes of congregations."[48] In chapel addresses by members of the faculty of the Meadville Theological School in 1909, there was general agreement that the social gospel concerned justice and mercy; however, Jesus was *not* a socialist and his kingdom was *not* of this world. "The social gospel for now, utilizing the truth of the New Testament," reminded Rev. Nicholas P. Gilman, professor of sociology and ethics at the school, "will emphasize the great institutions of human nature—the family, justice to the workman, and do away with the sins of corporations as worse than personal sins." Beyond this form of instruction, the New Church should remain neutral.[49]

By the 1912 presidential election, attitudes had begun to change, albeit ever so slowly. Writing in the *The New-Church Review,* Louis G. Hoeck, pastor of the Church of the New Jerusalem in Brooklyn, addressed the application of Christianity to the management of human affairs, and in particular to the nation's economic condition and the distribution of wealth. In all areas—from banking to questions of profit sharing, compulsory arbitration, postal savings banks, fixed wages, and the eight-hour workday—there was room for the application of religion according to love of one's neighbor. Of all the issues Hoeck highlighted, though, he considered monopoly to be the worst; it was evil in and of itself and not simply the abuse of a good thing. "Monopoly is an impossibility where all are equal and free," he wrote. "It destroys equality of opportunity to earn a living." Aligning himself with Roosevelt, Hoeck considered monopoly to be the "veritable antithesis of the Brotherhood of man in Christian Economics." Among its worst examples were the public utility corporations that supplied gas, electricity, telephone service, and street railroads.[50]

Of the seventy-six million people in the country, Hoeck pointed out, "seventy-six men, holding among them sixteen hundred directorships, are said to control fully one hundred of the greatest railroad, industrial and banking corporations, with a capital equal to one-fifth of the national wealth." Vast fortunes were being made without any return of the spoils to society. "Excessive profits gained through privilege, or gains reaped without giving anything in return, are robbery, and proportionally hurtful to the commonwealth." Monopoly was a corporate evil that needed to be addressed by the nation as a whole since the individual was powerless to deal with it. Government must work in the interests of the nation.[51] As did other social gospelers, Hoeck turned to Roosevelt as someone who had the courage and the stature to bring the nation's power to bear on monopolies. While it was not the duty of the Church to prescribe the nature of the reform, it was imperative that it denounce the evil as contrary to the Lord's commandments.[52]

In one of the more incisive analyses on the matter of the social gospel, Rev. William F. Wunsch compared L. B. De Beaumont's *Spiritual Reconstruction and the Religious Unrest of the Age* (1918) with Walter Rauschenbusch's *A Theology for the Social Gospel* (1917). De Beaumont, president of the Swedenborg Society in London, offered a view of reconstruction based on the theological works of Swedenborg but saw no reason to overhaul them simply to accommodate matters in the outside world. In his assessment of De Beaumont's position, Wunsch found little connection between Swedenborg's formulation of doctrines for a renewed Christianity and the moral matters confronting the modern world. "This theology Dr. De Beaumont proceeds agilely enough to sketch," remarked Wunsch, "but when he reaches the crux of the whole process of reconstruction,—bridging from the idea, especially if it is germinal, to the grown application to the present need,—he goes lame."[53] By contrast, Rauschenbusch presented a plan to rebuild in the name of the social gospel. Covering familiar Christian teachings, he focused on sin in the form of government despotism, the evils of states that focused on aggrandizement and militarism, and the predatory powers that motivated industry and finance. For Rauschenbusch, the solution came from the community, not from the individual. Only as a community could society realize the kingdom of God in its vision as the "larger neighbor," or, as Swedenborg would say, Universal Human. Wunsch found in Rauschenbusch's writings the very basis of Swedenborg's doctrine of the Universal Human: "Swedenborg's spiritual world is the warrant and reward and great consummation of the social gospel."[54]

Another member of the New Church, Rev. E. M. Lawrence Gould, pastor of the Church of the Neighbor in Brooklyn, explained that the history of civilization had been the story of the rise of democracy. Unfortunately, the average worker was far from receiving the full enjoyment of their rights. "The National Census for 1900 gives the average yearly wage of 700,000 textile workers as $315. . . . It says that the average yearly wage of 223,000 iron workers was $543, and that of the men employed in shoe factories was $473." To make matters worse, since most of the workers did not have a sufficient enough education to formulate a social program, they were forced to rely on self-appointed and professional interpreters who did not always work in their interests. In most European countries, labor parties had been established with the hope that a revolution could take place by political means. However, the religion that grew out of this philosophy had been deistic, acknowledging not a personal God but an impersonal force identified with evolution and sometimes with the collective spirit of the race. The New Church, Gould advised, must never become a partisan in that struggle. Still, there were aspects of it that the Church could support, including the importance of work and the spiritual dignity of honest labor.[55]

Though obviously not a substitute for religion, New Church reformers regarded sociology as the discipline most poised to serve society's temporal needs. Presuming a democratic theory of social change, they thought it possible for society to make tangible changes for socially sanctioned purposes. Thus, when the New Church spoke of social consciousness, it referred to society as an organism whose spiritual regeneration impacted the social and economic conditions of its citizens. As Rev. Hiram Vrooman, pastor of the Church of the New Jerusalem in Providence, Rhode Island, explained, "waves of social consciousness" were sweeping over American society and were indicative of a new age "wherein progress both natural and spiritual is unprecedented."[56]

By the later decades of the nineteenth and early years of the twentieth centuries, several highly respected members of the New Church had become outspoken advocates of reform—though not necessarily for socialism—pressuring the Church's publications to give space to their cause. This liberal contingent included Unitarian minister Benjamin F. Barrett; George Bush, professor of Hebrew and Oriental literature at New York University; Charles H. Mann, who saw usefulness as being a church's only purpose; and Chauncey Giles, pastor of New Church Societies in Cincinnati, New York, and Philadelphia, as well as the former editor of *The New-Church Messenger*. Also notable among this group were Lillian Beekman, teacher of science in the Academy Girls School at Bryn Athyn; Alfred H. Stroh of the Swedenborg Scientific Association; Lewis F. Hite, professor of philosophy at the New Church Theological School in Cambridge; and Frank Sewall, president of Urbana University. Finally, there were the pharmaceutical manufacturers Albert and Gustav Tafel; John Worcester, who was among the first in the Church to accept evolution; William F. Wunsch, professor at the New Church Theological School in Cambridge, Massachusetts; Paul Sperry, former president of the Swedenborgian denomination known informally as Convention; and John R. Swanton, one of the founding members of the Swedenborg Scientific Association.

Thomas A. King, pastor of the Chicago Society, who regarded the New Church as truly apostolic and catholic, urged it to become more socially conscious. "If we are a cult," he explained, "we can move away from the great centers of life, fence ourselves in, study Swedenborg's writings, condemn all that is not of ourselves, and go on thanking God that we are not as other men. Being a church, we must act as a church, and do the work of a church. We must live in the world and be a part of its great life, and in touch with men." King insisted that the Church retain its holy mission by bringing people to faith and repentance. By implication, this meant bringing its message to the poor, ignorant, and neglected people in the slums. "I have never had any sympathy whatever with the thought that the New Church is to be confined in its spiritual work, to the educated and refined men and women in the community.... As the Lord's representative in the world," it had to be a "living church with a catholic spirit, catholic heart, catholic outlook and work." Its mission was for all regardless of their condition—from educated to ignorant and openly sinful.[57]

James Reed, author of numerous Swedenborgian works and pastor of the Boston Society of the New Jerusalem, pointed to evidence on the natural plane of human experience that demonstrated the visible manifestations of a changed state in the life of humankind following the Last Judgment. On the basis of this postulate, he encouraged an awakened social consciousness, supporting public education; reforming prisons; and organizing hospitals for the poor, aged, and feeble-minded. All of these efforts were signs of a new age preparatory to the Universal Human. "One plain inference from the doctrine of the Greatest Man is that the common good is to be held superior to that of individuals." Individualism was not destroyed by collectivism, since personal duties and responsibilities were best realized in fellowship. Only when the actions of service became spontaneous expressions of love did they result in a wholesome influence on character. Falling back on the Swedenborgian aphorism, "All religion is of life, and the life of religion is to do good," Reed urged those with wealth to live in the consciousness of the Lord's presence.[58]

Retrenchment

The advocacy of a progressive solution to society's ills resulted in several unanticipated consequences. One notable example involved a special Swedenborgian edition of *The Christian Socialist* (March 15, 1910), whose editor, Rev. Edward Ellis Carr, printed special issues every several months that contained articles written by ministers and laypersons from a particular denomination or sect in support of Christian socialism.[59] Carr had already published many such special issues—Presbyterian, Baptist, Episcopal, Methodist, Church of Christ, Catholic, and Lutheran—but he lacked one from the New Church. So he reached out to Alfred J. Johnson of London; Rev. A. B. Francisco, pastor of the Humboldt Park Church in Chicago; Rev. Arthur Mercer, pastor of the Brooklyn Society; Rev. Herbert C. Small, pastor of the Indianapolis Society; and Rev. Hiram Vrooman of Rhode Island. They all accepted his invitation to address the problems of capitalism and called on the nation's theological schools, awakening them to the moral, political, and economic plight of the laboring class. Each rendered strong support for Christian socialism, arguing that its agenda aligned with Swedenborg's efforts to regenerate Christianity. In their articles, they made frequent reference to the doctrines of correspondences and usefulness, connecting civil and moral laws to the celestial world of divine purposes.[60]

Alfred J. Johnson challenged local, state, and national governments to provide the proper environment in which every person could perform useful actions for others. The practical application of the doctrine, he explained, passed under the name of socialism, whose objective was furtherance of the common good, meaning "to intervene and to provide fitting environment for all its citizens, and thus equal opportunities for all to develop those lives for which their individual capacities best fit them." The mutual roles of church and state were to make ideal citizens who, in turn, made good angels. Quoting Swedenborg, "He who is a civil and moral man can also be made spiritual, for what is civil and moral is the receptacle of what is spiritual."[61]

Rev. A. B. Francisco pointed out the degree to which Swedenborg had emphasized the Lord's regard for humanity "according to his use, and to men in the mass according to uses united in the form of a man." It was not the individual person but the "Giant Man," as once described by Louis F. Post, who appeared before the Lord.[62] Rev. Arthur Mercer added to this reasoning by emphasizing that the unjust industrial and social conditions that prevailed in the workplace should be confronted with love, community, and service.

> In an age of perfected machinery, of tremendous industrial development, of unexampled material opulence, with the wealth-producing power of society equal to any demand that human need could make upon it, we have conditions of unemployment at the base of our social structure, large numbers of people willing to work yet constantly on the verge of destitution. We have thousands of poor families compelled to set their women and little children at hard labor to eke out a scanty wage, and still below these a submerged class, steeped in hopeless poverty, which hatches out with the same inexorable fatality by which eggs produce chickens, every kind of moral delinquency, pauperism, vagabondage, vice, and

crime. While on these conditions as a foundation we have a social edifice filled with people enjoying every comfort, and, on the topmost floor of all, vast swollen fortunes and unexampled, idle, self-pampering luxury.[63]

Surely, Mercer argued, poverty was not of God but was a human-made artifice. Brooding over the theories of property ownership that simply justified the existing political and economic fabric, he saw nothing as being wasteful of human potential. The conditions of labor were evidence of "wage-slavery" and the oppression of the dispossessed. Worse yet, out of this displacement of wealth came the revenues that built churches. That the temples of God should be silent in light of such injustices was wrong. He called on the churches to accept culpability for their collusion with the wealthy classes and called on capitalists to Christianize their industries by replacing the existing laws of competition with those of love, mutuality, and cooperation.[64] Similarly, Rev. Herbert C. Small insisted that there could be no cure for poverty by continuing the existing system of capitalism, as it encouraged divisiveness by appealing to brute instincts and self-preservation. "The vision of the common good and the possibility of mutual service," he explained, "is destroyed by Capitalism."[65] Rev. Hiram Vrooman, who drew many of his beliefs from the settlements of Toynbee and Mansfield Hall in England, concluded the issue with a dire warning that a crisis of "significant proportions" would result unless immediate steps were taken to ensure cooperation of capital and labor on a national scale.[66]

While the British magazines *New-Church Quarterly, The New-Church Messenger*, and *The Church Reformer* spoke warmly of socialism and endorsed the articles printed in the special Swedenborgian issue of *The Christian Socialist*, the editors of New Church periodicals in the United States distanced themselves from what they saw as a false and misleading solution to society's problems.[67] "We have had to reject in the past, and shall have to do so in the future if they are offered, partisan papers intended by their writers simply to promote the propaganda of current political socialism," remarked H. Clinton Hay, managing editor of *The New-Church Review*, the official organ of the Massachusetts New-Church Union.[68] Lewis F. Hite, editor of *The New-Church Review,* not only rejected the articles but insisted that the authors' views not be mistaken as the official position of the church. "Not one of us would wish to see our Church organization turn aside from its distinctive use of preaching the Gospel . . . by unfolding the spiritual meaning of His Holy Word, to advocate, or even to discuss in a partisan spirit, the issues of the Republican or of the Democratic Party." Nor should the Church identify itself wholly with socialism since it would change the work given to it by the Lord. "The Church cannot become the State without ceasing to be the Church."[69]

In this and other editorials he wrote for *The New-Church Review,* Hite reflected the position of the New-Church Union in that he viewed socialism as both a tendency and a body of doctrine. In other words, it embodied a materialistic mode of thinking and living that imparted any number of compulsory changes to the body politic while, at the same time, intensifying the disparities between the classes, wage-earners, and employers. These matters, however serious, were for Caesar to address, not the Church. The separation was real and necessary. Left unsaid, but implied, was the belief that laws exist to maintain order and protect society against the ill-disposed and the rebellious.[70]

So concerned with the issue was the Cambridge Society of Swedenborgians in Boston that it offered a sample resolution explaining the Church's official position.

> Resolved, That fearing lest these assumptions on the part of the *Christian Socialist,* if silently acquiesced in, should place the New Church in a questionable light before the world, we deem it our imperative duty solemnly to declare, that as a Church, we have, and can have, no practical affiliation with any political or semi-political party, league, or movement whatever, for the reason that the Church's Divine mission is of a purely spiritual nature—assured that what the sincere acceptance of her heavenly doctrines fails to effect on the interrelations of man with man, no shrewdly devised scheme, no popular organization, in short, no mere "arm of flesh"

can possibly accomplish. That, while thus defining the true sphere of the Church, we as individuals, are free to coöperate with any and all who are wisely and conscientiously laboring for the best interests of the people.[71]

The Massachusetts New-Church Union warmly endorsed the resolution, reaffirming its position to have "no practical affiliation with any political or semi-political party, league, or movement whatever, for the reason that the Church's Divine mission is of a purely spiritual nature." Building on the position taken by the Union, the editors announced their intention to reject "partisan papers intended … to promote the propaganda of current political socialism."

The spiritual world being the world of causes, the cause of every form of government that can exist on earth must be there, the orderly uses of it flowing in from heaven and the disorderly uses from hell. And every angel has private property in perfect correspondence with his personal character—garments, furniture, house, land, flocks, gardens, workshops, or his own share in a general workshop in these days of division of labor, and his own tools and machinery, according to the needs and deserts of his use in the community. The common good is always composed of individual contributions which do not cease to be the property of the individual contributors by composing the common good. Indeed, they would become spiritually lifeless, useless, and worthless if they were to lose their organic relation to the individual contributor by ceasing to be his property.[72]

While encouraging members to put their religion into practice, many New Church leaders struggled to keep the functions of church and state separate. If the church endorsed, advocated, sanctioned, or otherwise authorized a particular political, industrial, or social measure, the leadership feared that its action could become a menace to civil liberty. Having been taught the importance of "discrete degrees," they were concerned that those in the New Church would lose sight of the differences separating spiritual and civil government.[73] The editor of *The New Christianity,* for example, stressed that the church, as an organization, had a limited sphere of duty. "She ought not to commit herself by formal resolution or enactment to any reform issue." This did not, however, apply to New Church individuals who, because of their love of justice, "ought to make them fearless in any needed application of justice to the affairs of men."[74]

In general, there seemed to be a consensus that the labor movement did not represent the breadth and depth of the New Church. Nor could economic determinism be a substitute for the spiritual condition of humankind. Better that New Church publications preach the importance of usefulness than force itself into the body politic.[75] As explained by Thomas Mower Martin,

> It is by no means [intended] that every minister of the New Church is to be a social and civil reformer, advocating in the pulpit or on the platform such remedies as, on the social plane are applied to the temperance question, or on the civil plane insisting on the single tax; but simply that he should teach the principles, as set forth in the New-Church doctrines, that inculcate the needful reforms on those planes, leaving the application of these principles to the citizens, just as he has hitherto left the application of the laws of spiritual life to the freedom and rationality of his hearers.[76]

"We are living in an age of free thought," announced Warren Goddard, Jr., instructor at the New Church Theological School. "An unconscious influx of new light from the unseen world has been slowly leading [us] away from all this to a state of greater freedom of thought." The result, however, had been mixed, with one of the effects being the prevalence of false views of life, which in turn lead to industrial and religious strife. Too many self-interested industrial combinations had participated in graft, bribery, and dishonesty. This, in turn, led opponents to find their answers in socialism, the single tax, free trade, and other forms of regulatory legislation. In the field of religion, some were even advocating for Christian Science and New Thought as means of drawing people away from materialism. For Goddard, however, it was important to concentrate on the doctrine of divine humanity and on alerting others to the power of this concept.[77]

By 1921, the church had found a moderately progressive approach to its dilemma, with Lewis F. Hite calling for a new interpretation of the works of Swedenborg that emphasized the meaning of the New Jerusalem on earth. The Bible, he argued, required a reinterpretation so that it might be applied to the specific social conditions of contemporary society. "If we are ever to have an enduring social philosophy, it must be developed out of the nature and life of true love; and it is the New-Church doctrine of love that must give us a New-Church social philosophy." Fearing the "clash of partisans," he implored the church to stand above the "smoke of heated passions" and establish a standard of literary and intellectual quality that rejected any and all articles written with "inflamed partisanship." Only those that began with the principle of divine love in the social, moral, and spiritual realms should be acceptable for publication. "Our doctrine . . . is an expansion of this [New Church] principle [of Divine Love] and takes the form, the Lord is Divine Love, Divine Wisdom, and Divine Use." Since their social philosophy was the development of universal love, it was "the Lord's love of the other through each that constitutes mutual love . . . [and] becomes, when extended to every other, the love of each for all and of all for each." The New Church's social philosophy should reflect the nature of mutual love as it is known in heaven. If followed, the occasions for hate and strife would go away, as would the enormous accumulations of capital. The world, he hoped, would someday look like one vast cooperative society in which "the love of use and service would in a large measure be substituted for the love of gain, the love of the neighbor for the love of self."[78]

Federal Council of Churches

As part of the social gospel movement, various federations formed at the city, county, state, and national levels, including many that were focused on religious issues. The federative idea carried any number of qualifying modifiers, such as *inter-church, inter-denominational, united,* and *general.* Charles Howard Hopkins's *The Rise of the Social Gospel in American Protestantism, 1865–1915* viewed the founding of the Federal Council of Churches as part of the flowering of the social gospel in American Christianity. Together with John A.

Hutchinson's *We Are Not Divided,* the two detailed the marriage of social services with denominational cooperation, the impetus of which originated with the Evangelical Alliance and the Institutional Church League founded in New York in 1894 to promote community awareness among urban churches. The League called for a conference in Philadelphia in 1900, which bore fruit in the National Federation of Churches and Christian Workers. In 1905, the National Federation sponsored the Interchurch Conference of thirty denominations, which drafted the constitution of what became the Federal Council of Churches, an ecclesiastically constituted entity intended for service rather than as an attempt to unite the denominations on the basis of theology or polity.[79]

The first draft of "The Social Creed of the Churches," as it was popularly called, was formulated by the General Conference of the Methodist Episcopal Church in 1908. In December of that year, the Federal Council of the Churches adopted the statement and would go on to reaffirm its ideals at their meetings in 1912 and 1916.[80]

1. Equal rights and justice for all men in all stations of life.

2. Protection of the family by the single standard of purity, uniform divorce laws, proper regulation of marriage, proper housing.

3. The fullest possible development of every child, especially by the provision of education and recreation.

4. Abolition of child labor.

5. Such regulation of the conditions of toil for women as shall safeguard the physical and moral health of the community.

6. Abatement and prevention of poverty.

7. Protection of the individual and society from the social, economic and moral waste of the liquor traffic.

8. Conservation of health.

9. Protection of the worker from dangerous machinery, occupational diseases and mortality.

10. The right of all men to the opportunity for self-maintenance, for safeguarding this right against encroachments of every kind, for the protection of workers from the hardships of enforced unemployment.

11. Suitable provision for the old age of the workers, and for those incapacitated by injury.

12. The right of employees and employers alike to organize; and for adequate means of conciliation and arbitration in industrial disputes.

13. Release from employment one day in seven.

14. Gradual and reasonable reduction of hours of labor to the lowest practicable point, and for that degree of leisure for all which is a condition of the highest human life.

15. A living wage as a minimum in every industry, and for the highest wage that each industry can afford.

16. A new emphasis upon the application of Christian principles to the acquisition and use of property, and for the most equitable division of the product of industry that can ultimately be devised.[81]

Though the New Church did not join the Federation until 1917, it had shown numerous signs of early interest. "Think what it would mean to have all the churches of the land united to promote temperance, to foster liberty, to oppose injustice, to expose and prevent civil and political corruption, [and] to regulate divorce," commented the editor of *The New-Church Messenger* in 1909. Being a member would place the New Church squarely amid the issues related to the welfare of both capital and labor alike, the abatement of child labor and prostitution, the substitution of peace for war, finding the best solution for the immigration problem, the race question, and all the other social and moral questions that confronted the country.[82]

In 1919, the editors of *The New-Church Review* published "The Church and Social Reconstruction," a document prepared by the Federal Council's Commission on the Church and Social Service. The document recognized that the world's social fabric had been severely torn due to the war, which was followed by serious industrial disorganization, unemployment, and famine. Needed above all was the reconstruction of international relations on the basis of cooperation, disarmament, and peace.[83] On the other hand, the Russian Revolution had raised the question of whether social reconstruction should be realized by constitutional methods or by class struggle and violence. In England and the United States, there was every reason to believe that social reconstruction would follow constitutional processes; but it remained unclear how other parts of the world could or would respond. If change was effected in accordance with the teachings of Christ, then it was assumed that it would be expressed through democracy rather than in class struggle. "The dictatorship of the proletariat in practice is a new absolutism in the hands of a few men, and is as abhorrent as any other dictatorship," reported the commission charged with providing the Federal Council's position on the matter.[84]

It would be wrong to assume that the social gospel movement was broad-based, given that large sections of the South and West remained either ignorant of its existence or opposed to its approach. The social gospel was a predominately urban phenomenon and so was alien to rural fundamentalists who stood their ground against liberal theology and progressive social thought. Supporters of the social gospel almost always came from the larger urban Episcopalian, Congregationalist, Methodist, and Baptist denominations. While the social gospel movement extended across denominations, seldom did its proponents constitute a majority of church membership. Even when they succeeded in passing resolutions supporting social gospel principles approved by the Federal Council (which merged in 1950 to form the National Council of Churches), the results carried little effect. This was particularly the case during the "Red Scare" era of postwar politics that brought into the open differences in perspective between the ameliorative wing of the social gospel and the few who, until the treaty of nonaggression between the Nazis and Soviets in August of 1939, served as the vanguard of Christianity's more active left-wing radicalism. For this latter group, only a regimented socialism was destined to succeed.

History suggests that the moral impulse of the social gospelers seldom extended beyond their rhetoric. Though they rang the changes on behalf of protosocialism, they remained caught up in a mushy form of meliorism that ignored the institutionalization of segregation and disfranchisement of the African American, supported ruinous forms of state paternalism, and demonstrated shameful cynicism when it came to middle-class biases. While railing against particular evils, the social gospelers generally had a greater affinity for the established order than they did for the indefiniteness and unanticipated consequences that would come out of systemic change. The juncture between religion, politics, and social responsibility collapsed into a kind of reformist hope that accorded with comfortable, cultured, and enlightened liberalism. As people who were raised more or less in comfort and prosperity, the social gospelers winced at actions or practices that amounted to more than wish-fulfillment. Unable to identify a middle ground between unrestricted individualism and scientific socialism, they satisfied themselves with the selective ownership of certain utilities while regarding competition as a benefit that should remain free of regulation.

Liberal theology's grand illusion—namely, its confidence that a combination of will and useful action would achieve what the old religion had left undone—remained unfulfilled in the opening decades of the twentieth century, leaving social gospelers with only fragmentary answers to life's vexing questions. The assumption that individuals would act with selfless love proved to be a "will-o'-the-wisp" and a chastening critique of utopian sentimentality. The conflict between self and God that provided the theological basis for sin and salvation retained its hold over those who shifted moral responsibility from the individual to society. Old theology, despite its neglect of questions addressing public morality, continued to reign unobstructed, while the social gospel opened the question of whether religion could offer moral insight into the need for social reconstruction.

The social gospelers' concern for humanity's natural and spiritual life went up in flames in the aftermath of the First World War. Reinhold Niebuhr, the American theologian and ethicist at Union Theological Seminary, dismissed the social gospel movement for its excessive optimism, its misplaced sense of sin, and its vision of a community of saints.[85] Niebuhr's message was both political and social in nature, pointing out that America's economy of abundance had been selfishly accumulated to produce profit for the few. The resulting inequality of wealth not only undermined democracy, but it allowed the churches to explain away their obligations to protect. While the social gospel philosophy expected that human beings were genuinely selfless and good, Niebuhrian realism judged them otherwise. The Christian socialism taught and practiced by the social gospelers had served as an alibi for the status quo rather than as a creed for change. Discounting the naïve belief that individual changes of the heart were sufficient enough to transform whole societies, Niebuhr looked to the ranks of the nonreligious left for solutions. Having first advocated socialist and working-class activism in the 1930s, he eventually adopted a neoorthodox stance that took aim at society's unrealistic utopianism. A trenchant critic of humanity's naïve views of its own nature, Niebuhr set a tone that endured through the Cold War politics of the 1940s and '50s, as he took literally the face of evil shown by Hitler and Stalin.[86]

6 Loose Ends

Can anyone fail to see quite clearly that the goals of creation are useful functions? Simply bear in mind that nothing can arise from God the Creator—nothing can be created, therefore—that is not useful. If it is to be useful, it must be for the sake of others. Even if it is for its own sake, it is still for others, because we are useful to ourselves in order to be fit to be useful to others.

(Swedenborg, *Divine Love and Wisdom* §308)

For the first three quarters of the nineteenth century, Swedenborgians were confident that their numbers would grow and "would mould the life of the world into heavenly order and beauty."[1] After a hundred years of existence, though, its ambitions had subsided and these dreams failed to materialize. In 1916, Swedenborgian Clarence W. Barron, publisher of the *Wall Street Journal,* spoke out strongly, noting that the New Church had made little progress in the United States during the previous two generations. While Methodists, Baptists, Presbyterians, and Episcopalians continued to thrive, membership in the New Church had seemingly peaked. "Was not the New Church an internal light by an internal way through the Word, illuminating men's lives, and had we any right to claim ourselves, more than others, to be the Church of the New Jerusalem?" Barron asked. Proud of the fact that he carried a copy of the Bible and a book of Swedenborg's writings wherever he went, he complained bitterly that too few New Church members were doing the same. Instead, they were reneging on contributing their "earthly substance" to publicly advance the Church's objectives, preferring instead to live their lives working to avoid criticism or debate.[2]

Due to the absence of strong vocal New Church leaders speaking out on such matters as slavery, state rights, emancipation, woman's place in society, and imperialism, these and other issues festered without resolution. In this regard, New Church members resembled the culture at large in that they preferred silence to the words of provocateurs and opinionated dissenters. While it minimized internal dissent, this ambivalence did little to advance the presence and purpose of the New Church in the contemporary world.

Early Fractures

At the beginning of its national existence, the United States contended with two competing philosophies: the humanitarian philosophy of the Enlightenment, with its belief in human perfectibility and egalitarian democracy, and the English philosophy of *laissez-faire*, with its belief that democracy was best managed under the custodianship of a few. Nowhere was this tension more evident than in the task of governance—both secular and ecclesiastical. Exemplary of this was the General Convention of the New Jerusalem (also known as the General Convention or simply Convention), which was organized in 1817 in Newton, Massachusetts. Governed as an episcopacy, the Convention met annually, but only its ministers had voting rights. As early as 1836, Rev. Richard DeCharms challenged the Convention's episcopal system of governance and, in 1840, founded what he called the Central Convention, which operated under a mixed set of rules. The resulting schism represented a long-simmering conflict between the Boston and Philadelphia branches of the New Church, the former proposing a spiritual allegiance to the General Convention, while the latter moved toward a more authoritarian form of governance. In 1852, the schism ended when the Central Convention dissolved following concessions made by the General Convention.[3]

Unhappy with the concessions, a conservative group known as the Academy Movement (instigated by DeCharms and William Henry Benade) was organized in 1859. Dedicated to the study of Swedenborg with an emphasis on the divine origins of his works, it was incorporated by the state of Illinois in 1861. Its fifteen "Associations," which were defined geographically and based on self-government, eventually brought to the fore the thorny question of whether Swedenborg spoke infallibly in matters of faith and science. Once again, tension arose as the New Church's Philadelphia members, who supported the divinely inspired and infallible nature of Swedenborg's writings, sparred with liberal members from New England who were more congregationally organized, were less clerical, and were more open-minded in their beliefs. In 1890, the General Church of Pennsylvania (later named General Church of the Advent of the Lord), with its stricter interpretation on the issues of baptism and leadership, broke from the General Convention, establishing its headquarters in Bryn Athyn, north of Philadelphia. Gifted with endowments from multi-industrialist John Pitcairn, Bryn Athyn became home to its theological school, college, and high school.

By contrast, the General Convention, also known as the Swedenborgian Church of North America and a member of the National Council of Churches of Christ, became the liberal wing of the New Church. Representing a loose affiliation of churches (often referred to as societies) and associations has meant that each society and member has the freedom to arrive at his or her individual or collective conclusions independent of the Convention. The many different locations of associations within this wing reflect the strong and sometimes contentious personalities of their leaders and faculty. The General Convention has placed great emphasis on the broader autonomy of its societies and, since 1970, the acceptance of women into ordination. Its theological and philosophical center moved from Waltham (New Church School) to Cambridge (New Church Theological School), and then to Newton, Massachusetts (Swedenborg School of Religion), before relocating in 2000 to become the Swedenborgian House of Studies at the Pacific School of Religion in Berkeley, California. In 2015, it would be renamed the Center for Swedenborgian Studies when it became affiliated directly with Berkeley's Graduate Theological Union.[4]

New Church Publications

The missionary activities of New Church members centered principally on founding the American Swedenborg Printing and Publishing Society (1850), which would later become known as the Swedenborg Foundation; opening Urbana University (1850); participating in the American Tract Society (1868); supporting a modest Board of Home and Foreign Missions (1880), which operated principally in the American South and West; and managing the New Church Board of Publications (1883). In its missionary efforts abroad, the American Swedenborg Printing and Publishing Society issued Swedenborg's works in English, a decided contrast from London's Swedenborg Society, which published them in the native languages, a factor that gave the latter society a much greater response level.[5]

Essentially, every member of the New Church—whether layperson or minister—sought to make visible where the Lord dwelt in and with humanity. The Lord's command to "go . . . and make disciples of all nations, baptizing them in the name of the Father and of the Son and of the Holy Spirit" (Matthew 28:19) "is the injunction that has come down through the Christian centuries to the New Christian Church."[6] In this regard, the Swedenborg Scientific Association, which was organized in 1898 and incorporated in 1906, was intended to preserve, translate, and publish the scientific and philosophical works of Swedenborg, as well as to promote their connection to modern science, philosophy, and theology. The founding of the association and its journal *The New Philosophy* (1898–present) marked the beginning of a renewed study into the works of Swedenborg.[7]

Making the argument that Swedenborg's theology did not by itself possess the necessary knowledge to seek interior spiritual and divine causes, Frank Sewall, president of the Swedenborg Scientific Association, insisted that Swedenborg's philosophical and scientific writings were inseparable from his theology. The work of producing and preserving Swedenborg's scientific works got underway with support from the Convention, the Academy of the New Church, the Swedenborg Society of London, and the Royal Swedish Academy of Sciences. Additional support came from the International Swedenborg Congress of 1910, the patronage of the king of Sweden, and contributions of scholars from across Europe and America.[8]

Above all else, the Swedenborgians labored to educate their fellow Americans through books, magazines, articles, editorials, lectures, and presentations. Lewis F. Hite wrote:

> If we are ever to have an enduring social philosophy, it must be developed out of the nature and life of true love; and it is the New-Church doctrine of love that must give us a New-Church social philosophy....
>
> [A member of the New Church] has an immense advantage in dealing with the complexities of the world, but he must be educated up to the level of his advantages before he may expect even a moderate degree of success; nevertheless he is bound to make the most of his advantage whether adequately educated or not. We are all, therefore, under obligation to make each his own contribution to a New-Church social philosophy....
>
> No doubt the imperfections of human nature would remain, and the vices of men, individual and organized, would still challenge our attention, and our efforts to overcome them. But ... the advent of democracy would be assured. Ignorance and vice would gradually yield to education, but the education would be higher and broader, deeper and more universal than it is now.[9]

With a mission that included the distribution of Swedenborg's writings to public libraries, colleges, theological seminaries, and reading rooms, the Church sought to make its way into the heart of American culture. As crusaders for reform, the Swedenborgians applied a mix of liberal, conservative, practical, and respectable solutions without scandal-mongering or sensationalizing. To be sure, their activities had a distinctly spiritual urgency to them in both content and motive. Some were even evangelical in tone and content, believing that Americans had reason to be optimistic and that if the results they predicted failed to rise to expectations, there were still new methods to try.[10]

Despite the enthusiasm to renew the New Church's missionary efforts through a revised list of publications, a report made as early as 1843 revealed both the zeal and frustration that attended an earlier effort. Only time would tell if their new endeavors would result in any demonstrable change.

Circulars have been addressed to New York University and to Columbia College, both in the city of New York, to which answers have been given expressive of a desire to receive the works; but they have not yet been sent, owing to the want of funds. Circulars have also been sent, during the past year, to the University of Pennsylvania; Jefferson College, Canonsburg, Pa.; St. Mary's College, Baltimore, Md.; St. John's College, Annapolis, Md.; and South Carolina College, Columbia, S. C.; but no answers have yet been received from either. Since the organization of the Book Committee, in 1839, between six hundred and seven hundred volumes have been distributed to sixty-eight different Libraries, mostly of Colleges; and many had been distributed previously, by the Missionary and Tract Board. Notwithstanding this, there still remains, according to a list in the American Almanac, sixty-eight Colleges and twenty-nine Theological Seminaries in the United States, to which none of the works have yet been supplied by this Convention.[11]

Political Biases

The political biases of America's New Church magazines and periodicals varied over time, depending on the editor, the publisher, and the topic at hand. Most publications contained references to the issue of temperance, the evils of tobacco, the single tax, and the sphere of women. Some went so far as to advocate for the Australian ballot; for opposition to vaccination; for discussion of mental healing; and for the Tuskegee approach to African-American education, "an education which is accomplishing more than all other influences combined toward solving the 'race problem' of the South." *The New Earth* (1889–1900), *The Echo* (1900), and *The New Christianity* (1888–98) lent their support to both Edward Bellamy's nationalism and Henry George's single tax. *The New-Church Review* (1894–1934), a quarterly published by the Massachusetts New-Church Union and lineal descendant of *The New Jerusalem Magazine* (1827–93), and *The New-Church Messenger* (1885–present), official organ of the General Convention of the New Jerusalem, were reflective of a broad mix of opinions in their choice of articles, editorials, and book reviews.[12]

In like manner, the British magazines *Uses: A Monthly New-Church Journal of Evolutionary Reform* (1896–1901), published by the New Church Socialist Society and edited by Thomas Duckworth Benson; *Morning Light: A New Church Weekly Journal* (1878–1904), published by James Speirs, agent for the Swedenborg Society; and *The Church Reformer* (1882) all advocated the single-tax theory, basing their support on Swedenborg's slogan, "All life is the life of use." These three magazines were popular among New Church members in the United States. Generally speaking, America's New Church periodicals were more conservative than were their British counterparts, many of which were outwardly socialist in their political leanings.

Less prominent political publications included *The Helper* (1888–1947), a pocket-size weekly published by the American New Church Tract and Publication Society in Philadelphia; *New Church Reading Circle* (1885–90), edited by Rev. S. C. Eby; *The New-Church League Journal* (1909–19), a monthly published by the American New-Church League in Chicago; *Sunday Afternoons* (1909–33), a weekly published in Chicago; the bi-monthly *New Church Life* (1881–present), originally published in Lancaster, Pennsylvania; and *The New Philosophy*. Similarly popular magazines were *New Church Independent and Monthly Review* (1853–1904), *New Church Pacific* (1888–95), and *The League* (1888–93). There were also publications intended for children and young adults, which included *New Church Magazine for Children* (1843–91), *Children's New-Church Magazine* (1864–90), and *Children's New-Church Messenger* (1885–1904).

Grand Bargain

Unlike their British and European cousins, American Swedenborgians failed to bridge the dark chasm of racism that lurked beneath its dominant white culture. There was neither concealment nor delicacy with regard to this matter. As historian Henry Adams critically observed, American society "offered the profile of a long, straggling caravan, stretching loosely towards the prairies, its few score of leaders far in advance and its millions of immigrants, negroes *[sic]*, and Indians far in the rear, somewhere in archaic time."[13] American reformers, including those from the New Church, harbored a blind eye when it came to the nation's culturally ingrained concepts of race inferiority.

As noted in chapter 5, above, many Northerners were prepared to make a "grand bargain" with their brethren in the South, allowing them to limit the African American's participation in government in exchange for set quotas of immigrants arriving from non-Western European peoples. The New Church teachings lent themselves in this context, since they showed that differences of temperament between the races allowed each of them to fulfill its place in the Universal Human. The Anglo-Saxon had no reason to despise the "affectional" African race, but this characterization of Swedenborg's did not apply to "the Africans in America, who are descended from savages captured near the coast and brought away as slaves." Thus, it was essential for white America to follow the advice of Booker T. Washington and the lessons learned at Hampton and Tuskegee that it was better for blacks to acquire "the education of the will to love useful work and do it well" than it was to turn their thought to voting and seeking office. Only then could their rights to life, liberty, and happiness be assured and not abridged by mob violence.[14]

In 1904, editor S. C. Eby noted that as African Americans sought to acquire the debts owed their ancestors, it was "quite within the ethics of the black man's righteousness to overreach and to evade, to cheat and to steal, as all being lawful for the weaker party in the effort to get even with the stronger." It seemed to Eby that too much of the energy of the African American was consumed in "the assertion and demonstration of the fact that the black man is as good as the white man." He concluded that the "law of use" remained the solution to the nation's social problem. "Let him look inwardly to the Lord, from such central place as he may find himself, and let him look outwardly to his work, doing those uses which lie ready to hand, with sincerity, cheerfulness, and love of the neighbor." It was important to remember that the African American was "vastly superior to the Anglo-Saxon in his capacity for the higher life" but that "love of service" was also an accurate definition of his character. "If our colored people once learned that the essence of religion is useful work and right relationship with the fellow-man, it would be impossible to prophesy the benefits that would accrue, not only to themselves, but to the entire nation of which they are a part. . . . The true point of view for the negro [sic], as for the rest of us, is that of seeking to understand in what way he can best contribute to the common good of the body to which he belongs."[15]

Women's Rights

Other aspects of the New Church's biases were exposed during the Chicago World's Fair of 1893, when Charles C. Bonney, a civic leader and lay member of the Swedenborgian Church, was appointed to plan a World's Congress Auxiliary exhibit to include the century's achievements in government, jurisprudence, finance, science, literature, education, and religion. To accomplish this objective, Bonney and his planning committee created a series of "parliaments," including a seventeen-day Parliament of Religions, with speakers who were invited to state their beliefs in a frank and catholic spirit. The Parliament opened on September 11, 1893, and ran to September 27, with representatives participating from a wide variety of religions and religious movements. "The spirit of co-operation in subordination to the common end, the realization of beauty and use, which resulted so nobly, to the surprise and admiration of the world, was only an ultimate manifestation of that which prevailed in the Religious Congresses."[16]

In preparing to contribute its particular contribution to the Parliament's events, the General Convention of the New Jerusalem identified several themes that it intended to present. These included "The Soul and its Future Life" by Rev. S. M. Warren, pastor of the New Jerusalem Church in Brooklyn, New York; "The Divine Basis of Co-operation between Men and Women" by Lydia Fuller Dickinson, a teacher and close friend of Frank Sewall, Henry James, Sr., and Chauncey Giles, president of the General Conference and editor of *The New Jerusalem Messenger;* "The Character and Degree of the Inspiration of the Christian Scriptures" by Rev. Frank Sewall, president of Urbana University; "The Incarnation of God in Christ" by Rev. Julian K. Smyth, pastor of the Church of the New Jerusalem in New York; "Reconciliation Vital, not Vicarious" by Rev. T. F. Wright, dean of the New Church Theological School in Bryn

Athyn; and "Swedenborg and the Harmony of Religions" by Rev. Lewis Pyle Mercer, pastor of the Chicago Society. In Rev. Mercer's published account of the Parliament, he noted that Dickinson's paper covered woman's relation to man, along with commentary on the question of women's suffrage. Though he included her paper in his official history, he redacted comments considered too controversial. "While many of her conclusions along this line can not be set forth as representing any consensus of interpretation of the teachings of the New Church," Mercer explained, "what she has to say of the original bond between man and woman, and the Divine basis of cooperation between them, together with her interpretation of the history of their relations and the meaning of the changes taking place, may rightfully appear here."[17]

Besides being called upon to formally present before the Parliament papers that were prepared by its delegates, each of the major religions was invited to organize auxiliary Congresses to deliver supplementary papers on the particulars of their respective beliefs and practices. With this in mind, the New Church Congress organized a program around five separate themes: "The Origin and Nature of the New Church," "Its Doctrines the True Basis of a Universal Faith and Charity," "The Planting of the New Church," "The Future of the New Church," and "Woman in the New Church."[18]

A subcommittee under the leadership of Miss A. E. Scammon—head of the Woman's Branch of the Auxiliary, which welcomed international visitors to the Parliament and to the city of Chicago—assumed responsibility for soliciting papers for the section titled "Woman in the New Church." Once prepared, explained Mercer, a review committee of New Church representatives decided on those papers "deemed most suitable to represent the teachings of the New Church as commonly interpreted among us." The committee's responsibility was to ensure that each of the papers chosen for presentation avoided issues of internal dispute within the Church, including that of the simmering role of the "new woman." Those approved for presentation included "Woman as Wife and Mother," "Education for Wife and Mother," "The Womanly Nature," "The

Ministry of Gentleness," and "The Feminine in the Church"—none of which challenged the Church's official position.[19] Several papers judged unrepresentative of its policies and practices were relegated to "Round-Table Conferences," which met in smaller afternoon sessions that included few outsiders. Though read and discussed, none of the papers were listed in the published program or included in the official history. Mercer's reasoning for their exclusion was that all papers approved for publication in the official history were "intended to awaken thought *in* the Church rather than to declare the thought *of* the Church." To her credit, Scammon's New Church Round-Table remained a fixture for introducing new ideas and issues into the Church.[20]

The right of women to attend New Church conventions as *bona fide* voting delegates remained a contentious issue over the decades. On occasion, boards and standing committees accepted a woman delegate or two, but they never did so officially. In fact, the Church postponed full recognition of women in committees until the passage in 1919 of the Nineteenth Amendment, which gave women the right to vote. While the Church demonstrated open-mindedness on sex education, it maintained a much more conservative stance on women's place in marriage and divorce. Except in the case of adultery, divorce was no solution to an unhappy marriage. Swedenborg's doctrine of degrees stood as a watchtower, with its dictum that true progress took place by slow incremental changes.[21]

In a review of Olive Schreiner's *Woman and Labour* (1911), New Church member Samuel S. Seward, Jr., objected to the author's arguments on the subject of woman's economic relation to society. The issue was not simply economic, as Schreiner had insisted, but spiritual as well. There were values and capacities at stake that went far beyond the author's emphasis on economic and physical capacities. "We must give these higher values the same place in our theories that they have in life," Seward insisted. The sexes were radically different in their spiritual natures, in their instinctive feelings, in their methods of approaching and using truth, and in the quality of their human impulses and affections. The real question was not whether women had the power or ability to do certain things, but it was how they were able to be the most useful in the largest sense. Here, each sex had its own special expressions and qualities that contributed toward life.[22]

Even progressive New Church magazines like *The New Christianity* found it difficult to support women's suffrage. While it opened its pages to all who wished to join in the debate, on balance, it gave most of its space to those who emphasized woman's more limited sphere of activity.[23] As late as 1914, Lewis F. Hite wrote that the demand on the part of women for "absolute individual freedom, irrespective of traditional ideas, social environment, or existing institutions" had been tragic in every sense of the word. Men and women had different restrictions, opportunities, functions, and capacities. "The right of a woman to preside gracefully at the breakfast table" was much more important than her need to preside at a public meeting.[24]

The Higher Criticism

German historical criticism of the Bible, known as the higher criticism, created yet another distraction for the New Church. Initiated by Johann Gottfried Eichhorn, professor of Oriental languages at Jena University and whose four-volume *Introduction to the Old Testament* (1780–83) became a breakthrough in the historical understanding of the Pentateuch, the higher criticism represented a textual examination that used philological, historical, and archaeological methods to address origin, authorship, and composition. Eichhorn approached scripture as a literary document that came down through history in a variety of divergent versions, having passed through the hands of many different authors. His approach was continued in due course by the groundbreaking works of Ludwig Feuerbach, author of *The Essence of Christianity* (1841), and David Strauss, author of *The Life of Jesus* (1846), among others. This predominantly positivist approach to scripture led to extensive questioning of its authenticity and intentionality. For too long, Swedenborgians chose to ignore the conclusions that were drawn by these efforts, preferring to rely instead on the revelatory views of its founder.

Though increasing numbers of Christians, including those of the New Church, had accepted scripture as being more allegorical than literal, the implications of historical criticism gave them pause. Many, for the first time, learned of the existence of multiple versions of scripture and of efforts by researchers to prepare the purest possible text using the tools of higher criticism. For their part, New Church members were "not disturbed by the discovery of the higher criticism [since they had] confidence in the Divine Providence that was in the formation of the letter of Divine Revelation in order that it might surely be a fitting vessel for a continuous spiritual meaning." They accused the higher critics of sweeping away the foundations of scripture and leaving little understanding of the historical Jesus. The trouble with both the conservative and liberal approaches to the higher criticism was "the loss of belief in the Divinity of the Lord Jesus, and the substitution of a theory of evolution of the Divine in all humanity . . . [making] . . . it difficult to believe in the miraculous and supernatural conception and life of the Son of God."[25]

Noting that traditional Christian doctrines, including incarnation and atonement, had been set aside or radically altered by the higher critics, Lewis F. Hite questioned whether Christianity had been improved or weakened by the investigations. He reluctantly concluded that modern thought was "deliberately and decidedly averse to the doctrine that Christ is God" and therefore discredited the very beliefs upon which the New Church was founded. "Christianity must in the end rest upon the fact that Christ is God." To believe otherwise changed Christianity by consigning to Christ characteristics other than interpreter, revealer, and medium of God. Even the name Jesus would "cease to be called for, and the religious world [would] settle down to a frank and quiet abandonment of all distinctively Christian professions." Christianity "must have a present, living Christ" or lose its very essence. It "must assert that Jehovah God in his fullness became man in Christ."[26]

H. Clinton Hay admitted that the higher critics had confirmed much of what Swedenborg had identified—namely, that the words in Genesis were not to be taken literally. "But now the liberty of the Bible student . . . is carrying him farther than we could wish" by excluding the important principle of correspondences as the key to the Bible's symbolism. Without this principle, there remained the chance that "nothing will be left of the old way of understanding the Bible," including the essential elements of liberal Christianity. Those in the New Church were "not disturbed by the discovery of the higher criticism," provided that it not cause one to relinquish belief in the divinity of Jesus or substitute the theory of evolution for the Divine in all humanity. Therein lied the nexus of the New Church's concern with this textual method.[27]

Philanthropy

Another issue periodically debated within New Church publications was the role of philanthropy and the presumed duties toward society of the great private fortunes produced by capitalism.[28] The topic moved to front and center with the pioneering role of Andrew Carnegie, who founded the Carnegie Steel Corporation in 1892. With the sale of his company in 1902 for $250 million, Carnegie became the world's wealthiest man. In an essay titled "Wealth," published in the *North American Review* in 1889 (before the founding of his corporation), Carnegie set forth his ethic of wealth responsibility, explaining that those who acquired wealth have the obligation to give most of it away. Later, in his autobiography (1920), he not only recounted his life's trials and triumphs, including his family's early association with Swedenborgianism, but he proposed that his "Gospel of Wealth" become the standard for subsequent generations of wealthy individuals to pursue.[29]

As a child, Carnegie recalled that his family was "not much hampered" by religious beliefs, noting that on both sides of his parents' families he could remember no one with orthodox Presbyterian views. Though his mother was an avid reader of William Ellery Channing, she did not attend church and refused to discuss religion at all. In fact, all the members of his family circle "had fallen away from the tenets of Calvinism."

> During my childhood the atmosphere around me was in a state of violent disturbance in matters theological as well as political. Along with the most advanced ideas which were being agitated in the political world—the death of privilege, the equality of the

citizen, Republicanism—I heard many disputations upon theological subjects which the impressionable child drank in to an extent quite unthought of by his elders. I well remember that the stern doctrines of Calvinism lay as a terrible nightmare upon me, but that state of mind was soon over, owing to the influences of which I have spoken. I grew up treasuring within me the fact that my father had risen and left the Presbyterian Church one day when the minister preached the doctrine of infant damnation.[30]

Carnegie remembered his father's reaction to such hellfire preaching: "If that be your religion and that your God, I seek a better religion and a nobler God." He recalled, too, that a small number of individuals had formed themselves into a Swedenborgian Society in Pittsburgh, which his father joined after leaving Presbyterianism. "I became deeply interested in the mysterious doctrines of Swedenborg," Carnegie admitted, so much so that his aunt "fondly looked forward to a time when I should become a shining light in the [Church of the] New Jerusalem, and I know it was sometimes not beyond the bounds of her imagination that I might blossom into what she called a 'preacher of the Word.'" Over time, his interest waned, though he continued to participate as a member of the Swedenborgian Society's choir.[31]

Carnegie's essay on wealth, which reflected the doctrine of stewardship and was a staple of Protestant moral teaching, precipitated a national conversation about the role and purpose of philanthropy and whether the rich were obligated to give away most of what they earned. From Carnegie's standpoint, inequality had proven its social benefits, as he accepted the basic premise that poverty and extreme wealth were the price that society paid for progress—a position opposed to those of Henry George and the social gospelers. *The New-Church Review* editor H. Clinton Hay joined in the discussion, recognizing the significant charitable gifts that Carnegie, Rockefeller, and the widow Olivia Sage had made to society. Hay was also no doubt aware of the patronage shown by the John Pitcairn family to the New Church in Bryn Athyn, Pennsylvania. Hay pointed out that since corporations employed individuals who were able to feed and clothe themselves and their families, these corporations operated as "an inexpressibly higher form of charity than that which provides food and clothing without employment, and thus pauperizes the beneficiaries." In effect, the Standard Oil Trust was "a work of charity, in the truest sense of the word, so far as the external form of usefulness is concerned, whatever may be the motives of the officers and managers of the corporation."[32]

For that reason, Hay questioned whether it was better to receive charitable contributions from a corporation, trust, or syndicate than it was from the US government. Would private philanthropy result in the government's neglect of its rightful responsibilities? Did private philanthropy become a form of "mistaken kindness" that allowed the government to invest in battleships rather than schools? Was this a true form of charity, or did it "do for the nation what it should be doing for itself"? Hay explained that "the true order of charity is for every man to be useful to all the rest of his fellow creatures, or society; to do what is right in every work and fulfill his duty in every office." This obligated employers to pay an honest wage and provide a favorable environment for work. "This fidelity to duty," Hay insisted, "is the charity taught in the New Church and by the Christian religion properly understood." If practiced, there would be no millionaires and no need for their benefactions. He found it fearfully inconsistent that great fortunes could be realized using cutthroat competition while, at the same time, creating circumstances that required the use of charity to conceal what these same entrepreneurs had done to the worker. Henry George would have approved of Hay's analysis.[33] And so, too, would have Swedenborg:

> Our body can behave morally and speak rationally, and yet our spirit can intend and think things that are the opposite of morality and rationality. It is clear from pretenders, flatterers, liars, and hypocrites that this is the nature of our earthly self. Clearly, people like this have a dual mind—their mind can be divided into two parts that do not agree.[34]

By contrast, Rev. Walter B. Murray, chairman of the New-Church Lecture and Publicity Bureau of Chicago, viewed wealth as a gift from God and therefore as an indication of divine favor. "We must not think that He condemns wealth," insisted Murray. "He condemned the possession of wealth when accumulated and held selfishly." While admitting that plutocracies had acted as barriers to social justice, ensuring inequality of opportunity, their existence did not imply that rich people ignored the conditions of the poor. "Individual rich men are often sincere Christians, as honest and sincere as any poorer man, and striving as hard as any other Christian to do good and establish the kingdom of God on earth." For that reason, plutocracy had nothing to do with the private motivations of the wealthy. As long as a truly democratic form of government prevailed, the Lord's bounties should not be confiscated. "Our use," Murray wrote, "is to be as the heart and lungs of the Church on earth ... animated wholly by the spirit of democracy, for in religion it is the spirit of brotherly love." It was therefore wrong to censure the rich, but only to judge their actions characterized by the love of neighbor.[35] We can see Swedenborg's ideas shining through in those of Murray:

> If we give the matter only a little rational thought, we can see what makes eminence and wealth blessings and what makes them curses. Specifically, they are blessings for people who do not set their heart on them and curses for people who do. To set one's heart on them is to love oneself in them, and not to set one's heart on them is to love the service they can perform and not oneself in them.[36]

When the bill to incorporate the Rockefeller Foundation came before the US Senate in 1910, it sparked a second round of discussions on the role of philanthropy. Reflecting on the role of the Foundation's proposed stewardship, the bill included the following phrase: "To promote the well-being and advance the civilization of the peoples of the United States and its Territories and possessions and of foreign lands, in the acquisition and dissemination of knowledge, in the prevention of suffering, and in the promotion of any and all the elements of human progress." At issue was not the disposition of funds but the fact that the Rockefeller Corporation, not the government, determined how the Foundation's funds were to be used.[37]

In passing the bill, opponents argued, the Senate would effectively transfer to a few individuals a function that rightfully belonged to the nation itself.

> There is something fearfully inconsistent in an order of things that creates great fortunes for the few by methods in which there is little if any genuine charity, and at the same time creates the need of alms-giving, or of a form of charity in which that needs to be done for others which they ought to be doing for themselves. There must be great spiritual loss in this for all concerned. Loss to those who have lived without charity in their business from day to day, for only so can spiritual character be formed which is the wealth and capital of eternal life.[38]

This genuine charity, as mentioned above, consists in being useful to others by making every effort to do the right thing in all situations and by responsibly performing one's duties.

The other half of the philanthropy question concerned whether or not there were social obligations of each individual to fellow humans. In addressing the question "Am I my brother's keeper?" James Reed, pastor of the Boston Society of the New Jerusalem, attempted to separate out the spiritual sense of the terminology from its bare literal meaning. While this statement was useful and regarded as "a Divine law of order," no such rule was true without qualification. "The fact is that each one was intended to be his brother's keeper, according to his ability, so far as his brother needs his care," he insisted. "But it is also the fact that there are certain things which his brother can most usefully do for himself." Danger lurked in government paternalism. "Government is organized for the sake of promoting the public or common good. It has nothing to do with individuals, except so far as their interests have to be viewed apart from the public interests." If the two could not be reconciled, it was wise to conclude that the best government was one that combined the largest common benefits with the smallest infraction of personal freedom. In this matter,

Reed insisted, the divine law of usefulness required the "completest exercise of individual freedom" as the basis of perfect cooperation. "To maintain a just balance between that which men do individually, as of themselves, and that which they do collectively, in coöperation with others, is a law of the greatest man, and the part of true wisdom."[39]

The Great War

For Rev. Walter B. Murray writing in 1916, the selfishness of people had made riches a curse, as it corrupted and destroyed the finer instincts of human nature. Though the desire to accumulate wealth was "an entirely legitimate ambition," those who did so for its own sake were often affected by its corrosive influence. "An unprejudiced study of our own republic will convince one that the influence of money has so controlled our legislation, our interpretation of laws, and our administration of them, that we have had in our midst a pluto-democracy." So great was this barrier to social justice that it ensured the perpetual inequality of opportunity for the world's citizens. "Are we to minimize the evils of plutocracy because we behold so many good men among the rich?" The selfish actions of the plutocracy could not be justified or washed away by their charity.[40] Murray, therefore, accused plutocracy, and German commercialism in particular, for instigating the First World War. He asked, "If plutocracy as a class spirit does oppose justice and opportunity, shall we not recognize it, and work rather for the spirit of democracy which we believe is destined to achieve social justice and a perpetual equality of opportunity?" And he answered these questions by saying that while New Church pastors should not teach partisan politics, they had every right to show their sympathy for the spirit of democracy.[41]

When President Wilson called upon Congress for a declaration of war, Rev. Howard C. Dunham reinforced his call by arguing that the New Church and democracy had been nurtured in a close and important relationship and that therefore it was essential to understand that democracy was the means by which the world prepared for the New Church. Therefore, "it is the interest and duty of the organized New Church to favor and promote democracy in every right and feasible way." It meant speaking out on women's suffrage; supporting initiative, referendum, and recall; abolishing unjust tariffs and taxes; and ending special privileges for the favored few. It also meant revising the land-holding laws of the world.[42]

> The great war in which we are now engaged, which was forced upon the world by the lingering remnants of autocracy, is, under Divine Providence, a war to advance the principles and objects of the Last Judgment. It is a war to advance the principles of democracy. It is a war to further the development of a new earth. It is a war to prepare this earth to become the basis and seminary of the all-glorious new heavens.[43]

With the words "The world must be made safe for democracy," a slogan to which many Americans rallied in the cause of the Allies, Swedenborgian E. H. Schneider warned that the New Church should take no side in the bloodbath, even though it might have a vital interest in the outcome. "The church does not say that we shall or shall not go to war, but it does teach in substance, as the Lord also taught, that we should submit our civil life to our civil government."[44] The same stance did not apply, however, to the creation of the League of Nations in 1920. "The unity in God ever works toward unity in mankind," George Henry Dole of Wilmington, Delaware, insisted. "A world Confederacy is coming, surely coming, and he who stands in the way of it will be ground to powder, because omnipotence, the very Spirit of God, is back of it."[45]

New Church polity differed in temperament from region to region. It included conservative, moderately progressive, and sometimes even radical elements—all of which reacted differently on matters of sociology, politics, morality, and economics. Depending on the issue, individual expressions proved as apologetic, defensive, or aggressively proactive as the particular issues demanded. Overall, members of the New Church were theologically liberal and, up to the period of the

Great Depression, socially progressive, considering Teddy Roosevelt to be their most respected model of a political leader. Successful at winning the hearts and minds of progressive Christians, they were supportive of the right of private property, critical of arbitrary rules and regulations, zealous in support of patriotism and nationalism, and vigilant in upholding the presumption that reason always stood on the side of tradition. Gone was the right of revolution, as they instead adhered to an ameliorative approach to change that was rooted in nature. Deductive and *a priori* in their reasoning, they viewed the course of human events as guided by an all-purposive power. The majority of New Church members retained a stronger allegiance to capitalism than they did to the demands of labor. Seeking an alternative to the extremes of *laissez-faire* economics and Marxist socialism, they struggled over their message. In the end, they left a fragmented legacy—some claiming roots in the social gospel and single-tax movements, others in harmless genteel rhetoric that did little to change the status quo. For virtually all these groups, the doctrine of usefulness cut through their arguments, and acting as a solvent despite their differences, it brought them to worship together on common ground.

7 Pragmatism

The community stagnates without the impulse of the individual.
The impulse dies away without the sympathy of the community.
(William James, *The Will to Believe*, 1896)

The distinguished historian Henry Steele Commager called the hopeful philosophy of pragmatism a central theme in the nation's experience and "the official philosophy of America."[1] While subsequent historians have questioned this statement, the popular culture seems content to view pragmatism as a distinctive characteristic of the nation's thought and culture. The case of "the vanishing pragmatist" may sit well with social critics, but pragmatism continues to reconstitute itself over and over as a homegrown explanation of the nation's hopes and dreams.[2] Its combination of experience, possibility, anti-elitism, experimentation, and democratic bias gives it a status to which few philosophies could ever aspire. Pragmatism's center of gravity is located within the aspirations of the nation's democratic society and its tendencies toward practicality, voluntarism, moralism, and openness. While it turns out to mean many things to many people, in the main, pragmatism offers a theory of meaning, a cluster of hopes, a way of helping to clarify ideas, and an openness to a range of options—all of which are latent not only in American optimism but also in its sense of exceptionalism.[3]

As the nation's most representative pragmatist, the philosopher and psychologist William James (1842–1910), the oldest son of the theologian and Swedenborgian Henry James, Sr., charmed critics and acolytes alike with his command of information, his ability to reduce issues to concrete terms, his avoidance of verbal conflict, and his ideas that were always meaningful in their consequences. Richard M. Gale identified what he interpreted as a tension between James's "Promethean pragmatism" and his "anti-Promethean mysticism," which exposed two different sides of his personality. On the former side, James exuded an expansive, abstract, and technical self; on the latter, he possessed a highly intuitive, experiential, and spiritual self. To understand him requires a thoughtful reflection on freedom, self, mysticism, ethics, and the nature of belief.[4]

The Making of a Mind

As "the unquiet son of an unquiet father," William James grew up in a bustling household filled with the untamed competitiveness of three male siblings, where family meals became a veritable bear garden animated by youthful horseplay and interspersed with adult discussions on morals, literature, and the arts.[5] His education benefited from his father's wide-ranging philosophical and theological interests, as it included books on a variety of subjects and visits paid to the household by Emerson, Thoreau, James John Garth Wilkinson, Bronson Alcott, and others of his father's generation. Freed from the standard fare of local schoolmasters, William's education followed the trail of his family's sojourns, as he and his siblings were deposited with a succession of private tutors in New York, London, Switzerland, and Paris.[6]

Despite his father's disapproval, William initially intended a life of painting and studied for a time with William Morris Hunt and his pupil, John La Farge, in Newport. After a year, he abandoned the effort and, at the age of nineteen, enrolled in the Lawrence Scientific School at Harvard, where he studied anatomy under Jeffries Wyman and Louis Agassiz. In 1864, he went to Harvard Medical School, where he took courses from Charles William Eliot in chemistry and from Edouard Brown-Séquard and Oliver Wendell Holmes, Sr., in physiology before breaking his studies to join an expedition to Brazil with Agassiz. Upon his return, and between bouts of depression, eye troubles, and digestive disorders, he resumed his medical studies, which included an internship at Massachusetts General Hospital. His principal diversion was his association with a group of young intellectuals (Oliver Wendell Holmes, Jr.; John Dewey; Chauncey Wright; Nicholas St. John Green; and Charles Sanders Peirce) who met regularly for conversation in what they called The Metaphysical Club. Not unlike his father's Saturday Club—which included Emerson; Nathaniel Hawthorne; Henry Wadsworth Long-fellow; Richard Henry Dana, Jr.; James Russell Lowell; and Charles Eliot Norton—The Metaphysical Club became a breeding ground for discourse that eventually drew William into philosophy and psychology. In 1867, he chose yet another moratorium from his medical studies so that he could read philosophy and attend university lectures in Germany. He finally completed his medical degree in 1869, but it was an anomaly of sorts since he never practiced medicine. No doubt the weight of being the oldest son complicated his search for identity and autonomy of person.[7]

Later that same year, William experienced a highly personal and existential crisis that threw his life into inner turmoil. Like his father who had faced a similar sickness of the soul (what Swedenborg called *vastation*) when the family was living in England in 1844, William underwent his own spiritual sickness. Troubled by the specter of scientific determinism and his own struggle to underscore the meaning of free will and voluntary choices in the face of resignation or fate, he found comfort in French philosopher Charles Renouvier's neo-Kantian essay on human freedom. It was Renouvier's philosophy that unburdened James from the dilemma of determinism by calling for the re-energizing of one's personal powers.[8]

James began his career in 1872, choosing not to practice medicine but instead to become an instructor of physiology at Harvard, where he devoted himself to the study of the human mind. As a physiologist, he came early to distrust the positivist philosophies of his day, drawn instead to the nature of experience as perceived from within and approaching his subject "with that freshness and lucidity of vision which comes alone to the man who is permitted to follow his soul's affinities whithersoever they lead him."[9] Physiology led him to the

emerging science of psychology, which, three years into his appointment, he began teaching. By 1878, he had contracted with Henry Holt
and Company to write *The Principles of Psychology*, which took twelve
years to complete. Though unable to follow his father's spiritual
journey into Swedenborgianism, William's science became increasingly subjected to spiritual filters that eventually led to his disavowal
of reductionist science in favor of a philosophy rooted somewhere
between idealism and empiricism.

James was trained as a scientist before he became a philosopher
and mystic. To his credit, he never let philosophy override the facts
of science or denigrate its significance. Instead, he chose to remove
the attribution of "materialist" from the word *scientist*, believing that
some form of pantheistic reality encompassed the unfinished picture
of a universe that he perceived as a mixture of theism and pluralism.
Like his father, who advocated a correspondence between material
things and their spiritual meaning, James raised the threshold of
awareness of individual responsibility and free will in order to connect
human actions and ideals. And just as Swedenborg had unearthed the
core of spiritual beliefs long concealed by ecclesiastical Christianity,
James looked beyond positivist knowledge of the material world in
his search for meaning and values.[10]

In his long introduction to *The Literary Remains of the Late Henry
James* (1885), William sought to distance himself from his father, an
effort that was nowhere more poignant than in the distinction he
made between their respective leanings toward monism and pluralism. Notwithstanding the effort, his intellectual debt to his father far
outweighed their differences. While he initially rejected his father's
beliefs as unwelcome detritus of a previous era, they eventually inter-
sected with his own. Over time, William drew nearer to his father's
conviction that there was a place in the world for the self-determinant
individual to stand apart from the withering forces that had captured
the minds and wills of his generation. His openness to a pluralistic world and his readiness to accept some form of supernaturalism
or providential signs in the universe were all aspects of their shared
convictions. Father and son were similarly drawn to Swedenborg's

doctrine of usefulness, the former appealing to the language of spirituality while the latter finding it through the more secular and practical framework of the psychology of belief. Both father and son, according to Paul J. Croce, applied probabilistic thinking to their insight, believing that the claim that something was "provable" was equivalent to saying that it was "probable" since there was no such thing as absolute objectivity. While nature was but a provisional shadow of reality, there was still enough in it to make one's ideas actionable.[11] "All my intellectual life I derive from you," William wrote to his father, "and though we have often seemed at odds in the expression thereof, I'm sure that there's a harmony somewhere, and that our strivings will combine."[12]

Pragmatic Theory

James was a radical empiricist to the core, relying on experience as the best and most appropriate pathway to truth. In his understanding of consciousness, he abandoned the duality of knower and known to better understand what it is that organisms do when in contact with objects, thereby making consciousness the moment of experience with the physical world. To use James's own words, "the body is the storm centre, the origin of co-ordinates, the constant place of stress in all that experience-train."[13] The human being was an organism that could be understood only within its natural environment. Unlike Locke, for whom the mind was a *tabula rasa*, soaking up sensations before connecting them to perceptions and choices, James viewed the mind as a creative component in the making of experience. He came to this position as a result of both the differences expressed by Asa Gray and Louis Agassiz over Darwin's *On the Origin of Species* and his own early publications that critiqued Thomas Henry Huxley's materialism and challenged Alfred R. Wallace's argument that humans were not subject to the same forces in natural selection as were the lower species.[14]

Several years later, in "Remarks on Spencer's Definition of Mind as Correspondence" (1878), James made a similar argument against the Neo-Lamarckism of Herbert Spencer when he assaulted his definition of life that called for a coercive "adjustment of inner to outer relations," a picture drawn so vast and simple that it proved "noxious" as a fail-safe formula.[15] Instead, James presented an alternative in the form of Darwin's independent forces being responsible for generating and selecting variations distinct from those environmental pressures that maintained or reinforced variations. Philosopher Matthew Crippen described the approach in this fashion: "James does on the epistemological level what Darwin does on the phylogenetic one. He allows for a separation between that which generates new content and that which causes it to inhere."[16] Years earlier, Ralph Barton Perry described James's approach somewhat differently, explaining that it "gropes about, advances and recoils, making many random efforts and many failures." Despite their different views, both were agreed in principle to the fact that James had used Darwin's idea of independent forces as an effective wedge unseating Spencer's Neo-Lamarckism.[17]

James's articulation of pragmatic theory began with his 1898 address at Berkeley titled "Philosophical Conceptions and Practical Results," later expanded and published as *Pragmatism: A New Name for Some Old Ways of Thinking* (1907), which he dedicated to the memory of John Stuart Mill, the philosopher from whom he learned the "pragmatic openness of mind."[18] With this and other publications, pragmatic philosophy earned a place in American philosophy. However, the depth and duration of that influence remains to this day a heavily contested topic, a debate that not the least of which concerns Charles Peirce's differences that led to his adoption of the term *pragmaticism* in 1904 as a means of distinguishing his own brand of thinking.[19] Unlike James, who interpreted pragmatism broadly as an overall theory of truth and a psychology of the conscious self, Peirce insisted on limiting pragmatism to a philosophical method of clarifying ideas by considering what practical effects they might have. Still, there was much upon which they agreed, including their understanding that God was a hypothesis that reasoning could never assure with certainty.[20]

According to James, "the philosophy which is so important in each of us is not a technical matter; it is our more or less dumb sense of what life honestly and deeply means. It is only partly got from books; it is our individual way of just seeing and feeling the total push and pressure of the cosmos."[21] For Howard V. Knox, James's statement constituted "a philosophic Declaration of Independence and a truly Jacobin vindication of the Rights of Man" in that it challenged the conception of philosophy long held sacred by the professionals in the discipline. "Refusing to treat philosophy as an idle pastime," or an exercise in "intellectual gymnastics," James demanded a connection between theory and life, a novel prospect for the professional philosopher.[22]

Pragmatism represented a philosophical movement whose theory of knowledge was based on the practical, voluntary, workable, and useful consequences of one's choices. Influenced by the jurist and social reformer Jeremy Bentham, whose consequentialist philosophy implied that morals, laws, and principles were tools for the attainment of human happiness, as well as by John Stuart Mill, whose utilitarianism advocated the rethinking of first principles based on how things are used and to what effect, James envisioned the convergence of their ideas on aspects of his pragmatic naturalism and moral perspective.[23] Instrumentalism joined with humanism and cognition to reach a judgment that was both emotionally satisfying and practical. Judgments derived from abstract or *a priori* information proved in the long run to be useless to the matters at hand and to their respective consequences.

Pragmatism humanized truth by leaving the term unfinished, an approximation sufficient in its probability to be counted as agreeing to certain ways of working for the fulfillment of human purposes. Truth is what could happen to an idea as the result of an individual's actions and social practices. "If there is to be truth . . . both realities and beliefs about them must conspire to make it."[24] Pragmatic truth required practical verification, thereby becoming "truth's cash-value in experiential terms." There was no single, comprehensive definition of truth; nor could there be. Rather than transcending experience, truth was mutable to particular situations. "The practical value of true ideas is thus primarily derived from the practical importance of their objects to us. Their objects are, indeed, not important at all times."[25]

Pragmatic truths were time-dependent, admitted to degrees of probability, and "worked" if they led to beneficial consequences in experience.[26]

The Age of Doing

William James's maxim that beliefs should be tested not by their origins but by their consequences gave birth to a generation of reformers whose outlook was both evolutionary and functional, impacting a diverse field of disciplines and changing dramatically the face of American social thought and action. The progressive movement, for example, was a period of social activism and political reform between 1890 and 1920 whose advocates sought to counter the callous indifference of the nation's institutions by demanding the centralization of power in the hands of a strong but democratically chosen government that would have the power to regulate industry, finance, transportation, agriculture, and labor. Calling for a new set of standards in business and politics, progressivism represented a social philosophy with roots deep in the American experience.

Often overlooked as being influential on America's pragmatic and progressive trends is Swedenborg's doctrine of usefulness. Both Peirce and James had ample contact with Swedenborg's ideas through Henry James, Sr., and through translations of Swedenborg by James John Garth Wilkinson. Like Swedenborg, James found little value in the shallow abstractions of contemporary religious beliefs. Focused on creeds and dogmas, the denominations seemed painfully unaware of their growing lack of relevance. Evident in James's writings was his concern for the lack of inner harmony in the self, something he diagnosed as being the hectic effect of modern life. Like Howells and Bellamy, he feared the end of the autonomous individual and the challenge of finding and retaining the self's moral fitness in modern society.[27]

With these values in its arsenal, pragmatism assumed a central role in American culture long before it became an academically designated school of thought. Its proponents were less concerned with truth than they were with its outcome, which was more or less uncertain. With experience being integral to the organic process of life, pragmatists refused to separate thought from action, or feeling from cognition. Instead of establishing a world of declared absolutes, they sought by means of the scientific method to develop a form of inquiry involving observation, experiment, hypothesis, and reflective reasoning that would identify the moral conduct of life in an environment subject to constant change.

Mind was the product of experience, or the interaction of the individual with his or her physical and social environment. As mind was not a passive function, it acquired its materials of knowledge through interaction with the community, whose experiences may or may not be limited. In this context, James's pragmatism best expressed its roots in American thought and culture, including the social theories of Henry James, Sr., to which it seemed most closely aligned. For James, a person's physical environment became a social tool by which individual moral judgments formed and acted out for good or bad. Within the uniqueness of each individual experience, moral conduct or choice was continually squared with the moment and not aligned to any universal norm. While literary naturalists created a rigidly deterministic environment within which victims acted out their fatalistic outcomes, pragmatism offered a visible demonstration of action over contemplation, over rationalization, and over ideology. Reflective of a nation of "doers," pragmatism was less a philosophy than it was a results-driven approach tied to creative intelligence, faith in the possibility of progress, and a cautious but optimistically constructive view of change. This was not the moral crusade of the social gospelers but a collective effort based on the alignment of purposes and effects, with the possibility of improvement lodged solidly in the importance of education, the primacy of experience, the willingness to believe, the commitment to action, and the moral acceptance of the consequences of those actions.

Pragmatism, which American scholar Woodbridge Riley once called "the philosophy of practicality ... whose prime criterion is success," was not so much a metaphysical system as it was a method to make ideas clear, instrumental, and personally satisfying.[28] Provided that one was willing to take chances, it became a philosophy of practicality and workability, of discovering truth for oneself, and of putting ideas to work. Pragmatism transcended individual human behavior to function on behalf of the broader humanity. Whether classified as humanism, functionalism, or empiricism, it sought "truth" as something grounded in experience, not as some mysterious Platonic ideal set apart from humankind. In an age of uncertainty, novelty, and strife, pragmatism told a story of freedom: refusing to adhere to otherworldly cosmologies, it relied on the role of the whole individual within the social fabric of the moment.

Pragmatism did not involve the revival of any Heraclitian doctrine that transformed nature into purposeless flux. As explained by Paul Croce, James defined reality moment by moment, sharing with his father the belief that providential action in the universe "was embedded within the natural world and within mankind." This position turned on his choice of a more humanistic science in place of the reductionist and positivist science of his age. He regarded his father's admiration of Swedenborg and his doctrines of correspondences and usefulness as meaningful mechanisms for unlocking the mysteries of the natural world.[29] In this manner, James broke from the scientific training of his teachers to find comfort in the spiritual world his father so loved. Such was the complexity of his view of science and the admiration he held for his father's spirituality. Though he began with reductionist science, it was far from the final word on the meaning of truth. Rather, his essay "The Will to Believe" became the centerpiece for his awareness of the conflicting forces that contributed to his perspective on life and its ultimate meaning.[30]

The Will to Believe

James's "The Will to Believe," an address to the Philosophical Clubs of Yale and Brown Universities published in 1896, represented a defense of faith (not necessarily religious faith) in which the individual made a voluntarily adopted statement possible or even true in the absence of certitude. It represented an act of consent wherein the individual trusted to believe what appeared as a real possibility. There was a transference made from what "ought" to be to what "is."

By acting "as if" something was true, even with limited evidence, the individual could make truth happen. As James explained, it was "the readiness to act in a cause the prosperous issue of which is not certified to us in advance." In a world of indeterminism, there was room for possibility and even probability. Even without guarantees, goals were possible.[31]

Written in response to Thomas Henry Huxley and philosopher and mathematician William K. Clifford, both of whom questioned any commitment to belief without sufficient evidence (judging such assent as self-deception, if not intellectual dishonesty), James argued that in choices of great personal significance, it was far better to rely on intuition than it was to suspend judgment. The consequences of avoiding moral choice could have much more severe outcomes. Choosing a specific course of action with insufficient evidence did not constitute self-deception or conceal the truth of the situation, since it could eventually lead to belief, which was not an option for those who suspended judgment based on unprovable evidence.[32] Even though one cannot always prove with reason and therefore cannot know with complete confidence that something is true, a seeker of truth can still believe, using judgment as a method and a justification for action. Belief was not fiction but instead operated within a combination of inferences, experiences, and intuition. Though he did not discuss the existence of God or advocate belief in religion, James's secular advocacy of belief offered affirmation of its importance as a broad and unparochial act of intention. This was in no way a defense of irrationality or wishful thinking; it was the willingness to act on options that the intellect was unable by itself to resolve.[33]

In its functioning, faith played an important part of reality. "Moral questions immediately present themselves as questions whose solution cannot wait for sensible proof," he wrote. "A moral question is a question not of what sensibly exists, but of what is good, or would be good if it did exist."[34] In acting on belief, or *willing to believe,* one creates the reality.

> A conception of the world arises in you somehow, no matter how. Is it true or not? you ask.

It *might* be true somewhere, you say, for it is not self-contradictory.

It *may* be true, you continue, even here and now.

It is *fit* to be true, it would be *well if it were true*, it *ought* to be true, you presently feel.

It *must* be true, something persuasive in you whispers next; and then—as a final result—

It shall be *held for true*, you decide; it *shall be* as if true, for *you*.

And your acting thus may in certain special cases be a means of making it securely true in the end.[35]

Faith was an instrument, a form of commitment for which one typically preferred to have as much knowledge as possible but which seldom offered an ideal set of circumstances before a decision was necessary. As James in quoting Kierkegaard stated, "we live forwards ... but we understand backwards."[36] It was not James's intention to replace religious faith, but rather to unveil the sources of its power, to show its connectedness with the world, and to provide refuge from the loneliness of the soul in its existential contact with the indeterminate vastness of the universe. In terms of its wishfulness, James's "The Will to Believe" stood within the same philosophical tradition as that within which fell Pascal's desperate wagering for the existence of God. Neither, however, served to illuminate the other. The former looked to the ethical, cultural, and aesthetic values that were brought into existence by a system of belief, while the latter simply represented a risk/benefit calculation devoid of any "passional" or intrinsic meaning for belief.[37]

Neither religious nor antireligious in its intentionality, pragmatism nonetheless favored religion, if only for its affirmative rather than skeptical outlook on life. Ultimate reality lay in immediate experience, which James described as "a radical empiricism ... which represents order as being gradually won and always in the making [and] rejects all doctrines of the Absolute."[38] As John Hick explained in his *Philosophy of Religion*, James argued "that the existence or nonexistence of God, of which there can be no conclusive evidence either way, was a matter of such momentous importance that anyone who so desired had the right to stake one's life upon the God hypothesis." For Hick, who categorized James's position as a form of traditional theism, this amounted to "an unrestricted license for wishful thinking."[39]

Actually, James had a much broader view of religion and belief than that, one that was suggestive and fluid, but nowhere clearly defined. His was an "open universe" where choices made a difference and ideals were realizable. As he explained in his lecture on "Pragmatism and Religion" (1906), an individual must be willing "to live on a scheme of uncertified possibilities which he trusts [and must be] willing to pay with his own person, if need be, for the realization of the ideals which he frames."[40] James invited readers to embrace life, allowing their hopes to outlive their fears. "Be not afraid of life," he told the Harvard Young Men's Christian Association in 1895, "believe that life *is* worth living, and your belief will help create the fact."[41]

Despite criticism from Bertrand Russell for lacking the technical rigor of a true philosophy, James's "The Will to Believe," or what he sometimes called the "*right* to believe," did not include views that either contradicted known facts or violated logic. Instead, it acted as a form of therapy that was designed to instigate the subject into constructive action. It represented a judgment about the truth-value of belief, the worth of life, and the implied goodness of the world.[42] Belief was an experience to be lived rather than an affirmation of any defined doctrine. As for the historical definition and attributes of God, these had no basis other than as a mechanically deduced vision erected as "aftereffects, secondary accretions upon those phenomena of vital conversation with the unseen divine [that occur] in the lives of humble private men."[43]

Recognizing that most data used to prove a scientific truth were gained in the laboratory *after* the truth itself was conjectured, James applied the same to faith, arguing that it is possible to will oneself into a belief by not only acting as if it were real but by generating data to support it.

Suppose . . . I am climbing in the Alps and . . . work myself into a position from which the only escape is by a terrible leap. Being without similar experience, I have no evidence of my ability to perform it successfully, but hope and confidence in myself make me sure I shall not miss my aim. . . . But suppose on the contrary, the . . . emotion of fear and mistrust preponderate . . . why, then I shall hesitate so long that at last, exhausted and trembling, launching myself in a moment of despair, I miss my foothold and roll into the abyss. In this case . . . the part of wisdom is clearly to believe what one desires, for the belief is one of the indispensable preliminary conditions of the realization of its object.[44]

Regardless of the particular perspective that one might have regarding the nature of the universe, it was important for the individual to act "as if he were individually helping to create the actuality of the truth whose metaphysical reality he is willing to assume." Anything less than passional assent was shameful. If every good person decided to wait for certitude, stagnation would ensue. The willingness to believe rather than disbelieve was the only practical approach to uniting beliefs and action. Either reap the positive benefits of belief or lose what possibilities it might have afforded. This was the logic of action—the choice between daring, and risking the chance of failure, or doing nothing and allowing opportunity to slip by.[45] Not taking a risk meant the difference between being a spectator and being an actor. "The visible world is but a part of a more spiritual and everlasting universe," observed Finnish philosopher Eino Kaila in 1912, "and our life gains its proper meaning from our being in touch, or in a harmonious relationship, with this." To do this, one must believe, regarding it as true even in the absence of sufficient evidence, and act accordingly. "If I tend not to dare anything simply because no one can *prove* the value of life to me, I surrender myself to doubt, and the victory of skepticism is sure, the world around me is pitch black."[46]

Throughout his life, James remained a radical empiricist, upholding his belief in experience as the most reliable guide to truth. Especially if it agreed with reality, truth became not only a measure for one's conduct but also a justification that life was worth living. There was a certain catholicity in his temperament and a healthy-mindedness in his ideas. Truth, he argued, may change, or, at the very least, newer theories may develop that challenge our existing understanding. Indeed, his seriousness as a philosopher and his readiness to argue his position radiated from his persona. As Arthur O. Lovejoy observed, James "found a place in which a man is imperatively called upon to take sides." Thus, while modestly calling pragmatism "a new name for some old ways of thinking," he belied the bewilderment it caused in the minds of those who sought to understand it.[47]

> Doubtless the chief service which be rendered to those of his contemporaries . . . was of a sort so general and pervasive that it is not easy to define. It lay in the bracing, stimulating, and mind-enlarging influence of his personality, in the contagion of openness of view and simplicity of utterance, of intellectual courage and intellectual candor, that proceeded from him; in the example of his constitutional inability to wear any bandages of either scientific or philosophic dogmatism over that vision turned straight to the face of immediate experience, of "raw, unverbalized life" in all its manifoldness and concreteness and richness of unexcluded possibilities.[48]

The Varieties of Religious Experience

James's *The Varieties of Religious Experience* (1902) naturally extended from those thoughts on religion that he provided in "The Will to Believe." In the latter, as noted above, he suggested that when given a choice between two hypotheses, it was important not to suspend judgment but to choose the one that most satisfied the individual's emotional and practical needs. In *Varieties*, James pushed things forward, focusing on the psychology or mental phenomena that accompanied the experience of religious belief. While most religious thinkers purported to believe in a part of selfhood that was permanent, immaterial, and dwelling freely within the physical body, which gave it a certain value or purpose beyond death, James made no such claim. Instead, the self was a fact of experience whose essential reality was in the consciousness of the moment.

James's *Varieties*, which he delivered at Edinburgh in 1899–1901 as part of the Gifford Lectures on Natural Religion, was a virtual *tour de force*, representing a synthesis of mind, faith, and belief. In it, James responded to three related questions: What does religion do? From whence did it come? And was it important that its claims be literally and objectively true? As he had not yet been defined by the professional community as either a physiologist, psychologist, or philosopher, he chose to glide from one discipline to the other without setting off the alarms of those interested in establishing distinct disciplinary boundaries and constraints. He emphasized the "experience" that an individual went through in response to a life crisis, as well as the transition from having a "sick soul" to reaching a state of "healthy-mindedness."[49]

James regarded the statements made by theologians and philosophers about religion to be ambiguous at best. Unless one could understand religious experience from the perspective of the subject, it carried little meaning. Similarly, he rejected the theological argument of God as the Absolute. All that was required to meet the practical needs of belief was that God be "both other and larger than our conscious selves. Anything larger will do, if only it be large enough to trust for the next step. It need not be infinite, it need not be solitary."[50] Above all else, this "otherness" needed to act catalytically to make individuals choose principled action that brought meaning to their existence. Whatever or however defined, God needed to be reasonable and useful. For without God, explained Gary Alexander, "James thinks that we will not be as moral as we possibly can be."[51]

James used the term *God* reluctantly, preferring a broader perspective that replaced religion's mythical dogmas and absolutes with *humanism*, which emphasized human experience as the source for moral guidance and an understanding of love, justice, peace, and social responsibility. In this sense, God became a symbol for the commitment to human ideals rather than a supernatural entity that was an object of belief. According to A. Eustace Haydon, who, along with John Dewey, was one of the signers of *Humanist Manifesto I* (1933), "More needful than faith in God is faith that man can give love, justice, peace and all his beloved moral values embodiment in human relations. Denial of this faith is the only real atheism. Without it, belief in all the galaxies of gods is mere futility. With it, and the practice that flows from it, man need not mourn the passing of the gods."[52]

Given that the existence of God could not be demonstrated or disproven by traditional means, James insisted that significance must be found in the quality of life caused by belief. He accepted the term *God* just so long as it both implied something *more* in the relation between the individual and the universe and resulted in a morally transformative experience. It would not, however, demand the preoccupation with anthropomorphism, interventionism, and redemptive attributes that was demonstrated by organized religion. There was a difference between the God of *revealed* religion, whose attributes were caught up in theological dogmatics, and the God of *natural* religion, whose relationship to the individual involved a connectedness to the panorama of life and its aggregate of human experience. God was a concept broader than that to which the religions claimed ownership. James's picture of the universe was always in an unfinished state, forever coming to terms with its different elements as it wrestled with moral will and the ongoing experiences of struggle, faith, and salvation. "Because God is not the absolute, but is himself a part when the system is conceived pluralistically," he wrote, "his functions can be taken as not wholly dissimilar to those of the other smaller parts—as similar to our functions consequently."[53]

James took exception to Thomas Henry Huxley's notion of agnosticism. In "The Sentiment of Rationality," an address delivered before the Harvard Philosophical Club in 1879 and published in *The Princeton Review* in 1882, he insisted that human beings must "take nothing as an equivalent for life but the fullness of living itself." When they choose to be only visitors and not dwellers, "[they] will never carry the philosophic yoke upon [their] shoulders." The choice of suspending judgment or belief was not an option. The same applied to Spencer's "Unknowable."

There can be no greater incongruity than for a disciple of Spencer to proclaim with one breath that the substance of things is unknowable, and with the next that the thought of it should inspire us with awe, reverence, and a willingness to add our co-operative push in the direction toward which its manifestations seem to be drifting. The unknowable may be unfathomed, but if it make such distinct demands upon our activity we surely are not ignorant of its essential quality.[54]

As for atheists who considered God a discredited myth that no longer deserved meaningful discussion, James offered them a more nuanced approach. Pragmatism's melioristic aspect looked not at religion's pernicious role in the history of human relations or at its blindness to modern science, but instead toward the richness of its diversity, its contributions to art and philosophy, and particularly its usefulness in serving human needs. If belief in God benefited the individual and society, the metaphysical issue as to whether God exists or not should take a back seat since this was an unanswerable question. The trouble with claiming ownership of "Truth" with a capital "T" was that it distracted people from working for the common good. "The real power of the pragmatic approach," wrote Andrew Fiala, "is that it reminds us that human life occurs within the shared practices and norms of a community." It celebrates the shared values and communal practices that result from those who practice religion's rituals and beliefs.[55] Though some forms of religiosity were clearly harmful, necessitating some measure of control over its adherents, such exceptions did not justify intolerance to the whole of religion's diversity.

James made sympathetic references to Jesus, but he did not identify with the label "Christian." Having rejected the abstract notions of an absolute God, opting instead for a finite God who worked in partnership with humanity, James left no room for the concepts of Christ and divine revelation. Instead, he constructed a framework in which belief was a matter of action, not contemplation, and where the individual stood as a participant, not simply as a spectator, in the world. Standing inside and not outside the decision-making process, the individual's choices became acts of faith that looked toward an uncertain future, hoping that it would confirm what they had the courage to risk.

Pluralism

James rejected the God of orthodoxy because he found him to be devoid of any practical purpose or meaning. God's existence by itself commanded no reverence. Instead, God needed to be a co-laborer with humankind in building a moral universe. Such a finite God, explained philosopher David Paulsen, was "pragmatically richer than belief in an absolutely unlimited God in that it provides greater virility and impetus to our moral endeavors."[56] James admitted to having "no living sense of commerce with a God. I envy those who have, for I know the addition of such a sense would help me immensely."[57] Busying himself instead with the prospect of improving the human condition individually and communally, he chose pluralism over either doing away with God (a "death-of-God" approach) or placing in God too much control. The traditional all-knowing and all-powerful God was irrelevant to human existence, but belief in God could result in a more ethically meaningful life. If God was the missing factor in unifying human ideals and choices, then James urged that God be put to such use.[58]

With the possible exception of Nietzsche's "God is dead" quote from his *Thus Spoke Zarathustra* (1883) and the theology that followed, few philosophers aside from James chose polytheism as a serious alternative to the monotheistic tradition in Western philosophy. He first made mention of this consideration in *Varieties* when expressing his compatibility with a pluralistic universe.

> Theism, whenever it has erected itself into a systematic philosophy of the universe, has shown a reluctance to let God be anything less than All-in-All. In other words, philosophic theism has always shown a tendency to become pantheistic and monistic, and to consider the world as one unit of absolute fact; and this has been at variance with popular or practical theism, which latter has ever been more or less frankly pluralistic, not to say polytheistic, and shown itself perfectly well satisfied with a universe composed of many original principles, provided we be only allowed to believe that the divine principle remains supreme, and that the others are subordinate.[59]

James's endorsement of both pluralism and polytheism was a response to the monistic worldview that seemed to turn life into a Greek tragedy with little room for free will. The only alternative, he explained, was "to cut loose from the monistic assumption altogether, and to allow the world to have existed from its origin in pluralistic form, as an aggregate or collection of higher and lower things and principles, rather than an absolute unitary fact."[60] This became his solution to the moral problem of evil and to God, its ultimate source. "Given the enormity of human ... suffering," explained Richard A. S. Hall, "James believes that God's goodness can be salvaged only if he is conceived of as limited in his natural powers."[61] Polytheism destroyed the divine hegemony of an all-powerful God by opening belief up to the possibility of embracing a more mystical and democratic theism, showing a degree of tolerance toward other religious systems, and demonstrating opposition to a more sovereign and monistic state of religious experience.

James was a religious pluralist who valued any religion that connected belief with the ethical life. It was not the existence or nonexistence of God, or an eternal moral law, that counted, but instead it was the empathy that humans expressed toward each other and the moral obligation to make things better that mattered in the end.[62] In his use of the term *plural universe,* James implied a reality comprised of many minds, as distinct from one absolute mind. His pluralism was a matter of no small importance, as he applied this idea in complex and varying ways to his epistemology, ethics, and views on religion.[63] In essence, he encouraged individuals to venture into religious pluralism, provided that the resulting fermentation supported the ideals of tolerance and healthy competition.[64]

James's pluralism contrasted sharply with the monism of Paul Carus, the stoicism of Buddhism, the dualism of Christian scholasticism, the absolutism of Josiah Royce, and the determinism of Calvinism. Desiring that pragmatism steer a middle course between these competing systems, he salvaged what terminology he could from the religious point of view, albeit expunged of its negative attributes. Still, at the end of the day, his position seemed to vacillate between advocating for human sufficiency and relying on the "otherness" that transcended personal experience.

Immortality

James's interest in immortality was, by his own admission, "a secondary point," though he certainly sympathized with those who found it to be an urgent impulse. The only thing to which he could attest with any intellectual clarity was that "we can experience union with *something* larger than ourselves and in that union find our greatest peace."[65] He accepted immortality within the framework of the pragmatist's will to believe, but he was personally troubled by neither its legitimacy nor the possibility of his own mortality.

> God is the producer of immortality; and whoever has doubts of immortality is written down as an atheist without farther trial. I have said nothing in my [Ingersoll] lectures about immortality or the belief therein, for to me it seems a secondary point. If our ideals are only cared for in 'eternity,' I do not see why we might not be willing to resign their care to other hands than ours. Yet I sympathize with the urgent impulse to be present ourselves, and in the conflict of impulses, both of them so vague yet both of them noble, I know not how to decide. It seems to me that it is eminently a case for facts to testify. Facts, I think, are yet lacking to prove 'spirit-return.'[66]

Philosopher Ralph Barton Perry suggested that James trended in his later years toward belief in immortality, experiencing a "growing faith in its reality."[67] One is reminded, however, of the French novelist Roger Martin du Gard's character Jean Barois, who, when faced with the immediacy of death in a sudden and unexpected traffic accident along the Boulevard Saint-Germain, burst out with the words "Hail, Mary, full of grace." Alarmed by what he interpreted as a momentary yet nonetheless alarming weakness, Barois prepared a testament of his beliefs in the event that another such event might cause him to revert in a weakened state to his former faith.[68] James admitted to the possibility of immortality, though he certainly did not do so in a manner compatible with Western religious tradition. Recognizing that belief in immortality represented one of humankind's "great spiritual needs," he found it disconcerting that mainline religions had appointed themselves its "official guardians," a role that possessed the pretended power of withholding it from those who did not accept their teachings.[69]

While most physiologists agreed that thought was a function of the brain, meaning that mental phenomena did not exist as independent variables in the world, James considered such strict scientific reasoning as flawed and that it was instead possible that the life of the mind might continue after the brain itself was dead. "When we think of the law that thought is a function of the brain, we are not required to think of productive function only; *we are entitled also to consider permissive or transmissive function.*" Thus consciousness could, in ways now unknown, continue intact and compatible "with the supernatural life behind the veil hereafter."

> Just how the process of transmission may be carried on, is indeed unimaginable; but the outer relations, so to speak, of the process, encourage our belief. Consciousness in this process does not have to be generated *de novo* in a vast number of places. It exists already, behind the scenes, coeval with the world. The transmission-theory not only avoids in this way multiplying miracles, but it puts itself in touch with general idealistic philosophy better than the production-theory does. It should always be reckoned a good thing when science and philosophy thus meet.[70]

In his explanation of the transmission-theory, James referenced mediums who allegedly could identify an individual's private thoughts or an apparition of something happening hundreds of miles away. He likewise referred to "the word 'influx,' used in Swedenborgian circles, [which] well describes [an] impression of new insight, or new willingness, sweeping over us like a tide." He also quoted Kant, who said that "the death of the body may indeed be the end of the sensational use of our mind, but only the beginning of the intellectual use. The body would thus be not the cause of our thinking, but merely a condition restrictive thereof, and, although essential to our sensuous and animal consciousness, it may be regarded as an impeder of our pure spiritual life."[71]

On the other hand, James playfully proposed how such an "intolerable number" of spiritual beings would exist if immortality were indeed true. The world would include "inconceivable billions of fellow-strivers," all of whom would make for an "inconveniently crowded stage." "Life is a good thing on a reasonably copious scale; but the very heavens themselves, and the cosmic times and spaces, would stand aghast, we think, at the notion of preserving eternally such an ever-swelling plethora and glut of it." While Christians might not have use for the heathen and the "swarms of alien kinsmen," James questioned whether this reasoning applied to God. If humankind wished to claim immortality, it should at least be tolerant of such claims as are made by *all* its members—past, present, and future—as "this is indeed a democratic universe." Not doing so would "be letting blindness lay down the law to sight."[72]

Given James's affirmation of the will to believe, individuals were justified in adopting immortality, even if it meant taking a personal "leap" to belief in light of insufficient evidence. If believing in immortality helped in coping with life and making the world a morally better place, then it was a ready-made solution. The metaphysical need to believe in immortality, explained Sami Pihlström of the University of Helsinki, "flow[s] from our mortality and the sorrow, distress, fear, horror, anxiety, or angst caused by it."[73] It would be difficult to say whether James's search for immortality was either a success or a failure. Certainly the idea of transhuman consciousness remained an ever-present hope. As mentioned above, his was not the absolute mind of, say, Carus's monism, but instead consisted of the plural seas of consciousness (a cosmic consciousness "like islands in the sea") that he set forth in his Ingersoll lecture on human immortality.[74]

On the whole, critics accused James of being too credulous, of accepting or at least admitting to the possibility of some form of paranormal communication (i.e., telepathy, clairvoyance, or premonition). James's friend Richard Hodgson likened the quality of the evidence to two distant persons who had only dead-drunk servants to act as their messengers.

Meliorism

Over the years, James became increasingly anti-institutional and anarchistic in his thinking, as he was alarmed by the number of people who had accepted a deterministic world in which the individual became the mere plaything of external forces. Championing personal freedom and active participation in the pursuit of democratic ideals, he spoke out publicly against certain events of the 1890s, especially the Spanish-American War, the Philippine-American War, the Dreyfus affair in France, attempts to annex Hawaii, and US meddling in Venezuelan affairs. Increasingly, he saw anonymous forces—governmental, military, corporate—assuming control over individual lives.[75] As he was already identified with psychical research, opposition to medical licensure laws, and support of mind-cure medicine, he came to politics naturally through his father's Christian socialism, Fourierism, and Swedenborgianism. Like his father, he advocated a vision that was deeply anti-institutional and was exemplified by his participation in the Anti-Imperialist League, his numerous letters to editors on social and political issues, and his public statements before the Massachusetts legislature against medical licensing. So strong was his reaction that he confided to William Dean Howells in 1900: "I am becoming more and more an individualist and anarchist and believer in small systems of things exclusively."[76]

James wondered how the individual became so powerless. How could democratic ideals and belief in personal freedom stand against such dominant and formidable forces? Was it possible to make a difference in the face of such odds? And how did one assert the importance of the individual in the context of a chance universe?[77] In answering these questions, he turned to both Swedenborg's doctrine of usefulness and the power of ideals to rekindle belief in the role of the individual. In doing so, he shared with his father a passionate approach to reform, arguing not for opportunistic solutions but for ones that were based in tolerance, pluralism, individual freedom, and faith in humanity's potential to create a better world.[78]

James's occasional anarchism remained highly intellectualized—a far cry from the Haymarket anarchists of his day. Based on the qualities of sympathy, love, and friendship, his democracy was more pacifist, individualist, and communitarian in nature. Indeed, his philosophy of pragmatism stood forthrightly against dogmatism, absolutism, and oppressions of all forms. As a theory of truth and a method for weighing values, it argued for a world where individuals, regardless of their place in it, played an active role. Encouraged by novelty and diversity, James embraced all possible worldviews over the tyranny of a single view. Opposing all absolutes as dangerous, he placed his faith in future possibilities rather than in any static point of view; and he encouraged activism, rather than indifference or revolution, as the preferred approach to reform.[79]

Philosophy was no longer an exercise of academics but a method of meliorist change that made room for hope and a belief that progress can be achieved through human effort. James's was a call to arms against theories that encouraged passiveness, acquiescence, and neglect of social evils. Instead of a single institutional philosophy, James gave each individual the self-determined opportunity to contribute to the realization of American ideals. Through individual and small group action distinct from the state or church, each individual could become a force in the affairs of society.[80]

With respect to the issues between capital and labor, pragmatism offered itself as a court of arbitration, settling disputes that festered as a result of arrogance on both sides. Adhering to no particular system or *a priori* path, it wove a course between these two adversaries by tracing each of their notions to its respective consequences. As James explained, "pragmatism unstiffens all our theories, limbers them up and sets each one at work."[81] It traced the specific consequences of a given hypothesis to their bare ends; and by its practical effects on the living, the hypothesis became fact. Truths that were reached through the pragmatic method represented an alignment of ideas with reality, valuing the ideas by the way they realized results. Pragmatism was a method for making a truth become *useful*—not for eternity but for now.

The melioristic approach became James's way of combating the extremes of optimism and pessimism. On the whole, explained religious scholar Wayne Proudfoot, "pragmatism inclines to meliorism, which stands between optimism and pessimism, where salvation is not assured."[82] In a pluralistic universe where God was finite and contingent upon a given environment, God became less God-like as humanity labored with God to realize change. Subordinating the true to the good in his escape from abstractions, James emphasized the power of the ideal in making individual actions morally worthwhile, and he sought to harmonize individuals with their work activity by means of what Scott R. Stroud of the University of Texas at Austin identified as an "experiential integrity."[83]

In addressing the question of how individuals were able to draw upon their own personal forces to overcome crises of will that kept them from acting out their hopes and goals, James's comments were reminiscent of Teddy Roosevelt's closing remarks in "The Strenuous Life," a speech that he gave before the Hamilton Club of Chicago in 1899: "Let us therefore boldly face the life of strife, resolute to do our duty well and manfully; resolute to uphold righteousness by deed and by word; resolute to be both honest and brave, to serve high ideals, yet to use practical methods. Above all, let us shrink from no strife, moral or physical, within or without the nation, provided we are certain that the strife is justified, for it is only through strife, through hard and dangerous endeavor, that we shall ultimately win the goal of true . . . greatness."[84] In other words, James's will to believe lent itself to invigorating those intent on transforming their inner ideals. It began with doubt, moved to action, and ended with belief. By convincing themselves that belief in action could make a positive difference, they changed their lives and the lives of others. Belief produced a transformative effect on the individual and on society. Being a meliorist meant giving meaning to the possibility that something might be produced by purposeful and sometimes even strenuous activities. As Ralph Barton Perry explained, "James attached intrinsic value to heroic action, and praised the life of conflict and struggle for the personal qualities it engendered."[85] James applauded the "strenuous life," but one that was not performed in service of the aggressiveness and martial virtues of empire-building. His activism came without the bellicose policies and injustices that accompanied the nation's raw use of power.[86]

The New Church Response

For Lewis F. Hite, editor of *The New-Church Review,* the elements of pragmatic philosophy were alive with "new impulses" and "fresh efforts." At last, there was a philosophy that corresponded with Swedenborg's doctrine of usefulness. From the days of Berkeley and Kant down through the closing years of the nineteenth century with Josiah Royce's *The World and the Individual* (1900), idealism had held sway over the discipline. The common sense ideas of the Scottish school, French positivism, and German materialism had all played second fiddle to idealism's approach to experience. Not until the introduction of pragmatism in the opening years of the twentieth century did a philosophy emerge that was capable of attacking the "vicious intellectualism" of the day by asserting the ability "to reduce the external world to order and bend it to our service." Hite reveled in the opportunity to abandon the conceptual world of Plato and "plunge into the blooming, buzzing confusion of sensible experience, and there make direct acquaintance with genuine reality." This "new realism," which he attributed to the work of John Dewey at Chicago, William James at Harvard, and F. C. S. Schiller at Oxford, placed emphasis on the instrumental function of thought.[87]

Pragmatism signaled an intellectual declaration of independence from the historical philosophies of the past, particularly from idealism. It was a method, explained Hite, "of solving our problems, of eliminating meaningless questions, and of choosing, and confining ourselves to, really important issues." It forced one to think in concrete terms and not be "hoodwinked . . . by big words and verbal abstractions." It offered "a theory of *meaning,* a theory of *truth,* and a theory of *knowledge*" that allowed for hypotheses and scientific generalizations to serve as instruments of human action. And provided that pragmatism could "enlarge its notion of 'practical,' and take the term 'consequences' as equivalent to possible experience," Hite felt that "knowledge, truth, and meaning alike [would] lead to God as their reality and fulfilment."[88]

This new realism asserted that purely rational considerations did not determine the issues of life. As a matter of practical existence, life was full of chances, of incomplete knowledge, and of hypotheses in which belief or disbelief was of little consequence. There were, on the other hand, matters, such as the existence of God, immortality, and even the credibility of Swedenborg, that involved moral decisions whose significance could not be ignored. One had to "take the chance or do without the truth. The fear of being in error is cowardly when we are faced with the opportunity to get the truth. Furthermore, taking the risk and making the choice may be just what is needed to bring the truth to pass. We thus take part in making truth, as Thomas Jefferson made democratic truth by the Declaration of Independence, or Swedenborg made religious truth by believing in his mission." By Hite's standard, James's will to believe was the proper way to make life worth living, provided that the satisfaction of combining will and choice gave character to each individual and meaning to the world by direct, creative, and determined actions. In short, the will to believe would "enable us to bring the primal chaos of experience into some sort of order; and we utilize this order in carrying out our purposes." Raw experience allowed one to identify, distinguish, separate, and combine characteristics, obtaining properties, such as hardness, toughness, and mass, that would help to formulate the relevant laws. And all such laws were "the outcome of mental operations upon the raw materials furnished by direct contact with the concrete world."[89]

According to Hite's analysis, James had drawn from the language of Swedenborg an understanding of life whose precise character derived from experience. Against the emptiness and unintelligibility of the Absolute, James affirmed a connectedness of subject and object to the actual world—a "world of actual experience [that] yields ample oneness of the felt and perceived sort." The world was "radically pluralistic," with nothing "added to it by superposing the absolute." Reality existed in the concreteness of immediate experience. "The real essence of rationality," concluded Hite, "lies precisely in the feeling, or the experience, of intimacy in the actual world." While the naturalists had created a rigid environment in which human beings lived to survive in passivity, the pragmatists had offered an infinite number of possibilities for the play of intelligence in life's experiences.[90]

Recognizing the instrumental nature of thought, James focused his attention on the immediacy of concrete experience rather than on those transcendent and mysterious forms of abstract knowledge. The object "no longer hangs in a remote and inaccessible realm," so "the truth, now like the object, is brought down from the ideal and abstract realm of eternal forms to the level of our passing experience." According to Hite, James's work was of monumental importance, furnishing an incisive introduction into the philosophy of existence, but in the end, his analysis of James's pragmatism was not without criticism:

> Truth and good constitute in Swedenborg's terms a distinct one. Pragmatism tends too much to subordinate truth. Truth and good are aspects of one life, one context of experience, as pragmatism insists; but this life, this context of experience, is not the mere flux of the moment: it is an infinitely complex organism, the type of which already exists in its completeness, but being infinite it contains within itself infinite possibilities of finite development and variation. Our concrete acquaintance with such an organism is given us in our actual experience of the combined functions of love, wisdom, and use.[91]

The Swedenborgian minister and president of Urbana University Frank Sewall (1837–1915), too, was drawn to James's insistence on the right to believe and therefore to his rejection of those devotees of pure science who chose agnosticism. Sewall admired James's position that truth was not an abstraction of mere thinking, but a form of conduct. Though James nowhere appealed to revealed thought or to the scriptures, Sewall respected his "valiant and generous plea for a man's psychological right to a religious belief."

> And if we may "accept on trust" a belief in the supernatural, may we not accept as legitimately "on trust" the fact of a written revelation of Divine Truth, nay, of an Incarnation of the Eternal Word in human form, and so likewise the fact of an ulterior revelation through special gifts of extraordinary seership both into the inner depths of Divine Truth within the parable of the Scriptures, and into those planes of spiritual existence which, though always

and closely encompassing all living beings, are necessarily not visible to organs of physical sense?[92]

Similarly, Rev. Paul Sperry, president of the General Convention and one of the leaders of the modernist movement within the New Church, explained in terms reminiscent of James not only that usefulness was good because it worked but that it worked because it was good. Doing things unselfishly had a place in the divine plan, in that progress was largely dependent upon human activity and service. The same was true of the spiritual world, where angelic life consisted of usefulness, each angel doing his or her part in the fulfillment of the divine plan. "The Lord's kingdom is a kingdom of uses," Sperry noted, "and everything which is to be a part of that system or kingdom must perform its proper function or use."[93] Unselfish usefulness, or the performance of a service outside of self, brought the deepest satisfactions to the human heart. Genuine love of the Lord and of one's neighbor furnished the only true impulse. That is to say, "only a good man can be truly useful." Usefulness was not realized by what was done, but by the way it was done, the fitness of the individual doing it, and the individual's efficiency in doing it. "We are useful as we carry out the possibilities of our nature," Sperry wrote, and "we are useless as we destroy our possibilities either by doing nothing . . . or by doing wrong and harmful things which destroy us spiritually and also injure our neighbor and dishonor our Creator."[94]

Usefulness had a fixed place in the divine plan and was the fulfillment of the Creator's intention of making humanity a pivotal force in the construction of the world. The stability of the angelic and natural worlds depended upon the members of each doing their part. Only then could there be the natural and spiritual advancement of humanity.

> The use is in a peculiar sense within the thing and awaits expression, or that it is a definite potential use which gives occasion for the existence of the thing. The use did not arise after the thing had been made; it was there inside of it, as it were its very soul waiting to be given the freedom of exercise. The deed clothes the use and

brings it out into serviceable contact with the world.... Therefore one is useful, not so much according to the specific thing he does, as according to the way he does it, the fitness of his doing it, the possibility of his real efficiency in doing it.[95]

Sperry identified "three ways of finding out how to be useful and at the same time of accomplishing real usefulness." First, ask the Creator to put oneself to work that is useful. Second, examine oneself inwardly so as to determine whether one has the desire, education, and experience to do a certain thing. And third, choose something based on one's best judgment. Usefulness did not demand genius, special talent, wealth, or honorable distinction; it only required honest effort. "If that love of being useful is in the heart of any one, be he prince or peasant, captain of industry or common laborer, legislator or humble citizen, that man has a valuable heritage, an opportunity to serve his fellow man, he has the secret of eternal happiness."[96] Usefulness existed in every environment and began as a small seed before developing into something great. Whoever was inspired by unselfish love was destined to recognize that which the Creator valued above all else. "If we recognize the real fact that no man of himself can do anything useful, and that every man's use is but the Lord's work in and through him, then we may recognize that pliability in the Lord's hands, ready yielding to the Divine manipulation is what makes a man to be useful." As Sperry pointed out, the Creator's rewards were distributed according to the spirit of an individual's usefulness, which not only had a practical importance in fulfilling a myriad of needs for civilization but also had a religious value as well. Here was the basis of humankind's covenant with the Creator. It was the covenant intended for membership in the community of the New Church.[97]

Sperry's support of pragmatism as a method of realizing "usefulness" brought the New Church into the forefront of those who aligned themselves with this new philosophy. Notwithstanding Richard Rorty's (his grandfather was Walter Rauschenbusch) trenchant critique of progressivism, which suggested that pragmatism was inherently conservative and that it sustained established institutions, there is ample reason to argue that the pragmatist's view of a better world represented a prophetic stand for purposive change through social engineering. What Rorty failed to understand was the Jeffersonians' inclination to utilize the power and scope of the federal government to achieve its ends.[98]

A formidable player in the biological and medical sciences, psychology, philosophy, and religion, James was gifted with the ability to bring wholly different and illuminating perspectives into each of these disciplines. Having a rich diversity of experience and knowledge, his study of humanity demonstrated a distinctive worldview. Although Van Wyck Brooks accused him of "destroying ethical morality and leaving the American mind to its own devices which, compared to the European . . . were hopelessly low-class," Alfred North Whitehead considered James to be one of the world's four greatest philosophers (along with Plato, Aristotle, and Leibniz) and his philosophy to be on par with Francis Bacon's experimentalism in human thinking.[99] As these two extremes suggest, James impelled readers in many different directions. For some, his philosophy represented the application of Darwin's evolutionary theory to the definition of truth; for others, it provided a foundation for scientific positivism; and still for others, it was viewed as a license to believe and make judgments without depending on either abstract reasoning or facts.

James was no system-maker dealing with broad generalizations; instead, he gloried in the things that could *not* be analyzed or systematized, preferring instead to embrace the novelty and multiplicity of life and the richness of data that defied easy scheme-making. His radical empiricism was itself an attack on the monistic philosophizing of his generation. Unlike Spencer, who in his senior years found his once highly touted synthetic philosophy crumbling before a generation of philosophers and social scientists, James found his ideas continuing to gain supporters even when he moved into metaphysical areas that were not typically recognized among devotees of science. His intense devotion to the search for truth and his treatment of any and all data found as significant made him one of the most influential psychologists in his day—and, as Dewey foretold, one of the greatest psychologists of all time.[100]

A virtual artist of the mind, this teacher of physiology and son of a Swedenborgian theologian felt impelled to treat the functioning brain and nervous system as an integrated organ of sensations and an instrument of action. In doing so, he brought the natural sciences into conversation with the fields of psychology and philosophy. Like an impressionistic painter, any distinctions he made between the material and the metaphysical, between the objective and the subjective, faded in the glare of light, suggesting forms hardly recognizable close up but exposing meaning and significance when viewed with the proper perspective. As a physiologist and philosopher, he expanded the boundaries of the mind by driving home the point that life was decided moment to moment and not as the dull mechanical outcome of a determinant chain of events. "In no revival of a past experience," James wrote, "are all the items of our thought equally operative in determining what the next thought shall be."[101] One understood life not by reducing it to intellectual categories or mechanical principles but by grasping intuitively the connection between the individual as knower and the individual as doer. It meant rejecting an absolute distinction between subject and object by recognizing the right to believe and running the risk of error (i.e., the courage to risk success and failure in the experience of testing or experimentation). James never claimed to be an ethical teacher, but he conveyed a moral atmosphere in his works that showed fully the character of the man.

8 Pastoral Clinical Movement

Work cure is the best of all psychotherapy, in my opinion. . . .
As well might we expect a patient to recover without food as to
recover without work. . . . The sound man needs work to keep
him sound, but the nervous invalid has an even greater need of
work to draw him out of his isolation, and to stop the miseries
of doubt and self-scrutiny, to win back self-respect and the
support of fellowship.

(Richard Clarke Cabot, *Psychotherapy*, 1909)

In Christianity, the priest's function has long been associated with restoration of both physical and spiritual health. With his power of forgiveness, this healer of souls could also extend his power to the healing of disease. Except for Roman Catholicism and fringe sects within Protestantism, religion since the age of Descartes has tended to defer the healing of the physical body to the natural sciences. Nevertheless, the mind, as distinct from the soul, has never been relinquished entirely to reductionist medicine. While prayer, faith healing, and experimental mind-cures have remained outliers to Christianity's earlier alliance with miracle-workers, the teachings of modern psychology have offered a window for religion to again assert its role, even if forced to take a back seat to reductionist medicine. That mind governs organ tissue and physiological functions by an effort of the will has made clear that below the plane of conscious mental life there is a vast unexplored region of unconscious thinking that influences health.

That said, the nonbiological aspects of healing remained a flash-point in the ongoing dialogue between religion and medicine in the late nineteenth and early twentieth centuries, as pastoral care claimed a role in the healing process that the medical profession reserved only for licensed physicians. As the visible arm of the social gospel, what became known as the pastoral clinical movement was a collaborative undertaking by American physicians and clergy that achieved in its treatment of functional diseases what Washington Gladden, Lyman Abbott, and Walter Rauschenbusch had done for child welfare and the labor movement. Predominantly Protestant in its perspective, the movement was stimulated by the Flexner Report of 1910, which urged that a clinical year be added to medical students' curriculum. This idea was subsequently applied to the placement of seminarians in hospitals and clinics as a way for them to learn about and work directly with physicians in the treatment of mental illnesses. In the clergy's search for a legitimate role in the field of healthcare, there were several questions that required answers: Could the ministerial ranks of American Protestantism claim a rightful leadership role with regard to discrete aspects of psychological and psychosomatic illnesses? To what degree could the clergy properly practice psychotherapy in its efforts to succeed at the "curing of souls"? What justified, let alone qualified, a minister—even one with a PhD—to undertake such a practice?

The Emmanuelists

The pastoral clinical movement had its official beginnings in 1925 at Worcester State Hospital in Massachusetts, developing from efforts that had begun decades, if not centuries, earlier by John Wesley, Cotton Mather, Swedenborgians, mesmerists, phrenologists, magnetizers, and the followers of the American spiritual teacher Phineas Parkhurst Quimby (1802–66), whose disciples included Mary Baker Eddy, founder of Christian Science, and the broad umbrella of unchurched mind-cure healers who were affiliated with the New Thought movement. The more immediate origins of the pastoral clinical movement were tied to the work of Elwood Worcester, rector of Boston's Emmanuel Church; his clerical colleague Samuel McComb;

internist Dr. Richard Clarke Cabot; psychiatrist Dr. Isador Coriat; and Dr. James Jackson Putnam, professor of neurology at Harvard. Their group effort, known as the Emmanuelists, represented a collaborative venture between conventional medicine and religion that sought to treat the psychiatric illnesses of marginalized and underserved patients—principally those suffering from neurasthenia, fear, anxiety, worry, and alcoholism. Their healing strategy was built upon the idea of surrender and a process of conversion that resulted in a new holism dedicated to love, usefulness, and moral reconstruction.[1]

Emmanuelism combined elements of mesmerism, transcendentalism, Shaker mysticism, and Quimbyism with the more recent work of William James and European experimental psychologists Wilhelm Wundt and Gustav Fechner to reveal a Christ who had the power not only to redeem but to heal.[2] Formed by a partnership between a select number of physicians who were willing to accept the limitations of reductionist medicine and an enthusiastic group of highly trained clergy who were intent on expanding their pastoral obligations, the program sought to revitalize an area of healing that had once been a vibrant part of early Christianity.[3] Popularized for a decade in the press and in magazines, Emmanuelism spread through more than forty ministries in several states and abroad, becoming a subject of intense interest in the years leading up to the dominance of Freudian psychiatry.[4]

Worcester was born into a clerical family of Swedenborgians and later attended Columbia University and the General Theological Seminary in New York, where he prepared for ordination into the Episcopal priesthood.[5] He then went abroad to earn his doctorate in psychology at the University of Leipzig, studying there with Wundt and Fechner. Fechner was interested in *Geisteswissenschaft* ("sciences of the mind"), a belief system which suggested that the relations between the material and spiritual worlds could be realized without reducing either of these realms to the terms of the other. Worcester cited Fechner as his source for the idea that mind, body, and spirit are interdependent, with each having functions exclusive of the others but all united in their action to address illness. Using this understanding as his rationale, Worcester set out to strike a balance between strict reductionist medicine, which explained psychological phenomena in terms of bodily states, and the extremes of Christian Science, "which explained away all bodily suffering or material deprivation by calling it mere mental error."[6] To achieve this, Worcester drew on John Dewey's and William James's contributions in clinical and educational matters, including those related to the psychology of religion and religious experience, to mediate between his objective and subjective tendencies.[7]

After accepting the pastorate of Emmanuel Church in Boston's Back Bay in 1904, Worcester decided to rekindle the healing ministry of Christianity by combining the power of Jesus "with the views and practices of modern science." Joining forces with Dr. Joseph Hersey Pratt of Massachusetts General Hospital and Dr. John D. Quackenbos, a fellow of the New Hampshire Society for the Prevention of Consumption, Worcester designed a group psychotherapy regimen of treatment for twenty-five of the city's poor and mostly black consumptives. The regimen, which was a precursor to the group techniques that would later be used in Alcoholics Anonymous, consisted of organized classes that were designed to instill morale and instruct on hygiene. As part of the class exercises, patients were taught methods that would help them to avoid communicating the disease to others. These methods were supplemented by readings from the Bible; hypno-suggestion; group pledges using the Apostles' Creed; prayers and lectures addressing the practical implications of worry, fear, and grief; and a religious mass or service. Samuel McComb, a Presbyterian minister who had trained in Ireland before attending lectures on psychology at Berlin and Oxford, joined in the endeavor and became a strong and loyal colleague.[8]

Following their success with consumptives, Worcester and McComb consulted with physicians in Boston and later in New York, Philadelphia, and Baltimore, seeking their support to expand the church's efforts to treat nervous and psychosomatic disorders. With the encouragement of psychiatrists Isador Coriat and Richard Clarke Cabot, they offered their parish facilities to those with moral or psychological problems who might wish to consult with them. Approximately two hundred sufferers ended up seeking their help, including many who required more than moral, educational, or suggestive treatment.[9] Their patients included not only those with nervous dyspepsia, neuralgia, neurasthenia, hypochondria, hysteria, and other troubles of the mind, but also those diagnosed with arteriosclerosis, hemiplegia, exophthalmic goiter, dementia praecox, locomotor ataxia, poliomyelitis, osteoarthritis, and tumors. In treating both organic and functional illnesses, the Emmanuelists went far beyond their initial objectives.[10]

With regimens comparable to biofeedback, spiritual meditation, and other holistic practices that are common today, Worcester and his colleagues introduced the power and influence of chaplaincy into the healing process.[11] For two years, he and his staff practiced innovative clinical treatments that, according to critics, grew increasingly nonscientific, as they drifted into Christian Science, Spiritualism, and dream analysis. Treatment also included Cabot's so-called "work cure," implying that work "unifies the personality, swings the centre out of self, occupies the thoughts, and furnishes normal and habitual expression to the new-born energies." Putting one's energies into useful, constructive work made for good "inner health" and served as a spiritual cleanser for troubled minds and "wounded hearts," thus bringing consolation and uplifting those who were suffering from complex and elusive problems.[12]

Lyman Pierson Powell, rector of St. John's Church in Northampton, Massachusetts, applied Christian faith to all nervous functional disorders. Using methods that were distinct from Christian Science but within the context of New Thought's suggestive psychotherapies, Powell recommended a re-energized Christianity that projected a vision of Christ healing one's body, mind, and soul. Supported by the editors of *Ladies' Home Journal, Good Housekeeping,* and *The Congregationalist,* he and other Emmanuelists offered a version of the social gospel that was directed at the healing process.[13]

Publications employed by Emmanuelists to explain their methods included the journal *Psychotherapy;* Paul Dubois's *The Psychic*

Treatment of Nervous Disorders (1905); Worcester, McComb, and Coriat's *Religion and Medicine* (1908), which became the official exposition of the movement and its practice; and Stanton Davis Kirkham's *The Philosophy of Self-Help: An Application of Practical Psychology to Daily Life* (1909).

CRITICS AND SUPPORTERS

Emmanuelism became a frequent topic of interest among women's clubs in the Northeast. For example, the Women's Council of the New York Association, which was affiliated with the New Church, met to discuss this movement in the Brooklyn Public Library in February of 1909. It opened with a discussion of *Religion and Medicine* before turning to Swedenborg's writings on the treatment of disease. This was followed by discourse centered on the differences between the Emmanuel Movement, Christian Science, and the emerging movement known as New Thought, which advocated healthy-mindedness through various methods of self-affirmation.[14]

For three years, Worcester and his staff treated patients at their church clinic, but this caused members of the medical community to question whether their program was dispensing medicine without a license. The suspicion held by doctors stemmed not simply from the program's advocacy of psychotherapy but also from the fact that nonphysicians were treating patients, and they were doing it *for free*. While psychiatry was finding a place in conventional medicine, the prospect of someone other than a licensed physician treating functional illnesses found few supporters within the medical community. Although he was an early advocate of Worcester's work, Harvard neurologist James Jackson Putnam shared in the wariness of his colleagues, eventually coming to regard Emmanuelism as a form of alternative medical authority that operated under the aegis of uncredentialed and untrained imitators. Even Richard Clarke Cabot, an early supporter of the Emmanuelists, gravitated toward a more doctor-dominated program at Massachusetts General Hospital, which is where he established the first social service department with social workers who did the work of the Emmanuelists but did so without the heavy hand of religious terminology. Ultimately, Cabot found it difficult to support ministers who could not tell the difference between religious therapy and some form of amateur psychiatry.[15]

On the authority and recommendations of American physician Silas Weir Mitchell, French neurologist Jean-Martin Charcot, and Swiss psychiatrist August Forel, the Emmanuelists also experimented with hypnosis. "Now we are surprised at this tendency to resort to hypnotism in Emmanuel Church," said H. Clinton Hay, "for at the outset Dr. Worcester and Dr. Putnam agreed upon the teachings of Dr. Paul Dubois, Professor of Neuropathology at the University of Berne," who did not approve of hypnotic therapy. Dubois's understanding "is in agreement with the teachings of the New Church in regard to freedom and reason, the precious jewels of human individuality," continued Hay, "for [these gifts] can be injured or even destroyed, in a sense, if we give up self-control for control by others." Given the nation's high regard for individualism and self-reliance at the time, the prospect of a patient's loss of control during hypnosis seemed a threat to the principles of rational psychotherapy.[16]

Defenders of Emmanuelism were typically members of the clergy who saw it not as a form of faith healing but as a legitimate form of psychotherapeutic treatment aimed at the reconstruction of the patient's moral and spiritual character, and thus within the purview of the ministry.[17] Faced, however, with mounting opposition, including a national effort to curb unregulated and unlicensed healers, Worcester was pressured into forming a medical advisory board whose members identified errors in the program's methods and promised a closer relationship between the physician and the clergyman.[18] To pacify critics, the Emmanuelists adopted the following rules:

(1) No person shall be received for treatment unless with the approval of, and having been thoroughly examined by, his family physician, whose report of the examination shall be filed with the minister's records. (2) No patient shall be referred for diagnosis or treatment to any specialist or assistant save with the advice and consent of the patient's own physician. (3) All patients who are not under the care of a physician must choose one, and put themselves in his care before they can receive instruction at Emmanuel Church.[19]

Under the revised protocols, *all* power rested with the physician to decide if a patient required referral to a neurologist or other specialist, or was suitable for treatment using moral and religious education. The board even went so far as to insist that Worcester discontinue any semblance of a church clinic, fearing the implication that it was a disguised form of medical treatment. Instead of treating disease, whether organic or functional, the church was directed to be "ready to assist in the moral and spiritual re-education of any person whom a physician asks him to see."[20]

Not all members of the medical profession found fault in the clergy's role. William Osler, Regis Chair of Medicine at Oxford, valued the Emmanuelists for their practical approach to faith. "A man must have faith in himself to be of any use in the world," he wrote. "There may be very little on which to base it—no matter, but faith in one's powers, in one's mission is essential to success." Noting the history of faith healing in the early Christian Church, the pious and simple sayings among the Peculiar People Christian movement in England, the alleged miracles at Lourdes, and the growth of Christian Science and homeopathy (the latter of which had its own Swedenborgian roots), Osler pointed out that each of these "deliciously credulous" examples owed their origin to the "chaotic mass of rubbish" doctors had forced on patients in their orgies of drugging, polypharmacy, and quack medicine. "It has done the profession good in awakening an interest in a too much neglected section of rational therapeutics," namely the relation of suggestion to the subconscious self. Osler endorsed the efforts of the Emmanuelists, noting that Dr. Joseph Hersey Pratt had been a former pupil of his. "I feel that our attitude as a profession should not be hostile," Osler concluded, "and we must scan gently our brother man and sister woman who may be carried away in the winds of new doctrine." The Emmanuelists were "active, earnest, capable" people at work on a problem, and it behooved the medical profession not to prejudge it.[21]

The Emmanuelists represented an offspring of New England's restless intellectual community who had dabbled in Spiritualism, telepathy, hypnotism, and other mind-over-body attractions. With churches having lost many of their historical roles and responsibilities, it was not at all strange that a few determined ministers would explore a combined medical and metaphysical treatment. The claims of the Emmanuelists differed little from those of Christian Scientists, except that the former worked *in concert with* the medical community. With the minister addressing the patient's moral and spiritual pathologies, and the physician looking at organic causation, the Emmanuelists informed the mind and educated the spirit by means of direct suggestion reinforced by faith. They hoped that in time doctors would endorse their healing regimen, as they intended a combined mental and moral program for those afflicted with various neuroses. The object was to maintain a healthy body, mind, and soul. As explained by historian Stow Persons, the movement represented a distinctive form of religio-therapy "that blended Christian faith in Christ's healing power with Jamesian mysticism, pre-Freudian psychiatry, and hypnosis." Before fading away, it produced a myriad of look-alike programs in Brooklyn, Boston, Philadelphia, Baltimore, Buffalo, Chicago, Detroit, Seattle, and San Francisco. Similar programs were formed in England, Ireland, Australia, South Africa, and Japan.[22]

Elwood Worcester practiced psychotherapy until his retirement in 1929, at which point he moved to New York to collaborate with Helen Dunbar at Columbia Presbyterian Hospital. The Emmanuel Movement eventually died out, and it was replaced by psychotherapeutic regimes administered by cadres of social workers, New Thought healers, trained psychologists, and Spiritualists.[23]

WORCESTER STATE HOSPITAL

Elwood Worcester's work among the Emmanuelists inspired Anton Boisen (1876–1965), considered the father of clinical pastoral education, to create a more holistic integration of psychoanalytic language and pastoral counseling. Unlike Worcester, however, Boisen never veered from recognizing the superiority of medical authority over nonmedical pastoral counseling.[24] A native of Indiana and a graduate of Indiana University, Boisen suffered from psychotic episodes (schizophrenia) before entering Union Theological Seminary in

New York, where he studied psychology under George Albert Coe, a longtime admirer of William James. After graduating in 1911, Boisen practiced ministerial work in both the Presbyterian and Congregational Churches before additional episodes of psychosis led to his hospitalization at Westboro State Hospital in Massachusetts. Upon his release, he went on to study the psychology of religion at Andover Theological Seminary. In 1925, he became a chaplain at Worcester State Hospital, a position he obtained through the support of physician and ethicist Richard Clarke Cabot and the hospital's superintendent, William D. Bryan, MD, the latter of whom was "an enlightened, dedicated administrator ... with a lively tradition of social awareness, educational and therapeutic innovation, and academic training in all disciplines including psychoanalysis."[25] Over the next several decades, Boisen, who ascribed his own recovery to the curative forces of religion, organized clinical training for seminary students at the hospital, taught ethics at Chicago Theological Seminary, and helped form the Council for the Clinical Training of Theological Students. His publications included *The Exploration of the Inner World* (1936), *Religion in Crisis and Custom* (1955), and *Out of the Depths* (1960).[26] Using his own experience, as well as drawing on the personal histories of George Fox, Emanuel Swedenborg,[27] and the biblical figures Ezekiel and Jeremiah, Boisen developed a perspective on mental illness and religion that became central to the core philosophy of the pastoral care movement. His acute interest in clinical observation and his own personal experience became the frame of reference for his choice of the case method.[28]

Recognizing a relationship—both good and bad—between mental illness and religious faith, Boisen urged that mental diseases be treated by utilizing a combination of reductionist knowledge and religious counseling. In the understanding of both normal and abnormal human experience, he thought it important to recognize the inner forces at work in shaping human behavior. Concerned with the lack of attention paid to the empirical data that one could gather about people's lives, Boisen teamed up with Richard Clarke Cabot to advocate the case history approach to ministerial training. Each patient became a "living document" whose values, beliefs, and behavior could come together in memory, self-examination, and judgment. While systematic observation and repeatable experiments were the warp and woof of scientific knowledge, mental and emotional responses to life situations made it difficult to organize human behavior into neat categories. The exactness and predictability possible in scientific knowledge failed to materialize when individuals faced exposure to psychological challenges. Each human being contained an assortment of experiences, complexities, tragedies, and possibilities whose solutions were not always scientific and technical, but psychological and religious as well.[29]

Assisting Anton Boisen in his clinical pastoral education efforts was the brilliant practical theoretician, psychiatrist, and Dantean scholar Helen Flanders Dunbar (1902–59), who had suffered from a variety of illnesses in her youth. A graduate of Bryn Mawr and Union Theological Seminary, she earned a PhD at Columbia University in medical science and an MD at Yale. She trained with Boisen at Worcester State Hospital and later worked with Carl Jung in Zurich, Switzerland. Besides directing the Council for the Clinical Training of Theological Students in New York City (1930–42)—as well as directing the Joint Committee on Religion and Medicine for the Federal Council of Churches and the New York Academy of Medicine (1931–36)—she taught at the New York Psychoanalytic Institute, played a central role in the founding of the American Psychosomatic Society in 1942, and was the first editor of APS's journal *Psychosomatic Medicine.* Her publications included *Emotions and Bodily Changes* (1935), *Psychosomatic Diagnosis* (1943), and *Mind and Body: Psychosomatic Medicine* (1947). A fervent believer in the interplay of mind and body, her holistic approach to unlocking psychosomatic illness proved invaluable to the advocates of pastoral counseling.[30]

As director of the Council for the Clinical Training of Theological Students, Dunbar was responsible for overseeing the training of seminarians whose objective was to treat the body, mind, and spirit as an intimately connected whole. Recognizing that the psychic component was a major determinant in chronic illnesses, she viewed the trained clergyman as someone who could complement the work of the medical doctor in the healing process; and it was this idea in particular that had brought her to Worcester State Hospital in 1925 to work with Boisen's groundbreaking enterprise. From her experiences with Boisen and with the clinical training of clergymen, she proceeded to reduce the impediments that separated medicine and religion by reconciling and recasting the roles of science and religion into a new and more balanced partnership. Her most important contribution to the field was the holistic and pragmatic approach to treating the patient that she brought to the imperfect nature of clinical decision-making.[31] As explained by Robert Charles Powell: "She considered her research on mind-body interaction and integration as highly practical, as providing knowledge relevant to physicians' practice albeit disseminated through clergy." A clinically trained clergy filled an essential role in preventive medicine.[32]

Another major contributor to the pastoral clinical movement was the physician, philosopher, and social worker Richard Clarke Cabot (1868–1939), who was destined to be a leader in the field. His father, who had been educated abroad, had lectured at the Cambridge Metaphysical Club and had been a close friend of Emerson. Nurtured in an atmosphere of wealth and privilege, which included receiving a superior education, Cabot dedicated his life to helping the less advantaged by becoming a Unitarian minister. He studied philosophy under William James, Josiah Royce, and George Herbert Palmer at Harvard before switching his studies to medicine. Married in the Swedenborgian Church in Waltham, Massachusetts, he and his wife Ella (a grandniece of James Russell Lowell; a graduate of Radcliffe and Harvard; and author of several books on ethics, religion, and education) shared a strong spiritual and intellectual commitment. An admirer of action-oriented pragmatism, Cabot began his medical career as house officer at Massachusetts General Hospital before becoming director of outpatient services, where he discovered that social, economic, and family environment affected the unhealthy status of many patients. As a teacher at Harvard Medical School, he invited social workers to assist with the nonphysiological aspects of patient health and introduced case analysis, which soon after became a standard teaching method for medical education. He also emphasized the importance of mentoring medical students as a way to form professional identity.[33]

Following his service in the United States Army Medical Reserve Corps in France during the First World War, Cabot returned to Boston where, hoping to organize the field of social ethics so that it would be comparable in standing with those of law and medicine, he developed a combined philosophy/sociology program at the Harvard Divinity School. There, he initiated a pastoral counseling program designed to transform the practice of social work from fixing clients' problems to helping them help themselves. He later became chair of Harvard's department of social ethics, adopting the clinic-pathological method to hospital social work. Author of "A Plea for a Clinical Year in the Course of Theological Study," he not only urged social workers into hospital settings but took seminarians away from their books to learn firsthand from patients who were suffering from physical and mental illnesses.[34]

The New Thought Movement

Outside the religious overtones of the Emmanuelists and the pastoral clinical efforts of Boisen, Dunbar, and Cabot were the parallel efforts of the New Thought movement, which William James called a "religion of healthy-mindedness." Drawing from both US native and foreign roots, New Thought espoused an intuitive belief that a healthy-minded attitude could be obtained through auto-suggestion, silence, and visualization and that it could overcome negativity, disease, and even poverty. The power of the mind could set an individual on a course of physical and mental health, interacting at the mind's subconscious level to repair the "sick soul."[35] Like the Emmanuelists, New Thoughters insisted that a single powerful mind could, by suggestion and other means, help another mind to overcome wrongful ways of thinking.[36] Although mainline Christian churches had divested themselves of their belief in their own therapeutic powers, mind-curists continued to use the techniques of silence, letting go, suggestion, guided imagery and visualization, breathing exercises, meditation, and other similar methods.[37]

The ideas and practices of New Thought—a mixture of liberal Christianity, transcendentalism, Spiritualism, and Swedenborgianism—held that the mental world was the only true reality and that the material world was its creation. According to Swedenborg, the activities and faculties of the body were maintained by divine influx. Each individual lived and had his being from the Lord. Thus, the health of the body constantly flowed from the Lord in a heavenly order, while disturbances arose from opposing influx, namely from the hells and from those in the spiritual world who were in opposition to the Lord's love and wisdom. Health and disease had a spiritual origin, the logical inference being that if the cause could be removed, the effect would cease to exist, and a cure could be established.[38]

James described New Thought's approach as "an intuitive belief in the all-saving power of healthy-minded attitudes as such, in the conquering efficacy of courage, hope, and trust, and a correlative contempt for doubt, fear, worry, and all nervously precautionary states of mind."[39] In his support for bringing psychology and religion together in dialogue, he identified Henry Wood and Horatio W. Dresser as the most successful representatives of this form of pastoral counseling. In espousing this hybrid philosophy that was simultaneously religious, synoptic, idealistic, optimistic, transformative, and eclectic in nature, James spoke of a harmony unfolding between the individual, God, and society that could free humans of their combative creeds and dogmas as well as of life's material impediments, including sickness and disease. The writings of both Wood and Dresser passed the pragmatic test of making a positive difference in the lives of those whose bodies and minds were restored to normalcy. Any idea or suggestion that kindled a condition of healthy-mindedness was worthy of consideration. When successful, "healthy-minded" individuals tended to be optimistic, seeing the world as good in contrast to those "sick souls" whose sense of sin, depression, and angst tore at their sense of self.[40] Those who believed in a transcendent source and enjoyed enhanced levels of emotional satisfaction often found a fuller sense of meaning in their lives. Emotions carried cognitive value that improved the quality of life.[41]

Horatio W. Dresser

In his day, there was probably no more steadfast and prolific proponent of Swedenborg's social psychology and the pastoral clinical movement than Horatio Willis Dresser (1866–1954). Born to parents who held strongly to the belief that healing and religion were intimately entwined, Dresser spent a lifetime speculating, testing, and practicing the interrelationship of these two disciplines. A prolific author schooled by some of the nation's best minds, he drew upon sources both ancient and modern to construct his view of the natural and spiritual worlds. A lifelong admirer of Swedenborg, he sought to fit his ideas and beliefs into the intellectual constructs of the modern world. One of the founders of the New Thought movement, he proved to be among its more popular and coherent spokespersons.[42]

Horatio's parents, Julius A. and Annetta G. Dresser, had once been patients of the healer Phineas Parkhurst Quimby, whose introspective experiences in the healing arts challenged the commonsense knowledge of the day. Beginning as an inquisitive mesmerist, Quimby analyzed not only his patients' but also his own experiences in the healing encounter, eventually replacing his mesmeric techniques with what he called the "silent method"—a treatment that encouraged patients to discover their own inner spiritual power so as to overcome disease and illness. Cured under Quimby's guidance, the Dressers moved to Boston, where they opened a mental healing practice based on the "Quimby System of Mental Treatment of Diseases." There, they wrote articles for various periodicals, defending their healing theories and techniques against the methods of another of Quimby's patients, Mary Baker Eddy. Unlike the Dressers, Eddy organized Quimby's methods into a church-based healing system initially named the Church of Christ, Scientist, and later simply as Christian Science.

As part of their practice, the Dressers offered a course consisting of twelve lectures that described health as being spiritual in nature and as the outer reflection of a person's inner world, or what they called "the Christ within." Following Quimby's format, they explained disease as consisting of false beliefs and opinions that were holding the body in bondage. The course discussed such topics as "the description and analysis of experiences illustrative of mental influence, point[ing] out the effect of erroneous opinions and beliefs"; "divine immanaence"; "the nature of matter"; "the subconscious after-effects of dynamic opinions and beliefs"; "the spiritual nature of man"; and the idea that "the spiritual life is continuous—that we already live in eternity." "The impression produced by the lectures was deeply religious."[43]

In honor of her mentor, Annetta published *The Philosophy of P. P. Quimby* (1895), a book of recollections outlining Quimby's life, philosophy, and healing methods, including portions of his unpublished manuscripts that she and others had edited. Four years later, Julius published *The True History of Mental Science* (1899), which contained a series of lectures that he delivered at the Church of the Divine Unity in Boston. Evident in these lectures was his deep regard for Plato, Emerson, and the healing practices of Quimby.[44]

Horatio, the oldest of the Dresser children, left primary school at thirteen to learn telegraphy and, three years later, was managing a railroad station on the Central Pacific line in Pinole, California. Later, he moved to New England, where he joined his parents in their mental healing practice in Boston, catering principally to an aging generation of Transcendentalists, Unitarians, Theists, and lapsed Eddyites. Gifted with strong communication skills, he became known among the town's Spiritualists as having mediumship abilities and a degree of telepathic powers.[45]

Horatio admired his parents' generation for having replaced the harsh protocols of conventional medicine with gentle reasoning and positive framing. The essential elements to bodily health and healthy-mindedness required a certain calmness to be generated by the healer, the patient's willingness to cooperate, a mind freed of inner discord, and an assumed "oneness" with God. To the extent that the diseased body or "sick soul" put faith into practice, the patient was capable of adjusting his or her inmost thoughts and external actions to the fullness of God's love.

In 1891, Horatio entered Harvard and, while a student there, wrote and delivered lectures under the title "Talks on Life in

Relation to Health." One of these talks, published as *The Immanent God: An Essay* (1895), referred to God as love and to evolution as God's method of creation, which he understood as a power and process to be shared with humanity once it had progressed sufficiently in intelligence and reasoning.[46] That same year, he published *The Power of Silence: A Study of the Values and Ideals of the Inner Life*, capturing much of what Quimby and his parents had been advocating in their healing practices.[47]

The Power of Silence offered a practical method for bringing "first principles" to the common seeker. Dresser explained the purpose of meditation, which he called the "power of silence" or "entering the silence," indicating how the mind could be a catalyst for mental healing. Disease and illness, which Dresser considered to be conditions of the *whole* person, were addressed by concentrating the mind on an uplifting thought or idea. He felt that the newly developed science of psychology offered valuable insight into this inner world of patients, as it allowed them to turn away from the hurrying world and—in a state of calmness, clarity, and intuitiveness—discover harmony within themselves and others. "He who thus knows himself," Dresser wrote, "whose motive is right, may go forth into the world unconcernedly; for the conditions we attract depend upon the attitude within." The soul's awakening became a turning point in life, sustaining and guiding the individual through times of struggle, doubt, and weakness.[48]

A devotee of Emerson, the prophet of self-reliance, Dresser celebrated individuality as an escape to freedom, a desire to attain a higher self that led ultimately to the Christ-ideal. The self-reliant individual was the Christ-centered soul operating in an environment of calm, self-possessed consciousness and self-realization. Humans were challenged to find their place in the world, to learn the wisdom surrounding their circumstances, and to become a center of force or consciousness that brought value to society. The Christ-ideal joined the individual and the Absolute together in unity. In his advocacy of individualism, Dresser viewed the world not as a stage for the individual to flaunt his ego, but as a place of social harmony and love born of the Christ-ideal.[49] To the degree that each person moved consciously toward self-analysis and interaction with other minds—avoiding creeds, dogmas, and customs along the way—one could realize true individuality and the fullness of human freedom. At such moments, the individual became the owner, not the property, of belief. Only then was he or she spiritually free to ascend into liberty and the broadening of life and self-understanding.[50]

Along with many in his generation, Dresser felt that a spiritual awakening was imminent in the world, a belief that was strongly encouraged by the convening of the Parliament of Religions, which he attended during the Columbian Exposition in 1893. The experience broadened his appreciation of many of the great religions of the world. An admirer of Victor Cousin's philosophy of eclecticism, he conceived of the world as a spiritual household in which all God's children could come together as one family in mutual respect, in a community of spirit, and in a devotion to righteousness. He hoped for a "religion of spirit" rather than one dedicated to creed or dogma—something that would be inclusive of all the sacred books of the West and the East. While many viewed the age as predominantly one of invention and discovery, a conclusion easily drawn from the technological discoveries that were introduced at the Columbian Exposition, Dresser thought the age would be far better known for being a time when no organism, society, institution, philosophy, religion, or nation stood apart from the process of evolution. Notwithstanding Darwin's theory of natural selection, he considered it absurd to think that evolution implied an absent God. Evolution may be the law of life, but it did not negate God's ontological presence.[51]

Dresser preferred theism, finding God *in,* rather than identical with, the world. Life, he explained, was a "continuous, divine communication" and not the detritus of some momentary event in the past. To the extent that creation was continuous, he urged, humanity should make efforts to adjust to it.[52] Evolution was a messy process that included the adaptation of a species by means of chance or random variations. Still, there remained an intervening providence that revealed itself to the world of humans, whose conscious intelligence stood as an independent force in nature and who, as moral beings, participated in the evolutionary process and its final product. Dresser invoked a mental evolution aimed at blunting the brutish aspects of life's struggles. In fact, God and humanity constituted a single intelligence that ultimately reconciled evolution in the concept of the Universal Human.[53]

It was during this seasoning of Dresser's spiritual interests that he helped organize the Metaphysical Club of Boston (1895) "to promote interest in and the practice of a true spiritual philosophy of life and happiness; to show that through right thinking one's loftiest ideas may be brought into perfect realization; [and] to advance the intelligent and systematic treatment of disease by mental methods." The club (not to be confused with the short-lived Metaphysical Club formed by Charles Peirce, William James, and Oliver Wendell Holmes, Jr., in Cambridge, Massachusetts) became a way station along the path to greater appreciation of the world's religions and growing interest in mental healing. It offered its members, which included Unitarian minister Loren B. Macdonald, Dr. J. W. Winkley, and Frederick Reed, a "silence room" for use to contemplate spiritual truths.[54]

Dresser also involved himself with the International Metaphysical League, whose early meetings helped launch the New Thought movement.[55] In addition, he helped found *The Journal of Practical Metaphysics* (1896–98), which advocated for a "more harmonious, rational, and ethical life." When the journal merged with the literary and political magazine *The Arena,* founded by Benjamin O. Flower, he served for a time as its associate editor before leaving in 1899 to start the magazine *The Higher Law* (1899–1902). Looking to expand his horizons, Dresser taught correspondence courses in spiritual philosophy, became proprietor from 1896 to 1898 of the Philosophical Publishing Company, and traveled abroad.

Dresser married Alice Mae Reed (1870–1961), a Wellesley graduate and high school teacher, whose brother, Frederick, managed the Greenacre Conferences in Eliot, Maine, a spiritual retreat center for the proponents of New Thought and the Baha'i faith. There, too, scholars from Hindu, Buddhist, Confucian, Parsi (Zoroastrian), Muslim, Christian, and Jewish faiths gathered in a spirit of friendship and openness to discuss their common interests in spirituality, revelation, and the lessons intended for the soul's happiness. Out of this endeavor came a flowering of scholarship that not only enhanced the growing reputation of New Thought but also incorporated greater amounts of Hindu and Buddhist thinking into different forms of mind-cure techniques.

In 1902, Dresser returned to Harvard, where he earned a master's degree in philosophy and, three years later, a PhD, studying under William James, Hugo Munsterberg, George Herbert Palmer, and Josiah Royce. From 1903 to 1911, he honed his teaching skills at Harvard, at Radcliffe, and, for a brief period as professor of applied psychology, at the Massachusetts College of Osteopathy. During that time he authored numerous books on spiritual and physical health, and he and his wife wrote articles for the popular magazine *Good Housekeeping* and for *The Journal of Home Economics*.[56]

Taking a cue from William James, who insisted that beliefs capable of supporting a good life could not be forged of mere thought but needed to be put to practice, Dresser spoke plainly about the value of New Thought, which promised increased self-knowledge, self-control, and social efficiency. The movement offered an optimistic attitude toward life, a belief in the goodness of humanity, of life, and of the world. "They believe that by looking for and affirming the good, by expecting the best from other people and from life, they will be able steadily to triumph over the ills of life, and become thoroughly sound and happy." In essence, the psychology behind New Thought was the belief that "we already are sane and harmonious sons of God, but are under misconception and ignorance," including the assumption that we are bodies possessing souls when, in truth, "we are spiritual beings born to have dominion over the flesh."[57]

> The deeper truth which the New Thought devotees were striving for when they affirmed that everything could be changed by a mental attitude, and that there need be no more sickness, poverty, sorrow or suffering, was this: God who gives us this experience which we call life bestows it for our health, for our good and our joy, but we in our ignorance have rebelled and created friction. If we have given way to hate, to anger and selfishness, it will not

suffice to affirm that as children of God we know only love, think only kind thoughts; we must actually love, really be kind, truly serve. Only by changing in life, in conduct, in what we habitually love, can we really make progress. Although everything the mind curers have taught us can be used, with radical modifications, the important point is to press on to the new Christian consciousness of our time. . . . Within you and me, the divine love and wisdom reside. . . . When the love of that which is noble, good, divine, becomes the prevailing will, then the desired changes will follow.[58]

In 1911, Dresser accepted the position of professor of philosophy and education at Ursinus College in Pennsylvania, where he taught until 1913 and then resigned to enroll at the New Church Theological School in Cambridge to pursue his interest in Swedenborgianism. His later writings included *The Future Life* (1914), *The Religion of the Spirit in Modern Life* (1914), *The Victorious Faith* (1917), a collection of essays titled *The Spirit of New Thought* (1917), and *Handbook of the New Thought* (1917), the last two of which are considered the best statements on New Thought beliefs and practices.[59]

The First World War was a harsh blow to the hopes and dreams of New Thoughters, as the flower of American youth lost their lives in the ensuing inferno. Supportive of the nation's noble efforts to make the world safe for democracy, Dresser enlisted for service in the Fourth French Army as director of a *Foyer du Soldat*, a program arranged between the YMCA and the French Army directed at improving soldier morale by providing books, stationery, entertainment, and canteen service to the troops. Acquitting himself without letting go of the ideals that had brought the nation into the war, he returned to become a minister in the General Convention and pastor of a Swedenborgian Church in Portland, Maine.

The immediate years following his return from Europe were busy, filled with efforts to further the purposes of the New Thought movement, which had lost much of its momentum in the aftermath of the war. Seeking to establish a place for himself in the field of applied psychology, he contracted with Thomas Y. Crowell Company to produce a set of textbooks connecting the different branches of psychology. These included *Psychology in Theory and Application* (1924), *Ethics in Theory and Application* (1925), *A History of Ancient and Medieval Philosophy* (1926), *A History of Modern Philosophy* (1928), and *Outlines of the Psychology of Religion* (1929).

During the 1920s, Dresser began work on a manuscript tentatively titled *The Psychology and Philosophy of Emanuel Swedenborg*, which he intended as a textbook built around Swedenborg's law of correspondences and divine influx. Taking into account the disciplinary developments that had occurred in the intervening century, he borrowed from a selection of Swedenborg's writings, interspersing them with modern psychology. Using the law of correspondences and divine influx as starting points to a proper understanding of human behavior, Dresser explained the nature of the soul, the relationship between psychology and ethics and between ethics and religion, the concept of regeneration, and how human beings lived in two worlds—one material and temporary, the other spiritual and eternal. Building on this, Dresser reasoned that despite Darwin's theory of natural selection and certain contemporary theories of psychology, there was no reason to deny that the goal of human life was union with God, where the "self" retained its individuality alongside the blessedness of similar souls in a heavenly society. Swedenborg's psychology, with its "upward look to the Divine," had made inner life the primary concern of human activity. To the extent that influx flowed into the body, it followed a quest that ended not with bodily death but with a communion of souls in a world of pure spiritual essence.[60] As understood by the law of correspondences, the sense organs were connected by "interior sight" to the spiritual world and to the purposes and ends of divine influx. "The body is inwardly so organized," explained Dresser, "as to carry out in minute detail the spirit's behests," receiving direction from its source in the Divine.[61]

Beginning with God as universal love and wisdom, love became the central motive of human activity in Dresser's conception of psychology. "Man's being from moment to moment is sustained by this indwelling Love, infilling his own love-nature, renewing him so that each pulsation of life, each rhythm of activity within him, is from the same Divine source." The psychology of the soul was an expression of God's love, which, in turn, affected the life of both the mind and the body. To the extent that humans lived in accordance with that love, their interiors opened to divine influx and the body acted in perfect harmony (i.e., correspondence) with the divine intent. In such a state, health was the natural condition and disease its contradiction. Here, too, manifestations of love radiated from the individual like the fragrance of a flower and formed a person's signature sphere that could be recognizable to all.[62]

From love, divine influx, and the law of correspondences, Dresser turned to wisdom and the doctrine of usefulness. Given that all being existed for a purpose in the divine economy, all things existed through cause, end, and usefulness. The universe, recognized as a complexity of divine purposes, "consists of constant useful functions produced by wisdom under love's initiative."[63] Into this creative life humanity fulfilled its ends, each individual perceiving the world differently from another. The same wine that became the occasion of evil in one person became instrumental to another in the form of a sacrament. The same money that was the "root of all evil" offered the means to the good life elsewhere.[64] The life that each individual built by his or her perception of the good and true became known through the "loves" that were reflected in their deeds and, over time, in the "fiber" of the individual.[65] In one's deeds, one saw the practical implications of the succession of activities from inmost to outermost. And in one's useful actions could be seen the intersection between will and understanding, which constituted the rational mind. Love of the Lord was expressed through love of neighbor (i.e., service, deeds, or works done on behalf of one's neighbor). Love of the Lord was "inseparable from service for the Lord's sake."[66]

During the years that Dresser worked on the Swedenborg manuscript, he found himself implementing many of the practices of the Emmanuelists, who regarded disease as something other than what conventional medicine called the product of germs; it "seizes a man from outside, almost without regard to the state of mind and body."

Here, he explained, was the great tragedy of modern medicine.[67] Having studied the works of Jung and Adler, he concluded that human infirmities were best attacked by a combination of religion, psychology, and medicine. This motivation caused him to join the Associated Clinic of Religion and Medicine, later renamed the Associated Counseling Service, a consortium of churches and clinics in Brooklyn where, from 1931 to 1953, he offered his services in applied psychology and contributed articles in *The New-Church Messenger* under a section called "With the Consulting Psychologist."[68]

Dresser spent his later years at the Church of the Savior Unitarian in Brooklyn, offering personal counseling and enjoying the friendship of pastor John Howland Lathrop, who encouraged him to lead the Emmanuel Movement initiative following Worcester's retirement.[69] Dresser declined the offer, choosing instead to continue writing on the general topic of health and inner control. For more than a decade, he focused almost entirely on topics associated with applied psychology. Exemplary texts of this nature were his *Fatigue* (1930), *Nervousness* (1930), *Overcoming Worry* (1930), *Knowing and Helping People* (1933), *The Conquest of Fear* (1935), *Spiritual Healing from a New Church Viewpoint* (1940s), and *Emotional Conflicts* (1940s). Less rigid than many about the reality of disease, he claimed both Christian and secular methods of healing, including auto-suggestion, silence, meditation, redirection of attention, love, work, service, visualization, and positive thinking. He died in Boston in 1954 at the age of eighty-eight and left an abiding legacy in healing the "sick soul" with New Thought and the ideas of Swedenborg.

The legacy left by the pioneering work of Worcester, Cabot, Boisen, Dunbar, and Dresser continued to inspire conversations between religion and psychiatry, offering provocative areas of disagreement as well as areas of common ground. The task of discovering meaning in the face of personal suffering, and understanding the experience of mental illness, including its confessional or personal narrative stories, led to a general agreement on the mutual benefits that accrue from a dialogue between medicine and religion. Carried out in different theoretical suppositions and settings, the core of the pastoral clinical movement remained focused on curbing the destructive impulses of the patient. Trained in ethical and "meaning-of-life" issues, pastors moved away from the hurtful moralism tied to past practices and embraced a greater pluralism, supporting the sensitivity of people of many faiths and beliefs. Today, pastoral clinical work is divided among trained ministers; professional psychologists and psychotherapists; and a broad band of laitized paraprofessionals, celebrity healers, and self-help gurus. Included in this latter group are increasing numbers of clergy who represent themselves as both diagnosticians and counselors. However, pastoral counseling and psychotherapy are quite different, as are the respective responsibilities associated with each of these disciplines. Notwithstanding these changes to the landscape, today's pastoral clergy are largely nondenominational and nondogmatic in their approaches, with their utilitarian techniques revealing strong and enduring ties to the traditional objectives of the social gospel.[70]

Conclusion: American Spirit

We . . . with our evolutionary theories and our mechanical philosophies, already know nature too impartially and too well to worship unreservedly any god of whose character she can be an adequate expression. . . . To such a harlot we owe no allegiance.

(William James, *Is Life Worth Living?*, 1896)

It seems only right that this book should end where it began, showing the connection among a few gifted individuals whose words changed the world intellectually, artistically, and even materially. Ralph Waldo Emerson was such a figure; so, too, were Henry James, Sr., and his son, William James, whose contributions as a philosopher and psychologist bridged the nineteenth and twentieth centuries. Arthur O. Lovejoy compared William James to Emerson, saying that they were the most influential American writers on philosophy and the only two with wide international standing, resulting in generations of disciples who carried forward their ideas.[1] Emerson was much beloved by Henry James, Sr., and his family. His complete writings were among William James's most treasured books, and they became the stepping-off point for his eventual belief system. As Frederic I. Carpenter explained, William James marked and annotated Emerson's writings, placing them into three distinct categories: those that revealed unique contributions; those that he considered counter to his own philosophy; and those that supported his action-oriented pragmatism. James read Emerson not just out of general interest but because he was considered the nation's intellectual godfather and an integral part of the American mind. "Throughout his life," noted

Carpenter, "James praised the pragmatic Emerson, but disapproved the transcendentalist."[2] His admiration of the sage remained strong, provided he endorsed the interaction of thought and experience and so long as his divination of experience pointed to the future. Emerson's *Representative Men*, a paean to Swedenborg's doctrine of usefulness, stood for the ascendant role of ideas transformed into purposive action. When, however, his words were lost in billowy clouds of transcendental fluff, James lost interest. It was not that he disapproved of Emerson's ideals or ends, but that the abstractness of those ideals was often misplaced.[3]

As mentioned in chapter 1, above, Emerson identified the first half of the nineteenth century as the age of Swedenborg, considering it an alignment of Swedenborg's mysticism with the period's affection for idealism. The doctrines of correspondences and usefulness served as a counterforce to an age addicted to materialism, offering in its place the prospect of divine influx and the visionary writings of its Transcendentalist poets and authors—all of which were intended to sublimate selfhood for the more encompassing Universal Human.[4] Swedenborgianism became a storehouse filled with the collective expressions of the soul and its connection to society, including the celebration of human dignity, an impatience with obsolete rules, and the growth of each individual from self-love to love of the Divine and of others. Those influenced by Swedenborg's writings carried away from them an appreciation of the nonduality of mind and body, a preference for imagination over reason, a recognition of the primacy of spirit over matter, a sense of self-sufficiency and purpose, and an openness to challenging the status quo.

Emerson declared truth to be ideal and undefinable; James, on the other hand, insisted that it was specific, definable, and embodied in its use. Neither conception had a systematic quality, suggesting the unfinished nature of the universe. Neither was anxious to make commitments for future generations, binding them to a particular belief or rule of conduct. As a champion of individualism and the instrumental application of thought to human knowledge, James encouraged a level of nonconformity that paid dividends, offering a fresh alternative to the dogmatic philosophizing of his day. An imaginative and open-minded thinker who was gifted with the discerning eye of an artist, the curiosity and skepticism of a scientist, and the heart of a humanist, James celebrated the practical benefits of belief, the determining factor of experience in the conduct of life, and each person's ability to affect the future in a meaningful way. Provisional in his views, he advocated a form of pluralism that functioned as a solvent to life's competing propositions, claiming a middle course between empiricism and rationalism.

Among Swedenborgians there existed an antinomian path that, while not always followed, dispensed with conventional claims and arguments by triggering a conversation that was productive of more radically altered options to life's problems. In their conversation on the human condition, their message was simple and straightforward, namely, that religion should guide people toward an awareness of society's obligations to the least among humankind. Essentially, they carried their faith, empathy, and imagination into public life with the hope of binding humankind together in grace—a view of life in which the transcendence of all spilled beyond its boundaries to encompass humanity's capacity for collective improvement, love, and service.

Swedenborg himself refused to live in the closed universe of his day; instead, he was forever challenging its intellectual boundaries with bold new perspectives. He sought a type of wisdom that distanced himself from the sectarianism of his age by valuing the imagination and not the impoverished vocabulary of accepted notions. He was extraordinarily gifted in his ability to ask questions that turned on what it meant to be human, which is to say that his questions went to the very heart of personal and collective morality. Rather than complacently accepting the reigning worldview, he drew from the discoveries of past and present scholarship to challenge, revise, and reinvent the religious and secular beliefs of his age. This is the legacy that Swedenborg left to his followers.

As Swedenborg's beliefs were carried into the twentieth century via the philosophy of pragmatism, they continued a common thread that had been running through the body politic: exercising a dislike of tradition and speculative intellectualism and resurrecting an emotional tie to individualism and to direct and unimpeachable experience. Whether accentuated in the virtues of Henry James, Sr.'s, Christian socialism, Edward Bellamy's nationalism, Henry George's single tax, the social gospeler's "brotherhood of man," or John Dewey's "great community," the preference for peaceful, noncoercive forms of societal reconstruction involved making each individual a potential agent of change.

Central to the nation's vision was an emblematic hopefulness that beliefs were rules for action, truth was an outcome of human action, and democracy stood malleable to change.[5] The world was a place of openness and possibility, where truth was an event inseparably bound to actions and social practices that work and where the plurality of experience ruled out the viciousness of extremes. The Swedenborgian doctrines of correspondences and usefulness that were found in America's reform tradition became the keys to unlocking the connection between actions and their deeper meaning. Here was the nexus of political voluntarism, moralism, and a readiness to challenge the status quo. Religion remained, but the old gods were exchanged for a secular spirituality that focused on human ideals and values in an age of democracy and science. Pragmatism not only fit the terms of usefulness, but it also divinized the world, leaving human beings to build an ethic not of ends but of means, valuing experience and their imaginative vision of the ideal.[6]

Appendix

Use **was the** term Swedenborg employed to emphasize the practical character of humanity's work. All purposive activity led to beneficial results for one's neighbor, to the good of the community, and to the overall good in God's kingdom at large. Being useful meant to be of service. In its universality, God's kingdom was explicitly one of ends and modes of service for the good of the human race. In an informative explanation of this concept from his unpublished manuscript on the ideas of Emanuel Swedenborg, Horatio W. Dresser laid out the parameters of the doctrine of usefulness:

> In every created thing there is this endeavor to produce the activities for which it exists. Thus, even in outermost, things such as stony, saline, oily, or metallic things in the mineral kingdom, there is implicit both the end and the beginning of all these activities. The end is the endeavor to be what the thing was created to be, as the bud tends to burst into the fully open flower and produce fruit after its kind. Grasses and herbs, plants, shrubs, and trees constitute a higher level of ends than minerals. Hence, the vegetable kingdom is the middle one: things in that kingdom serve each and all things in the animal kingdom, nourishing and vivifying the bodies of animals. Thus, the animal kingdom is "first" in rank, in contrast with the vegetable kingdom as "last." So, in turn, there are series from lowest things through the middle, to the highest

within the animal kingdom. Thus, it is, that man is highest in the scale of created natural things. The forms for receiving life on the various levels constitute the basis for service of each thing.

Whatever life or thing comes from the Lord, thus, has its practical fitness in the scale or system. It is characteristic of life to be for real utility: the useless can have no life and is cast away. The useful is seen especially in doing what is good and true. For the end which a thing fulfills is the good for which it stands in the scale of goods making up the whole system. The form of a thing is, in lesser degree, the clue to its value. A tree, as a form established for certain ends, fulfills a certain service in the natural world. But animals, being higher in the scale, have forms which vary according to the excellence of the values which they embody; and these forms are more explicitly seen as goods. The realization of goodness is the great objective of the whole kingdom of beings and things which manifest Love and Wisdom.

The service is the exercise or realization in ends achieved, in actual deeds making explicit the goods and truths. Thus, the works of charity verify the reality of love for the neighbor which a man professing such love actually feels. The joy of service is in the actual deed done. The value is in the function, and the function has place in the great system of functions in the [Universal Human].

Again, the activity which a man loves determines his life. It is not the mere fact of service which is decisive. For "uses" may be infernal as well as heavenly. An evil-minded man may be extremely practical in carrying out his scheme. Rogues, thieves, and villains stand together and constitute a sort of brotherhood. Thus, in external form beings and things may simulate activities which embody worthy ends. We must then penetrate beneath the form, and the bare fact of utility, to the kind of service made concrete in this or that group of deeds, and view the deeds according to their effect on human welfare. Hence, the importance of the motive, the type of love.

Furthermore, knowledge conduces to service; but there are different types of knowledge. Although knowledge may suggest the service, to will and to do is actually to serve. Knowing, understanding, and being wise are not ends or values in themselves; but most have service as their end, and this "use" must be worthy. It is the *internal* man who has been formed to serve the Lord through all the activities which love to God and man demand of us. The soul is to be cared for that it may thus serve, loving spiritual truth for its service-value.

Therefore, not even in the other life is man rewarded for any other motive than for the realization of this central purpose of his being as a member of the race fulfilling a function which, when actually worthy of a reward, puts him within the [Universal Human]. No man, for instance, is rewarded for his good actions if these were done for the sake of his own gain, honor, and reputation. It is always the end for which deeds are done that is significant. Actions acquire worth in relation to ends. Insofar as man is living for ends, in the larger sense of contributory functions, he is already in the other life. Therefore, the truly useful man is one who, loving the good in his neighbor, works for the good from the purest motive. The term "use" is to be carefully distinguished from mere utility or utilitarianism, as if the highest motive were the greatest happiness of the greatest number. It is always functional goodness, never pleasure, satisfaction, or happiness, which determines the value of the service and its significance in social psychology.

We repeat, therefore, knowing is in a measure divided from willing until we attain their unity through what we actually do. There are many impulses in human nature which conflict with the will even after we have enjoyed special instruction. We often postpone the more serious endeavor to seek first the kingdom of God, and the righteousness essential to it, because we still cling to the idea that the heavenly order of life begins in the life after death. There is, of course, no ground for this delay, since the whole of our earth-life is a preparation, and we are each year making ready for places we are to occupy in the ever-dawning future. The heavenly order is not an affair of time, but of affection and service. It begins whenever we will. The spiritual is in process within the natural.

Again, we delay because we idealize the past only, and put true receptivity far from us in the golden days when men walked and talked with God. The race seems to have wandered so far since those precious days that there is little hope. But what is the meaning of this wonderful record of the race's spiritual history if not that each of us is passing through some period in the same history? Of what value are great promises unless they are true for us whoever we are and wherever we are on life's journey?

Since God's world is a kingdom of purposes, the Divine descends into humanity to make us useful individuals, and ascends through us toward the perfect. We have every reason to look to our common promptings and our common occu-pations for evidences that the spiritual is being brought out through the natural. It is not the disciples alone who, seek-ers for fish in the sea, are called to be fishers of men, but every-one since our natural life can be transfigured by beauty, love of truth, and the expression of goodness.

One reason we so often fail to take the step from knowing to doing is that we do not put our will into the common natural activities with the realization that we are already in a measure occupying places in the [Universal Human]. We still put Sun-day too far from weekdays, sacred things from secular, heav-enly occupations from earthly. In veriest truth, the actual state of soul with each of us, weekdays or Sundays, turns upon *what we love most* and work for. Each of us is already using the will we wish for.... It is always a question of use or misuses, as in the case of one who has inherited a large fortune.

Summarizing, we observe that what is chiefly new or different in this doctrine of the [Universal Human], is the new light cast on the whole principle by the application of correspondence as a descriptive law. By this approach, the ideal of heavenly societies, envisaged as one man from the Divine point of view, is more definitely articulated. The approach to social life here on earth, in the light of descending heavenly influences, is also made more concrete, that is, by the correspondential principle terminating in "uses" as means to social service at its best. The functional ideal of society, thus finding formulation afresh, was for centuries the inspiration of Christians. Each man was regarded as a member of this hierarchy of ascending social groups actuated by Divine purpose in creation because of his relation to the heavenly order of reality, and also because, as an organ in the social whole here on earth, he could contribute to the welfare of the corporate groups in which (through the "body of Christ") he participated. The individual was said to exist for the whole, and the whole for the individual. Our mutual relationships and obligations unite and bind us through love toward God and for man as dwelling with God. This mutuality unites us as denizens in the City of God. The threefold groupings of this heavenly order date from Plato, the idea of Christian membership in the organic sense from Paul, and that of the city of God from Augustine. Swedenborg discloses a view of this organic correlation by more direct appeal to the human body as the type of social relatedness. The problem for his followers is to connect this doctrine with current social psychology. In contemporary efforts for social reform, we find the idea of progressive social betterment substituted for the most part for Augustine's view. Much emphasis is put on the struggle for social justice here on earth, in contrast with the alleged aristocracy of the City of God.[1]

Endnotes

Introduction

1. Read Ernst Benz, *Emanuel Swedenborg: Visionary Savant in the Age of Reason* (West Chester, PA: Swedenborg Foundation, 2002).

2. O. B. Frothingham, "Swedenborg," in *North American Review* 134 (1882): 615.

3. Emanuel Swedenborg, *Divine Love and Wisdom* (West Chester, PA: Swedenborg Foundation, 2010 [1763]), §154.

4. Emanuel Swedenborg, *True Christianity*, 2 vols. (West Chester, PA: Swedenborg Foundation, 2010–11 [1771]), §694.

5. Swedenborg, *Divine Love and Wisdom* §303.

6. Emanuel Swedenborg, *Apocalypse Explained*, 6 vols. (West Chester, PA: Swedenborg Foundation, 1994–97 [1785–89]), §1194.

7. Read Arthur O. Lovejoy, *The Great Chain of Being: A Study of the History of an Idea* (Cambridge: Harvard University Press, 1936); E. M. W. Tillyard, *The Elizabethan World Picture* (London: Chatto and Windus, 1943); Allen Debus, *Man and Nature in the Renaissance* (Cambridge: Cambridge University Press, 1978); Edward P. Mahoney, "Lovejoy and the Hierarchy of Being," in *Journal of the History of Ideas* 48 (1987): 211–30.

8. Emanuel Swedenborg, *Secrets of Heaven*, 2 vols. (West Chester, PA: Swedenborg Foundation, 2010, 2012 [1749]), §1807; Swedenborg, *Divine Love and Wisdom* §339.

9. Swedenborg, *True Christianity* §67; Swedenborg, *Divine Love and Wisdom* §317.

10. Swedenborg, *Divine Love and Wisdom* §310; Emanuel Swedenborg, *Arcana Coelestia* (West Chester, PA: Swedenborg Foundation, 1998 [1749–56]), §4223.

11. Emanuel Swedenborg, *Secrets of Heaven* (Unpublished section translation by Lisa Hyatt Cooper, [1749–56]), §6073.

12. Swedenborg, *Secrets of Heaven* §997; Swedenborg, *Arcana Coelestia* §7038.

13. Swedenborg, *Apocalypse Explained* §1193.
14. Swedenborg, *Divine Love and Wisdom* §§237, 254, 331–33, 339.
15. Ibid., §264.
16. Swedenborg, *Secrets of Heaven* (Unpublished section translations by Lisa Hyatt Cooper), §§7038, 9297:4.
17. Emanuel Swedenborg, *Divine Love* (New York: Swedenborg Foundation, 1914 [1762–63]), §6.
18. Emanuel Swedenborg, *New Jerusalem* (West Chester, PA: Swedenborg Foundation, 2016 [1758]), §§65–107.
19. Swedenborg, *True Christianity* §§373–75.
20. Swedenborg, *Divine Love and Wisdom* §§154, 349–57.
21. Matthew Bowman, "Sin, Spirituality, and Primitivism: The Theologies of the American Social Gospel, 1885–1917," in *Religion and American Culture: A Journal of Interpretation* 17 (2007): 96.
22. Examples include: "The Use of Environment," in *The New Christianity* 3 (1890): 164; "The Nature, Origin and Use of Evil," in *The New Christianity* 3 (1890): 225–26, 241–42, 257–58, 276–77; John Doherty, "The Beauty of Use," in *The New Christianity* 2 (1889): 9–10; "The Use of Doctrine," in *The New Christianity* 2 (1889): 178–79; J. S. David, "The Love of Use in Labor," in *The New Christianity* 2 (1889): 325–26; John Filmer, "The Usefulness of Poverty," in *The New Christianity* 8 (1895): 12.
23. Read Edward K. Spann, *Brotherly Tomorrows: Movements for a Cooperative Society in America, 1820–1920* (New York: Columbia University Press, 1989). See also "Spiritual Growth Through Usefulness," in *The New Christianity* 10 (1897): 141.
24. William James, "Philosophical Conceptions and Practical Results" (1898), in Russell B. Goodman, ed., *Pragmatism: Critical Concepts in Philosophy*, vol. 1 (London and New York: Routledge, 2005), 61–62.
25. William Blake, "The French Revolution" (1791), in William Blake, *The Selected Poems of William Blake* (Hertfordshire: Wordsworth Edition, 1994), 207; Peter J. Lineham, "The English Swedenborgians: 1770–1840: A Study in the Social Dimensions of Religious Sectarianism" (PhD diss., University of Sussex, 1978), 272.

1 Love's Affections

1. Ralph H. Orth and Alfred R. Ferguson, eds., *The Journals and Miscellaneous Notebooks of Ralph Waldo Emerson*, 16 vols. (Cambridge: Harvard University Press, 1977), vol. XIII, 335.
2. F. O. Matthiessen, *American Renaissance: Art and Expression in the Age of Emerson and Whitman* (New York: Oxford University Press, 1941), viii.
3. Read David George Goyder, *A Concise History of the New Church* (London: T. Goyder, 1827).

4. Thomas A. King, "The Church and the Slums," in *The New-Church Review* 14 (1907): 414, 415, 416.

5. See Cyriel Odhner Sigstedt, *The Swedenborg Epic: The Life and Works of Emanuel Swedenborg* (London: The Swedenborg Society, 1981), 389; Abbé Barruel, *Memoirs Illustrating the History of Jacobinism* (Hartford: Hudson and Goodwin, 1799); Marsha Keith Schuchard, "Swedenborg, Jacobitism, and Freemasonry," in Brock and Glenn, eds., *Swedenborg and His Influence,* 359–77; Marsha Keith Schuchard, *Emanuel Swedenborg, Secret Agent on Earth and in Heaven: Jacobites, Jews and Freemasons in Early Modern Sweden* (Leiden: Brill, 2011); Marsha Keith Schuchard, "The Secret Masonic History of Blake's Swedenborg Society," in *Blake: An Illustrated Quarterly* 26 (1992): 40–51; Robert Rix, *William Blake and the Cultures of Radical Christianity* (London: Ashgate Publishing Co., 2007), 105–6. See also Robert Hindmarsh, *Rise and Progress of the New Jerusalem Church in England, America, and Other Parts* (London: Hodson and Son, 1861); Carl Th. Odhner, *Robert Hindmarsh; A Biography* (Philadelphia: Academy Book Room, 1895).

6. Read Daniel W. Goodenough, "A Trust from God: A Survey of Swedenborg's Political Thought," in Brock and Glenn, eds., *Swedenborg and His Influence,* 135–53.

7. R. L. Tafel, *Documents Concerning the Life and Character of Emanuel Swedenborg,* 2 vols. (London: Swedenborg Society, 1877), vol. II, 735–39; Hindmarsh, *Rise and Progress of the New Jerusalem Church in England, America, and Other Parts,* 41–49. See also Marsha Keith Schuchard, "Freemasonry, Secret Societies, and the Continuity of the Occult Traditions in English Literature" (PhD diss., University of Texas at Austin, 1975); Samuel Beswick, *Swedenborg Rite and the Great Masonic Leaders of the Eighteenth Century* (New York: Kessinger Publishing, 1994 [1870]).

8. There is evidence of a nineteenth-century fringe Masonic order called the Swedenborg Rite (1871–1908), whose members included individuals from the United States, Canada, France, Germany, India, Egypt, Romania, and England. See Albert Gallatin Mackey and H. L. Haywood, *Encyclopedia of Freemasonry,* 2 vols. (New York: Kessinger Publishing, 2003), vol. II, 997; Augustus Row, "Illuminati of Avignon, or Swedenborg Rite," in *Masonic Biography and Dictionary* (Philadelphia: J. B. Lippincott and Co., 1868), 139.

9. Clarke Garrett, "Swedenborg and the Mystical Enlightenment in Late Eighteenth-Century England," in *Journal of the History of Ideas* 45 (1984): 67–81; Clarke Garrett, *Respectable Folly: Millenarians and the French Revolution in France and England* (Baltimore: Johns Hopkins Press, 1975); Inge Jonsson, *Emanuel Swedenborg* (New York: Twayne Publishers, 1971); Kathleen Raine, *Blake and Tradition,* 2 vols. (Princeton: Princeton University Press, 1968); Clarke Garrett, "The Spiritual Odyssey of Jacob Duché," in *Proceedings of the American Philosophical Society* 119 (1975): 143–55.

10. John Gould Fletcher, "William Blake," in *North American Review* 218 (1923): 522.

11. Read Glen E. Brewster, "'Out of Nature': Blake and the French Revolution Debate," in *South Atlantic Review* 56 (1991): 7–22; William Richey, "The French Revolution: Blake's Epic Dialogue with Edmund Burke," in *ELH* 59 (1992): 817–37; Edmund Burke, *Reflections of the Revolution in France* (Harmondsworth: Penguin, 1984).

12. J. P. R. Wallis, "Blake," in A. W. Ward and A. R. Waller, eds., *The Cambridge History of English Literature. Vol. XI. The Period of the French Revolution* (Cambridge: Cambridge University Press, 1914), 187–90. See also J. G. Davies, *The Theology of William Blake* (Oxford: Clarendon Press, 1948).

13. Read Jon Mee, *Dangerous Enthusiasm: William Blake and the Culture of Radicalism in the 1790s* (Oxford: Clarendon Press, 1992); Jon Mee, "Apocalypse and Ambivalence: The Politics of Millenarianism in the 1790s," in *South Atlantic Quarterly* 95 (1996): 671–97.

14. Rix, *William Blake and the Cultures of Radical Christianity,* 98.

15. From "Of National Characters," in David Hume, *Essays and Treatises on Several Subjects,* 4 vols. (London: Printed for A. Millar, in the Strand; and A. Kincaid and A. Donaldson, in Edinburgh, 1753), vol. I, 291.

16. Swedenborg, *True Christianity* §§13, 52, 54; Emanuel Swedenborg, *Heaven and Hell* (West Chester, PA: Swedenborg Foundation, 2010 [1758]), §303.

17. Read Lovejoy, *Great Chain of Being.*

18. Emanuel Swedenborg, *Spiritual Experiences* (New York: Swedenborg Foundation, n.d. [1747–65]), §§4783, 4777.

19. Swedenborg was not a social reformer theologian in the modern sense, and he did not speak out against the slave trade in any of his writings, either published or unpublished. This is despite the fact that ten million slaves were merchandized in eighteenth-century England, which is where he spent thirteen years working on his spiritual books and where placards announcing the sale of sub-Saharan Africans were common and publicly visible. See James F. Lawrence, "A World Apart: The American Antislavery Issue," in Anders Hallengren, ed., *The Moment Is Now: Carl Bernhard Wadström's Revolutionary Voice on Human Trafficking and the Abolition of the African Slave Trade* (West Chester, PA: Swedenborg Foundation, 2019), 157–78.

20. Swedenborg, *True Christianity* §§800–50.

21. Emanuel Swedenborg, *Last Judgment (Posthumous)* (Bryn Athyn, PA: General Church of the New Jerusalem, 1997), §118.

22. Emanuel Swedenborg, *A Treatise Concerning the Last Judgment, and the Destruction of Babylon* (London: R. Hindmarsh, 1788), vi, vii, viii. Thus, Swedenborg's idea of a "last judgment" was not so much an apocalyptic ending of human history as it was the opening of a new chapter of a divinely inspired theory of history.

23. August Nordenskjöld, *A Plan for a Free Community upon the Coast of Africa under the Protection of Great Britain; but Entirely Independent of All European Laws and Governments* (London: Robert Hindmarsh, 1789). The work was later republished by Wadström as *Plan for a Free Community at Sierra Leona, upon the Coast of Africa, under the Protection of Great Britain; with an Invitation to all Persons Desirous of Partaking the Benefits Thereof* (London: T. and J. Egerton, 1792).

24. Carl Bernhard Wadström, *An Essay on Colonization, Particularly Applied to the Western Coast of Africa, with Some Free Thoughts on Cultivation and Commerce* (London: Darton and Harvey, 1794–95).

25. James John Garth Wilkinson, *The African and True Christian Religion: His Magna Charta* (London: J. Speirs, 1892); Marguerite Beck Block, *The New Church in the New World: A Study of Swedenborgianism in America* (New York: Henry Holt and Company, 1932), 83–87. In the case of Carter, he was already abolitionist from his earlier Baptist inspiration, and he never explicitly cites his conversion to Swedenborgianism as his reason for emancipating slaves, including on the manumission document itself wherein he declares that he has long been against slavery. However, Block reasons that the timing of his recent conversion indicates that Swedenborg's ideas must have had something to do with it.

26. Rev. Howard C. Dunham, "The New Church and Democracy," in *The New-Church Review* 25 (1918): 231.

27. Richard DeCharms, *Some Views of Freedom and Slavery in the Light of the New Jerusalem* (Philadelphia: Published by Author, 1855); Richard DeCharms, *A Discourse on the True Nature of Freedom and Slavery* (Philadelphia: A. H. Jones, 1850).

28. "The New Church and Social Reform," in *The New Jerusalem Messenger* 1 (1855): 30.

29. J. R. Hibbard, "Illinois Association, Superintendent's Report," in *The New Jerusalem Magazine* 34 (1861): 215.

30. "What Are the Teachings of the New Church with Regard to Slavery?," in *The New Jerusalem Magazine* 37 (1865): 472–83.

31. Alfred Kazin, "The Father of Us All," in *The New York Review of Books* 28 (1982): 3.

32. Read Francis H. Underwood, "Ralph Waldo Emerson," in *North American Review* 130 (1880): 479–98.

33. John O. McCormick, "Emerson's Theory of Human Greatness," in *The New England Quarterly* 26 (1953): 291–314. The French educator Victor Cousin's (1792–1867) philosophical system known as eclecticism represented a reaction against the materialism of the eighteenth-century Enlightenment by attempting to bring all the known philosophies into a single synthesis. Together with transcendentalism, which was also eclectic in nature, the philosophy of eclecticism very much colored American intellectual history through the first half of the nineteenth century.

34. Ralph Waldo Emerson, *Representative Men,* in *Emerson's Complete Works,* 12 vols. (Boston: Houghton, Mifflin and Co., 1883), vol. IV, 12.

35. Ralph Waldo Emerson, *Essays and Lectures,* Joel Porte, ed. (New York: Library of America, 1983), 618; Emerson, *Representative Men,* 25, 29.

36. Emerson, *Essays and Lectures,* 618.

37. Read Judith N. Shklar, "Emerson and the Inhibitions of Democracy," in *Political Theory* 18 (1990): 601–14.

38. Emerson, *Representative Men,* 41–87.

39. Ibid., 143–77.

40. Ibid., 181–209.

41. Ibid., 213–45.

42. Ibid., 249–76. In his second novel, *Wilhelm Meister's Apprenticeship,* Goethe had stressed the importance of "learning by doing."

43. Clarence Hotson, "Sampson Reed, a Teacher of Emerson," in *The New England Quarterly* 2 (1929): 249–77; Clarence Hotson, "Emerson and the Swedenborgians," in *Studies in Philology* 27 (1930): 517; E. W. Emerson and W. E. Forbes, eds., *Journals of Ralph Waldo Emerson with Annotations,* 10 vols. (Boston: Houghton Mifflin Co., 1909), vol. II, 25.

44. Emerson, *Representative Men,* 100; Hotson, "Emerson and the Swedenborgians," 517–45.

45. Emerson, *Representative Men,* 91–139.

46. Ibid., 128, 129.

47. Frothingham, "Swedenborg," 615.

48. Block, *New Church in the New World,* 145.

49. John Goddard, "'Swedenborg the Mystic': Is Emerson's Characterization Correct?," in *The New-Church Review* 21 (1914): 323, 332.

50. Frederic Harold Young, *The Philosophy of Henry James, Sr.* (New York: Bookman Associates, 1951), 3.

51. Paul Jerome Croce, "Mankind's Own Providence: From Swedenborgian Philosophy of Use to William James's Pragmatism," in *Transactions of the Charles S. Peirce Society* 43 (2007): 492.

52. Henry James, *The Secret of Swedenborg: Being an Elucidation of His Doctrine of the Divine Natural Humanity* (Boston: Fields, Osgood, & Co., 1869), 67; Austin Warren, *The Elder Henry James* (New York: Macmillan, 1934), 194. Read also Paul J. Croce, "A Scientific Spiritualism: The Elder James's Adaptation of Emanuel Swedenborg," in Brock and Glenn, eds., *Swedenborg and His Influence,* 251–62.

53. Henry James, *Substance and Shadow: Or Morality and Religion in Their Relation to Life: An Essay upon the Physics of Creation* (Boston: Ticknor and Fields, 1863), 159–60. In *Substance and Shadow,* the term *shadow* attests to the projection of a mere appearance, not a reality. James identifies religion as one of the greatest of these shadows, as it undermines the rays of divine

truth that lay open the path of human destiny—namely, that of society, fellowship, and equality. By emasculating and stultifying the gospel with their ecclesiastical pretensions, religion's clergy corrupted political and religious life.

54. Julia A. Kellogg, *The Philosophy of Henry James* (New York: John W. Lovell Co., 1883), 11, 13, 18, 20.

55. Henry James, Sr., *Society the Redeemed Form of Man, and the Earnest of God's Omnipotence in Human Nature: Affirmed in Letters to a Friend* (Boston: Houghton, Osgood and Co., 1879), 158; Dwight W. Hoover, *Henry James, Sr. and the Religion of Community* (Grand Rapids, MI: William B. Eerdmans Publishing Co., 1969), 107.

56. Read Henry James, "Letter to a Swedenborgian," in *Tracts for the New Times* (New York: AMS Press, 1983 [1847]); Henry James, *The Church of Christ Not an Ecclesiasticism: A Letter of Remonstrance to a Member of the Soi-Disant New Church* (New York: Redfield, 1854).

57. James, *Substance and Shadow,* 220.

58. Henry James, *The Social Significance of Our Institutions: An Oration Delivered by Request of the Citizens at Newport, R.I., July 4, 1861* (Boston: Ticknor and Fields, 1861), 29, 31.

59. Henry James, *Lectures and Miscellanies; Or, Man's Experience and Destiny* (New York: Redfield, 1852), 3–6, 9, 10, 11, 20.

60. Ibid., 11, 45.

61. Ibid., 368–69.

62. James, *Social Significance of Our Institutions,* 25, 26.

63. James, *Lectures and Miscellanies,* 54, 61, 63, 66–69, 72, 93.

64. Ibid., 87, 92.

65. Read James Duban, *The Nature of True Virtue: Theology, Psychology, and Politics in the Writings of Henry James, Sr., Henry James, Jr., and William James* (Madison: Farleigh Dickinson University Press, 2001). See also T. D. Benson, "Evolution of Socialism," in *The New Christianity* 11 (1898): 93.

66. Henry James, *Moralism and Christianity; Or Man's Experience and Destiny. In Three Lectures* (New York: J. S. Redfield, 1850), 80–82, 89.

67. Read James Duban, "'A Reverent and Obedient Evolution': Jonathan Edwards, the New Science, and the Socialism of Henry James, Sr.," in *Journal of Speculative Philosophy* 23 (2009): 244–61; James Duban, "Charles Darwin, Henry James, Sr., and 'Evolution,'" in *Harvard Library Bulletin* 7 (1996): 45–62.

68. Young, *Philosophy of Henry James, Sr.,* 284, 312.

69. James, *Moralism and Christianity,* 9.

2 Incantatory Delusions

1. John Humphrey Noyes, *History of American Socialisms* (Philadelphia: J. B. Lippincott and Co., 1870), 550.

2. Morris Hillquit, *History of Socialism in the United States* (New York: Funk & Wagnalls Company, 1906), 103; http://thecommonlife.com/files/books/American%20Communities.pdf (accessed June 22, 2015). Other communities included Raritan Bay Union in Perth Amboy, New Jersey; the Prairie Home Colony near West Liberty in Logan County, Ohio; and the Swedenborgian societies at Yellow Springs, Jasper, Canton, and Leraysville.

3. Noyes, *History of American Socialisms*, 42–58.

4. Read Arthur E. Bestor, Jr., *American Phalanxes: A Study of Fourierist Socialism in the United States, with Special Reference to the Movement in Western New York* (New Haven: Yale University, 1938); Arthur E. Bestor, Jr., *Backwoods Utopias: The Sectarian Origins and the Owenite Phase of Communitarian Socialism in America, 1663–1829* (Philadelphia: University of Pennsylvania Press, 1967); Carl J. Guarneri, *The Utopian Alternative: Fourierism in Nineteenth-Century America* (Ithaca, NY: Cornell University Press, 1991); Carl J. Guarneri, "The Associationists: Forging a Christian Socialism in Antebellum America," in *Church History* 52 (1983): 36–49.

5. Robert Owen, "Address, April 27, 1825," in *The New-Harmony Gazette* 1 (October 1, 1825): 1–2.

6. Even when the word *socialism* entered the lexicon, it remained elusive, carrying various linguistic burdens suggestive of different political, religious, and economic explanations. Its three main sources of thought derived from the Saint-Simonians, Fourierists, and Owenites, even though their terminology remained fluid. By 1840, the word *socialist* had become common currency; and then, after 1848, a division had formed between those who favored the label *socialist* and those who preferred the label *communist*, in the tradition of Karl Marx and Friedrich Engels. With this division came different overtones of revolutionary militancy, partisanship, and ownership. Later, still, brought the coinage of newer words such as *nationalize*, which was the result of Bellamy's publication of *Looking Backward; Fabianism*, which appeared in 1900; *syndicalism*, which was introduced at about the same time in France and Italy; and *populist*, which formed out of the People's Party in the United States in 1892. Read Arthur E. Bestor, Jr., "The Evolution of the Socialist Vocabulary," in *Journal of the History of Ideas* 9 (1948): 259–302.

7. Originating in Germany, the Harmony Society established itself in Harmony, Pennsylvania (1805–14), before moving to Harmony, Indiana (1814–25), and then returning to Economy, Pennsylvania (1825–98). Its members were known as Rappites, named after founder George Rapp (1775–1847), and they were essentially separatists who were unwilling to accept the forms of Christian worship prevalent in Germany at the time. See Hillquit, *History of Socialism in the United States*, 103.

8. Read R. G. Garnett, *Cooperation and the Owenite Socialist Communities in Britain, 1825–45* (Manchester, England: Manchester University Press, 1972); J. F. C. Harrison, *Robert Owen and the Owenites in Britain and America: The Quest for the New Moral World* (London: Routledge and Kegan Paul, 1969); Noyes, *History of American Socialisms*, 15, 38.

9. Noyes, *History of American Socialisms*, 59–65.

10. Jonathan Becher, *Charles Fourier: The Visionary and His World* (Berkeley: University of California Press, 1986), 166. Spiritualism made its entrée into the Western world in the mid-nineteenth century. In his *The History of Spiritualism*, Sir Arthur Conan Doyle distinguished between those advocating Spiritualism on behalf of Swedenborg and those who chose to become Spiritualists in their own right. Swedenborg warned others against contacting this world because the spirits reveled in fooling the unwary, but few heeded his admonition, preferring to contact the dead and thus participating in a Spiritualist movement that succeeded beyond belief. See Arthur Conan Doyle, *The History of Spiritualism*, 2 vols. (London: Cassell and Company Ltd., 1926).

11. Noyes, *History of American Socialisms*, 15–17.

12. Block, *New Church in the New World*, 153–54; Noyes, *History of American Socialisms*, 259–66.

13. Read Becher, *Charles Fourier;* Nicholas V. Riasanovsky, *The Teaching of Charles Fourier* (Berkeley: University of California Press, 1969); Albert Brisbane, *Social Destiny of Man; Or, Association and Reorganization of Industry* (Philadelphia: C. F. Stollmeyer, 1840); Albert Brisbane, *Association; Or, a Concise Exposition of the Practical Part of Fourier's Social Science* (New York: Greeley and McElrath, 1843).

14. Charles Crowe, "Christian Socialism and the First Church of Humanity," in *Church History* 35 (1966): 93–106.

15. See Parke Godwin, *A Popular View of the Doctrines of Charles Fourier* (New York: J. S. Redfield, 1844), 17. For criticism, see James John Garth Wilkinson to Henry James, Sr., August 1846, in Clement John Wilkinson, *James John Garth Wilkinson: A Memoir of His Life, with a Selection from His Letters* (London: Kegan Paul, Trench, Trübner & Co., 1911), 55.

16. Emerson, "New England Reformers," in *Emerson's Complete Works*, vol. III, 239; "Man the Reformer," in *Emerson's Complete Works*, vol. I, 236–37.

17. Emerson, "American Civilization," in *Emerson's Complete Works*, vol. XI, 279.

18. E. P. Peabody, "Plan of the West Roxbury Community," in *The Dial* 2 (1842): 361–72.

19. Both William Ellery Channing and Swedenborg were noted for their unusually similar interests in scientific and spiritual pursuits, even though Channing had reputedly never read Swedenborg's works. According to Channing's nephew, William Henry Channing, and his son, Dr. William

Francis Channing, neither in conversations nor in writings had William Ellery had the least allusion to the life or doctrines of Swedenborg. William Francis admitted that at least one volume of Swedenborg's works had been in his father's library, but he was unsure what it would have been. "My father could have drawn very little directly from Swedenborg, as he never made him a study, nor expressed interest in, or obligation to, his works," observed William Francis. On the other hand, a Mrs. Mowatt recounted that she and her husband had been reading aloud from Swedenborg's *Divine Providence* when William Ellery, who had been listening, remarked that he had read a portion of Swedenborg's works but had not drawn any conclusions as yet of his doctrines. In that there were no references in William Ellery's writings to Swedenborg, especially considering the entire domain of the latter's theological writings, Benjamin Barrett felt that while the two men were in agreement on many points, they had come to their beliefs from widely different processes. Both William Ellery and Swedenborg loved and honored the Word and listened reverently to its whisperings, thus opening their "interiors" to the illuminating influences of heaven and its angels. Both saw the errors of the old theologies, exalted the righteousness of life, and valued love of the Lord and one's neighbor above all else. Generous and catholic in spirit, they both insisted that the true church was much larger than any single sect, denomination, or creed. See B. F. Barrett, *Swedenborg and Channing: Showing the Many and Remarkable Agreements in the Beliefs and Teachings of these Writers* (Philadelphia: Claxton, Remsen and Haffelfinger, 1879), xi, xiii, 285–88.

20. Van Wyck Brooks, *America's Coming-of-Age* (New York: B. W. Huebsch, 1915), 89. William Ellery Channing's famous sermon is cited as the most explicit expression of transcendentalism: "The universe, I know, is full of God. The heavens and earth declare his glory. In other words, the effects and signs of power, wisdom, and goodness, are apparent through the whole creation. But apparent to what? Not to the outward eye; not to the acutest organs of sense; but to a kindred mind, which interprets the universe by itself.... We see God around us because He dwells within us." See William E. Channing, "Likeness to God," in *The Works of William E. Channing, D. D.* (Boston: American Unitarian Association, 1898), 293–94.

21. Quoted in Hillquit, *History of Socialism in the United States,* 105–6.

22. Charles Lane, "Brook Farm," in *The Dial* 4 (1844): 352, 354.

23. Saul K. Padover, "Ralph Waldo Emerson: The Moral Voice in Politics," in *Political Science Quarterly* 74 (1959): 334–50.

24. Joel Myerson, "An Annotated List of Contributions to the Boston *Dial*," in *Studies in Bibliography* 26 (1973): 133–66.

25. David A. Zonderman, "George Ripley's Unpublished Lecture on Charles Fourier," in *Studies in the American Renaissance* (1982): 185; Charles R. Crowe, *George Ripley: Transcendentalist and Utopian Socialist* (Athens: University of Georgia Press, 1967), 70.

26. George Willis Cooke, "'The Dial': An Historical and Biographical Introduction, with a List of the Contributors," in *Journal of Speculative Philosophy* 19 (1885): 225–65, 322–23.

27. Block, *New Church in the New World*, 150.

28. [Ralph Waldo Emerson], "Fourierism and the Socialists," in *The Dial* 3
(1842): 87.

29. William Henry Channing (1810–84) was ordained in 1835 and installed in
a Unitarian church in Cincinnati. As explained by his biographer Octavius
Brooks Frothingham, he exemplified "a worshiper and a worker, a philosophical theist and an ardent friend of human brotherhood." His education
began at the Latin School in Boston, where under the charge of Benjamin
Gould, he mastered Homer's *Iliad,* Virgil, Cicero, Caesar, and Tacitus.
From there he moved on to Harvard, where in 1829 he graduated in the
company of classmates Oliver Wendell Holmes and James Freeman
Clarke. Although he received no honors or prizes for his learning, Rev.
Channing had close enough relationships to the leaders of his class that he
was elected into the Phi Beta Kappa Society. In 1830, he began to study for
the ministry, delving into such topics as free will, providence, the Gnostics,
the skepticism of David Hume, and even phrenology. He reached the conclusion that: "Where God is there is heaven, and God is everywhere.
Heaven is all that is perfect, all that is beautiful, true, good; heaven lies
about us now and ever." See Octavius Brooks Frothingham, *Memoir of William Henry Channing* (Boston: Houghton, Mifflin and Co., 1886), 7, 76.

30. Quoted in Frothingham, *Memoir of William Henry Channing,* 177.

31. "A Call to the Friends of Social Reform in New England," in *The Present* 1
(1843): 207–10.

32. Ibid., 282, 285.

33. P., "Social Reform," in *The Present* 1 (1843): 318–22.

34. George Ripley, Minot Pratt, and Charles A. Dana, "Brook Farm Association," in *The Present* 1 (1844): 350–53.

35. Elizabeth Peabody, "Fourierism," in *The Dial* 4 (1844): 473–83.

36. Ibid., 474–76, 479, 483.

37. Quoted in Frothingham, *Memoir of William Henry Channing,* 207. Between
both *The Phalanx* and *The Harbinger,* William Henry Channing wrote
some thirty-nine articles.

38. Noyes, *History of American Socialisms,* 529–32. With this decision, *The Phalanx* turned over its subscription list to *The Harbinger,* which, published
weekly, proceeded to publish through five volumes edited and printed at
Brook Farm (June 14, 1845, to October 30, 1847), and the last two and a
half in New York (November 6, 1847, to February 10, 1849).

39. Quoted in Frothingham, *Memoir of William Henry Channing,* 207. Here
again, the same persons who wrote for *The Dial* also wrote for *The Harbinger.* Moreover, the same spirit guided it. Ripley, Dwight, and Dana were

able editors and managed its publication in much the same literary tone as did Peabody. Clearly, their zeal was no less earnest.

40. Brisbane eventually returned to the United States and retook his leadership role following the fire and subsequent collapse of the Brook Farm phalanx.

41. Read Charles Arthur Hawley, "Swedenborgianism and the Frontier," in *Church History* 6 (1937): 203–22.

42. Godwin, *Popular View of the Doctrines of Charles Fourier,* 106–7.

43. Ibid., 115, 116, 118.

44. See Hugh Doherty, "To the Editor of the New Jerusalem Magazine, Boston, U.S.," in *The Phalanx* (September 7, 1844): 264.

45. Dan McKanan, "Making Sense of Failure: From Death to Resurrection in Nineteenth-Century Communitarianism," in *Utopian Studies* 18 (2007): 159–92.

46. Read William Hall Brock, "Phalanx on a Hill: Responses to Fourierism in the Transcendentalist Circle" (PhD diss., Loyola University of Chicago, 1995), chapter 6. Read Charles Julius Hempel, *The True Organization of the New Church as Indicated in the Writings of Emanuel Swedenborg and Demonstrated by Charles Fourier* (New York: William Radde, 1848). The synthesis was even made by the Spiritualist and clairvoyant Andrew Jackson Davis, who plagiarized from both Fourier and Swedenborg for his own purposes. See Andrew Jackson Davis, *The Magic Staff: An Autobiography* (New York: J. S. Brown and Co., 1859).

47. Swedenborg, *Arcana Coelestia* §3900:9; [Emerson and Brisbane], "Fourierism and the Socialists," 86–96; William H. Channing, "Fourier and Swedenborg," in *The Present* 1 (1844): 431.

48. David A. Zonderman, "George Ripley's Unpublished Lecture on Charles Fourier," in *Studies in the American Renaissance* (1982): 189.

49. Henry James, Sr., never joined the Brook Farm Phalanx as a bona fide member. As a radical individualist, membership would have violated his most intimate sense of self-worth. He remained detached from the actual workings of Fourier's associationism, as the technical aspects of socialism never quite fit his views. He understood spiritual socialism entirely on his own terms. Nevertheless, he was an advocate of Christian socialism as humanity's truest means of redemption, contributing liberally to *The Harbinger* to spell out Swedenborg's philosophy and its applicability to Fourier's social science. While *The Harbinger* was intended to propagate Fourierism, it instead influenced the surge of Swedenborgianism. Spiritualism was deemed more important and was deeper in the hearts of its members than was the scientific orderliness of socialism.

By the time most of the Fourierist communities folded, the publication of Charles Julius Hempel's *The True Organization of the New Church as Indicated in the Writings of Emanuel Swedenborg and Demonstrated by Charles Fourier* came as a belated tribute to the combined work of these figures. According to Hempel, the doctrines of both men "cannot remain separate." Not only did Fourier's scientific series align with the spiritual heavens of the Universal Human, but the arrangements that Fourier discovered became essential elements in understanding the passions of the soul and the conjunction of the inner and outer selves. When Hempel's book was published, Fourierism had all but disappeared, ending any further efforts to demonstrate the relevance of Fourier and Swedenborg.

50. Henry James, "Reply to New Jerusalem Magazine," in *The Harbinger* 6 (1847): 54–55.

51. Guarneri, "Associationists," 42.

52. John Dwight, "The Idea of a Divine Social Order," in *The Harbinger* 6 (1848): 170; Charles A. Dana, *A Lecture on Association, in Its Connection with Religion* (Boston: Benjamin H. Greene, 1844).

53. Guarneri, "Associationists," 41.

54. James, *Moralism and Christianity,* 44–45. By morality, James meant the sentiment of selfhood within a state of conscious freedom or rationality, thus giving the individual ownership of his words and deeds. See James, *Substance and Shadow,* 3.

55. James, *Substance and Shadow,* 106.

56. Between 1842 and 1846, William Henry Channing divided his time between preaching in Brooklyn, New York, and preaching at West Roxbury in the pulpit of Theodore Parker. It was in Brooklyn where he became friends of Horace Greeley, Henry James, Sr., and Margaret Fuller.

57. Ralph Waldo Emerson, "New England Reformers," in *Essays: Second Series* (Boston: Phillips, Sampson, and Company, 1855), 243–45, 247, 249, 252.

58. Ibid., 255–59.

59. Noyes, *History of American Socialisms,* 554.

60. "Fire at Brook Farm," in *The Harbinger* 2 (1846): 221.

61. "To Our Friends," in *The Harbinger* 2 (1846): 237–38. Read Perry Miller, "Errand into the Wilderness," in *William and Mary Quarterly* 10 (1953): 3–32.

62. Sterling F. Delano, "The Boston Union of Associationists (1846–1851): 'Association Is to Me the Great Hope of the World,'" in *Studies in the American Renaissance* (1996): 5–40.

63. Read Lindsay Swift, *Brook Farm: Its Members, Scholars, and Visitors* (New York: Macmillan Co., 1900).

64. Read Dan McKanan, "Making Sense of Failure: From Death to Resurrection in Nineteenth-Century American Communitarianism," in *Utopian Studies* 18 (2007): 159–92; Christopher Clark, *The Communitarian Movement: The Radical Challenge of the Northampton Association* (Ithaca, NY: Cornell University Press, 1995); John Thomas Codman, *Brook Farm: Historic and Personal Memoirs* (New York: AMS Press, 1971 [1894]); Sterling F. Delano, *Brook Farm: The Dark Side of Utopia* (Cambridge, MA: Harvard

University Press, 2004); George Ripley, "The Angels of the Past," in *The Christian Examiner and Religious Miscellany* 42 (1847): 343–44.

65. Guarneri, *Utopian Alternative*, 242.

66. Delano, "Boston Union of Associationists," 10.

67. Ibid., 15–17.

68. Quoted in Frothingham, *Memoir of William Henry Channing*, 213–14.

69. With some thirty-three individuals signing a statement of the Religious Union, the members met on Sunday evenings for conversation, music, and prayer. Their weekly discussions addressed such questions as the war with Mexico, the spiritual world, education of children, human nature, reforms of the day, the work of prayer, and questions on the Union's management. At their gatherings, members also listened to passages from Fourier, Henry James, Hempel, and *The Harbinger*. On occasions, the group participated in a communion exercise that included a temporary altar, candles, and dishes of fruit and biscuits. The members even inducted, ordained, and sent out missionaries to spread the cause of associationism to other regions of the country. During much of this time, William Henry Channing was traveling from New England to Ohio to spread the gospel of the new Union. By December 1850, the Religious Union's meetings and services ended with hardly a whimper, as the leading spirits of associationism occupied themselves with other issues. Though exhausted from his missionary work on behalf of the organization, William Henry remained passionate about its promise, focusing his efforts on the Raritan Bay Union project. Like others, however, he turned his thoughts and energies to clairvoyance, psychometry, Spiritualism, women's rights, and temperance reform, as well as eventually to abolitionism and a plan for a Fugitive Slave League. He also spent considerable time in Rochester, New York, known as the last station on the Underground Railroad between the Southern states and Canada. This cause, along with the war with Mexico, the passage of the Fugitive Slave Bill, and the annexation of Texas, brought him to an uncompromising commitment to the extermination of slavery. "Let us then make a common sacrifice to remove it, and so discharge our common duty to the slaves, the slave-holders, the freemen of the North, and the whole Union," he wrote in a letter to Samuel P. Chase in 1853 (Quoted in Frothingham, *Memoir of William Henry Channing*, 261).

70. Alfred Cridge quoted in Noyes, *History of American Socialisms*, 498. At the forced sale of the North American Phalanx, shareholders received sixty-six cents on the dollar. See Hillquit, *History of Socialism in the United States*, 103.

71. Quoted in Frothingham, *Memoir of William Henry Channing*, 215–18. In time, William Henry Channing came to realize that his convictions on religion were gone. Jesus was not the person he reputed to be; the Gospels were unreliable; and Christianity was not a divine institution. Neither was there revelation from heaven nor grounds for an ordained priesthood. "In a

word," wrote Frothingham, "he became a deist, and resigned his [ministry in Cincinnati] accordingly." He "had come to the conclusion that 'Christianity' was not the religion of Jesus Christ" (Frothingham, *Memoir of William Henry Channing,* 150).

72. "Correspondence," in *The Harbinger* 3 (1846): 86.

73. "Celebration of Fourier's Birthday in Boston," in *The Harbinger* 4 (1847): 297–98.

74. "The Swedenborg Association," in *The Harbinger* 3 (1846): 63.

75. "Swedenborg's Scientific Writings," in *The Harbinger* 3 (1846): 71–72.

76. "Review," in *The Harbinger* 4 (1847): 327, 328.

77. Ibid., 329, 330.

78. Read John L. Thomas, "Romantic Reform in America, 1815–1865," in *American Quarterly* 17 (1965): 656–81.

79. Read Matei Calinescu, *Five Faces of Modernity: Modernism, Avant-garde, Decadence, Kitsch, Postmodernism* (Durham: Duke University Press, 1987), 107–8; Charles Fourier, "Socialism in France," in Robert Owen, *New Moral World: Or Gazette of the Universal Community Society of Rational Religionists* 6 (1839): 754. The subject of the Last Judgment did not mean the destruction of the world nor the proposition that further procreation of humankind would cease at this moment. Instead, Swedenborg believed the Last Judgment signified that all who were born from the beginning of creation to the end of the Church were judged in 1757. At this time, the former heavens passed away, affecting those only of the Reformed who professed a belief in God. Those who did not believe and condemned the Word were cast into hell. The Reformed were then arranged according to countries and according to their differences of love. Upon death, every individual went to the society of his/her own love, conjoined with those of similar love.

80. Guarneri, "Associationists," 37.

81. Ronald A. Bosco and Joel Myerson, eds., *The Later Lectures of Ralph Waldo Emerson, Vol. 1: 1843–54* (Athens: University of Georgia Press, 2001), 162. Read Charles Howard Hopkins, *The Rise of the Social Gospel in American Protestantism, 1865–1915* (New Haven: Yale University Press, 1940); James A. Dombrowski, *The Early Days of Christian Socialism in America* (New York: Octagon Books, 1966 [1937]).

3 In Search of a Vision

1. The second half of the nineteenth century became a vivid display of eclectic talent: Henry Hobson Richardson and Louis Sullivan in architecture; Jeffries Wyman and Clarence King in science; Winslow Homer, Thomas Eakins, and Albert P. Ryder in painting; William Graham Sumner and Lester Ward in sociology; Oliver Wendell Holmes in law; Henry George in economics; and William James and John Dewey in philosophy.

2. Walt Whitman, *Democratic Vistas* (London: Walter Scott, 1888), 11, 13.

3. Rev. G. Lawrence Allbutt, "The Attitude to Be Taken to the Darwinian Doctrine of the Origin of Species," in *The New-Church Review* 26 (1919): 534–35.

4. Henry S. Nash, "Religion, Revelation, and Moral Certitude," in *The Biblical World* 31 (1908): 369.

5. The anonymously published *Vestiges of the Natural History of Creation* (1844) had been written by Robert Chambers, an Edinburgh writer and publisher of *Chambers's Edinburgh Journal*. In it he proposed a vast sequence of developmental change in the universe, with the eventual appearance of humanity through progressive change from primates.

6. Darwin based his theory of natural selection on plausibility—a methodological change of tectonic magnitude. His hypothesis rested on the accumulation of data with which he built the argument for species development. Both probabilistic concepts and statistical reasoning were integral parts of his evolutionary theory, revealing how populations could be expected to evolve and capturing important biological generalizations (selection, mutation, migration, drift) that would otherwise have been missed in the randomness of the data. Read Barbara L. Horan, "The Statistical Character of Evolutionary Theory," in *Philosophy of Science* 61, no. 1 (1994): 76–95; Marcel Weber, "Determinism, Realism, and Probability in Evolutionary Theory," in *Philosophy of Science* 68, no. 3, Suppl. (2001): S213–S224; Roberta L. Millstein, "Interpretations of Probability in Evolutionary Theory," in *Philosophy of Science* 70, no. 5 (2002): 1317–28; David L. Hull, "Deconstructing Darwin: Evolutionary Theory in Context," in *Journal of the History of Biology* 38, no. 1 (2005): 137–52.

7. D. H. Meyer, "American Intellectuals and the Victorian Crisis of Faith," in *American Quarterly* 27, no. 5 (1975): 591.

8. James Moore, "Deconstructing Darwinism: The Politics of Evolution in the 1860s," in *Journal of the History of Biology* 24, no. 3 (1991): 353–408.

9. John Passmore, "Darwin's Impact on British Metaphysics," in *Victorian Studies* 3, no. 1 (1959): 51.

10. At the time of his recommendation to the post on the HMS Beagle, Darwin admitted that he had not "the least doubt the strict and literal truth of every word in the Bible" (Quoted in Nora Barlow, ed., *The Autobiography of Charles Darwin, 1809–1882* [New York: Harcourt, Brace, 1958], 57).

11. Francis Darwin, ed., *The Life and Letters of Charles Darwin,* 2 vols. (New York: D. Appleton, 1896), vol. I, 147.

12. For examples, see James C. Livingston, "Darwin, Darwinism, andTheology: Recent Studies," in *Religious Studies Review* 8 (1982): 105–16; Maurice Mandelbaum, "Darwin's Religious Views," in *Journal of the History of Ideas* 19 (1958): 363–78; Dov Ospovat, "God and Natural Selection: The Darwinian Idea of Design," in *Journal of the History of Biology* 15 (1980):

169–95; Frank Burch Brown, "The Evolution of Darwin's Theism," in *Journal of the History of Biology* 19 (1986): 1–45.

13. Darwin to Gray, November 26, 1860, in "Darwin Correspondence Project," https://www.darwinproject.ac.uk/letter/DCP-LETT-2998.xml (accessed January 24, 2016).

14. Bernard Lightman, "Darwin and the Popularization of Evolution," in *Notes and Records of the Royal Society of London* 64, no. 1 (2010): 11–16.

15. Quoted in Thomas Henry Huxley, "Mr. Darwin's Critics [1871]," in *Darwiniana: Essays* (New York: D. Appleton and Co., 1896), 126.

16. John C. Greene, "Darwin and Religion," in *Proceedings of the American Philosophical Society* 103 (1959): 721. Alfred R. Wallace remained a loyal defender of natural selection until 1869, when he began attending séances and his conversion to Spiritualism drew him in a direction that Darwin and his supporters could not support, let alone understand. Not having family wealth or the essential breeding and education expected of gentlemen naturalists meant that even though Wallace was the co-originator of the theory of natural selection, his Fellowship in the Royal Society would come late, not until 1893.

17. The term *dysteleology* was invented by Haeckel to explain the purposelessness in natural selection. Read Edward Aveling, *The Creed of an Atheist* (London: Free Thought Publishing Co., 1881); Edward Aveling, *The Student's Darwin* (London: Freethought Publishing Co., 1881); Robert G. Ingersoll, *Works of Robert G. Ingersoll*, 13 vols. (New York: Dresden, 1909–15), vol. IV, 463–64; Ernst Haeckel, *Riddle of the Universe at the Close of the Nineteenth Century* (New York: Harper and Brothers, 1900).

18. Read Charles R. Darwin, *The Descent of Man, and Selection in Relation to Sex* (New York: Appleton and Co., 1871), 67.

19. Edmund Swift, Jr., *Evolution and Natural Selection in the Light of the New Church* (Philadelphia: American New Church Tract and Publication Society, n.d.), 3.

20. L. I. Tafel, "New Church and Evolution," in *The New-Church Messenger* 110 (1916): 107.

21. Block, *New Church in the New World*, 310–16; Linda Simonetti Odhner, "Recapitulation Theories and Man's Place in the Universe," in Brock and Glenn, eds., *Swedenborg and His Influence*, 199–226. See also John R. Swanton, *Emanuel Swedenborg: Prophet of the Higher Evolution* (New York: New Church Press, 1928).

22. Read John Henry Barrows, ed., *The World's Parliament of Religions, an Illustrated and Popular Story of the World's First Parliament of Religions, Held in Chicago in Connection with the Columbian Exposition of 1893*, 2 vols. (Chicago: The Parliament Publishing Co., 1893).

23. Laurie Shannon, "'The Country of Our Friendship': Jewett's Intimist Art," in *American Literature* 71, no. 2 (1999): 227–62.

24. Parsons was a classmate of Sampson Reed, who introduced Emerson and other Transcendentalists to Swedenborg. Read Josephine Donovan, "Jewett and Swedenborg," in *American Literature* 65, no. 4 (1993): 732–33. Read also Theophilus Parsons, *The Infinite and the Finite* (Boston: Roberts Brothers, 1872); Theophilus Parsons, *Outlines of the Religion and Philosophy of Swedenborg* (Boston: Roberts Brothers, 1876).

25. Annie Fields, ed., *Letters of Sarah Orne Jewett* (Boston: Houghton Mifflin Company, 1911), 47.

26. Donovan, "Jewett and Swedenborg," 735.

27. Fields, ed., *Letters of Sarah Orne Jewett*, 21–22.

28. Frank Norris, *The Octopus* (New York: Sagamore Press, Inc., 1957), 401.

29. See Joseph Schiffman, ed., "Mutual Indebtedness: Unpublished Letters of Edward Bellamy to William Dean Howells," in *Harvard Library Bulletin* 12 (1958).

30. Read Arthur E. Morgan, *Edward Bellamy* (New York: Columbia University Press, 1944); Arthur E. Morgan, *The Philosophy of Edward Bellamy* (New York: King's Crown Press, 1945).

31. Andover Theological Seminary, the leading center of Edwardian Calvinism, was founded in 1808 in response to the "drift" of Harvard's Divinity School to Unitarianism. Among the leading advocates of the New Theology, or Progressive Orthodoxy, was William Jewett Tucker (1839–1926), who hoped to retain the core of Protestant theology while, at the same time, seeking accommodation with modern scientific thought.

32. "The Religion of Solidarity" was not published until 1940 by Arthur E. Morgan, whose *Edward Bellamy* insisted that it represented a definitive expression of Bellamy's faith and social philosophy. The same opinion was held by Sylvia E. Bowman in *The Year 2000: A Critical Biography of Edward Bellamy* (New York: Bookman, 1958) and Joseph Schiffman's introduction to *Edward Bellamy: Selected Writings on Religion and Society* (New York: Liberal Arts Press, 1955).

33. Edward Bellamy, "The Religion of Solidarity," in Arthur E. Morgan, *The Religion of Solidarity with a Discussion of Edward Bellamy's Philosophy* (Yellow Springs, Ohio: Antioch Bookplate Co., 1940), 18, 19. For an alternative interpretation, read Thomas A. Sancton, "Looking Inward: Edward Bellamy's Spiritual Crisis," in *American Quarterly* 25 (1973): 538–57; Samuel Haber, "The Nightmare and the Dream: Edward Bellamy and the Travails of Socialist Thought," in *Journal of American Studies* 36 (2002): 417–40. See also Joseph Schiffman, "Edward Bellamy's Religious Thought," in *PMLA* 68 (1953): 716–32.

34. Bellamy, "Religion of Solidarity," 21, 22, 24, 29, 30, 31, 36.

35. Ibid., 40, 41, 42, 43.

36. Read Edward Bellamy, *The Duke of Stockbridge: A Romance of Shays' Rebellion* (New York: Silver, Burdett and Co., 1900).

37. Edward Bellamy, "Remarks," in *The Nationalist* I (1889): 1.

38. Herbert Spencer, *First Principles* (New York: D. Appleton and Co., 1898), 584.

39. See Richard Hofstadter, *Social Darwinism in American Thought* (Philadelphia: University of Pennsylvania Press, 1944).

40. Read Philip Foner, *History of the Labor Movement in the United States*, 2 vols. (New York: International Publishers, 1947); Ronald L. Filippelli, *Labor Conflict in the United States: An Encyclopedia* (New York: Garland Publishers, 1990).

41. Read *Andover Review* XIV (1890): 236–53.

42. Joseph Schiffman, "Edward Bellamy's Altruistic Man," in *American Quarterly* 6 (1954): 195–209.

43. Read Walter Aldine Smith, "The Religion of Edward Bellamy" (M.A. thesis, Columbia University, 1937).

44. Quoted in Rudolf Kirk and Clara Kirk, "Howells and the Church of the Carpenter," in *The New England Quarterly* 32 (1959): 185–206; Howard H. Quint, *The Forging of American Socialism* (Indianapolis: Bobbs-Merrill Co., 1964), 80.

45. John H. Franklin, "Edward Bellamy and Nationalism," in *The New England Quarterly* 11 (1938): 739–72; Francis A. Walker, "Mr. Bellamy and the New Nationalist Party," in *The Atlantic Monthly* 65 (1890): 248–62.

46. S. David, "What is Nationalism," in *The New Christianity* 3 (1890): 377–78, 794–95.

47. Elizabeth Sadler, "One Book's Influence: Edward Bellamy's *Looking Backward*," in *The New England Quarterly* 17 (1944): 530–55; Allyn B. Forbes, "The Literary Quest for Utopia: 1880–1900," in *Social Forces* 6 (1927): 179–89. Read also Sylvia E. Bowman, *Edward Bellamy Abroad: An American Prophet's Influence* (New York: Twayne Publishers, 1962).

48. Stephen Graham, *Tramping with a Poet in the Rockies* (New York: D. Appleton and Co., 1922), v–vi.

49. Vachel Lindsay, *The Golden Book of Springfield* (New York: Macmillan Co., 1920), 6–7, 22, 23.

50. Quoted in Block, *New Church in the New World*, 346.

51. R. L. Tafel, *Socialism and Reform in the Light of the New Church: Lectures* (London: James Speirs, 1891), 11, 32, 50, 53, 66, 91, 99.

52. Ibid., 4.

53. Ibid., 124–25, 137–38.

54. Ibid., 141–42.

55. Read Charles J. Tull, *Father Coughlin and the New Deal* (Syracuse: Syracuse University Press, 1965); Charles J. Tull, *The Townsend Crusade: An Impartial Review of the Townsend Movement and the Probable Effects of the Townsend Plan* (New York: The Committee on Old Age Security of the 20th Century

Fund, Inc., 1936); Joseph Dorfman, *Thorstein Veblen and His America* (New York: Viking Press, 1947), 68, 388.

56. William Cooper Howells, *Recollections of Life in Ohio from 1813 to 1840* (Cincinnati: Robert Clarke Co., 1895), iv, vi, 42, 104, 158; Susan Goodman and Carl Dawson, *William Dean Howells: A Writer's Life* (CA: University of California Press, 2005), 12.

57. William Dean Howells, *Literary Friends and Acquaintances: A Personal Retrospect of American Authorship* (New York: Harper and Brothers Publishers, 1900), 228. Read also Paul Abeln, *William Dean Howells and the Ends of Realism* (New York: Routledge, 2005).

58. Delmar Gross Cooke, *William Dean Howells: A Critical Study* (New York: E. P. Dutton and Co., 1922), 9.

59. Letter dated January 27, 1889, in Kirk and Kirk, "Howells and the Church of the Carpenter," 193.

60. William Dean Howells, *A Boy's Town* (New York: Harper and Brothers Publishers, 1890), 20–21.

61. Read O. W. Firkins, "William Dean Howells," in *The Sewanee Review* 29 (1921): 171–76.

62. Read Emanuel Swedenborg, *The Doctrine of Life for the New Jerusalem: from the Commandments of the Decalogue* (New York: American Swedenborg Printing and Publishing Society, 1891). See also Walter J. Meserve, "Truth, Morality, and Swedenborg in Howells' Theory of Realism," in *The New England Quarterly* 27 (1954): 252–57.

63. Read Hannah Graham Belcher, "Howells's Opinions on the Religious Conflicts of His Age as Exhibited in Magazine Articles," in *American Literature* 15 (1943): 262–78. The Church of the Carpenter was founded by Rev. William Dwight Porter Bliss and his Society of Christian Socialists in Boston. Bliss, an eager follower of Henry George, Laurence Gronlund, and Edward Bellamy, advocated nationalism, the single tax, socialism, and pro-labor issues from his monthly publication *The Dawn*. Read Kirk and Kirk, "Howells and the Church of the Carpenter," 185–206.

64. Read Everett W. MacNair, *Edward Bellamy and the Nationalist Movement, 1889 to 1894* (Milwaukee: Fitzgerald, 1957).

65. Joseph Schiffman, ed., "Mutual Indebtedness: Unpublished Letters of Edward Bellamy to William Dean Howells," in *Harvard Library Bulletin* 12 (1958): 372–73.

66. Meserve, "Truth, Morality, and Swedenborg in Howells' Theory of Realism," 253.

67. Mildred Howells, *Life in Letters of William Dean Howells*, 2 vols. (Garden City: Doubleday, Doran and Co., 1928), vol. I, 165.

68. William Dean Howells, *The Leatherwood God* (New York: The Century Co., 1916), 74–76.

69. William Dean Howells, *Italian Journeys* (Boston: Houghton and Mifflin and Co., 1907), 144, 150–52, 355.

70. William Dean Howells, *Ragged Lady* (Toronto: W. J. Gage, 1899), 256.

71. Read Howells's review of H. C. Lea's *History of the Inquisition in the Middle Ages* in "Study," in *Harper's Monthly* 76 (1888): 640.

72. Read Howells's comments in *Harper's Monthly* 80 (1890): 484.

73. Howells's supporters included Sarah Orne Jewett, Frank Norris, Theodore Dreiser, Floyd Dell, Stephen Crane, and Randolph Bourne, who all relished the truthfulness of Tolstoy.

74. Clare R. Goldfarb, "William Dean Howells: An American Reaction to Tolstoy," in *Comparative Literature Studies* 8 (1971): 317–37.

75. William Dean Howells, "Easy Chair," in *Harper's Magazine* 127 (October 1913): 798.

76. Read William Dean Howells, *A Hazard of New Fortunes* (New York: Harper and Brothers Publishers, 1889); William Dean Howells, *A Traveler from Altruria: Romance* (New York: Harper and Brothers Publishers, 1894); William Dean Howells, *Through the Eye of the Needle: A Romance* (New York: Harper and Brothers Publishers, 1907).

77. James, *Society the Redeemed Form of Man.*

78. Ralph Waldo Trine, *In the Fire of the Heart* (New York: McClure, Phillips and Co., 1906), 316–36.

79. Read Francesca Bordogna, "Inner Division and Uncertain Contours: William James and the Politics of the Modern Self," in *The British Journal for the History of Science* 40 (2007): 505–36.

80. William H. Mayhew, "An Altruistic World," in *The New-Church Review* 14 (1907): 583–87.

81. Howells, *Traveler from Altruria*, 299–300.

82. William Dean Howells, *Years of My Youth* (New York: Harper and Brothers Publishers, 1917), 106; William Dean Howells, "Easy Chair," in *Harper's Monthly* 140 (1920): 279.

83. Alfred Russel Wallace, *Man's Place in the Universe* (New York: McClure, Phillips and Co., 1903), 258–77; William Dean Howells, "Easy Chair," in *Harper's Monthly* 108 (1903): 640–44.

84. Belcher, "Howells's Opinions on the Religious Conflicts of His Age as Exhibited in Magazine Articles," 262–78.

85. William Dean Howells, "What Shall It Profit?," in *Harper's Monthly* 82 (1891): 384.

86. W. F. Taylor, "On the Origin of Howells's Interest in Economic Reform," in *American Literature* 2 (1930): 3–14; Conrad Wright, "The Sources of Mr. Howells's Socialism," in *Science and Society* 2 (1938): 514–17.

87. George Arms, "The Literary Background of Howells's Social Criticism," in *American Literature* 14 (1942): 26–76.

88. D. H. Lawrence, "Why the Novel Matters," in D. H. Lawrence, *Selected Criticism* (New York: Viking Press, 1956), 105.

4 Single Tax

1. Quoted in Charles A. Madison, "Henry George, Prophet of Human Rights," in *South Atlantic Quarterly* 43 (1944): 360.

2. George's literary abilities, first recognized by Noah Brooks, moved him in 1866 from a printer job at the *San Francisco Times* to a reporter's desk. Before long, he became an editorial writer and then editor-in-chief and managing editor.

3. Quoted in Louis F. Post, *The Prophet of San Francisco* (Chicago: L. S. Dickey & Co., 1904), 16.

4. Read George W. Bishop, Jr., "The Message of Henry George: A Social Philosopher's Indictment of Monopoly and Privilege as Causes of Poverty," in *American Journal of Economics and Sociology* 34 (1975): 129–38.

5. George R. Geiger, "The Forgotten Man: Henry George," in *The Antioch Review* 1 (1941): 302.

6. Henry George, *Social Problems* (London: Kegan Paul, Trench and Co., 1884), 34, 37.

7. Ibid., 15, 21, 22, 31, 194.

8. https://en.wikipedia.org/wiki/Henry_George (accessed May 18, 2020).

9. Leo G. Mazow, "George Inness, Henry George, the Single Tax, and the Future Poet," in *American Art* 18 (2004): 61.

10. Read T. J. Jackson Lears, *No Place of Grace: Antimodernism and the Transformation of American Society, 1880–1920* (New York: Pantheon, 1981); Raymond Geiger, *The Philosophy of Henry George* (New York: Macmillan Co., 1933).

11. Henry George, *Progress and Poverty: An Inquiry into the Cause of Industrial Depressions, and of Increase of Want with Increase of Wealth. The Remedy* (4th ed.; New York: D. Appleton and Co., 1886 [1879]), 3, 8, 9.

12. Ibid., 198–99, 224. In his concept of distribution, George dismissed the "iron law of wages" theory offered by classical economist Thomas Robert Malthus, which stated that real wages could never rise above the level of subsistence. George argued that instead of being drawn from capital, wages came from the product of the labor for which they were paid. Nevertheless, he was in substantial accord with the classical school of economics and in particular with David Ricardo's law of rent, although he disagreed with Ricardo's treatment of the law as correlative to the law of wages.

13. See William Thomas Thornton, *On Labour, Its Wrongful Claims and Rightful Dues* (London: Macmillan and Co., 1869); Francis Amasa Walker, *The Wages Question: A Treatise on Wages and the Wages Class* (London: Macmillan and Co., 1876).

14. George, *Progress and Poverty,* 249, 255, 265, 266.

15. Ibid., 308, 364. The words "life, liberty and the pursuit of happiness" were taken from Locke's phrase "life, liberty and property" in his *Two Treatises*

of Civil Government (1689). Jefferson considered his choice of "pursuit of happiness" as synonymous with the term *property*, only more pleasant sounding.

16. Dominic Candeloro, "Louis F. Post and the Single Tax Movement, 1872–98," in *American Journal of Economics and Sociology* 35 (1976): 415–30.

17. George, *Progress and Poverty*, 410.

18. Robert Bannister, *Social Darwinism: Science and Myth in Anglo-American Social Thought* (Philadelphia: Temple University Press, 1979), 219–23.

19. George, *Progress and Poverty*, 457.

20. Ibid., 433, 436, 439, 452–53.

21. Ibid., 480, 484, 488.

22. Ibid., 494, 496, 505, 507–8.

23. http://www.wealthandwant.com/HG/Moses.html (accessed May 18, 2020). Read also Aharon H. Shapiro, "Moses—Henry George's Inspiration," in *The American Journal of Economics and Sociology* 47 (1988): 493–501.

24. Quoted in Edmund Yardley, ed., *Addresses at the Funeral of Henry George* (Chicago: The Public Publishing Co., 1905), 41.

25. Bob Lawson-Peebles, "Henry George the Prophet," in *Journal of American Studies* 10 (1976): 41.

26. Duke of Argyll, "The Prophet of San Francisco," in *The Nineteenth Century* 15 (1884): 537–58.

27. See Henry George, *An Open Letter to Pope Leo XIII* (New York: Charles L. Webster and Co., 1893). George's ideas, which were similar to Alfred Russel Wallace's in *Land Nationalization, Its Necessity and Its Aims* (New York: Charles Scribner's Sons, 1892), were best represented by the Land Nationalization Society and the English League for the Taxation of Land Values in Great Britain. The Land Reform Union, better known as "The League," and the Single Tax League formed a few years after the publication of *Progress and Poverty*.

28. Henry George, *The Science of Political Economy* (New York: Doubleday and McClure Co., 1898), 198, 383, 391.

29. George, *Progress and Poverty*, 288–89, 319.

30. Charles R. McCann, Jr., "Apprehending the Social Philosophy of Henry George," in *American Journal of Economics and Sociology* 67 (2008): 67–88.

31. George, *Social Problems*, 47, 55, 66, 76, 77.

32. Ibid., 75, 104, 112, 123–34, 261.

33. Henry George, *Our Land and Land Policy: Speeches, Lectures, and Miscellaneous Writings* (New York: Doubleday and McClure Co., 1902), 153.

34. Both George and LeConte were friends and fellow Californians whose Neo-Lamarckian beliefs took precedence over their views on geological and human evolution. Both explained evolution as a process that gathered in strength to the point of rapid change or catastrophe at which time God

sometimes intervened to move it in either an upward advance or a downward spiral. Humankind, set apart from the animal kingdom, had a mental power capable of making a difference if utilized and so directed. By contrast, natural selection proved much too materialistic for George to accept. In its place, he held that a divine mind stood behind the evolutionary process, directing both nature and humanity to some foreordained end. While there was no guarantee of human progress at any one time, the conditions under which people in various civilizations lived, and their effort to respond, made the difference between progress and failure. Not every civilization provided sufficient stimulus for its members to make it the basis of their exertions. Those, however, who did, much like the giraffe who stretched its neck for food among the higher boughs of trees, were able to survive. See Edward J. Pfeifer, "The Scientific Source of Henry George's Evolutionary Theories," in *Pacific Historical Review* 36 (1967): 397–403. Read Edward J. Pfeifer, "The Genesis of American Neo-Lamarckism," in *Isis* 56 (1965): 156–67; George W. Stocking, Jr., "Lamarckianism in American Social Science: 1890–1915," in *Journal of the History of Ideas* 23 (1962): 239–56.

35. George, *Progress and Poverty*, 474–96.

36. Ibid., 126.

37. For religious aspects of George and Bellamy, read Dombrowski, *Early Days of Christian Socialism in America*, 35–49, 84–95.

38. Michael Silagi and Susan N. Faulkner, "Henry George and Europe: The Far-Reaching Effect of the Ideas of the American Social Philosopher at the Turn of the Century," in *American Journal of Economics and Sociology* 45 (1986): 201–13.

39. "First Annual Convention of the Single Tax Party of the United States," in *The Single Tax Review* 19 (1919): 105–12. Read Arthur Nichols Young, *The Single Tax Movement in the United States* (Princeton: Princeton University Press, 1916).

40. "The Late Charles Hardon," in *The Single Tax Review* 17 (1917): 298.

41. Examples include: "Money, Land and Monopoly," in *The New Christianity* 8 (1895): 172–73; "Justice of the Single Tax," in *The New Christianity* 10 (1897): 28–29; "Reply to a Letter from an Illinois Farmer," in *The New Christianity* 10 (1897): 61–62; "Progress of the Single Tax," in *The New Christianity* 10 (1897): 77; S. U. J. Chubb, "The Single Tax and Its Relation to the Christian Religion," in *The New Christianity* 10 (1897): 122–23; "Henry George," in *The New Christianity* 10 (1897): 161; James E. Mills, "Henry George's Answer to Herbert Spencer and the Land Question," in *The New Christianity* 6 (1893): 25–26.

42. M. Cebelia L'Hommedieu, "John Filmer," in *Land and Freedom* 29 (1929): 72. (*Land and Freedom* was formerly *The Single Tax Review*.)

43. "Spiritual Significance of the Single Tax," in *The New Earth* 7 (1896): 13–15; L. E. Wilmarth, "The Various Planes of Desire and Thought to

Which the Single Tax Appeals," in *The New Earth* 7 (1896): 18–20; "Planks from George's Mayoralty Platform," in *The New Earth* 8 (1897): 91–92.

44. Only when Bellamy published his book *Equality* did the Swedenborgians find a more redeeming value to his nationalism, considering it the best presentation yet made concerning the ideology's ethical basis. Nonetheless, nationalism was always thought to be too utopian. See "Nationalism and the Single Tax," in *The New Earth* 2 (1891): 3, 10–11, 39, 53–54; "Endorsement of Bellamy's *Equality*," in *The New Earth* 8 (1897): 66–67; "Book Review," in *The New Earth* 7 (1896): 70–71.

45. L. E. Wilmarth, "The Harmony of the New Political Economy with the Teachings of Swedenborg," in *The New Earth* 1 (1889): 5–6.

46. L. E. Wilmarth, "Use Quite Distinct from Ownership," in *The New Earth* 1 (1890): 6–7.

47. J. B. Spiers, "In the South," in *The New-Church Messenger* 96 (1909): 11.

48. Gregory S. Jackson, "'What Would Jesus Do?' Practical Christianity, Social Gospel Realism, and the Homeletic Novel," in *PLMA* 121 (2006): 641–61. Other exemplary books include John H. W. Stuckenberg's *Christian Sociology* (New York: Funk and Wagnalls Co., 1880); Joseph Hine Rylance's *Lectures on Social Questions. Competition, Communism, Cooperation, and the Relation of Christianity to Socialism* (New York: T. Whittaker, 1880); Bishop Samuel Smith Harris's *The Relation of Christianity to Civil Society* (New York: T. Whittaker, 1883); Josiah Strong's *Our Country: Its Possible Future and Present Crisis* (New York: Baker and Taylor, 1885); George C. Lorimer's *Studies in Social Life: A Review of the Principles, Practices, and Problems of Society* (Chicago: Belford, Clark and Co., 1886); Philip S. Moxom's *The Industrial Revolution: A Sermon* (P. S. Moxom, 1886); Auguste J. F. Behrend's *Socialism and Christianity* (New York: Baker and Taylor, 1886); Minot J. Savage's *Social Problems* (Boston: G. H. Ellis, 1886); Francis N. Zabriskie's *The Bible a Workingman's Book* (New York: R. F. Bogardus, 1888); George D. Herron's *The Christian Society* (New York: Fleming H. Revell Co., 1894); Henry Vedder's *Socialism and the Ethics of Jesus* (New York: Macmillan, 1912).

49. H. C. H., "Socialism and the New Church," in *The New-Church Review* 17 (1910): 600–1.

50. George Inness, Jr., *Life, Art, and Letters of George Inness* (New York: The Century Co., 1917), 10, 61. See also Mary Phillips, "The Effect of Swedenborgianism on the Later Paintings of George Inness," in Brock and Glenn, eds., *Swedenborg and His Influence*, 427–37.

51. Sally M. Promey, "The Ribband of Faith: George Inness, Color Theory, and the Swedenborg Church," in *American Art Journal* 26 (1994): 44–65.

52. Eugene Taylor, "The Interior Landscape: George Inness and William James on Art from a Swedenborgian Point of View," in *Archives of American Art Journal* 37 (1997): 2–3.

53. Quoted in Elliott Daingerfield, *George Inness: The Man and His Art* (New York: Privately Printed, 1911), dedications.

54. George Inness, "Colors and Their Correspondences," in *The New Jerusalem Messenger* 13 (1867): 78–79.

55. Swedenborg, *Divine Love and Wisdom* §374.

56. Mazow, "George Inness, Henry George, the Single Tax, and the Future Poet," 58–77; Inness, Jr., *Life, Art, and Letters of George Inness,* 62. See also Adrienne Baxter Bell, *George Inness and the Visionary Landscape* (New York: National Academy of Design, 2003).

57. "Advertisement," in *The New Earth* 4 (1893): 8; "Mr. Post's Lecture on Taxation," in *The New Earth* 4 (1893): 31.

58. Louis F. Post, *Social Service* (New York: A. Wessels, 1909), dedication; Dominic Candeloro, "From the Narrow Single Tax to Broad Progressivism: The Intellectual Development of Louis F. Post, 1898–1913," in *American Journal of Economics and Sociology* 37 (1978): 329.

59. "Discussion by the Hon. Louis F. Post," in *The New-Church Messenger* 121 (1921): 42.

60. Carrie A. Foster, *The Women and the Warriors: The U.S. Section of the Women's International League for Peace and Freedom, 1915–1946* (Syracuse, NY: Syracuse University Press, 1995), 124; "Louis Post," in the American Catholic History Research Center and University Archives, http://cuomeka. wrlc.org/exhibits/show/immigration/documents/bio-post (accessed March 13, 2015).

61. Candeloro, "Louis F. Post and the Single Tax Movement," 425.

62. "Socialism Defined by a Socialist," in *The New Earth* 9 (1898): 92.

63. Catharine Nugent, ed., *Life Work of Thomas L. Nugent* (Chicago: Laird and Lee, 1896), 81.

64. Quoted in Nugent, ed., *Life Work of Thomas L. Nugent,* 112, 113, 117, 335.

65. Correspondence of Rev. E. Payson Walton in Nugent, ed., *Life Work of Thomas L. Nugent,* 94. See also Alice Thacher Post, "Thomas Nugent," in *The New Earth* 7 (1896): 95.

66. Quoted in Nugent, ed., *Life Work of Thomas L. Nugent,* 97–98, 316.

67. Ibid., 83, 84.

68. Ibid., 85, 86.

69. Nugent, ed., *Life Work of Thomas L. Nugent,* 34, 55–58.

70. Quoted in Nugent, ed., *Life Work of Thomas L. Nugent,* 297. Merl Curti, *The Growth of American Thought* (New York: Harper and Brothers Publishers, 1943); Ralph Henry Gabriel, *The Course of American Democratic Thought* (New York: Ronald Press Co., 1956); William Warren Sweet, *The Story of Religion in America* (New York: Harper and Brothers, 1939).

71. Quoted in Nugent, ed., *Life Work of Thomas L. Nugent,* 73, 315–16.

72. Wayne Alvord, "T. L. Nugent, Texas Populist," in *The Southwestern Historical Quarterly* 57 (1953): 65–81. Read also Octavius Brooks Frothingham, *The Religion of Humanity* (New York: D. G. Francis, 1873); Theodore Thornton Munger, *The Freedom of Faith* (Boston: Houghton, Mifflin and Co., 1883); Washington Gladden, *Applied Christianity: Moral Aspects of Social Questions* (Boston: Houghton, Mifflin and Co., 1886); Lyman Abbott, *Christianity and Social Problems* (Boston: Houghton, Mifflin and Co., 1896).

73. Nugent, ed., *Life Work of Thomas L. Nugent*, 113, 121.

74. Quoted in Nugent, ed., *Life Work of Thomas L. Nugent*, 110, 155, 157–59, 160, 167.

75. Nugent, ed., *Life Work of Thomas L. Nugent*, 63, 204–5, 261, 285, 290–91.

76. Quoted in Nugent, ed., *Life Work of Thomas L. Nugent*, 73, 74, 246.

77. Ibid., 87, 100.

78. George R. Geiger, "Forgotten Man," 291–307.

5 Social Gospel

1. Read Paul A. Carter, *The Decline and Revival of the Social Gospel: Social and Political Liberalism in American Protestant Churches, 1920–1940* (Ithaca, NY: Cornell University Press, 1956); Hopkins, *Rise of the Social Gospel in American Protestantism;* Aaron I. Abell, *The Urban Impact on American Protestantism, 1865–1900* (Cambridge, MA: Harvard University Press, 1943); Robert T. Handy, ed., *The Social Gospel in America, 1870–1920: Gladden, Ely, Rauschenbusch* (New York: Oxford University Press, 1966); Donald K. Gorrell, *The Age of Social Responsibility: The Social Gospel in the Progressive Era, 1900–1920* (Macon, GA: Mercer University Press, 1988).

2. "The Failure of Protestantism in New York City," in *The New Christianity* 8 (1895): 130; "Some Proceedings of the M. E. General Conference," in *The New Christianity* 5 (1892): 82; "The Church in the World," in *The New Christianity* 3 (1890): 282–83; C. M. Morse, "The Church and the Working Man," in *The New Christianity* 2 (1889): 123–24. Read Harold A. Durfee, *The Theologies of the American Social Gospel* (Park College, MO: Union Theological Seminary, 1951).

3. Sidney Fine, "Richard T. Ely, Forerunner of Progressivism, 1880–1901," in *Mississippi Valley Historical Review* 37 (1951): 599–624.

4. John Wright Buckham, *Progressive Religious Thought in America: A Survey of the Enlarging Pilgrim Faith* (Boston: Houghton Mifflin Co., 1919), 12.

5. Read Henry May, *The Protestant Churches and Industrial America* (New York: Harper, 1949); Hopkins, *Rise of the Social Gospel in American Protestantism;* William Hutchinson, *The Modernist Impulse in American Protestantism* (Cambridge, MA: Harvard University Press, 1976); Reinhold Niebuhr, *Reflections on the End of an Era* (New York: Scribner's, 1934);

Carter, *Decline and Revival of the Social Gospel;* Donald Meyer, *The Protestant Search for Political Realism, 1919–1941* (Middletown, CT: Wesleyan University Press, 1988); Robert T. Handy, *The American Religious Depression, 1925–1935* (Philadelphia: Fortress Press, 1968); Ronald White and C. Howard Hopkins, *The Social Gospel: Religion and Reform in Changing America* (Philadelphia: Temple University Press, 1976); Abell, *Urban Impact on American Protestantism;* Paul A. Carter, *The Spiritual Crisis of the Gilded Age* (DeKalb: Northern Illinois University Press, 1971); Sydney Ahlstrom, *A Religious History of the American People* (2nd ed.; New Haven: Yale University Press, 2004); Susan Curtis, *A Consuming Faith: The Social Gospel and Modern American Culture* (Baltimore: Johns Hopkins University Press, 1991); Robert Crunden, *Ministers of Reform: The Progressives' Achievement in American Civilization, 1889–1920* (New York: Basic Books, 1982).

6. Examples include W. D. P. Bliss, "What is Christian Socialism," in *The New Christianity* 3 (1890): 76–77; "Christian Socialism," in *The New Christianity* 3 (1890): 189; W. D. P. Bliss, "Jesus Christ and Christian Socialism," in *The New Christianity* 3 (1890): 203–4; W. H. Muller, "Socialism in a Nutshell," in *The New Christianity* 3 (1890): 300; "Effects of Alcohol on the Mind," in *The New Christianity* 8 (1895): 76–77; "Poverty a Prime Cause of Intemperance," in *The New Christianity* 8 (1895): 108–9; "Prohibition," in *The New Christianity* 9 (1896): 43–44; "Alcohol and the Brain," in *The New Christianity* 6 (1893): 28; "Temperance and Reform," in *The New Christianity* 6 (1893): 43–45; John Ellis, "Single Tax, Intoxicating Drinks and Poverty," in *The New Christianity* 6 (1893): 60; "Initiative and Referendum," in *The New Christianity* 8 (1895): 107.

7. Matthew Bowman, "Sin, Spirituality, and Primitivism," 95–126.

8. The Society of Christian Socialists was formally organized in Boston in 1889 with a declaration of principle: "To awaken members of Christian churches to the fact that the teachings of Jesus Christ lead directly to some specific form or forms of socialism; that, therefore, the Church has a definite duty upon this matter, and must, in simple obedience to Christ, apply itself to the realization of the social principles of Christianity." Its leaders included Rev. William D. P. Bliss; Prof. George D. Herron, chair of applied Christianity at Iowa College; and economist Richard T. Ely at the University of Wisconsin. In 1894, Herron and Ely organized the American Institute of Christian Sociology, which was intended to furnish literature to support the educational arm of the churches and their colleges. See Hillquit, *History of Socialism in the United States*, 292, 320.

9. Washington Gladden, *Recollections* (Boston: Houghton Mifflin Co., 1909), 252, 255, 299, 300, 301–2.

10. Washington Gladden, *Being a Christian: What It Means and How to Begin* (Boston: Pilgrim Press, 1885), 15–21.

11. Buckham, *Progressive Religious Thought in America*, 228.

12. Washington Gladden, *Tools and the Man: Property and Industry under the Christian Law* (Boston: Houghton, Mifflin, 1893), 255. Washington Gladden, *Christianity and Socialism* (New York: Eaton and Mains, 1905), 145, 153.

13. Gladden, *Recollections*, 63, 429.

14. Gladden, *Applied Christianity*, 10, 15, 18, 19, 29, 33, 37.

15. Ibid., 79.

16. Ibid., 96, 169, 171, 180–209.

17. Ibid., 221.

18. Gladden, *Recollections*, 308, 313, 314.

19. Gladden, *Christianity and Socialism*, 44, 58–59, 73. In his use of the term "practical vassalage," Gladden made the point that in the question of the workers' livelihood and welfare, those actions most often taken were decided without their consultation.

20. Gladden, *Recollections*, 346, 390–97.

21. Ibid., 154, 176, 197, 218.

22. Quoted in Buckham, *Progressive Religious Thought in America*, 230, 231.

23. Gladden, *Tools and the Man*, 86. Read also Orestes A. Brownson, *The Works of Orestes A. Brownson: Controversy. Vol. 5*, Henry F. Brownson, ed. (Detroit: Thorndike Nourse and Henry F. Brownson, 1884), 131.

24. Gladden, *Tools and the Man*, 280.

25. Read Nathaniel Southgate Shaler, *The Neighbor: The Natural History of Human Contacts* (Boston: Houghton, Mifflin and Co., 1904); Stow Persons, *American Minds: A History of Ideas* (New York: Holt, Rinehart and Winston, 1958), 276–97. See also R. T. Berthoff, "Southern Attitudes Toward Immigration, 1865–1914," in *Journal of Southern History* 17 (1951): 328–60; Walter L. Fleming, "Immigration to the Southern States," in *Political Science Quarterly* 20 (1905): 275–94; Bert J. Loewenberg, "Efforts of the South to Encourage Immigration, 1865–1900," in *South Atlantic Quarterly* 33 (1934): 363–85; Barbara M. Solomon, "Intellectual Background of the Immigration Restriction Movement in New England," in *The New England Quarterly* 25 (1952): 47–59; Edward Saveth, "Race and Nationalism in American Historiography: The Late Nineteenth Century," in *Political Science Quarterly* 64 (1939): 421–41.

26. Gladden, *Recollections*, 374.

27. Read William James, *The Meaning of Truth* (London: Longmans, Green, and Co., 1909).

28. Abbott, *Christianity and Social Problems*, 23, 35.

29. "Dr. Abbott's Beliefs," in *The New Christianity* 3 (1890): 56; "Lyman Abbott Believes in the Supreme Divinity of Christ," in *The New Christianity* 3 (1890): 169–70; "Notes and Comments," in *The New Christianity* 3 (1890): 184; "Mr. Abbott is Right," in *The New Christianity* 3 (1890): 264;

"Abbott on the Blood of Christ," in *The New Christianity* 2 (1889): 377–78; "Notes and Comments," in *The New Christianity* 1 (1888): 216.

30. Quoted in H. Clinton Hay, "The New Knowledge of God," in *The New-Church Review* 21 (1914): 167–68.

31. Abbott, *Christianity and Social Problems*, 125, 133.

32. Ibid., 51, 60, 87, 95–96, 365, 366–67.

33. Ibid., 78, 175, 183.

34. Ibid., 198, 204, 240, 260–67.

35. Ibid., 276, 288, 291.

36. David A. Shannon, *The Socialist Party of America: A History* (New York: Macmillan, 1955), chapters 1 and 2.

37. Quoted in Dores R. Sharpe, *Walter Rauschenbusch* (New York: Macmillan, 1942), 91–92; Paul Minus, *Walter Rauschenbusch: American Reformer* (New York: Macmillan, 1988), 60–65; Jacob H. Dorn, "The Social Gospel and Socialism: A Comparison of the Thought of Francis Greenwood Peabody, Washington Gladden, and Walter Rauschenbusch," in *Church History* 62 (1993): 82–100.

38. Casey Nelson Blake, "Christianity and the Social Crisis: A Middle-Class Church Grown Lazy and Comfortable," in *Commonweal Magazine* (October 26, 2007), http://paloaltocatholic.net/christianity-and-the-social-crisis (accessed July 7, 2015).

39. Walter Rauschenbusch, *Christianity and the Social Crisis* (New York: The Macmillan Co., 1907), 91, 344, 371, 413.

40. Walter Rauschenbusch, *Christianizing the Social Order* (New York: The Macmillan Co., 1912), 321.

41. Walter Rauschenbusch, *A Theology for the Social Gospel* (New York: The Macmillan Co., 1917), 2, 5, 43.

42. Ibid., 114.

43. Ibid., 77, 81, 97, 108.

44. Read Minus, *Walter Rauschenbusch*.

45. Thomas Mower Martin, "The Duty of the New Church to Social Reform," in *The New-Church Review* 17 (1910): 238. See also G. Reiche, "The New Church and the Present Time," in *The New Christianity* 7 (1894): 131–32; "The Clergy in Politics," in *The New Christianity* 3 (1890): 363; S., "What Has the Christian Minister to Do with Questions Political and Social?," in *The New Christianity* 1 (1888): 388–89; "The Future of New Church," in *The New Christianity* 9 (1896): 65–66.

46. "Practical Christianity," in *The New Christianity* 4 (1891): 27–28.

47. Martin, "Duty of the New Church to Social Reform," 236–44.

48. S., "What Has the Christian Minister to Do with Questions Political and Social?" 388–89.

49. "Religion and Life," in *The New-Church Review* 16 (1909): 628.

50. Louis G. Hoeck, "Christian Economics," in *The New-Church Review* 19 (1912): 65–67.

51. Ibid., 67–68.

52. Ibid., 72.

53. Rev. William F. Wunsch, "Swedenborg and Theological Reconstruction," in *The New-Church Review* 26 (1919): 424–25.

54. Quoted in Wunsch, "Swedenborg and Theological Reconstruction," 428, 430.

55. Rev. E. M. Lawrence Gould, "The Labor Movement and the New Church," in *The New-Church Review* 23 (1916): 398, 401, 402.

56. Hiram Vrooman, "The Relation of Theology to Sociology," in *The New-Church Review* 17 (1910): 514, 515.

57. King, "Church and the Slums," 416–18.

58. James Reed, "Fundamental Laws of Social Order," in *The New-Church Review* 17 (1910): 498, 499, 501, 505, 507.

59. Protestant Episcopal edition, March 1, 1907; Methodist special edition, Sept 1, 1908; Catholic special edition, January 15, 1909; Lutheran special edition, December 1, 1909; Swedenborgian edition, March 15, 1910.

60. H. C. H., "The Church and Social Unrest," in *The New-Church Review* 14 (1907): 588–92.

61. Alfred J. Johnson, "The Sociological Aspect of New Church Truth," in *The Christian Socialist* 7 (1910): 1–2.

62. A. B. Francisco, "Grand Man and Modern Socialism," in *The Christian Socialist* 7 (1910): 2–3.

63. Arthur Mercer, "Christian Economics According to Swedenborg," in *The Christian Socialist* 7 (1910): 3.

64. Ibid., 4.

65. Herbert C. Small, "Socialism vs. Capitalism as a Moral and a Spiritual Force in Society," in *The Christian Socialist* 7 (1910): 5–6.

66. Rev. Hiram Vrooman, "The Question of Interest or Usury," in *The Christian Socialist* 7 (1910): 7–8; A. L. M., "A Pastoral Alliance," in *The New Christianity* 10 (1897): 19.

67. H. C. H., "Socialism and the New Church," 602; "Christian Sociology," in *The New-Church Magazine* 3 (1884): 232–40; "Religious and Social Progress," in *The New-Church Magazine* 3 (1884): 192–97, 547–53.

68. H. C. H., "Socialism and the New Church," 606.

69. Ibid., 601.

70. Lewis F. Hite, "The New-Church Point of View," in *The New-Church Review* 30 (1923): 82–97.

71. Quoted in H. C. H., "Socialism and the New Church," 602.

72. H. C. H., "Socialism and the New Church," 602, 604, 606.

73. Ibid., 601.

74. "The Duties of the Church to Matters of Reform," in *The New Christianity* 7 (1894): 114.

75. Gould, "Labor Movement and the New Church," 396–408.

76. Martin, "Duty of the New Church to Social Reform," 242.

77. Warren Goddard, Jr., "The Spirit of the Age and What It Lacks," in *The New-Church Review* 14 (1907): 548, 549, 551.

78. Lewis F. Hite, "A New-Church Social Philosophy," in *The New-Church Review* 28 (1921): 206–7, 208, 209, 214, 216.

79. Hopkins, *Rise of the Social Gospel in American Protestantism;* John A. Hutchinson, *We Are Not Divided: A Critical and Historical Study of the Federal Council of the Churches of Christ in America* (New York: Round Table Press, 1941).

80. Samuel McCrea Cavert, "The Social Ideals of the Churches," in *The New-Church Review* 28 (1921): 199–201. In May 1908, thirty-two separate Christian denominations met in Philadelphia to form the Federal Council of Churches. Among their collaborative issues were immigration reform, labor reform, temperance, the abolition of child labor, and improvements for the poor.

81. Quoted in Cavert, "Social Ideals of the Churches," 200.

82. "Other Sheep," in *The New-Church Messenger* 96 (1909): 18. The commissions included Evangelism, Social Service, Christian Education, Temperance, International Justice and Good Will (formerly Peace and Arbitration), Church and Country Life, Inter-Church Federations, and Relations with the Orient. The committees included Foreign Missions, Home Missions, Family Life and Religious Rest Day, and Ministerial Relief and Sustentation. See H. K. Carroll, *Federal Council Year Book* (New York: Missionary Education Movement, 1917), 2–3.

83. Commission on the Church and Social Service, Federal Council of the Churches of Christ in America, "The Church and Social Reconstruction," in *The New-Church Review* 26 (1919): 433–50.

84. Ibid., 436.

85. Reinhold Niebuhr, *Moral Man and Immoral Society: A Study in Ethics and Politics* (New York: Charles Scribner's Sons, 1932), chapter 1; Niebuhr, *Reflections on the End of an Era*, 48.

86. Arthur Schlesinger, Jr., "Forgetting Reinhold Niebuhr," in *The New York Times* (September 18, 2005). Read Robin W. Lovin, *Reinhold Niebuhr and Christian Realism* (Cambridge: Cambridge University Press, 1995); Reinhold Niebuhr, *Faith and History: A Comparison of Christian and Modern Views of History* (New York: Charles Scribner's Sons, 1949); Reinhold Niebuhr, *The Children of Light and the Children of Darkness: A Vindication of Democracy and a Critique of Its Traditional Defense* (New York: Charles Scribner's Sons, 1944); Reinhold Niebuhr, *The Nature and Destiny of Man* (New York: Scribner's, 1941–43).

6 Loose Ends

1. Dunham, "New Church and Democracy," 230.
2. Clarence W. Barron, "Defects in New-Church Organization," in *The New-Church Review* 23 (1916): 355, 359; Kenneth L. Fisher, *110 Minds that Made the Market* (Hoboken, NJ: John Wiley and Sons, 2007), 56–57.
3. Block, *New Church in the New World*, 196–204; "Communication," in *The New Jerusalem Magazine* 15 (1842): 450–51.
4. See Richard R. Gladish, "Retrospective of the New Church Theological School, 1866? 1966," in *Studia Swedenborgiana*, http://www.baysidechurch. org/studia/default.asp?ArticleID=60&VolumeID=27&AuthorID=14&detail=1 (accessed June 18, 2019).
5. F. M. Billings, "Foreign Missions," in *The New-Church Review* 17 (1910): 590–94.
6. H. Clinton Hay, "Missionary Work in the New Church," in *The New-Church Review* 17 (1910): 26–31. The missionary work of the New Church included efforts in Michigan, Minnesota, Kansas, Missouri, Texas, Maryland, Virginia, Tennessee, Georgia, Florida, the Washington Territory, and the provinces of Nova Scotia and New Brunswick. See "Annual Report of the Board of Home and Foreign Missions," in *Journal of the Sixty-Ninth Annual Session of the General Convention of the New Jerusalem* (Boston: Massachusetts New-Church Union Press, 1899), 51.
7. Alfred H. Stroh, "Results of Four Missions to Sweden (1902–18)," in *The New-Church Review* 26 (1919): 251. *The New Philosophy* journal later moved to the Swedenborgian House of Studies in Berkeley, California.
8. Frank Sewall, "The Swedenborg Scientific Association: Its Aims and Its Achievements," in *The New Philosophy* 15 (1912): 95. Read also John S. Haller, Jr., *Man and His Muse: The Swedenborgian World of Rev. Frank Sewall* (Amazon Books, 2019), chapter 7.
9. Hite, "New-Church Social Philosophy," 207, 212, 216.
10. New Church book rooms were opened in Baltimore, Boston, Brooklyn, Chicago, Cincinnati, Minneapolis, New York, Philadelphia, San Francisco, St. Louis, and the District of Columbia. See "New-Church Book Rooms," in *The New-Church Messenger* 110 (1916): 218.
11. Z. Hyde, "Report of the Book Committee," in *The New Jerusalem Magazine* 16 (July 1843): 418.
12. Asa E. Goddard, "Some Lessons from Hampton and Tuskegee," in *The New-Church Review* 18 (1911): 102. In an 1891 issue of *The New-Church Messenger*, for example, the publication's most extreme position included an editorial titled "The Socialism Taught in the Doctrines of the New Church." See "The General Convention Committed to Socialism," in *The New Christianity* 4 (1891): 35.

13. Henry Adams, *The Education of Henry Adams* (New York: Houghton Mifflin Co., 1918), 237. See also John S. Haller, Jr., *Outcasts from Evolution: Scientific Attitudes of Racial Inferiority, 1859–1900* (Urbana, IL: University of Illinois Press, 1971).

14. T. F. W., "The Negro Problem," in *The New-Church Review* 14 (1907): 122–24; Goddard, "Some Lessons from Hampton and Tuskegee," 86–102; "Miscellaneous," in *The New Christianity* 10 (1897): 12; W. M. Goodner, "The Church in Relation to Social Problems," in *The New Christianity* 1 (1888): 140–41; A. C., "The Weakness and Strength of the Negro Race," in *The New Christianity* 10 (1897): 125–26; "Tuskegee," in *The New Christianity* 11 (1898): 61; "A Hopeful Utterance from the South," in *The New Christianity* 8 (1895): 42; "New Method of Negro Development in the South," in *The New Christianity* 8 (1895): 173–74.

15. Rev. S. C. Eby, "The Black Man and His Qualitative Force," in *The New-Church Messenger* 87 (1904): 57–58.

16. Rev. L. P. Mercer, ed., *The New Jerusalem in the World's Religious Congresses of 1893* (Chicago: Western New-Church Union, 1894), xii.

17. Ibid., 82–83.

18. Ibid., 71–73.

19. Ibid., 129.

20. Ibid. The Parliament of Religions that met in Chicago during the Columbian Exposition of 1893 was the idea of Charles C. Bonney, a New Church member who served as the Parliament's president. Believing that a new era of religious peace and progress was rising over the world and "dispelling the dark clouds of sectarian strife," he brought together what he hoped would be a fraternity of religious leaders to uphold the importance of a "brotherhood of religions" that would "worship God and love man in every clime." See C. C. Bonney, "Worshipers of God and Lovers of Man," in Barrows, ed., *World's Parliament of Religions*, vol. 1, 67–72.

21. Examples of the mix of opinions include Ida C. Hultin, "Woman's Sphere," in *The New Christianity* 10 (1897): 187; "Women in Public Meetings," in *The New Christianity* 11 (1898): 81; Alice Stone Blackwell, "The Newest New Woman," in *The New Christianity* 11 (1898): 171; Robert H. Debeck, "If an Individual Is a Church, What Is a Husband and Wife?," in *The New Christianity* 8 (1895): 102–3, 184; "Mental Differences Between the Sexes," in *The New Christianity* 8 (1895): 109; "Women against Women's Suffrage," in *The New Christianity* 2 (1889): 252.

22. Samuel S. Seward, Jr., "Schreiner's 'Woman and Labor,'" in *The New-Church Review* 19 (1912): 407–25; "An Announcement," in *The New-Church Messenger* 121 (1921): 303.

23. Lydia Fuller Dickinson, "Equal Spiritual Opportunity," in *The New Christianity* 8 (1895): 90–91; Ella G. Ives, "Why One Woman Would Vote," in *The New Christianity* 5 (1892): 156–57.

24. L. F. H., "Woman's Rights and the New Freedom," in *The New-Church Review* 21 (1914): 275, 280, 282.

25. H. C. H., "The Bible and the Higher Criticism," in *The New-Church Review* 17 (1910): 277, 278.

26. L. F. H., "Christianity and Modern Thought," in *The New-Church Review* 17 (1910): 280–82, 285.

27. H. C. H., "Bible and the Higher Criticism," 275–80. During the World's Fair in St. Louis in 1904, the Swedenborg House offered a series of New Church lectures on the higher criticism by Rev. J. C. Ager of Brooklyn, New York. As a scholarly and spiritual undertaking, he insisted that the effort had been long overdue, arguing that when properly understood, it carried forward the true internal and spiritual meaning of the scriptures in much the same manner that Swedenborg had done a century earlier. For nearly fifteen hundred years, the Catholic Church failed to discover the real meaning of the scriptures and, as a consequence, turned to Church doctrine as the most competent authority. Protestantism, on the other hand, gave rise to multiple interpretations and multiple creeds due to its insistence on a strictly literal interpretation of the scriptures. In Ager's opinion, there was no ground for distrusting the Bible, provided that one separated what was historically accurate from the meaning that was spiritually and emotionally intended. Many of the stories were myths reflecting "tribal origins and movements." The essential content of all revelation, he argued, was not the actual fact but the spiritual wisdom behind the stories. Keeping this in mind, it was not the historicity of the story that counted but the intent of its creator. "Belief in the Divine authorship of the Bible is not dependent upon our knowing who the men were through whom the literal sense was written, or upon previous proof that they were inspired men. The only proof we need that the letter of Scripture is inspired is 'the good tidings of great joy' which it brings to human souls." See Rev. J. C. Ager, "The Bible and the Higher Criticism," in *The New-Church Messenger* 87 (1904): 244–45; Albert J. Edmonds, "The Higher Criticism and the New Church," in *The New Christianity* 11 (1898): 107–8; S. Beswick, "The Higher Criticism and Swedenborg," in *The New Christianity* 6 (1893): 57.

28. See "Pauperism and Philanthropy," in *The New Earth* 4 (1894): 27; "No Beggars or Peddlers Allowed to Apply to the Charity Organizations," in *The New Earth* 4 (1894): 26; "The Disease of Charity," in *The New Earth* 3 (1892): 17; "What Is True Charity?," in *The New Christianity* 3 (1890): 270; W. H. Wood, "Charity," in *The New Christianity* 1 (1888): 403.

29. Carnegie further elaborated on his "Wealth" essay with *The Gospel of Wealth and Other Timely Essays* (1900).

30. Andrew Carnegie, *Autobiography of Andrew Carnegie* (Boston: Houghton Mifflin Co., 1920), 22–23.

31. Ibid., 23, 50–51.

32. H. C. H., "Philanthropies of Millionaires," in *The New-Church Review* 17 (1910): 286. See also "Foolish Criticism of the Rich," in *The New Christianity* 10 (1897): 43–44.

33. H. C. H., "Philanthropies of Millionaires," 287, 288.

34. Swedenborg, *True Christianity* §443:2.

35. Rev. Walter B. Murray, "Plutocracy versus Democracy," in *The New-Church Review* 23 (1916): 200–11.

36. Emanuel Swedenborg, *Divine Providence* (West Chester, PA: Swedenborg Foundation, 2010 [1764]), §217:2.

37. H. C. H., "Philanthropies of Millionaires," 286.

38. Ibid., 289.

39. James Reed, "Am I My Brother's Keeper?," in *The New-Church Review* 16 (1909): 352, 358, 359.

40. Murray, "Plutocracy versus Democracy," 201, 204, 205, 210.

41. Ibid., 200–11; Paul H. Friesen, "Review of Socialism and Christianity in Early 20th Century America," in *American Society of Church History* (May 30, 2009).

42. Dunham, "New Church and Democracy," 236, 237.

43. Ibid., 234–35.

44. E. H. Schneider, "The New Church and Democracy," in *The New-Church Review* 25 (1918): 366.

45. George Henry Dole, "The New Church and the League of Nations," in *The New-Church Messenger* 118 (1920): 6.

7 Pragmatism

1. Henry S. Commager, *The American Mind: An Interpretation of American Thought and Character Since the 1880s* (New Haven: Yale University Press, 1950), 97, 443.

2. David A. Hollinger, "The Problem of Pragmatism in American History," in *Journal of American History* 67 (1980): 88–107; James Campbell, "One Hundred Years of Pragmatism," in *Transactions of the Charles S. Peirce Society* 43 (2007): 1–15.

3. Morton White, *Social Thought in America: The Revolt against Formalism* (New York: Oxford University Press, 1949); Darnell Ruckor, *The Chicago Pragmatists* (Minneapolis: University of Minnesota Press, 1969); Cushing Strout, *The Pragmatic Revolt in American History: Carl Becker and Charles Beard* (New Haven: Yale University Press, 1958).

4. The differences between and among pragmatism's leading representatives are essentially variations on a theme, determined in part by their different interests and choices of application. Despite the metaphysical idealism of Charles Peirce, the radical empiricism of William James, and the empirical naturalism of John Dewey and George Herbert Mead, their convergences

led toward, not away from, a generally common perspective that was ultimately *pragmatic* in its effects. For contrasting opinions, read Charles W. Morris, "Peirce, Mead, and Pragmatism," in *The Philosophical Review* 47 (1938): 109–27; Frederick J. E. Woodbridge, "The Promise of Pragmatism," in *The Journal of Philosophy* 26 (1929): 541–52; Richard M. Gale, *The Divided Self of William James* (Cambridge: Cambridge University Press, 1999). Others, like James O. Pawelski, viewed James as steering a course between a rationalistic system that was not sufficiently empirical and an empirical system that was too materialistic to account for ethics, settling on a pluralistic moralism based on a spiritualistic but nonprovidential faith in the democratic individual. Read James O. Pawelski, "William James's Divided Self and the Process of Its Unification: A Reply to Richard Gale," in *Transactions of the Charles S. Peirce Society* 39 (2003): 645; James O. Pawelski, "William James and the Journey Toward Unification," in *Transactions of the Charles S. Peirce Society* 40 (2004): 795; David Baggett, "On a Reductionist Analysis of William James's Philosophy of Religion," in *The Journal of Religious Ethics* 28 (2000): 423–48.

5. William James (1771–1832), the Scots-Irishman and patriarch of the James family, immigrated to Albany, New York, in 1789, where he made a fortune investing in business and real estate, including the Erie Canal, leaving to his heirs a trust fund estimated at three million dollars. Henry James, Sr., one of William's twelve children and a person of independent mind, refused to take up what his father considered to be a respectable vocation (see chapter 1, above). Disinherited, he had to fight in the courts for more than a decade before receiving his portion of the estate, which enabled him to live a life unconditioned by the expediency of making a living. In place of having to choose a career to provide for his family, he became a theologian, lecturer, and writer, assembling a very idiosyncratic set of theological and social assets that were reflective of the spirituality of Swedenborg and the socialism of Charles Fourier. His children included William (1842–1910), the philosopher and psychologist; Henry (1843–1916), the novelist and man of letters; Garth Wilkinson (1845–83), named for his father's Swedenborgian colleague in England; Robertson (1846–1910), a chronic alcoholic and museum curator; and Alice (1848–92), who suffered from lifelong invalidism but whose literary gifts brought her closest to her two older brothers.

6. Ralph Barton Perry, *The Thought and Character of William James,* 2 vols. (Boston: Little, Brown, and Co., 1935), vol. 1, 105.

7. Read L. Menand, *The Metaphysical Club: A Story of Ideas in America* (Boston: Houghton Mifflin, 2006).

8. Cushing Strout, "William James and the Twice-Born Sick Soul," in *Daedalus* 97 (1968): 1062–82. As his first act of freedom, William James said, he chose to believe that his will was free. He was encouraged to do this by reading Charles Renouvier, who considered himself to be a "Swedenborg of history" (Charles Renouvier, *Uchronie [l'utopie dans l'histoire]: Esquisse*

historique apocryphe du développement de la civilisation européenne tel qu'il n'a pas été, tel qu'il aurait pu être [1st ed., Paris, 1876], iii). In his diary entry of April 30, 1870, William wrote, "I think that yesterday was a crisis in my life. I finished the first part of Renouvier's second *Essais* and see no reason why his definition of free will—'the sustaining of a thought *because I choose to* when I might have other thoughts'—need be the definition of an illusion. At any rate, I will assume for the present—until next year—that it is no illusion. My first act of free will shall be to believe in free will." See Perry, *Thought and Character of William James*, vol. 1, 323.

9. Howard V. Knox, "William James and His Philosophy," in *Mind* 22 (1913): 231.

10. Croce, "Mankind's Own Providence," 490–508.

11. Ibid., 498.

12. Quoted in Perry, *Thought and Character of William James*, vol. 1, 130.

13. William James, *Essays in Radical Empiricism* (London: Longmans, Green, and Co., 1912), 170.

14. William James, "Lectures on the Elements of Comparative Anatomy," in *North American Review* 100 (1865): 290–98; William James, "The Origin of the Human Races," in *North American Review* 101 (1865): 261–63.

15. William James, "Remarks on Spencer's Definition of Mind as Correspondence," in *Journal of Speculative Philosophy* 12 (1878): 1–18.

16. Matthew Crippen, "William James on Belief: Turning Darwinism against Empiricistic Skepticism," in *Transactions of the Charles S. Peirce Society* 46 (2010): 482.

17. Ralph Barton Perry, "The Philosophy of William James," in *The Philosophical Review* 20 (1911): 3.

18. William James, *Pragmatism: A New Name for Some Old Ways of Thinking* (New York: Longmans, Green, and Co., 1907), dedication page.

19. Campbell, "One Hundred Years of Pragmatism," 1–15; James Mark Baldwin, "The Limits of Pragmatism," in *Psychological Review* 11 (1904): 30–60; Charles Hartshorne, Paul Weiss, and Arthur W. Burks, eds., *Collected Papers of Charles Sanders Peirce*, 8 vols. (Cambridge, MA: Harvard University Press, 1931–58), vol. 5, 414. *Collected Papers*, an effort to bring some level of unity to his writings, was based on lectures delivered at the Lowell Institute in Boston and at Columbia University. The effort proved unsatisfying to critics like Lovejoy, who made clear his opinion in the essay "The Thirteen Pragmatisms" (1908). Read Arthur O. Lovejoy, *The Thirteen Pragmatisms and Other Essays* (Baltimore: Johns Hopkins University Press, 1963).

20. Gary Alexander, "The Hypothesized God of C. S. Peirce and William James," in *The Journal of Religion* 67 (1987): 304–21.

21. James, *Pragmatism*, 4.

22. Knox, "William James and His Philosophy," 237.

23. Read John Stuart Mill, *On Liberty* (Boston: Ticknor and Fields, 1863); Jeremy Bentham, *An Introduction to the Principles of Morals and Legislation* (Oxford: Clarendon Press, 1907).

24. William James, *Pragmatism and the Meaning of Truth* (Cambridge, MA: Harvard University Press, 1975), 273, 283–84.

25. James, *Pragmatism*, 200, 203.

26. H. S. Thayer, "On William James on Truth," in *Transactions of the Charles S. Peirce Society* 13 (1977): 3–19.

27. Read Gerald E. Myers, *William James, His Life and Thought* (New Haven: Yale University Press, 1986), chapter 12; Eugene Fontinell, *Self, God, and Immortality: A Jamesian Investigation* (Philadelphia: Temple University Press, 1986); Wesley Cooper, *The Unity of William James's Thought* (Nashville, TN: Vanderbilt University Press, 2002).

28. Woodbridge Riley, *American Thought: From Puritanism to Pragmatism and Beyond* (Gloucester, MA: Peter Smith, 1959), 279.

29. Croce, "Mankind's Own Providence," 490–93. Read also Eugene Taylor, "William James on Darwin: An Evolutionary Theory of Consciousness," in *Annals of the New York Academy of Sciences* 602 (1990): 7–33.

30. Paul Croce, "From History of Science to Intellectual History: The Probabilistic Revolution and the Chance-Filled Universe of William James," in *Intellectual History Newsletter* 13 (1991): 11–32.

31. William James, *The Will to Believe and Other Essays in Popular Philosophy* (New York: Dover Publications, 1956), 90.

32. G. L. Doore, "William James and the Ethics of Belief," in *Philosophy* 58 (1983): 353–64.

33. Michael R. Slater, *William James on Ethics and Faith* (Cambridge: Cambridge University Press, 2009), 32; H. S. Thayer, "The Right to Believe: William James's Reinterpretation of the Function of Religious Belief," in *The Kenyon Review* 5 (1983): 89–105.

34. James, *Will to Believe*, 22.

35. William James, *A Pluralistic Universe* (New York: Longmans, Green, and Co., 1920 [1909]), 328–29.

36. James, *Pragmatism and the Meaning of Truth*, 107.

37. Phil Cox, "William James's Epistemological 'Gamble,'" in *Transactions of the Charles S. Peirce Society* 36 (2000): 284–96; James, *Will to Believe*, 11. See also Blaise Pascal, *Pensées de Pascal: Précédées de Sa Vie* (Paris: Librairie de Firmin Didot Fréres, 1855).

38. Henry James, ed., *The Letters of William James*, 2 vols. (Boston: The Atlantic Monthly Press, 1920), vol. 2, 203, 204.

39. John Hick, *Philosophy of Religion* (Englewood Cliffs, NJ: Prentice-Hall, 1990), 59. For an opposite position, read Ludwig F. Schlecht, "Re-reading 'The Will to Believe,'" in *Religious Studies* 33 (1997): 217–25.

40. William James, *Pragmatism and Other Writings* (New York: Penguin Books, 2000), 17, 130.

41. Ibid., 240.

42. Bertrand Russell, *A History of Western Philosophy* (New York: Simon and Schuster, 1945), 814; W. Richard Comstock, "William James and the Logic of Religious Belief," in *The Journal of Religion* 47 (1967): 187–209.

43. William James, *The Varieties of Religious Experience: A Study in Human Nature* (New York: Longmans, Green, and Co., 1928 [1902]), 447.

44. William James, "Rationality, Activity and Faith," in *The Princeton Review* (July to December 1882): 74–75.

45. James, *Will to Believe*, 91, 99.

46. Eino Kaila and Heikki A. Kovailanen, "William James: The Philosopher of America," in *Transactions of the Charles S. Peirce Society* 47 (2011): 139–40.

47. James, *Pragmatism*, title page. Read also Arthur O. Lovejoy, "William James as Philosopher," in *International Journal of Ethics* 21 (1911): 143.

48. Lovejoy, "William James as Philosopher," 151.

49. Read Donald Capps, *Men, Religion, and Melancholia: James, Otto, Jung, and Erickson* (New Haven: Yale University Press, 1997); Anne Harrington, *The Cure Within: A History of Mind-Body Medicine* (New York: Norton, 2008); R. W. B. Lewis, *The Jameses: A Family Narrative* (New York: Farrar, Straus, and Giroux, 1991).

50. James, *Varieties of Religious Experience*, 425, 525.

51. Alexander, "Hypothesized God of C. S. Peirce and William James," 312.

52. A. Eustace Haydon, *Biography of the Gods* (New York: Macmillan Co., 1941), 329.

53. James, *Pluralistic Universe*, 318.

54. James, *Will to Believe*, 69, 86. Sam Harris, Richard Dawkins, Christopher Hitchens, and Victor J. Stenger took strident exception to religious fundamentalism but were also critical of agnosticism, treating it as an untenable alternative to religious faith. Read Richard Dawkins, *The God Delusion* (Boston: Houghton Mifflin Co., 2008); Sam Harris, *The End of Faith: Religion, Terror, and the Future of Reason* (New York: W. W. Norton and Co., 2004); Christopher Hitchens, *God Is Not Great: How Religion Poisons Everything* (New York: Twelve, 2007); Victor J. Stenger, *The New Atheism: Taking a Stand for Science and Reason* (New York: Prometheus Books, 2009); Scot D. Yoder, "Making Space for Agnosticism: A Response to Dawkins and James," in *American Journal of Theology and Philosophy* 34 (2013): 135–53.

55. Andrew Fiala, "Militant Atheism, Pragmatism, and the God-Shaped Hole," in *International Journal for Philosophy of Religion* 65 (2009): 147. Read also John Dewey, *A Common Faith* (New Haven: Yale University

Press, 1934); Harris, *End of Faith;* Hitchens, *God Is Not Great;* Richard Rorty, *Philosophy and Social Hope* (New York: Penguin, 1999).

56. David Paulsen, "The God of Abraham, Isaac, and (William) James," in *Journal of Speculative Philosophy* 13 (1999): 125.

57. James, ed., *Letters of William James,* vol. 2, 211.

58. Read John K. Roth, "William James, John Dewey, and the 'Death-of-God,'" in *Religious Studies* 7 (1971): 53–61.

59. James, *Varieties of Religious Experience,* 131.

60. Ibid., 132.

61. Richard A. S. Hall, "The Polytheism of William James," in *The Pluralist* 4 (2009): 21.

62. Michael R. Slater, "Pragmatism, Realism, and Religion," in *The Journal of Religious Ethics* 36 (2008): 653–81.

63. Michael R. Slater, "William James's Pluralism," in *The Review of Metaphysics* 65 (2011): 63.

64. James, *Will to Believe,* 263–98.

65. James, *Varieties of Religious Experience,* 524, 525.

66. Ibid., 524.

67. Ralph Barton Perry, *The Thought and Character of William James: Briefer Version* (New York: Harper and Row, 1964 [1935]), 268.

68. Roger Martin du Gard, *Jean Barois* (New York: Bobbs-Merrill Co., 1969 [1913]), 252.

69. William James, *Human Immortality: Two Supposed Objections to the Doctrine* (London: Archibald Constable & Co., 1906), 9.

70. Ibid., 24–25, 26, 32, 39, 47–48.

71. Ibid., 54–55, 57.

72. Ibid., 61, 64, 68, 70–71, 75, 83, 87.

73. Sami Pihlström, "William James on Death, Mortality, and Immortality," in *Transactions of the Charles S. Peirce Society* 38 (2002): 612.

74. James, *Pluralistic Universe,* 310; William James, *Memories and Studies* (New York: Longmans, Green, and Co., 1911), 204; James, *Varieties of Religious Experience,* 389

75. Deborah J. Coon, "'One Moment in the World's Salvation': Anarchism and the Radicalization of William James," in *Journal of American History* 83 (1996): 70–99.

76. William James to William Dean Howells, Nov. 16, 1900, quoted from the William Dean Howells Papers at Harvard University in Coon, "'One Moment in the World's Salvation,'" 71.

77. Coon, "'One Moment in the World's Salvation,'" 70–99; William James, "The Philippine Tangle," in William James, *Essays, Comments and Reviews,* Frederick H. Burkhardt, Fredson Bowers, and Ignas K. Skrupskelis, eds. (Cambridge, MA: Harvard University Press, 1987), 154–58.

78. Read James, *Pluralistic Universe;* John L. Thomas, *Alternative America: Henry George, Edward Bellamy, Henry Demarest Lloyd and the Adversary Tradition* (Cambridge, MA: Harvard University Press, 1983); Crunden, *Ministers of Reform.*

79. James, *Memories and Studies,* 95–96.

80. Perry, *Thought and Character of William James,* vol. 2, 383.

81. James, *Pragmatism,* 53.

82. Wayne Proudfoot, "William James on an Unseen Order," in *The Harvard Theological Review* 93 (2000): 60.

83. Scott R. Stroud, "William James on Meliorism, Moral Ideals, and Business Ethics," in *Transactions of the Charles S. Peirce Society* 45 (2009): 379.

84. Teddy Roosevelt, "The Strenuous Life," at http://www.bartleby.com/58/1.html (accessed January 7, 2016).

85. Ralph Barton Perry, *In the Spirit of William James* (Bloomington, IN: Indiana University Press, 1958), 147. Read also "Andrew F. Smith, William James and the Politics of Moral Conflict," in *Transactions of the Charles S. Peirce Society* 40 (2004): 135–51.

86. James Livingston, *Pragmatism and the Political Economy of Cultural Revolution, 1850–1940* (Chapel Hill: University of North Carolina Press, 1994); Robert L. Beisner, *Twelve Against Empire: The Anti-Imperialists, 1898–1900* (New York: McGraw-Hill, 1968). See Daniel W. Bjork, *The Compromised Scientist: William James in the Development of American Psychology* (New York: Columbia University Press, 1983); Howard Feinstein, *Becoming William James* (Ithaca, NY: Cornell University Press, 1984); Bruce Kuklick, *The Rise of American Philosophy, Cambridge, Massachusetts, 1860–1930* (New Haven: Yale University Press, 1977); James Kloppenberg, *Uncertain Victory: Social Democracy and Progressivism in European and American Thought, 1870–1920* (New York: Oxford University Press, 1986); Frank Lentricchia, *Ariel and the Police: Michel Foucault, William James, Wallace Stevens* (Madison: University of Wisconsin Press, 1988); Livingston, *Pragmatism and the Political Economy of Cultural Revolution;* Cornel West, *The American Evasion of Philosophy: A Genealogy of Pragmatism* (Madison: University of Wisconsin Press, 1989).

87. Lewis F. Hite, "Professor James' Radical Empiricism," in *The New-Church Review* 17 (1910): 258, 259, 260.

88. Lewis F. Hite, "'What Is Pragmatism?,'" in *The New-Church Review* 16 (1909): 426, 427, 429.

89. Hite, "Professor James' Radical Empiricism," 261–63, 265.

90. Ibid., 267, 269, 270–71.

91. Ibid., 266, 274.

92. Frank Sewall, "Professor William James on the 'Worth of Living,'" in Frank Sewall, *Swedenborg and Modern Idealism: A Retrospect of Philosophy from Kant to the Present Time* (London: J. Speirs, 1902), 179, 181. See also

Frank Sewall, *The New Metaphysics: Or, the Law of End, Cause, and Effect, with Other Essays* (London: J. Speirs, 1888); Frank Sewall, *The New Ethics: An Essay on the Moral Law of Use* (New York: G. P. Putnam's Sons, 1881).

93. Rev. Paul Sperry, "The Practical Value of Being Useful," in *The New-Church Review* 23 (1916): 553.

94. Ibid., 554, 555.

95. Ibid., 553, 555.

96. Ibid., 556.

97. Ibid., 557, 558, 560.

98. James T. Kloppenberg, "Pragmatism: An Old Name for Some New Ways of Thinking?," in *The Journal of American History* 83 (1996): 123. See also Richard Rorty, *Consequences of Pragmatism* (Minneapolis: University of Minnesota Press, 1982), xliii; Richard Rorty, *Achieving Our Country: Leftist Thought in the Twentieth Century* (Cambridge: Harvard University Press, 1997).

99. Jane Mayhall paraphrasing Van Wyck Brooks in "William James and the Modern World," in *The Antioch Review* 8 (1948): 292. Alfred North Whitehead, *Modes of Thought* (New York: The Free Press, 1938), 3.

100. Andrew J. Reck, "The Influence of William James on John Dewey in Psychology," in *Transactions of the Charles S. Peirce Society* 20 (1984): 87–117.

101. William James, *Psychology, Briefer Course* (New York: Henry Holt and Co., 1913), 262.

8 Pastoral Clinical Movement

1. Ray Stanndard Baker, *The Spiritual Unrest* (New York: Frederick Stokes Co., 1910), 192; Katherine McCarthy, "Psychotherapy and Religion: The Emmanuel Movement," in *Journal of Religion and Health* 23 (1984): 101; John Gardner Greene, "The Emmanuel Movement, 1906–1929," in *The New England Quarterly* 7 (1934): 494–532. See also Susan E. Myers-Shirk, *Helping the Good Shepherd: Pastoral Counselors in a Psychotherapeutic Culture, 1925–1975* (Baltimore: Johns Hopkins University Press, 2009); Charles E. Hall, *Head and Heart: The Story of the Clinical Pastoral Education Movement* (Decatur, GA: Journal of Pastoral Care Publications, Inc., 1993).

2. Read Allan McLane Hamilton, "The Religio-Medical Movements," in *North American Review* 189 (1909): 223–32; Edgar Draper, *Psychiatry and Pastoral Care* (NJ: Prentice-Hall, Inc., 1965).

3. Elwood Worcester and Samuel McComb, *The Christian Religion as a Healing Power: A Defense and Exposition of the Emmanuel Movement* (New York: Moffat, Yard and Co., 1909), 6; Raymond J. Cunningham, "The Emmanuel Movement: A Variety of American Religious Experience," in *American Quarterly* 14 (1962): 57.

4. Baker, *Spiritual Unrest*, 192.

5. Though Worcester was raised in the Episcopalian tradition of his mother that was practiced in his family upbringing, he was also through his father's side a nephew and cousin to the Swedenborgian Worcester clergy clan, whom in his autobiography he calls "practical mystics" and about whom he details fascinating interactions starting in childhood and continuing well into his career. See Elwood Worcester, *Life's Adventure: The Story of a Varied Career* (New York: Charles Scribner's Sons, 1932), 8–13.

6. McCarthy, "Psychotherapy and Religion," 95. Read Elwood Worcester, *Life's Adventure;* Elwood Worcester and Samuel McComb, *Body, Mind and Spirit* (Boston: Marshall Jones Co., 1931); Elwood Worcester, Samuel McComb, and Isador H. Coriat, *Religion and Medicine: The Moral Control of Nervous Disorders* (New York: Moffat, Yard and Co., 1908).

7. Curtis W. Hart, "Present at the Creation: The Clinical Pastoral Movement and the Origins of the Dialogue between Religion and Psychiatry," in *Journal of Religion and Health* 49 (2010): 536–46.

8. Elwood Worcester, *Life's Adventure,* 278–79.

9. Lyman Pierson Powell, *The Emmanuel Movement in a New England Town* (New York: G. P. Putnam's Sons, 1909), 12.

10. Neurasthenia, or nervous exhaustion, was a condition identified by Dr. George Miller Beard, who offered proof of this new disease by pointing to the baleful effects of weakness and exhaustion that attended many of society's leading scientists, industrialists, bankers, and intellectuals. Perceived initially as a male disorder, it was thought to result from the body's inability to sustain the increased pace of life. As Canadian physician William Osler noted that medicines were of little avail in treating neurasthenia, American physician Silas Weir Mitchell chose to treat his patients with a combination of rest, isolation, massage, electricity, and placebos. His so-called "rest cure," however, failed to serve the needs of many patients, and this led Dr. Richard Clarke Cabot at Massachusetts General Hospital to explore in 1905 the substitution of a "work cure" designed to fill the time of those sufferers who he believed would benefit more from work than rest. Read John S. Haller, Jr., "Neurasthenia: The Medical Profession and the 'New Women' of the Late 19th Century," in *New York State Journal of Medicine* LXXI (February 15, 1971): 472–82.

11. Richard Clarke Cabot, "New Phases in the Relation of the Church to Health," in *Outlook* 88 (1908): 505; R. L. Hartt, "Christian Science without Mystery," in *World's Work* 15 (1907): 9648–53.

12. L. P. Powell, *Emmanuel Movement in a New England Town,* 8, 14, 18, 19.

13. The Emmanuelists had mixed feelings regarding Christian Science, recognizing and celebrating its exuberant reaction to philosophical materialism but, at the same time, viewing it as "singularly uninformed" as to the history of philosophy and psychology. They considered Mary Baker Eddy's theology "crude and her therapeutics dangerously indiscriminating." Nevertheless, at the back of its "manifest absurdities" stood the belief that "God

is all in all." With Eddy's death, the Emmanuelists hoped that those who succeeded her would "purge the movement of some of its objectionable features." It was for these reasons that the Emmanuelists saw themselves as having found the right residuum of truth from both Christianity and medicine. Read L. P. Powell, *Emmanuel Movement in a New England Town*, 145–46.

14. "Brooklyn, N.Y.," in *The New-Church Messenger* 96 (1909): 124.

15. McCarthy, "Psychotherapy and Religion," 102–3; Robert Charles Powell, "Emotionally, Soulfully, Spiritually 'Free to Think and Act': The Helen Flanders Dunbar (1902–59) Memorial Lecture on Psychosomatic Medicine and Pastoral Care," in *Journal of Religion and Health* 40 (2001): 100.

16. H. Clinton Hay, "Healing at Emmanuel Church, Boston," in *The New-Church Review* 14 (1907): 252.

17. Albert B. Shields, "The Emmanuel Movement in America," in *The British Medical Journal* 1 (1909): 1153.

18. "Reviews and Criticism: Mental Healing and the Emmanuel Movement," in *The Psychological Clinic* 2 (1908–9): 212–23.

19. "The Emmanuel Movement," in *The British Medical Journal* 1 (1909): 430.

20. Ibid. See also Sanford Gifford, *The Emmanuel Movement: The Origins of Group Treatment and the Assault on Lay Psychotherapy* (Boston: Harvard University Press, 1997).

21. William Osler, "The Faith that Heals," in *The British Medical Journal* 2 (1910): 1470, 1472. Regarding homeopathy's Swedenborgian roots, see John S. Haller, Jr., *Swedenborg, Mesmer, & the Mind/Body Connection* (West Chester, PA: Swedenborg Foundation, 2010), 198–210.

22. Persons, *American Minds*, 423.

23. Sanford Gifford, "Review," in *Isis* 92 (2001): 428–29.

24. Anton T. Boisen, *The Exploration of the Inner World: A Study of Mental Disorder and Religious Experience* (New York: Harper and Brothers, 1936), 8.

25. Hart, "Present at the Creation," 539.

26. Read Anton T. Boisen, *Out of the Depths* (New York: Harper, 1960); Edward E. Thornton, *Professional Education for Ministry: A History of Clinical Pastoral Education* (Nashville, TN: Abingdon, 1970).

27. Boisen placed Swedenborg among a select historical group of "successful explorers" who had come through a personal crisis involving hallucinations yet had emerged to complete a reintegration of their personality onto a higher spiritual plane. He considered Swedenborg to be a mystical genius and acknowledged his influence on Emerson, Brook Farm, American transcendentalism in general, and William James's *The Varieties of Religious Experience*. Boisen admired Swedenborg's ethical foundation in his doctrine of usefulness, which guides people to have the best interest of others as foremost in their living. See Robert David Leas, *Anton Theophilus Boisen: His Life, Work, Impact, and Theological Legacy* (Denver, CO: Journal of

Pastoral Care Publications, Inc., 2009), 32–34; Robert David Leas, *Boisen, Mysticism, Swedenborg, and Exceptional Mental and Spiritual States* (Berkeley: Studia Swedenborgiana Press, 2010), 1–3.

28. Curtis W. Hart, "Notes on the Psychiatric Diagnosis of Anton Boisen," in *Journal of Religion and Health* 40 (2001): 423–29.

29. Harry C. Meserve, "Anton Boisen and the Cure of Souls," in *Journal of Religion and Health* 32 (1993): 3–8; David A. Steere, "Anton Boisen: Figure of the Future," in *Journal of Religion and Health* 8 (1969): 359–74.

30. Read Robert Charles Powell, "Healing and Wholeness: Helen Flanders Dunbar (1902–1959): An Extra-Medical Origin of the American Psychosomatic Movement" (PhD diss., Duke University, 1974).

31. Robert C. Powell, "Helen Flanders Dunbar and a Holistic Approach to Psychosomatic Problems," in *Psychiatric Quarterly* (Summer, 1978): 136; Curtis W. Hart, "Helen Flanders Dunbar: Physician, Medievalist, Enigma," in *Journal of Religion and Health* 35 (1996): 47–58.

32. R. C. Powell, "Emotionally, Soulfully, Spiritually 'Free to Think and Act,'" 107.

33. Hart, "Present at the Creation," 536–46.

34. Ibid., 544–46. Read "A Plea for a Clinical Year in the Course of Theological Study," in Richard Clarke Cabot, *Adventures on the Borderlands of Ethics* (New York and London: Harper and Brothers, 1926).

35. James, *Varieties of Religious Experience*, 92–93, 118.

36. Max Eastman, "The New Art of Healing," in *The Atlantic Monthly* 101 (1908): 645.

37. Donald F. Duclow, "William James, Mind-Cure, and the Religion of Healthy-Mindedness," in *Journal of Religion and Health* 41 (2002): 45–56. The pastoral counseling of Horatio W. Dresser in the 1930s was due to James's influence, bringing together psychology and religion into a search for "healthy-mindedness."

38. H. Clinton Hay, "Mental Healing," in *The New-Church Review* 15 (1908): 64, 67; "How to Think Healing Thoughts," in *The New Christianity* 10 (1897): 100; L. K., "Healing Thought," in *The New Christianity* 6 (1893): 9–10; Swedenborg *True Christianity* §154; Swedenborg, *Arcana Coelestia* §2004; Swedenborg, *Heaven and Hell* §§37, 38, 208, 296, 297. Swedenborgians were later attracted to psycho-analysis as "a highly successful method of curing the milder forms of mental disease, and also those physical diseases which have a mental or psychic origin. . . . Swedenborg himself to some extent anticipated psycho-analysis, as he did so many modern discoveries. . . . In a letter to Eric Benzelius under the date of September 8th, 1714, he includes, 'A method of ascertaining the desires and the affections of the minds of men by analysis.' . . . The central fact established by psycho-analysis, namely that every act and word springs from a deeply hidden and unconscious motive, as well as from those motives which come into con-

sciousness, is a most striking confirmation of the teaching of Swedenborg concerning the 'ruling love'" (E. M. Lawrence Gould, "Psycho-Analysis," in *The New-Church Review* 23 [1916]: 251, 260, 261). See also Swedenborg, *Heaven and Hell* §58.

39. James, *Varieties of Religious Experience*, 94–95.

40. Ibid., 157.

41. Ellen Kappy Suckiel, "William James on the Cognitivity of Feelings, Religious Pessimism, and the Meaning of Life," in *Journal of Speculative Philosophy* 17 (2003): 30–39.

42. James, *Varieties of Religious Experience*, 94.

43. Horatio W. Dresser, *Health and the Inner Life: An Analytical and Historical Study of Spiritual Healing Theories, with an Account of the Life and Teachings of P. P. Quimby* (New York: G. P. Putnam's Sons, 1906), 123–27.

44. See Julius A. Dresser, *The True History of Mental Science; the Facts Concerning the Discovery of Mental Healing* (Boston: Ellis, 1899); Annetta Dresser, *The Philosophy of P. P. Quimby, with Selections from His Manuscripts and a Sketch of His Life* (Boston: G. H. Ellis, 1895).

45. Horatio W. Dresser, *The Open Vision: A Study of Psychic Phenomena* (New York: Thomas Y. Crowell Company, 1920), 172. Horatio's siblings included Ralph Howard (1872–73); Jean Paul (1877–1935), who became a minister in the Church of the New Jerusalem; and Philip Seabury (1885–1960), who became a popular writer in the New Thought movement.

46. Horatio W. Dresser, *The Immanent God: An Essay* (Boston: Published by the Author, 1895), 17, 25.

47. *National Cyclopædia of American Biography*, vol. XI (New York: James T. White & Company, 1901), 110.

48. Horatio W. Dresser, *The Power of Silence: A Study of the Values and Ideals of the Inner Life* (New York and London: G. P. Putnam's Sons, 1906 [1895]), 184–87, 311. Horatio W. Dresser, *In Search of a Soul: A Series of Essays in Interpretation of the Higher Nature of Man* (New York and London: G. P. Putnam's Sons, 1899 [1897]), 46.

49. Dresser, *In Search of a Soul*, 127–28, 132, 180–82.

50. Ibid., 171; Horatio W. Dresser, *Voices of Freedom: And Studies in the Philosophy of Individuality* (New York and London: G. P. Putnam's Sons, 1899), 158, 171–96, 199.

51. Dresser, *In Search of a Soul*, 74.

52. Dresser, *Power of Silence*, 30, 42–43.

53. Horatio W. Dresser, *Man and the Divine Order: Essays in the Philosophy of Religion and in Constructive Idealism* (New York and London: G. P. Putnam's Sons, 1903), 354, 363.

54. Quoted in Horatio W. Dresser, *A History of the New Thought Movement* (New York: Thomas Y. Crowell Company, 1919), 171, 182, 195. Read also Barrows, ed., *World's Parliament of Religions*, vol. 1.

55. After its reorganization in 1906, the League became a federation of New Thought Centers. Two years later, the League became the National New Thought Alliance, whose conventions offered workshops on practical metaphysics, consciousness, psychology, and individuality. In 1914, the Alliance changed its name to the International New Thought Alliance (INTA). See Dresser, *History of the New Thought Movement*, 200.

56. Horatio W. Dresser, "An Invitation," in *Good Housekeeping* 50 (1910): 472–73; Mrs. Horatio Dresser, "The Food Economy Kitchen and Its Value in the Community," in *The Journal of Home Economics* 13 (1921): 33–35.

57. Horatio W. Dresser, "A Talk to Our Policyholders," in *Good Housekeeping* 51 (1910): 432.

58. Ibid., 433, 434.

59. Ronald Hughes, ed., *Phineas Parkhurst Quimby: His Complete Writings and Beyond* (Howard City, MI: Phineas Parkhurst Quimby Resource Center, 2009), 106. One example of Dresser's articles during this period was "The Age of John Locke," in *Home Progress* 6 (1916–17): 53–59.

60. Horatio W. Dresser, *The Psychology and Philosophy of Emanuel Swedenborg*, 2 vols., John S. Haller, Jr., ed. (*Creative Works* Collection, Southern Illinois University Carbondale, 2018), vol. 1, 17, 39. See also Swedenborg, *Secrets of Heaven* §687.

61. Dresser, *Psychology and Philosophy of Emanuel Swedenborg*, vol. 1, 17, 110–11.

62. Ibid., 17–18, 159.

63. Swedenborg, *True Christianity* §47.

64. Dresser, *Psychology and Philosophy of Emanuel Swedenborg*, vol. 2, 114.

65. See Swedenborg, *Arcana Coelestia* §3570.

66. Dresser, *Psychology and Philosophy of Emanuel Swedenborg*, vol. 2, 132. See also the appendix on page 245 of the present volume.

67. Horatio W. Dresser, *A Message to the Well and Other Essays and Letters on the Art of Health* (New York and London: G. P. Putnam's Sons, 1910), 21.

68. Hughes, ed., *Phineas Parkhurst Quimby*, 121.

69. C. Alan Anderson, *Healing Hypotheses: Horatio W. Dresser and the Philosophy of New Thought* (New York: Garland Publishing, Inc., 1993), 108–9. http://www.ppquimby.com/anderson/chapter_4.htm#iii.%20Middle%20and%20Later%20Years (accessed January 17, 2011). "John Howland Lathrop," at http://www25.uua.org/uuhs/duub/articles/johnhlathrop.html (accessed January 17, 2011).

70. Ernest E. Bruder, "New Directions in Clinical Pastoral Training," in *Journal of Religion and Health* 10 (1971): 121–37; Ernest E. Bruder, "Major Issues Currently Impeding Clinical Pastoral Education," in *Journal of Religion and Health* 11 (1972): 299–312; Stephen G. Prichard, Stephen M. Price, James M. Murphy, John Messerschmitt, and William G. Brockman, "Pastoral Counseling," in *Journal of Religion and Health* 13 (1974): 40–56; John

B. Houck and David M. Moss, "Pastoral Psychotherapy, the Fee-for-Service Model, and Professional Identity," in *Journal of Religion and Health* 16 (1977): 172–82; David M. Moss, "Priestcraft and Psychoanalytic Psychotherapy: Contraction or Concordance?," in *Journal of Religion and Health* 18 (1979): 181–88; Homer U. Ashby, Jr., "Values and the Moral Contest of Pastoral Counseling," in *Journal of Religion and Health* 20 (1981): 176–85; Robert L. Randall, "Self Psychology in Pastoral Counseling," in *Journal of Religion and Health* 28 (1989): 7–15; Richard Dayringer, "The Image of God in Pastoral Counseling," in *Journal of Religion and Health* 51 (2012): 49–56.

Conclusion: American Spirit

1. Lovejoy, "William James as Philosopher," 145.

2. Read Frederic I. Carpenter, "William James and Emerson," in *American Literature* 11 (1939): 42–44.

3. It was Emerson's vagueness that James, the proverbial moralist, found most objectionable. For example, it was sometimes difficult to separate the abstractness of Emerson's transcendentalism from the practical consequences that fed the popular mind. Emerson's description of "The Young American," read before the Mercantile Library Association of Boston in 1844, was not recognition of the "gritty" struggles of the poor and laboring classes overcoming the challenges of life, but of an idea that tallied with his abstract conviction that Nature was guiding the nation toward some mystical concept of justice and humanity. While the eloquence of his words spoke of action and most certainly resonated with his audience, they were used to empower American imperialism and destiny, something of which James could not approve. While Emerson suggested that citizens had a responsibility to lead, others took his idealism and transformed it into schemes of greed. "The Young American exists both as a literary construct and a real world phenomenon," wrote Brady Harrison, but it was used in ways Emerson had not anticipated, with "other truly young Americans . . . stepping forward to lead the nation in the construction of empires." Emerson, "The Young American," in *Essays and Lectures*, 217; Brady Harrison, "The Young Americans: Emerson, Walker, and the Early Literature of American Empire," in *American Studies* 40 (1999): 75–97.

4. Matthiessen, *American Renaissance*, viii.

5. Colin Koopman, "Pragmatism as a Philosophy of Hope: Emerson, James, Dewey, Rorty," in *Journal of Speculative Philosophy* 20 (2006): 106–16.

6. Frothingham, "Swedenborg," 600–16.

Appendix

1. Dresser, *Psychology and Philosophy of Emanuel Swedenborg*, vol. 2, 143–47.

300   Endnotes

Bibliography

Aaron, Daniel. *Men of Good Hope.* New York: Oxford University Press, 1951.

Abbott, Lyman. *Christianity and Social Problems.* Boston: Houghton, Mifflin and Co., 1896.

Abell, Aaron I. *The Urban Impact on American Protestantism, 1865–1900.* Cambridge, MA: Harvard University Press, 1943.

Abeln, Paul. *William Dean Howells and the Ends of Realism.* New York: Routledge, 2005.

Abzig, Robert H. *Cosmos Crumbling: American Reform and the Religious Imagination.* New York: Oxford University Press, 1994.

Adams, Henry. *The Education of Henry Adams.* New York: Houghton Mifflin Co., 1918.

Ahlstrom, Sydney. *A Religious History of the American People.* 2nd ed. New Haven: Yale University Press, 2004.

Anderson, C. Alan. *Healing Hypotheses: Horatio W. Dresser and the Philosophy of New Thought.* New York: Garland Publishing, Inc., 1993.

Arthur, Timothy Shay. *Ten Nights in a Bar-Room and What I Saw There.* Philadelphia: Porter and Coates, 1882 [1854].

Aveling, Edward. *The Creed of an Atheist.* London: Free Thought Publishing Co., 1881

_____. *The Student's Darwin.* London: Freethought Publishing Co., 1881.

Baker, Ray Stanndard. *The Spiritual Unrest.* New York: Frederick Stokes Co., 1910.

Bannister, Robert. *Social Darwinism: Science and Myth in Anglo-American Social Thought.* Philadelphia: Temple University Press, 1979.

Barlow, Nora, ed. *The Autobiography of Charles Darwin, 1809–1882.* New York: Harcourt, Brace, 1958.

Barrett, B. F. *Swedenborg and Channing: Showing the Many and Remarkable Agreements in the Beliefs and Teachings of these Writers.* Philadelphia: Claxton, Remsen and Haffelfinger, 1879.

Barrows, John Henry, ed. *The World's Parliament of Religions, an Illustrated and Popular Story of the World's First Parliament of Religions, Held in Chicago in Connection with the Columbian Exposition of 1893*. 2 vols. Chicago: The Parliament Publishing Co., 1893.

Barruel, Abbé. *Memoirs Illustrating the History of Jacobinism*. Hartford: Hudson and Goodwin, 1799.

Becher, Jonathan. *Charles Fourier: The Visionary and His World*. Berkeley: University of California Press, 1986.

Behrend, Auguste J. F. *Socialism and Christianity*. New York: Baker and Taylor, 1886.

Beisner, Robert L. *Twelve Against Empire: The Anti-Imperialists, 1898–1900*. New York: McGraw-Hill, 1968.

Bell, Adrienne Baxter. *George Inness and the Visionary Landscape*. New York: National Academy of Design, 2003.

Bentham, Jeremy. *An Introduction to the Principles of Morals and Legislation*. Oxford: Clarendon Press, 1907.

Benz, Ernst. *Emanuel Swedenborg: Visionary Savant in the Age of Reason*. West Chester, PA: Swedenborg Foundation, 2002.

Berger, Pierre. *William Blake: Mysticism and Poetry*. London: Chapman and Hall, 1914.

Bestor, Arthur E., Jr. *American Phalanxes: A Study of Fourierist Socialism in the United States, with Special Reference to the Movement in Western New York*. New Haven: Yale University, 1938.

_____. *Backwoods Utopias: The Sectarian Origins and the Owenite Phase of Communitarian Socialism in America, 1663–1829*. Philadelphia: University of Pennsylvania Press, 1967.

Beswick, Samuel. *Swedenborg Rite and the Great Masonic Leaders of the Eighteenth Century*. New York: Kessinger Publishing, 1994 [1870].

Bjork, Daniel W. *The Compromised Scientist: William James in the Development of American Psychology*. New York: Columbia University Press, 1983.

Blake, William. *Poems of William Blake*. William Butler Yeats, ed. New York: The Book League of America, Inc., 1938.

_____. *The Selected Poems of William Blake*. Hertfordshire: Wordsworth Edition, 1994.

Block, Marguerite Beck. *The New Church in the New World: A Study of Swedenborgianism in America*. New York: Henry Holt and Company, 1932.

Boisen, Anton T. *The Exploration of the Inner World: A Study of Mental Disorder and Religious Experience*. New York: Harper and Brothers, 1936.

_____. *Out of the Depths*. New York: Harper, 1960.

_____. *Religion in Crisis and Custom*. New York: Harper, 1955.

Bosco, Ronald A., and Joel Myerson, eds. *The Later Lectures of Ralph Waldo Emerson, Vol. 1: 1843–54*. Athens: University of Georgia Press, 2001.

Bowman, Sylvia E. *Edward Bellamy: A Critical Biography.* New York: Bookman Associates, 1958.

———. *Edward Bellamy Abroad: An American Prophet's Influence.* New York: Twayne Publishers, 1962.

———. *The Year 2000: A Critical Biography of Edward Bellamy.* New York: Bookman, 1958.

Brisbane, Albert. *Association; Or, a Concise Exposition of the Practical Part of Fourier's Social Science.* New York: Greeley and McElrath, 1843.

———. *Social Destiny of Man; Or, Association and Reorganization of Industry.* Philadelphia: C. F. Stollmeyer, 1840.

———. *Theory of the Functions of the Human Passions, Followed by an Outline View of the Fundamental Principles of Fourier's Theory of Social Science.* New York: Miller, Orton, and Mulligan, 1856.

Brisbane, Redella, ed. *Albert Brisbane, a Mental Biography.* Boston: Arena, 1893.

Brock, Erland J., and E. Bruce Glenn, eds. *Swedenborg and His Influence.* Bryn Athyn, PA: Academy of the New Church, 1988.

Brock, William Hall. "Phalanx on a Hill: Responses to Fourierism in the Transcendentalist Circle." PhD diss., Loyola University of Chicago, 1995.

Brooks, Van Wyck. *America's Coming-of-Age.* New York: B. W. Huebsch, 1915.

Brown, William Adams. *Christian Theology in Outline.* New York: Charles Scribner's Sons, 1906.

———. *Is Christianity Practicable?* New York: Charles Scribner's Sons, 1916.

Brownson, Orestes A. *The Spirit-Rapper: An Autobiography.* Boston: Little, Brown, 1854.

———. *The Works of Orestes A. Brownson: Controversy. Vol. 5.* Henry F. Brownson, ed. Detroit: Thorndike Nourse and Henry F. Brownson, 1884.

Buckham, John Wright. *Progressive Religious Thought in America: A Survey of the Enlarging Pilgrim Faith.* Boston: Houghton Mifflin Co., 1919.

Burke, Edmund. *Reflections of the Revolution in France.* Harmondsworth: Penguin, 1984.

Burkholder, Robert E., and Joel Myerson. *Ralph Waldo Emerson: An Annotated Secondary Bibliography.* Pittsburgh: University of Pittsburgh Press, 1985.

Cabot, Richard Clarke. *Adventures on the Borderlands of Ethics.* New York and London: Harper and Brothers, 1926.

Calinescu, Matei. *Five Faces of Modernity: Modernism, Advant-garde, Decadence, Kitsch, Postmodernism.* Durham: Duke University Press, 1987.

Cameron, Kenneth Walter, ed. *Emerson Among His Contemporaries: A Harvest of Estimates, Insights, and Anecdotes from the Victorian Literary World and an Index.* Hartford, CT: Transcendental Books, 1967.

Cameron, Kenneth Walter, ed. *Emerson, Thoreau and Concord in Early Newspapers: Biographical and Historical Lore for the Scholar and General Reader.* Hartford, CT: Transcendental Books, 1958.

Caplan, Eric. *Mind Games: American Culture and the Birth of Psychotherapy.* Berkeley: University of California Press, 1998.

Capper, Charles. *Margaret Fuller: An American Romantic Life.* vol. 1. New York: Oxford University Press, 1992.

Capps, Donald. *Men, Religion, and Melancholia: James, Otto, Jung, and Erickson.* New Haven: Yale University Press, 1997.

Carnegie, Andrew. *Autobiography of Andrew Carnegie.* Boston: Houghton Mifflin Co., 1920.

_____. *The Gospel of Wealth and Other Timely Essays.* New York: Century, 1900.

Carroll, H. K. *Federal Council Year Book.* New York: Missionary Education Movement, 1917.

Carter, Paul A. *The Decline and Revival of the Social Gospel: Social and Political Liberalism in American Protestant Churches, 1920–1940.* Ithaca, NY: Cornell University Press, 1956.

_____. *The Spiritual Crisis of the Gilded Age.* DeKalb: Northern Illinois University Press, 1971.

Cashdollar, Charles D. *The Transformation of Theology, 1830–1890: Positivism and Protestant Thought in Britain and America.* New Jersey: Princeton University Press, 1989.

Cayton, Mary Kupiec. *Emerson's Emergence: Self and Society in the Transformation of New England, 1800–1845.* Chapel Hill: University of North Carolina Press, 1989.

Chai, Leon. *The Romantic Foundations of the American Renaissance.* Ithaca, NY: Cornell University Press, 1987.

Channing, William E. *The Works of William E. Channing, D. D.* Boston: American Unitarian Association, 1898.

Chevigny, Bell Gale. *The Woman and the Myth: Margaret Fuller's Life and Writings.* Rev. ed. Boston: Northeastern University Press, 1994.

Clark, Christopher. *The Communitarian Movement: The Radical Challenge of the Northampton Association.* Ithaca, NY: Cornell University Press, 1995.

Codman, John Thomas. *Brook Farm: Historic and Personal Memoirs.* New York: AMS Press, 1971 [1894].

Commager, Henry S. *The American Mind: An Interpretation of American Thought and Character Since the 1880s.* New Haven: Yale University Press, 1950.

Cooper, Wesley. *The Unity of William James's Thought.* Nashville, TN: Vanderbilt University Press, 2002.

Crowe, Charles R. *George Ripley: Transcendentalist and Utopian Socialist.* Athens: University of Georgia Press, 1967.

Crunden, Robert. *Ministers of Reform: The Progressives' Achievement in American Civilization, 1889–1920.* New York: Basic Books, 1982.

Curti, Merl. *The Growth of American Thought.* New York: Harper and Brothers Publishers, 1943.

Curtis, Susan. *A Consuming Faith: The Social Gospel and Modern American Culture.* Baltimore: Johns Hopkins University Press, 1991.

Daingerfield, Elliott. *George Inness: The Man and His Art.* New York: Privately Printed, 1911.

Dana, Charles A. *A Lecture on Association, in Its Connection with Religion.* Boston: Benjamin H. Greene, 1844.

Darwin, Charles R. *The Descent of Man, and Selection in Relation to Sex.* New York: Appleton and Co., 1871.

_____. *On the Origin of Species by Means of Natural Selection.* London: John Murray, Albemarle Street, 1859.

Darwin, Francis, ed. *The Life and Letters of Charles Darwin.* 2 vols. New York: D. Appleton, 1896.

Davies, J. G. *The Theology of William Blake.* Oxford: Clarendon Press, 1948.

Davis, Andrew Jackson. *The Magic Staff: An Autobiography.* New York: J. S. Brown and Co., 1859.

Dawkins, Richard. *The God Delusion.* Boston: Houghton Mifflin Co., 2008.

De Beaumont, L. B. *Spiritual Reconstruction and the Religious Unrest of the Age.* London: Swedenborg Society, 1918.

Debus, Allen. *Man and Nature in the Renaissance.* Cambridge: Cambridge University Press, 1978.

DeCharms, Richard. *A Discourse on the True Nature of Freedom and Slavery.* Philadelphia: A. H. Jones, 1850.

_____. *Some Views of Freedom and Slavery in the Light of the New Jerusalem.* Philadelphia: Published by Author, 1855.

Delano, Sterling F. *Brook Farm: The Dark Side of Utopia.* Cambridge, MA: Harvard University Press, 2004.

Dewey, John. *A Common Faith.* New Haven: Yale University Press, 1934.

Dombrowski, James A. *The Early Days of Christian Socialism in America.* New York: Octagon Books, 1966 [1937].

Dorfman, Joseph. *Thorstein Veblen and His America.* New York: Viking Press, 1947.

Doyle, Arthur Conan. *The History of Spiritualism.* 2 vols. London: Cassell and Company Ltd., 1926.

Draper, Edgar. *Psychiatry and Pastoral Care.* NJ: Prentice-Hall, Inc., 1965.

Dresser, Annetta. *The Philosophy of P. P. Quimby, with Selections from His Manuscripts and a Sketch of His Life.* Boston: G. H. Ellis, 1895.

Dresser, Horatio W. *Health and the Inner Life: An Analytical and Historical Study of Spiritual Healing Theories, with an Account of the Life and Teachings of P. P. Quimby.* New York: G. P. Putnam's Sons, 1906.

_____. *A History of the New Thought Movement.* New York: Thomas Y. Crowell Company, 1919.

_____. *The Immanent God: An Essay.* Boston: Published by the Author, 1895.

_____. *In Search of a Soul: A Series of Essays in Interpretation of the Higher Nature of Man.* New York and London: G. P. Putnam's Sons, 1899 [1897].

_____. *Man and the Divine Order: Essays in the Philosophy of Religion and in Constructive Idealism.* New York and London: G. P. Putnam's Sons, 1903.

_____. *A Message to the Well and Other Essays and Letters on the Art of Health.* New York and London: G. P. Putnam's Sons, 1910.

_____. *The Open Vision: A Study of Psychic Phenomena.* New York: Thomas Y. Crowell Company, 1920.

_____. *The Power of Silence: A Study of the Values and Ideals of the Inner Life.* New York and London: G. P. Putnam's Sons, 1906 [1895].

_____. *The Psychology and Philosophy of Emanuel Swedenborg.* 2 vols. John S. Haller, Jr., ed. *Creative Works* Collection, Southern Illinois University Carbondale, 2018.

_____. *A True History of Mental Science: A Lecture Delivered at the Church of the Divine Unity, Boston, Mass., on Sunday Evening Feb. 6, 1887.* Boston: A. Mudge, 1887.

_____. *Voices of Freedom: And Studies in the Philosophy of Individuality.* New York and London: G. P. Putnam's Sons, 1899.

Dresser, Julius A. *The True History of Mental Science; the Facts Concerning the Discovery of Mental Healing.* Boston: Ellis, 1899.

Duban, James. *The Nature of True Virtue: Theology, Psychology, and Politics in the Writings of Henry James, Sr., Henry James, Jr., and William James.* Madison: Farleigh Dickinson University Press, 2001.

Dubois, Paul. *The Psychic Treatment of Nervous Disorders.* New York and London: Funk & Wagnalls Company, 1905.

Dunbar, Helen Flanders. *Emotions and Bodily Changes.* New York: Columbia University Press, 1935.

_____. *Mind and Body: Psychosomatic Medicine.* New York: Random House, 1947.

_____. *Psychosomatic Diagnosis.* New York: P. B. Hoeber, Inc., 1943.

Durfee, Harold A. *The Theologies of the American Social Gospel.* Park College, MO: Union Theological Seminary, 1951.

Eaton, A. H. *The Oregon System.* Chicago: A. C. McLurg and Co., 1912.

Eby, Samuel C. *Swedenborg's Service to Philosophy.* Peoria, IL: J.W. Franks and Sons, 1891.

Edel, Leon. *Henry James: The Untried Years: 1843–1870.* New York: Avon, 1978.

Edwards, Jonathan. *The Nature of True Virtue.* Ann Arbor: University of Michigan Press, 1960 [1765].

_____. *A Treatise Concerning Religious Affections.* London: C. H. Kelly, 1898 [1746].

Egbert, Donald Drew, and Stow Persons, eds. *Socialism and American Life*. 2 vols. Princeton: Princeton University Press, 1952.

Eggleston, W. G. *People's Power and Public Taxation*. Portland, OR: Multnomah Print Co., 1910.

Emerson, E. W., and W. E. Forbes, eds. *Journals of Ralph Waldo Emerson with Annotations*. 10 vols. Boston: Houghton Mifflin Co., 1909.

Emerson, Ralph Waldo. *Emerson's Complete Works*. 12 vols. Boston: Houghton, Mifflin and Co., 1883.

_____. *Essays and Lectures*. Joel Porte, ed. New York: Library of America, 1983.

_____. *Essays: Second Series*. Boston: Phillips, Sampson, and Company, 1855.

Evans, Christopher H. *The Kingdom Is Always But Coming: A Life of Walter Rauschenbusch*. Grand Rapids, MI: William B. Eerdmans, 2004.

Faulkner, H. U. *The Quest for Social Justice, 1898–1914*. New York: The Macmillan Co., 1931.

Feinstein, Howard. *Becoming William James*. Ithaca, NY: Cornell University Press, 1984.

Fellman, Michael. *The Unbounded Frame: Freedom and Community in Nineteenth Century American Utopianism*. Westport, CT: Greenwood Press, 1973.

Fields, Annie, ed. *Letters of Sarah Orne Jewett*. Boston: Houghton Mifflin Company, 1911.

Filippelli, Ronald L. *Labor Conflict in the United States: An Encyclopedia*. New York: Garland Publishers, 1990.

Fisher, Kenneth L. *110 Minds that Made the Market*. Hoboken, NJ: John Wiley and Sons, 2007.

Foner, Philip. *History of the Labor Movement in the United States*. 2 vols. New York: International Publishers, 1947.

Fontinell, Eugene. *Self, God, and Immorality: A Jamesian Investigation*. Philadelphia: Temple University Press, 1986.

Foster, Carrie A. *The Women and the Warriors: The U.S. Section of the Women's International League for Peace and Freedom, 1915–1946*. Syracuse, NY: Syracuse University Press, 1995.

Frothingham, Octavius Brooks. *George Ripley*. Boston: Houghton, Mifflin and Co., 1882.

_____. *Memoir of William Henry Channing*. Boston: Houghton, Mifflin and Co., 1886.

_____. *The Religion of Humanity*. New York: D. G. Francis, 1873.

_____. *Transcendentalism in New England: A History*. Philadelphia: University of Pennsylvania Press, 1972 [1876].

Fuller, Margaret. *Woman in the Nineteenth Century*. New York: Norton, 1971 [1855].

Gabriel, Ralph Henry. *The Course of American Democratic Thought*. New York: Ronald Press Co., 1956.

Gale, Richard M. *The Divided Self of William James*. Cambridge: Cambridge University Press, 1999.

Garnett, R. G. *Cooperation and the Owenite Socialist Communities in Britain, 1825–45*. Manchester, England: Manchester University Press, 1972.

Garrett, Clarke. *Respectable Folly: Millenarians and the French Revolution in France and England*. Baltimore: Johns Hopkins Press, 1975.

Geiger, Raymond. *The Philosophy of Henry George*. New York: Macmillan Co., 1933.

George, Henry. *An Open Letter to Pope Leo XIII*. New York: Charles L. Webster and Co., 1893.

_____. *Our Land and Land Policy, National and State*. San Francisco: White & Bauer, 1871.

_____. *Our Land and Land Policy: Speeches, Lectures, and Miscellaneous Writings*. New York: Doubleday and McClure Co., 1902.

_____. *Progress and Poverty: An Inquiry into the Cause of Industrial Depressions, and of Increase of Want with Increase of Wealth. The Remedy*. 4th ed. New York: D. Appleton and Co., 1886 [1879].

_____. *The Science of Political Economy*. New York: Doubleday and McClure Co., 1898.

_____. *Social Problems*. London: Kegan Paul, Trench and Co., 1884.

Gide, Charles. *Selections from the Works of Fourier*. London: Swan Sonnenschein and Co., 1901.

Gifford, Sanford. *The Emmanuel Movement: The Origins of Group Treatment and the Assault on Lay Psychotherapy*. Boston: Harvard University Press, 1997.

Girgus, S. B. *The American Self: Myth, Ideology and Popular Culture*. Kansas: University of Kansas Press, 1981.

Gladden, Washington. *Applied Christianity: Moral Aspects of Social Questions*. Boston: Houghton, Mifflin and Co., 1886.

_____. *Being a Christian: What It Means and How to Begin*. Boston: Pilgrim Press, 1885.

_____. *Christianity and Socialism*. New York: Eaton and Mains, 1905.

_____. *Recollections*. Boston: Houghton Mifflin Co., 1909.

_____. *Ruling Ideas of the Present Age*. Boston and New York: Houghton, Mifflin and Company, 1895.

_____. *Social Facts and Forces*. New York: G. P. Putnam's Sons, 1897.

_____. *Tools and the Man: Property and Industry under the Christian Law*. Boston: Houghton, Mifflin, 1893.

_____. *Working People and Their Employers*. Boston: Lockwood, Brooks, and Company, 1876.

Gladish, Robert K. *Swedenborg, Fourier, and the America of the 1840's.* Bryn Athyn, PA: Swedenborg Scientific Association, 1983.

Godwin, Parke. *A Popular View of the Doctrines of Charles Fourier.* New York: J. S. Redfield, 1844.

Gohdes, Clarence L. F. *The Periodicals of American Transcendentalism.* Durham: Duke University Press, 1931.

Goodman, Russell B., ed. *Pragmatism: Critical Concepts in Philosophy.* vol. 1. London and New York: Routledge, 2005.

Goodman, Susan, and Carl Dawson. *William Dean Howells: A Writer's Life.* CA: University of California Press, 2005.

Gorrell, Donald K. *The Age of Social Responsibility: The Social Gospel in the Progressive Era, 1900–1920.* Macon, GA: Mercer University Press, 1988.

Gosling, Francis. *Before Freud: Neurasthenia and the American Medical Community, 1870–1910.* Urbana, IL: University of Illinois Press, 1987.

Gougeon, Len. *Virtue's Hero: Emerson, Antislavery, and Reform.* Athens: University of Georgia Press, 1990.

Goyder, David George. *A Concise History of the New Church.* London: T. Goyder, 1827.

Graham, Stephen. *Tramping with a Poet in the Rockies.* New York: D. Appleton and Co., 1922.

Grattan, C. Hartley. *The Three Jameses.* London: Longmans, 1932.

Greeley, Horace, and H. J. Raymond. *Association Discussed, or the Socialism of the Tribune Examined.* New York: Harper and Brothers, 1847.

Guarneri, Carl J. *The Utopian Alternative: Fourierism in Nineteenth-Century America.* Ithaca, NY: Cornell University Press, 1991.

Haeckel, Ernst. *Riddle of the Universe at the Close of the Nineteenth Century.* New York: Harper and Brothers, 1900.

Hale, Nathan G., Jr. *The Rise and Crisis of Psychoanalysis in the United States: Freud and the Americans, 1917–1985.* New York: Oxford University Press, 1995.

Hall, Charles E. *Head and Heart: The Story of the Clinical Pastoral Education Movement.* Decatur, GA: Journal of Pastoral Care Publications, Inc., 1993.

Hallengren, Anders, ed. *The Moment Is Now: Carl Bernhard Wadström's Revolutionary Voice on Human Trafficking and the Abolition of the African Slave Trade.* West Chester, PA: Swedenborg Foundation, 2019.

Haller, John S., Jr. *Man and His Muse: The Swedenborgian World of Rev. Frank Sewall.* Amazon Books, 2019.

———. *Outcasts from Evolution: Scientific Attitudes of Racial Inferiority, 1859–1900.* Urbana, IL: University of Illinois Press, 1971.

———. *Swedenborg, Mesmer, & the Mind/Body Connection.* West Chester, PA: Swedenborg Foundation, 2010.

Handy, Robert T. *The American Religious Depression, 1925–1935.* Philadelphia: Fortress Press, 1968.

_____, ed. *The Social Gospel in America, 1870–1920: Gladden, Ely, Rauschenbusch.* New York: Oxford University, 1966.

Hanson, John Wesley, ed. *The World's Congress of Religions.* Chicago: Monarch Book Co., 1894.

Harrington, Anne. *The Cure Within: A History of Mind-Body Medicine.* New York: Norton, 2008.

Harris, Sam. *The End of Faith: Religion, Terror, and the Future of Reason.* New York: W. W. Norton and Co., 2004.

Harris, Samuel Smith. *The Relation of Christianity to Civil Society.* New York: T. Whittaker, 1883.

Harrison, J. F. C. *Robert Owen and the Owenites in Britain and America: The Quest for the New Moral World.* London: Routledge and Kegan Paul, 1969.

Hartshorne, Charles, Paul Weiss, and Arthur W. Burks, eds. *Collected Papers of Charles Sanders Peirce.* 8 vols. Cambridge, MA: Harvard University Press, 1931–58.

Haydon, A. Eustace. *Biography of the Gods.* New York: Macmillan Co., 1941.

Hempel, Charles Julius. *The True Organization of the New Church as Indicated in the Writings of Emanuel Swedenborg and Demonstrated by Charles Fourier.* New York: William Radde, 1848.

Herron, George D. *The Christian Society.* New York: Fleming H. Revell Co., 1894.

Hick, John. *Philosophy of Religion.* Englewood Cliffs, NJ: Prentice-Hall, 1990.

Hillquit, Morris. *History of Socialism in the United States.* New York: Funk & Wagnalls Company, 1906.

Hindmarsh, Robert. *Rise and Progress of the New Jerusalem Church in England, America, and Other Parts.* London: Hodson and Son, 1861.

Hitchens, Christopher. *God Is Not Great: How Religion Poisons Everything.* New York: Twelve, 2007.

Hite, Lewis F. *Swedenborg's Historical Position.* Boston: Massachusetts New-Church Union, 1928.

Hofstadter, Richard. *Social Darwinism in American Thought.* Philadelphia: University of Pennsylvania Press, 1944.

Hoopes, Ames. *Consciousness in New England: From Puritanism and Ideas to Psychoanalysis and Semiotics.* Baltimore: Johns Hopkins University Press, 1989.

Hoover, Dwight W. *Henry James, Sr. and the Religion of Community.* Grand Rapids, MI: William B. Eerdmans Publishing Co., 1969.

Hopkins, Charles Howard. *The Rise of the Social Gospel in American Protestantism, 1865–1915.* New Haven: Yale University Press, 1940.

Horton, Walter Marshall. *The Significance of Swedenborg for Contemporary Theology.* New York: The Swedenborg Publishing Association, 1938.

Howells, Mildred. *Life in Letters of William Dean Howells.* 2 vols. Garden City: Doubleday, Doran and Co., 1928.

Howells, William Cooper. *Recollections of Life in Ohio from 1813 to 1840.* Cincinnati: Robert Clarke Co., 1895.

Howells, William Dean. *A Boy's Town.* New York: Harper and Brothers Publishers, 1890.

_____. *Italian Journeys.* Boston: Houghton and Mifflin and Co., 1907.

_____. *The Leatherwood God.* New York: The Century Co., 1916.

_____. *Literary Friends and Acquaintances: A Personal Retrospect of American Authorship.* New York: Harper and Brothers Publishers, 1900.

_____. *Ragged Lady.* Toronto: W. J. Gage, 1899.

_____. *Through the Eye of the Needle: A Romance.* New York: Harper and Brothers Publishers, 1907.

_____. *A Traveler from Altruria: Romance.* New York: Harper and Brothers Publishers, 1894.

_____. *Years of My Youth.* New York: Harper and Brothers Publishers, 1917.

Hughes, Ronald, ed. *Phineas Parkhurst Quimby: His Complete Writings and Beyond.* Howard City, MI: Phineas Parkhurst Quimby Resource Center, 2009.

Hughley, J. Neal. *Trends in Protestant Social Idealism.* New York: King's Crown, 1948.

Hume, David. *Essays and Treatises on Several Subjects.* 4 vols. London: Printed for A. Millar, in the Strand; and A. Kincaid and A. Donaldson, in Edinburgh, 1753.

Hutchinson, John A. *We Are Not Divided: A Critical and Historical Study of the Federal Council of the Churches of Christ in America.* New York: Round Table Press, 1941.

Hutchinson, William. *The Modernist Impulse in American Protestantism.* Cambridge, MA: Harvard University Press, 1976.

Huxley, Thomas Henry. *Darwiniana: Essays.* New York: D. Appleton and Co., 1896.

Ingersoll, Robert G. *Works of Robert G. Ingersoll.* 13 vols. New York: Dresden, 1909–15.

Inness, George, Jr. *Life, Art, and Letters of George Inness.* New York: The Century Co., 1917.

James, Henry, ed. *The Letters of William James.* 2 vols. Boston: The Atlantic Monthly Press, 1920.

James, Henry, Sr. *Christianity the Logic of Creation.* New York: Appleton, 1857.

_____. *The Church of Christ Not an Ecclesiasticism: A Letter of Remonstrance to a Member of the* Soi-Disant *New Church.* New York: Redfield, 1854.

_____. *Lectures and Miscellanies; Or, Man's Experience and Destiny.* New York: Redfield, 1852.

_____. *The Literary Remains of the Late Henry James.* William James, ed. New Jersey: Literature House, 1885.

_____. *Moralism and Christianity; Or Man's Experience and Destiny. In Three Lectures.* New York: J. S. Redfield, 1850.

_____. *The Nature of Evil, Considered in a Letter to the Rev. Edward Beecher, D.D., Author of "The Conflict of Ages."* New York: Appleton, 1855.

_____. *The Old and New Theology, Two Lectures.* London: Longman, Green, Longman, & Roberts, 1861.

_____. *The Secret of Swedenborg: Being an Elucidation of His Doctrine of the Divine Natural Humanity.* Boston: Fields, Osgood, & Co., 1869.

_____. *The Social Significance of Our Institutions: An Oration Delivered by Request of the Citizens at Newport, R.I., July 4, 1861.* Boston: Ticknor and Fields, 1861.

_____. *Society the Redeemed Form of Man, and the Earnest of God's Omnipotence in Human Nature: Affirmed in Letters to a Friend.* Boston: Houghton, Osgood and Co., 1879.

_____. *Substance and Shadow: Or Morality and Religion in Their Relation to Life: An Essay upon the Physics of Creation.* Boston: Ticknor and Fields, 1863.

_____. *Tracts for the New Times.* New York: AMS Press, 1983 [1847].

_____. *What Constitutes the State?* New York: J. Allen, 1846.

James, William. *Essays, Comments and Reviews.* Frederick H. Burkhardt, Fredson Bowers, and Ignas K. Skrupskelis, eds. Cambridge, MA: Harvard University Press, 1987.

_____. *Essays in Radical Empiricism.* London: Longmans, Green, and Co., 1912.

_____. *Human Immortality: Two Supposed Objections to the Doctrine.* London: Archibald Constable & Co., 1906.

_____. *Is Life Worth Living?* Philadelphia: S. Burns Weston, 1896.

_____. *The Meaning of Truth.* London: Longmans, Green, and Co., 1909.

_____. *Memories and Studies.* New York: Longmans, Green, and Co., 1911.

_____. *A Pluralistic Universe.* New York: Longmans, Green, and Co., 1920 [1909].

_____. *Pragmatism: A New Name for Some Old Ways of Thinking.* New York: Longmans, Green, and Co., 1907.

_____. *Pragmatism and the Meaning of Truth.* Cambridge, MA: Harvard University Press, 1975.

_____. *Pragmatism and Other Writings.* New York: Penguin Books, 2000.

_____. *The Principles of Psychology.* New York: Henry Holt and Company, 1890.

_____. *Psychology, Briefer Course.* New York: Henry Holt and Co., 1913.

_____. *The Varieties of Religious Experience: A Study in Human Nature.* New York: Longmans, Green, and Co., 1928 [1902].

_____. *The Will to Believe and Other Essays in Popular Philosophy.* New York: Dover Publications, 1956.

Jewett, Sarah Orne. *Country By-Ways.* Boston: Houghton, Mifflin, 1881.

_____. *The Country of the Pointed Firs.* Boston: Houghton, Mifflin, 1896.

_____. *Deephaven.* Boston: James R. Osgood, 1877.

Johnson, Tom Loftin. *My Story.* New York: B. W. Huebsch, 1911.

Jones, Ernest. *Papers on Psycho-Analysis.* New York: William Ward and Co., 1913.

Jonsson, Inge. *Emanuel Swedenborg.* New York: Twayne Publishers, 1971.

Jung, C. G. *The Theory of Psychoanalysis.* New York: Journal of Nervous and Mental Diseases Publishing Co., 1915.

Kellogg, Julia A. *The Philosophy of Henry James.* New York: John W. Lovell Co., 1883.

King, Henry Churchill. *The Theology and the Social Consciousness.* New York: Macmillan Co., 1902.

Kirkham, Stanton Davis. *The Philosophy of Self-Help: An Application of Practical Psychology to Daily Life.* New York and London: G. P. Putnam's Sons, 1909.

Kloppenberg, James. *Uncertain Victory: Social Democracy and Progressivism in European and American Thought, 1870–1920.* New York: Oxford University Press, 1986.

Kuklick, Bruce. *The Rise of American Philosophy, Cambridge, Massachusetts, 1860–1930.* New Haven: Yale University Press, 1977.

Kumar, Krishan. *Utopia and Anti-Utopia in Modern Times.* London: Basil Blackwell, 1987.

Lawrence, D. H. *Selected Criticism.* New York: Viking Press, 1956.

Lears, T. J. Jackson. *No Place of Grace: Antimodernism and the Transformation of American Society, 1880–1920.* New York: Pantheon, 1981.

Leas, Robert David. *Anton Theophilus Boisen: His Life, Work, Impact, and Theological Legacy.* Denver, CO: Journal of Pastoral Care Publications, Inc., 2009.

_____. *Boisen, Mysticism, Swedenborg, and Exceptional Mental and Spiritual States.* Berkeley: Studia Swedenborgiana Press, 2010.

Lentricchia, Frank. *Ariel and the Police: Michel Foucault, William James, Wallace Stevens.* Madison: University of Wisconsin Press, 1988.

Lewis, R. W. B. *The Jameses: A Family Narrative.* New York: Farrar, Straus, and Giroux, 1991.

Lindsay, Vachel. *The Golden Book of Springfield.* New York: Macmillan Co., 1920.

Lineham, Peter J. "The English Swedenborgians: 1770–1840: A Study in the Social Dimensions of Religious Sectarianism." PhD diss., University of Sussex, 1978.

Livingston, James. *Pragmatism and the Political Economy of Cultural Revolution, 1850–1940.* Chapel Hill: University of North Carolina Press, 1994.

Lloyd, Caroline Augusta. *Henry Demarest Lloyd, 1847–1903: A Biography.* 2 vols. New York: Knickerbocker Press, 1912.

Lorimer, George C. *Studies in Social Life: A Review of the Principles, Practices, and Problems of Society.* Chicago: Belford, Clark and Co., 1886.

Lovejoy, Arthur O. *The Great Chain of Being: A Study of the History of an Idea.* Cambridge: Harvard University Press, 1936.

_____. *The Thirteen Pragmatisms and Other Essays.* Baltimore: Johns Hopkins University Press, 1963.

Lovin, Robin W. *Reinhold Niebuhr and Christian Realism.* Cambridge: Cambridge University Press, 1995.

Machen, J. Gresham. *Christianity and Liberalism.* New York: Macmillan, 1923.

Macintosh, Douglas Clyde. *Theology as an Empirical Science.* New York: Macmillan, 1927.

Mackey, Albert Gallatin, and H. L. Haywood, *Encyclopedia of Freemasonry.* 2 vols. New York: Kessinger Publishing, 2003.

MacNair, Everett W. *Edward Bellamy and the Nationalist Movement, 1889 to 1894.* Milwaukee: Fitzgerald, 1957.

Mannheim, Karl. *Ideology and Utopia: An Introduction to the Sociology of Knowledge.* New York: Harcourt, 1985.

Manuel, Frank E. *The New World of Henri Saint-Simon.* Cambridge: Harvard University Press, 1979.

_____. *The Prophets of Paris.* Cambridge: Harvard University Press, 1956.

Martin du Gard, Roger. *Jean Barois.* New York: Bobbs-Merrill Co., 1969 [1913].

Marty, Martin E. *The New Shape of American Religion.* New York: Harper, 1959.

Marx, Leo. *The Machine in the Garden: Technology and the Pastoral Ideal in America.* London: Oxford University Press, 1964.

Mathews, Shailer. *Faith of Modernism.* New York: Macmillan, 1924.

_____. *The Spiritual Interpretation of History.* Cambridge, MA: Harvard University Press, 1927.

Matthiessen, F. O. *American Renaissance: Art and Expression in the Age of Emerson and Whitman.* New York: Oxford University Press, 1941.

May, Henry. *The Protestant Churches and Industrial America.* New York: Harper, 1949.

McClay, W. M. *The Masterless: Self and Society in Modern America.* Chapel Hill: University of North Carolina Press, 1994.

Mee, Jon. *Dangerous Enthusiasm: William Blake and the Culture of Radicalism in the 1790s.* Oxford: Clarendon Press, 1992.

Menand, L. *The Metaphysical Club: A Story of Ideas in America.* Boston: Houghton Mifflin, 2006.

Mercer, L. P., ed. *The New Jerusalem in the World's Religious Congresses of 1893.* Chicago: Western New-Church Union, 1894.

Meyer, Donald. *The Protestant Search for Political Realism, 1919–1941.* Middletown, CT: Wesleyan University Press, 1988.

Mill, John Stuart. *On Liberty.* Boston: Ticknor and Fields, 1863.

Miller, J. I. *Democratic Temperament: The Legacy of William James.* Lawrence, Kansas: University Press of Kansas, 1997.

Miller, Robert Moats. *American Protestantism and Social Issues, 1919–1939.* Chapel Hill: University of North Carolina, 1958.

_____. *Bishop G. Bromley Oxnam: Paladin of Liberal Protestantism.* Nashville, TN: Abingdon Press, 1990.

Minus, Paul. *Walter Rauschenbusch: American Reformer.* New York: Macmillan, 1988.

Morgan, Arthur E. *Edward Bellamy.* New York: Columbia University Press, 1944.

_____. *The Philosophy of Edward Bellamy.* New York: King's Crown Press, 1945.

_____. *The Religion of Solidarity with a Discussion of Edward Bellamy's Philosophy.* Yellow Springs, OH: Antioch Bookplate Co., 1940.

Moxom, Philip S. *The Industrial Revolution: A Sermon.* P. S. Moxom, 1886.

Munger, Theodore Thornton. *The Freedom of Faith.* Boston: Houghton, Mifflin and Co., 1883.

Myers, Gerald E. *William James, His Life and Thought.* New Haven: Yale University Press, 1986.

Myers-Shirk, Susan E. *Helping the Good Shepherd: Pastoral Counselors in a Psychotherapeutic Culture, 1925–1975.* Baltimore: Johns Hopkins University Press, 2009.

National Cyclopædia of American Biography. vol. XI. New York: James T. White & Company, 1901.

Niebuhr, H. Richard. *The Kingdom of God in America.* New York: Harper, 1959 [1937].

Niebuhr, Reinhold. *The Children of Light and the Children of Darkness: A Vindication of Democracy and a Critique of Its Traditional Defense.* New York: Charles Scribner's Sons, 1944.

_____. *Faith and History: A Comparison of Christian and Modern Views of History.* New York: Charles Scribner's Sons, 1949.

_____. *The Irony of American History.* New York: Charles Scribner's Sons, 1952.

_____. *Moral Man and Immoral Society: A Study in Ethics and Politics.* New York: Charles Scribner's Sons, 1932.

_____. *The Nature and Destiny of Man.* New York: Charles Scribner's Sons, 1941–43.

_____. *Reflections on the End of an Era.* New York: Charles Scribner's Sons, 1934.

Nordenskjöld, August. *A Plan for a Free Community upon the Coast of Africa under the Protection of Great Britain; but Entirely Independent of All European Laws and Governments.* London: Robert Hindmarsh, 1789.

Norris, Frank. *The Octopus.* New York: Sagamore Press, Inc., 1957.

Norton, Charles Eliot, ed. *The Correspondence of Thomas Carlyle and Ralph Waldo Emerson.* 2 vols. Boston: Ticknor and Co., 1888.

Noyes, John Humphrey. *History of American Socialisms.* Philadelphia: J. B. Lippincott and Co., 1870.

Nugent, Catharine, ed. *Life and Work of Thomas L. Nugent.* Chicago: Laird and Lee, 1896.

Odhner, Carl Th. *Robert Hindmarsh; A Biography.* Philadelphia: Academy Book Room, 1895.

Orth, Ralph H., and Alfred R. Ferguson, eds. *The Journals and Miscellaneous Notebooks of Ralph Waldo Emerson.* 16 vols. Cambridge: Harvard University Press, 1977.

Orvis, Marianne (Dwight). *Letters from Brook Farm, 1844–1847.* Amy L. Reed, ed. Philadelphia: Porcupine, 1972.

Owen, Alex. *The Place of Enchantment: British Occultism and the Culture of the Modern.* Chicago: University of Chicago Press, 2004.

Parrington, Vernon. *The Romantic Revolution in America. Vol. 2 of Main Currents in American Thought: An Interpretation of American Literature from the Beginnings to 1920.* New York: Harcourt, 1927.

Parsons, Theophilus. *The Infinite and the Finite.* Boston: Roberts Brothers, 1872.

_____. *Outlines of the Religion and Philosophy of Swedenborg.* Boston: Roberts Brothers, 1876.

Pascal, Blaise. *Pensées de Pascal: Précédées de Sa Vie.* Paris: Librairie de Firmin Didot Fréres, 1855.

Pellarin, Charles. *Life of Charles Fourier.* New York: W. H. Graham, 1848.

Perry, Ralph Barton. *In the Spirit of William James.* Bloomington, IN: Indiana University Press, 1958.

_____. *The Thought and Character of William James.* 2 vols. Boston: Little, Brown, and Co., 1935.

_____. *The Thought and Character of William James: Briefer Version.* New York: Harper and Row, 1964 [1935].

Persons, Stow. *American Minds: A History of Ideas.* New York: Holt, Rinehart and Winston, 1958.

Pittenger, Mark. *American Socialists and Evolutionary Thought, 1870–1920.* Madison, Wis.: University of Wisconsin Press, 1993.

Poole, Susan Flagg. *Lost Legacy: Inspiring Women of Nineteenth-Century America.* West Chester, PA: Chrysalis Books, 1999.

Post, Louis F. *The Prophet of San Francisco.* Chicago: L. S. Dickey & Co., 1904.

_____. *Social Service.* New York: A. Wessels, 1909.

Powell, Lyman Pierson. *The Emmanuel Movement in a New England Town.* New York: G. P. Putnam's Sons, 1909.

Powell, Robert Charles. "Healing and Wholeness: Helen Flanders Dunbar (1902–1959): An Extra-Medical Origin of the American Psychosomatic Movement." PhD diss., Duke University, 1974.

Quint, Howard H. *The Forging of American Socialism.* Indianapolis: Bobbs-Merrill Co., 1964.

Raine, Kathleen. *Blake and Tradition.* 2 vols. Princeton: Princeton University Press, 1968.

Rall, Harris Franklin. *The Coming Kingdom.* New York: Methodist Book Concern, 1924.

Rauschenbusch, Walter. *Christianity and the Social Crisis.* New York: The Macmillan Co., 1907.

_____. *Christianizing the Social Order.* New York: The Macmillan Co., 1912.

_____. *A Theology for the Social Gospel.* New York: The Macmillan Co., 1917.

Reed, Sampson. *Observations on the Growth of the Mind; with Remarks on Some Other Subjects.* Gainesville, FL: Scholars Facsimiles and Reprints, 1970.

Renouvier, Charles. *Essais de Critique Générale.* Paris: Librairie Philosophique de Ladrange, 1864.

_____. *Uchronie [l'utopie dans l'histoire]: Esquisse historique apocryphe du développement de la civilisation européenne tel qu'il n'a pas été, tel qu'il aurait pu être.* 1st ed., Paris, 1876.

Reynolds, Larry J. *European Revolutions and the American Literary Renaissance.* New Haven: Yale University Press, 1988.

Riasanovsky, Nicholas V. *The Teaching of Charles Fourier.* Berkeley: University of California Press, 1969.

Riley, Woodbridge. *American Thought: From Puritanism to Pragmatism and Beyond.* Gloucester, MA: Peter Smith, 1959.

Rix, Robert. *William Blake and the Cultures of Radical Christianity.* London: Ashgate Publishing Co., 2007.

Rorty, Richard. *Achieving Our Country: Leftist Thought in the Twentieth Century.* Cambridge: Harvard University Press, 1997.

_____. *Consequences of Pragmatism.* Minneapolis: University of Minnesota Press, 1982.

_____. *Philosophy and Social Hope.* New York: Penguin, 1999.

Rose, Anne C. *Transcendentalism as a Social Movement, 1830–1850.* New Haven, CT: Yale University Press, 1981.

Row, Augustus. *Masonic Biography and Dictionary.* Philadelphia: J. B. Lippincott and Co., 1868.

Ruckor, Darnell. *The Chicago Pragmatists.* Minneapolis: University of Minnesota Press, 1969.

Russell, Bertrand. *A History of Western Philosophy.* New York: Simon and Schuster, 1945.

Rylance, Joseph Hine. *Lectures on Social Questions. Competition, Communism, Cooperation, and the Relation of Christianity to Socialism.* New York: T. Whittaker, 1880.

Sams, Henry W., ed. *Autobiography of Brook Farm.* Englewood Cliffs, NJ: Prentice-Hall, 1958.

Sandeman, Robert. *Letters on Theron and Aspasio.* New York: John S. Taylor, 1838.

Savage, Minot J. *Social Problems.* Boston: G. H. Ellis, 1886.

Schiffman, Joseph, ed. *Edward Bellamy: Selected Writings on Religion and Society.* New York: Liberal Arts Press, 1955.

Schlesinger, Arthur M., Jr. *The Age of Jackson.* Boston: Little, Brown and Company, 1945.

_____. *A Pilgrim's Progress: Orestes A. Brownson.* Boston: Little, Brown and Company, 1966 [1939].

Schneider, Herbert Wallace. *A History of American Philosophy.* New York: Columbia University Press, 1946.

_____. *Meditations in Season on the Elements of Christian Philosophy.* London: Oxford University Press, 1938.

Schneider, Herbert Wallace, and George Lawton. *A Prophet and a Pilgrim: Being the Incredible History of Thomas Lake Harris and Laurence Oliphant; Their Sexual Mysticisms and Utopian Communities Amply Documented to Confound the Skeptic.* New York: Columbia University Press, 1942.

Schuchard, Marsha Keith. *Emanuel Swedenborg, Secret Agent on Earth and in Heaven: Jacobites, Jews and Freemasons in Early Modern Sweden.* Leiden: Brill, 2011.

_____. "Freemasonry, Secret Societies, and the Continuity of the Occult Traditions in English Literature." PhD diss., University of Texas at Austin, 1975.

Sewall, Frank. *The New Ethics: An Essay on the Moral Law of Use.* New York: G. P. Putnam's Sons, 1881.

_____. *The New Metaphysics: Or, the Law of End, Cause, and Effect, with Other Essays.* London: J. Speirs, 1888.

_____. *Swedenborg and Modern Idealism: A Retrospect of Philosophy from Kant to the Present Time.* London: J. Speirs, 1902.

Shaler, Nathaniel Southgate. *The Neighbor: The Natural History of Human Contacts.* Boston: Houghton, Mifflin and Co., 1904.

Shannon, David A. *The Socialist Party of America: A History.* New York: Macmillan, 1955.

Sharpe, Dores R. *Walter Rauschenbusch.* New York: Macmillan, 1942.

Sigstedt, Cyriel Odhner. *The Swedenborg Epic: The Life and Works of Emanuel Swedenborg.* London: The Swedenborg Society, 1981.

Slater, Michael R. *William James on Ethics and Faith.* Cambridge: Cambridge University Press, 2009.

Smith, Walter Aldine. "The Religion of Edward Bellamy." M.A. thesis, Columbia University, 1937.

Spann, Edward K. *Brotherly Tomorrows: Movements for a Cooperative Society in America, 1820–1920*. New York: Columbia University Press, 1989.

Spencer, Herbert. *First Principles*. New York: D. Appleton and Co., 1898.

Spencer, Michael. *Charles Fourier*. Boston: Twayne, 1981.

Spiller, Robert E., et al. *Literary History of the United States*. 3 vols. New York: Macmillan, 1948.

Steffens, Lincoln. *The Struggle for Self-Government*. New York: McClure, Phillips, 1906.

Stenger, Victor J. *The New Atheism: Taking a Stand for Science and Reason*. New York: Prometheus Books, 2009.

Strong, Josiah. *Our Country: Its Possible Future and Present Crisis*. New York: Baker and Taylor, 1885.

Strout, Cushing. *The New Heavens and the New Earth: Political Religion in America*. New York: Harper and Row, 1974.

_____. *The Pragmatic Revolt in American History: Carl Becker and Charles Beard*. New Haven: Yale University Press, 1958.

Stuckenberg, John H. W. *Christian Sociology*. New York: Funk and Wagnalls Co., 1880.

Swank, Scott Trego. "The Unfettered Conscience: A Study of Sectarianism, Spiritualism, and Social Reform in the New Jerusalem Church, 1840–1870." Doctoral dissertation, University of Pennsylvania, 1970 [MS, microfilm, e-book].

Swanton, John R. *Emanuel Swedenborg: Prophet of the Higher Evolution*. New York: New Church Press, 1928.

Swedenborg, Emanuel. *Apocalypse Explained*. 6 vols. West Chester, PA: Swedenborg Foundation, 1994–97 [1785–89].

_____. *Apocalypse Revealed*. 2 vols. West Chester, PA: Swedenborg Foundation, 1997 [1766].

_____. *Arcana Coelestia*. West Chester, PA: Swedenborg Foundation, 1998 [1749–56].

_____. *Divine Love*. New York: Swedenborg Foundation, 1914 [1762–63].

_____. *Divine Love and Wisdom*. West Chester, PA: Swedenborg Foundation, 2010 [1763].

_____. *Divine Providence*. West Chester, PA: Swedenborg Foundation, 2010 [1764].

_____. *The Doctrine of Life for the New Jerusalem: from the Commandments of the Decalogue*. New York: American Swedenborg Printing and Publishing Society, 1891.

_____. *Heaven and Hell*. West Chester, PA: Swedenborg Foundation, 2010 [1758].

_____. *Last Judgment (Posthumous)*. Bryn Athyn, PA: General Church of the New Jerusalem, 1997.

_____. *Marriage Love*. Unpublished section translation by George F. Dole [1768]. §183:3.

_____. *New Jerusalem*. West Chester, PA: Swedenborg Foundation, 2016 [1758].

_____. *Secrets of Heaven*. 2 vols. West Chester, PA: Swedenborg Foundation, 2010, 2012 [1749].

_____. *Secrets of Heaven*. Unpublished section translations by Lisa Hyatt Cooper. [1749–56]. §§6073, 7038, 9297:4.

_____. *Spiritual Experiences*. New York: Swedenborg Foundation, n.d. [1747–65].

_____. *A Treatise Concerning the Last Judgment, and the Destruction of Babylon*. London: R. Hindmarsh, 1788.

_____. *True Christian Religion*. New York: E. P. Dutton and Co., 1933 [1771].

_____. *True Christianity*. 2 vols. West Chester, PA: Swedenborg Foundation, 2010–11 [1771].

Sweet, William Warren. *The Story of Religion in America*. New York: Harper and Brothers, 1939.

Swift, Edmund, Jr. *Evolution and Natural Selection in the Light of the New Church*. Philadelphia: American New Church Tract and Publication Society, n.d.

Swift, Lindsay. *Brook Farm: Its Members, Scholars, and Visitors*. New York: Macmillan Co., 1900.

Tafel, R. L. *Documents Concerning the Life and Character of Emanuel Swedenborg*. 2 vols. London: Swedenborg Society, 1877.

_____. *Socialism and Reform in the Light of the New Church: Lectures*. London: James Speirs, 1891.

Tanner, Duncan. *Political Changes and the Labour Party, 1900–1918*. Cambridge: Cambridge University Press, 1990.

Temple, William. *Nature, Man, and God*. London: Macmillan, 1934.

Thomas, John L. *Alternative America: Henry George, Edward Bellamy, Henry Demarest Lloyd and the Adversary Tradition*. Cambridge: Harvard University Press, 1983.

Thornton, Edward E. *Professional Education for Ministry: A History of Clinical Pastoral Education*. Nashville, TN: Abingdon, 1970.

Thornton, William Thomas. *On Labour, Its Wrongful Claims and Rightful Dues*. London: Macmillan and Co., 1869.

Tillyard, E. M. W. *The Elizabethan World Picture*. London: Chatto and Windus, 1943.

Toksvig, Signe. *Emanuel Swedenborg: Scientist and Mystic*. New Haven: Yale University Press, 1948.

Tomkins, E. Berkeley. *Anti-Imperialism in the United States: The Great Debate, 1890–1920*. Philadelphia: University of Pennsylvania Press, 1970.

Trachtenberg, Alan. *The Incorporation of America: Culture and Society in the Gilded Age.* New York: Hill and Wang, 1982.

Trine, Ralph Waldo. *In the Fire of the Heart.* New York: McClure, Phillips and Co., 1906.

Tull, Charles J. *Father Coughlin and the New Deal.* Syracuse: Syracuse University Press, 1965.

_____. *The Townsend Crusade: An Impartial Review of the Townsend Movement and the Probable Effects of the Townsend Plan.* New York: The Committee on Old Age Security of the 20th Century Fund, Inc., 1936.

Tuveson, Ernest Lee. *Redeemer Nation: The Idea of America's Millennial Role.* Chicago: University of Chicago Press, 1968.

Vedder, Henry. *Socialism and the Ethics of Jesus.* New York: Macmillan, 1912.

Wadström, Carl Bernhard. *An Essay on Colonization, Particularly Applied to the Western Coast of Africa, with Some Free Thoughts on Cultivation and Commerce.* London: Darton and Harvey, 1794–95.

_____. *Plan for a Free Community at Sierra Leona, upon the Coast of Africa, under the Protection of Great Britain; with an Invitation to all Persons Desirous of Partaking the Benefits Thereof.* London: T. and J. Egerton, 1792.

Walker, Francis Amasa. *The Wages Question: A Treatise on Wages and the Wages Class.* London: Macmillan and Co., 1876.

Wallace, Alfred Russel. *Land Nationalization, Its Necessity and Its Aims.* New York: Charles Scribner's Sons, 1892.

_____. *Man's Place in the Universe.* New York: McClure, Phillips and Co., 1903.

Ward, A. W., and A. R. Waller, eds. *The Cambridge History of English Literature. Vol. XI. The Period of the French Revolution.* Cambridge: Cambridge University Press, 1914.

Warren, Austin. *The Elder Henry James.* New York: Macmillan, 1934.

Weisenburger, Francis P. *Ordeal of Faith: The Crisis of Church-Going America, 1865–1900.* New York: Philosophical Library, 1959.

Welch, Richard E., Jr. *Response to Imperialism: The United States and the Philippine-American War.* Chapel Hill: University of North Carolina Press, 1979.

West, Cornel. *The American Evasion of Philosophy: A Genealogy of Pragmatism.* Madison: University of Wisconsin Press, 1989.

Westbrook, Robert B. *Democratic Hope: Pragmatism and the Politics of Truth.* New York: Cornell University Press, 2005.

White, Morton. *Social Thought in America: The Revolt against Formalism.* New York: Oxford University Press, 1949.

White, Ronald, and C. Howard Hopkins. *The Social Gospel: Religion and Reform in Changing America.* Philadelphia: Temple University Press, 1976.

White, William. *Emanuel Swedenborg: His Life and Writings.* 2 vols. London: Simpkin, Marshall and Co., 1867.

Whitehead, Alfred North. *Modes of Thought.* New York: The Free Press, 1938.

Whitman, Walt. *Democratic Vistas.* London: Walter Scott, 1888.

Wilkinson, Clement John. *James John Garth Wilkinson: A Memoir of His Life, with a Selection from His Letters.* London: Kegan Paul, Trench, Trübner & Co., 1911.

Wilkinson, James John Garth. *The African and True Christian Religion: His Magna Charta.* London: J. Speirs, 1892.

_____. *Emanuel Swedenborg: A Biographical Sketch.* London: Otis Clapp, 1849.

Worcester, Elwood. *Life's Adventure: The Story of a Varied Career.* New York: Charles Scribner's Sons, 1932.

Worcester, Elwood, and Samuel McComb. *Body, Mind and Spirit.* Boston: Marshall Jones Co., 1931.

_____. *The Christian Religion as a Healing Power: A Defense and Exposition of the Emmanuel Movement.* New York: Moffat, Yard and Co., 1909.

Worcester, Elwood, Samuel McComb, and Isador H. Coriat. *Religion and Medicine: The Moral Control of Nervous Disorders.* New York: Moffat, Yard and Co., 1908.

Worcester, Samuel H. *Index to the Apocalypse Explained of Emanuel Swedenborg.* 2 vols. New York: American Swedenborg Printing and Publishing Society, 1889.

Wunsch, William F., and Julian K. Smyth (comp.). *The Gist of Swedenborg.* Philadelphia: J. B. Lippincott and Co., 1920.

Yardley, Edmund, ed. *Addresses at the Funeral of Henry George.* Chicago: The Public Publishing Co., 1905.

Young, Arthur Nichols. *The Single Tax Movement in the United States.* Princeton: Princeton University Press, 1916.

Young, Frederic Harold. *The Philosophy of Henry James, Sr.* New York: Bookman Associates, 1951.

Zabriskie, Francis N. *The Bible a Workingman's Book.* New York: R. F. Bogardus, 1888.

Index

A

Abbott, Lyman, 67, 133–36, 141, 216; on capitalism's ills, 136; on individualism, 134, 135, 136; on Jesus's teachings, 135–36; and New Church, 134–35; on property, 135–36; on sin, 134; social gospel/Christian socialism of, 125, 135; on value of labor, 135–36; writings of, 134

abolitionism, 10, 12–13, 264n69; associationism on, 50; Emerson on, 55; New Church on, 13–15

Academy Movement, 160–61

Academy of the New Church, 162

Adams, Henry, 165

Addams, Jane, 137

Adler, Alfred, 238

Agassiz, Louis, 182, 185

Ager, Rev. J. C., 285n27

agnosticism, 290n54; Darwin's, 65, 66, 68; William James on, 197

Alcoholics Anonymous, 218

Alcott, Bronson, 4

Alcott, Louisa May, 3–4

Alexander, Gary, 196

American Christian Commission, 131

American Institute of Christian Sociology, 278n8

American Missionary Association, 133

American Swedenborg Printing and Publishing Society, 162

American Tax Reform League, 113

American Tract Society, 162

American Union of Associationists, 50, 57–58

Andover Theological Seminary, 73, 224, 268n31

angels, hierarchy of, 11–12

Anti-Imperialist League, 204

The Arena, 233

Arthur, Timothy Shay, xxiv

Associated Clinic of Religion and Medicine, 238

Brisbane, Albert, 39, 44, 56, 79; as associationist, 45, 58; as Fourierist, 36, 39–40, 50; influences on, xxiv, 39, 45

Brook Farm, xxv, 35, 42–45; as association, 46, 47–48, 50, 125; William Ellery Channing and, 42; Rev. William Henry Channing and, 49; Christian socialism at, 55, 125; fire destroys, 56–58; founded, 42; as Fourierist phalanx, 38, 47–49, 52; influences on, 42, 52; inhabitants of, 46, 55; journal of (*The Dial*), 44–45; purpose of, 43; as Swedenborgian, 52–55, 295–96n27

Brooks, Van Wyck, 43, 212

Brotherhood of the Kingdom, 138

Brown, Solyman, 39, 52

Brown-Séquard, Edouard, 182

Brownson, Orestes A., 42, 132

Bryan, Dr. William D., 224

Bryn Athyn, 69, 146, 161, 167–68, 173

Buckley, Arabella, 67

Buddhism, 200, 233–34

Burke, Edmund, 7, 17, 31

Bush, George, xxiii, 13, 146

Bushnell, Horace, 127

C

Cabot, Ella, 226

Cabot, Richard Clarke, 218, 220–21, 226–27, 238; and pastoral care, 217, 224–25; on psychotherapy, 215; "work cure" of, 215, 219, 294n10

Cambridge Society of Swedenborgians, 150–51

Campbell, George Douglas (Duke of Argyll), 104–5

Canton Phalanx, 38–39

capitalism: Christianity v., 139; ills of, 123, 127, 136, 139, 205; inequalities in, 126, 127, 138. *See also* labor

Carlyle, Thomas, 17, 21, 23, 41

Carnegie, Andrew, 172–73

Carpenter, Frederic I., 241–42

Carr, Rev. Edward Ellis, 147

Carter, Col. Robert, 13, 255n25

Carus, Paul, 70; and monism, 200, 203

Cather, Willa, 71

Center for Swedenborgian Studies, 161

Chambers, Robert, 266n5

Channing, William Ellery, 41, 45, 172, 259–60n19; and Brook Farm, 42, 49; on transcendentalism, 260n20

Channing, William Francis, 259–60n19

Channing, Rev. William Henry, xxiv, 48, 58, 259–60n19, 261n29, 263n56; and abolitionism, 264n69; and associationism and Fourierism, 45–46, 47, 49–50, 52, 55, 58, 59; as deist, 264–65n71

Chapman, John (Johnny Appleseed), 81

Cousin, Victor, 17, 39, 232, 255n33
Crane, Stephen, 87, 93, 271n73
Crippen, Matthew, 186
Croce, Paul, 23–24, 185, 190
Thomas Y. Crowell Company, 235–36
Crusoe, Robinson (pseud.), 80

D

Daedalus Hyperboreus, xvi
Dana, Charles A., 3, 40, 50, 53, 58, 261–62n39
Dana, Richard Henry, Jr., 183
Darwin, Charles: agnosticism of, 65, 66, 68; influence of, 65–66, 67, 232, 266n6;
    interpreted, 65, 66–67; William James on, 186; on natural selection, 68, 232,
    266n6; New Church on, 68–69; *On the Origin of Species* of, 64, 67, 185
Davis, Andrew Jackson, 262n46
Dawn, The, 79, 270n63
DeBeaumont, L. B., 144
DeCharms, Rev. Richard, 13, 14, 160
degrees, doctrine of, xvi, xvii, xviii–xix, xx, xxiii, 53, 151, 169
Dell, Floyd, 271n73
democracy, 135, 145; Emerson on, 15, 16; Henry James, Sr., on, 26–28, 30, 31; New
    Church on, 177–78; pragmatism based in, 181; social gospel achieved by, 156
Dewey, John, 84, 96, 183, 196, 207, 218, 286–87n14; great community of, 105, 244; on
    William James, 213
Dial, The, 44–45, 48, 49
Dickinson, Lydia Fuller, 167, 168
Doherty, Hugh, 51–52
Dole, George Henry, 178
Doyle, Sir Arthur Conan, 259n10
Dreiser, Theodore, 71, 72, 86, 93, 271n73
Dresser, Alice Mae Reed, 233, 234
Dresser, Annetta G., 229–30
Dresser, Horatio Willis, 228, 229–38, 296n37; Emmanuel movement and, 237–38;
    on evolution, 231, 232–33; on God, 231, 232, 236–37; influences on, 229, 231, 232,
    234, 237–38; on meditation, 231; as a medium, 230; on natural selection, 236;
    New Thought founded by, 229, 233, 234–35; as pastoral counselor, 228, 229–38;
    on psychology, 231, 236–37; on self-reliant individual, 231–32; on spiritual
    awakening, 232; on Swedenborg, 229, 236, 237–38, 245–49; as theist, 232–33;
    on usefulness, 237, 245–49; in World War I, 235; at World's Parliament of
    Religions, 232; writings of, 231, 234, 235, 236, 237–38
Dresser, Jean Paul, 297n45
Dresser, Julius A., 229–30
Dresser, Philip S., 297n45
Dresser, Ralph Howard, 297n45
Drummond, Henry, 67, 78
Dubois, Paul, 219–20, 221

Duché, Rev. Jacob, 6
du Gard, Roger Martin, 201
Dunbar, Helen Flanders, 223, 225–26, 227, 238
Dunham, Rev. Howard C., 177–78
Dwight, John Sullivan, 52, 53, 55, 261–62n39

E
Eby, Rev. S. C., 165, 166–67
Echo, The, 109, 164
Eckhart, Meister, xvii
eclecticism, 232, 255n33
Eddy, Mary Baker, 216, 229, 294–95n13
education, of African Americans (Tuskegee approach), 133, 164, 166
Edwards, Jonathan, 29, 32, 74, 129
Eichhorn, Johann Gottfried, 170
Eliot, Charles William, 182
Ely, Richard T., 79, 88, 136, 137, 278n8
Emerson, Ralph Waldo, 15–23, 61, 86, 92, 183, 241; on associationism, 45; on
    benevolence, 15; on the Church, 41–42; on community, 55–56; on democracy,
    15, 16; edits *The Dial,* 44–45; essays of, 15, 16; on genius, 17–18, 19–20; on great
    men, 17–23; influence of, 24, 73, 230, 231; influences on, ix, xxiii, 16–17, 31, 73,
    295–96n27; William James on, 241–42, 299n3; optimism of, 16–17; Over-soul
    of, 74; on quest for perfection, 41–42; on reform/dissent, 55–56; on self-reliant
    individual, 15, 16, 54, 65, 74; on Swedenborg, xxv, 4, 17, 20–23, 45, 242; on
    usefulness, ix, 17–18, 31, 242; "The Young American" of, 299n3
Emmanuel movement, 216–23; as alternative medicine, 220; Christian Science
    and, 219, 220, 294–95n13; clergy's role in v. physician's role, 217, 221–22; Horatio
    Willis Dresser and, 237–38; as faith-healing, 217, 219, 221–22; hypnosis in,
    221; on mind-cure, 217, 227; New Church on, 220–21; publications of, 219–20;
    rules of treatment in, 221–22; as spiritualism, 219; women in, 220; Dr. Elwood
    Worcester and, 222, 223
empiricism, 185, 212; experience as basis of, 189–90, 192, 195–96, 208, 209
Encyclopedists, 34
Engels, Friedrich, 258n6
England, 4; Swedenborgianism in, 53, 59, 144, 162, 165
English League for the Taxation of Land Values, 273n27
Enlightenment (Age of), 6, 8, 9, 10–11, 160
Evangelical Alliance, 154
Evans, Warren Felt, xxiv
evolution, 64–65; in arts and letters, 69–72; as chance, 64, 65; directed, 106–7,
    273–74n34; Horatio Willis Dresser on, 231, 232–33; and Emerson's individual,
    65; Henry George on, 102, 106–7, 273–74n34; as God's work, 232–33; to justify
    imperialism, 65; via natural selection, 66–67; New Church on, 67–69; progress
    as outcome of, 102; religion and, 134; Herbert Spencer on, 76; uncertainty in,
    65; Wallace on, 91. *See also* Darwin, Charles

F

Fabianism, 82, 89, 125, 139, 258n6
Fairfax, Thomas, 13
faith: -healing, 217, 218, 219, 221–22, 223 (*see also* mind-cure); William James
    defends, 188, 189, 190–95, 243; justification/salvation by, xvii, 5; science
    reconciled with, 91
Farmers' Alliance, 115, 117, 119
Fechner, Gustav, 217
Federal Council of Churches, 153–56, 282n80; New Church and, 155–56; social
    creed of, 154–55
Feuerbach, Ludwig, 170
Fiala, Andrew, 198
Filmer, John, 108
Fiske, John, 91, 132
Fletcher, John Gould, 7
Flexner Report, 216
Flower, Benjamin O., 70, 233
Forel, August, 221
forms, doctrine of, xvi, xviii
Fourier, Charles, xxv, 34–35, 36, 37–40, 45, 79; divine social code of, 53; on
    harmonie, 36; ideas of compared to Swedenborg's, 46–47, 48, 49, 50–53, 54–55,
    60–61, 262–63n49; social science of, 262–63n49; universal analogy of, 52;
    writings of, 37–38, 46–47
Fourierism, 34, 37–40, 45, 49–50, 51, 54, 204, 258n6; and associationism, 45, 47–50,
    51; communities/phalanxes of, 35, 38–39, 47–49, 50, 52, 54, 58–59, 125, 129;
    disciples/followers of, 36, 39, 45, 46, 49, 50–51, 58; journal of (*The Harbinger*),
    59–60, 262–63n49; as materialistic, 52; New Church and, 38–39, 54; as
    Spiritualism, 38. *See also* associationism; Owenism
Fox, George, 17, 224
Fox sisters, 4
Francisco, Rev. A. B., 147, 148
Freemasonry, 5, 6
Freneau, Philip, xxiii
Friends of Social Reform, 46–47, 49
Frothingham, Octavius Brooks, xvii, 261n29
Fugitive Slave League, 264n69
Fuller, Margaret, 41, 42, 44

G

Gale, Richard M., 182
Garland, Hamlin, 71, 79, 93, 99
Garrison, William Lloyd, Jr., 99
Geiger, George R., 119
General Church of Pennsylvania, 161
General Church of the Advent of the Lord, 161

H

Haeckel, Ernst, 67, 267n17
Hale, Edward Everett, 78
Hall, Prescott F., 132
Hall, Richard A. S., 200
Harbinger, The, 50, 51, 53, 56, 58, 59–60, 261n38, 261–62n39, 262–63n49
Hardon, Charles, 108
Harmony Society, 258n7
Harrison, Brady, 299n3
Hawthorne, Nathaniel, 183
Hay, H. Clinton, 69, 110, 149, 221; on charity, 174; on the higher criticism, 171–72; on philanthropy, 173–74
Haydon, A. Eustace, 196–97
healing: Christian Science on, 222, 223; by Jesus, 217, 219; of mind, 215, 216, 218, 219, 238–39; mind controls, 218; New Thought on, 216; religion's function in, 215–16, 224–26, 238–39
healthy-mindedness, 220, 227, 228, 296n37
Hedge, Frederic Henry, 42
Hegel, G. W. F., 39
Hempel, Charles Julius, 52, 53, 262–63n49
Hermann, F. B. von, 100
Herrick, Robert, 71
Herron, George D., 278n8
Hick, John, 192–93
higher criticism, 170–72, 285n27
Hillman, Harry W., 80
Hindmarsh, Robert, 5
Hinduism, 233–34
Hite, Lewis F., 146, 150; on divine love, 153; on the higher criticism, 171; on the New Jerusalem, 153; on pragmatism, 207–9; on social philosophy, 153, 163; on women, 170
Hobart, Nathaniel, 21
Hodgson, Richard, 203
Hoeck, Louis G., 143–44
Holmes, Oliver Wendell, Jr., 183, 233
Holmes, Oliver Wendell, Sr., 182, 261n29
homeopathy, 55, 222, 295n21
Homestead Act, 98
Hopkins, Charles Howard, 153
Hopkins, Mark, 127
Howe, Edward Watson, 71
Howe, Julia Ward, 4, 78–79
Howells, William Cooper, xxiii, 13, 52, 84–85, 87
Howells, William Dean, xxvi, 72, 78, 84–92, 93, 188, 204; on American plutocracy, 90; and Fiske, 91; on individual in society, 89–90; influences on, xxiii, 84–85, 86,

87, 89, 90, 91, 92, 99; literary criticism by, 85–86, 88–89; on ministerial role, 87–88; novels of, 86–87, 89, 90–92; optimism of, 87; poetry of, 91–92; on religion, 87, 90, 91; on social gospel, 88; as socialist thinker, 86; on Tolstoy, 88–89; on usefulness, 85, 89
Hume, David, 9
Hunt, William Morris, 182
Hutchinson, John A., 153–54
Huxley, Thomas Henry, 75, 185, 191, 197
Hyatt, Alpheus, 106

I

immigration, 121; restricted, 132–33, 165–67
Immigration Restriction League, 132
individual: Abbott on, 134, 135, 136; Emerson's self-reliant, 15, 16, 54, 65, 74; equality of each, 117; Henry James, Sr., on, 54; William James on, 181, 204–6
Industrialism, 76–77, 139; ills of, 95–96
influx, divine, xvi, xvii, xix, 4, 11, 228; Horatio Willis Dresser on, 236–37; Henry James, Sr., on, 54
Ingersoll, Robert G., 67
Inness, George, 110–13; influences on, 112–13
Inness, George, Jr., 113
Institutional Church League, 154
Intellectual Repository, The, xi–xii
International Metaphysical League, 233
International New Thought Alliance. *See* National New Thought Alliance
International Swedenborg Congress of 1910, 162
Ireland, land system in, 113

J

James, Alice, 287n5
James, Garth Wilkinson, 287n5
James, Henry, Jr. (novelist), 30, 86, 93, 287n5
James, Henry, Sr., 23–31, 89–90, 114, 167, 181, 188, 287n5; on Apostolic Christianity, 24; Christian socialism of, 23, 29, 54–55, 244, 262–63n49; on church as corrupt, 26; on community, 26; on correspondences doctrine, 25, 54, 190; on democracy, 26–28, 30, 31; on disinterested benevolence, 29; on divine influx, 54; on Divine-Natural-Humanity, 24, 26, 27, 29–30, 32; on Emerson, 24; and Fourierism, 53, 54–55; on God, 25; and *The Harbinger*, 262–63n49; influence of, 32, 41, 73, 115, 116, 125, 128, 129, 184, 185, 189, 190, 204; influences on, xxiv, 23, 24–25, 29, 30, 31–32, 53, 184–85, 241; on Jesus, 25; on knowledge through revelation, 25; on material v. spiritual force, 25; on monism and pluralism, 184; on nature, 30; New Church on, 109; on pride, 25–26; on property, 28; religious epiphany of, 23; and Saturday Club, 183; on shadow, 256–57n53; on Universal Human, 27, 28, 30, 31; on usefulness, 23, 28, 31–32, 184–85; writings of, 24
James, Robertson, 287n5

La Farge, John, 182
laissez-faire, 110, 126–27, 128, 160
land. *See* George, Henry, land policy/single tax of
Land Nationalization Society, 273n27
Land Reform League of California, 99
Land Reform Union, 273n27
Lane, Charles, 43, 44
Lanier, Sidney, 71
Last Judgment, 12, 61, 254n22, 265n79
Lathrop, John Howland, 238
Lawrence, D. H., 92
League of Nations, 178
LeConte, Joseph, 106, 273–74n34
Leo XIII (Pope), 105
Leraysville Phalanx, 38–39
Lindsay, Vachel, 80–81
Linnaeus, Carolus, 68
Lloyd, Henry Demarest, 63
Locke, John, 10, 100, 185, 272–73n15
London, Jack, 72, 107
Longfellow, Henry Wadsworth, 183
love, xxi, xxii, xxiii, 3; divine, 153, 236–37
Lovejoy, Arthur O., 195, 241, 288n19
Low, Seth, 131
Lowell, James Russell, 86, 183

M
Malthus, Thomas Robert, 29, 100, 132, 272n12
Manchester School of Economics, 100
Manhattan Single Tax Club, 113
Mann, Charles H., 146
Martin, Thomas Mower, 142, 143, 152
Martin, Rev. William, 109
Marx, Karl, 29, 86, 99, 128, 258n6
Marxism, 114, 125, 138
Massachusetts New-Church Union, 149–50, 151, 164
materialism, 4, 242; of natural selection, 67
Mather, Cotton, 216
Mather, Ralph, 6
Matthiessen, Francis Otto, 4
Mazzini, Giuseppe, 137
McComb, Samuel, 216, 218–19, 220
McGlynn, Father Edward, 104
Mead, George Herbert, 286–87n4
Mercer, Rev. Arthur, 147, 148–49

religion: associationism as servant of, 51; Darwin affects, 64–65, 67; in harmony with science, 67–68, 69; healing function of, 215–16, 224–26, 238–39; politics separate from, 115, 116–17, 118–19; as shadow, 256–57n53; and social gospel movement, 129–30

Religious Union, 58, 264n69

Renouvier, Charles, 183, 287–88n8

Retina, The, 52, 84

Ricardo, David, 132, 272n12

Riis, Jacob, 137

Riley, James Whitcomb, 99

Riley, Woodbridge, 189

Ripley, George, 40, 44; and Brook Farm, 42, 45, 46, 56–57; edits *The Harbinger,* 53, 58, 261–62n39; as missionary, 53

Rix, Robert, 8

Robertson, Frederick, 127

Rockefeller, John D., 173, 174, 175–76

Roe, Daniel, 37

Rølvaag, O. E., 71

Romanes, George John, 67

Roosevelt, Theodore, 130–31, 137, 206; and New Church, 143, 144, 179

Rorty, Richard, 211–12

Rousseau, Jean-Jacques, 10, 34

Royce, Josiah, 200, 207, 226, 234

Ruskin, John, 41

Russell, Bertrand, 193

Ryan, Daniel J., 136

S

Sage, Olivia, 173

Saint-Simon, Henri de, 39, 258n6

Salvation Army, 134

Sandeman, Robert, 23

Saturday Club, 183

Scammon, Miss A. E., 168, 169

Schiller, F. C. S., 207

Schindler, Solomon, 80

Schmidt, Nathaniel, 138

Schneider, E. H., 178

Schreiner, Olive, 169–70

Schuchard, Marsha Keith, 5–6

series, doctrine of, xvi, xvii, xviii–xix

Sewall, Frank, 146, 162, 167, 209–10

Seward, Samuel S., Jr., 169–70

Shakers, 36, 71, 217

Shakespeare, William, 17, 19–20

Sharp, Granville, 12

Shaw, George Bernard, 99
Sheldon, Charles, 109–10
sin: as collective, not individual, xxiii, 123–24, 139, 140; as a disease, 134
Sinclair, Upton, 84
Single Tax League, 273n27
slavery, 9–15; Swedenborg on, 10, 31, 166, 254n19. *See also* abolitionism
Small, Rev. Herbert C., 147, 149
Smith, Adam, 99, 132
Smyth, Rev. Julian K., 167
social Darwinism, 65, 75, 76, 133
social gospel movement, xxvii, xxviii, 8, 121–58, 244; action as basis of, 137;
    combines sociology and religion, 129–30; communitarianism as forerunner of,
    61; democracy aids in, 156; and Federal Council of Churches, 153–56; Henry
    George in, 104; on healing of mind, 219; Jesus's teachings as basis of, 114, 123,
    124, 125, 127, 130, 135–36, 137, 138–39, 140, 143; on kingdom of God, 124; leaders of
    (*see* Abbott, Lyman; Gladden, Washington; Rauschenbusch, Walter); as liberal
    theology, 156–58; as Neo-Lamarckian, 122; New Church and, 125, 141–56; and
    pastoral clinical movement, 239; as precursor to progressivism, 130; on sin, 124;
    targets of, 157; as urban, 156; usefulness doctrine in, 61, 124; on wealth, 122–23;
    World War I puts an end to, 158
social reform/social thought, ix, x, 78–80, 163. *See also* Christian socialism; social
    gospel movement
socialism, 125, 128, 130, 258n6; Bellamy influences, 75; Henry George on, 105;
    New Church and, 82–84, 114, 165; Robert Owen reforms, 34–35, 36, 37. *See also*
    Christian socialism
Society of Christian Socialists, 79, 138, 270n63, 278n8
sociology, 129–30, 145
Speirs, James, 165
Spencer, Herbert, 29, 75, 104, 212; as Neo-Lamarckian, 185–86; on progress, 102; as
    social Darwinist, 76; on survival of the fittest, 64, 76; Unknowable of, 197–98
Spencer, S. H., 108
Sperry, Rev. Paul, 146, 210–11
Spiers, Rev. Junius B., 109
Spiritualism, 4; in Emmanuel movement, 219; and Fourierism, 38; William James
    on, 202, 203; as Swedenborgian, 259n10; Wallace's, 267n16
Standard Oil Trust, 174
Stone, Lucy, 79
Strauss, David, 170
Strindberg, August, 6
Stroh, Alfred H., 146
Strong, Augustus Hopkins, 140
Stroud, Scott R., 206
Sumner, William Graham, 75
Suzuki, Daisetz T., 112
Swanton, John R., 69, 146